# The Effect of Directives Within the Area of Direct Taxation on the Interpretation and Application of Tax Treaties

**Series on International Taxation**

VOLUME 84

*Series Editors*

Prof. Ruth Mason, University of Virginia School of Law
Prof. Dr Ekkehart Reimer, University of Heidelberg

*Introduction & Contents*

The Series on International Taxation deals with a wide variety of topics in the global tax arena. The authors include many of the field's leading experts as well as talented newcomers. Their expert views and incisive commentary have proven highly useful to practitioners and academics alike.

*Objective*

The volumes published in this series are aimed at offering high-quality analytical information and practical solutions to international tax practitioners.

*Readership*

Practitioners, academics and policy makers in international tax law.

*Frequency of Publication*

2-3 new volumes published each year.

*The titles published in this series are listed at the end of this volume.*

# The Effect of Directives Within the Area of Direct Taxation on the Interpretation and Application of Tax Treaties

Mees Vergouwen

Wolters Kluwer

*Published by:*
Kluwer Law International B.V.
PO Box 316
2400 AH Alphen aan den Rijn
The Netherlands
E-mail: lrs-sales@wolterskluwer.com
Website: www.wolterskluwer.com/en/solutions/kluwerlawinternational

*Sold and distributed by:*
Wolters Kluwer Legal & Regulatory U.S.
920 Links Avenue
Landisville, PA 17538
United States of America
E-mail: customer.service@wolterskluwer.com

*Printed on acid-free paper.*

ISBN 978-94-035-0907-5

e-Book: ISBN 978-94-035-0917-4
web-PDF: ISBN 978-94-035-0927-3



Printed in the Netherlands.

# Table of Contents

# List of Abbreviations

| | |
|---|---|
| Arbitration Directive | Council Directive (EU) 2017/1852 of 10 October 2017 on tax dispute resolution mechanisms in the European Union |
| ATAD1 | Council Directive (EU) 2016/1164 of 12 July 2016 laying down rules against tax avoidance practices that directly affect the functioning of the internal market |
| ATAD2 | Council Directive (EU) 2017/952 of 29 May 2017 amending Directive (EU) 2016/1164 as regards hybrid mismatches with third countries |
| CJEU | Court of Justice of the European Union |
| DSC | Dutch Supreme Court |
| ECtHR | European Court of Human Rights |
| EU | European Union |
| EU Charter | Charter of Fundamental Rights of the European Union |
| Extra-EU Treaties | Tax treaties concluded between a state that is, at the time of this book, a Member State and a state that is not, at the time of this book, a Member State (i.e., a third state) |
| ICJ | International Court of Justice |
| ICJ Statute | Statute of the International Court of Justice |
| ICSID | International Centre for Settlement of Investment Disputes |
| ILC | International Law Commission |
| Interest and Royalties Directive | Council Directive 2003/49/EC of 3 June 2003 on a Common System of Taxation Applicable to Interest and Royalty Payments made between Associated Companies of Different Member States |
| Intra-EU Treaties | Tax treaties concluded between two contracting states that are, at the time of this book, Member States |
| Member State | A state that is, at the time of this book, a member of the European Union |

| | |
|---|---|
| Merger Directive | Council Directive 2009/133/EC of 19 October 2009 on the common system of taxation applicable to mergers, divisions, partial divisions, transfers of assets and exchanges of shares concerning companies of different Member States and to the transfer of the registered office of an SE or SCE between Member States |
| Mutual Assistance Directive | Council Directive 2011/16/EU of 15 February 2011 on administrative cooperation in the field of taxation and repealing Directive 77/799/EEC |
| OECD Model | OECD Model Tax Convention on Income and on Capital |
| Parent-Subsidiary Directive | Council Directive 2011/96/EU of 30 November 2011 on the common system of taxation applicable in the case of parent companies and subsidiaries of different Member States, as amended by Council Directives 2014/86/EU and 2015/121. |
| PCA | Permanent Court of Arbitration |
| TEU | Treaty on European Union |
| TFEU | Treaty on the Functioning of the European Union |
| Treaty of Lisbon | Treaty of Lisbon amending the Treaty on European Union and the Treaty establishing the European Community, signed at Lisbon, 13 December 2007 |
| Treaty of Maastricht | Treaty on the European Union, signed at Maastricht, 7 February 1992 |
| Treaty of Rome | Treaty of Rome, singed at Rome, 25 March 1957 |
| UN | United Nations |
| UN Charter | Charter of the United Nations |
| VCLT 1969 | Vienna Convention on the Law of Treaties, done at Vienna on 23 May 1969 |
| VCLT 1986 | Vienna Convention on the Law of Treaties between States and International Organizations or Between International Organizations, done at Vienna on 21 March 1986 |

# PART I Introduction

CHAPTER 1

# Introduction

## 1.1 SUBJECT OF THIS STUDY

The subject of this study is determining the effect of directives within the area of direct taxation adopted on the basis of Article 115 TFEU (hereinafter: the 'Directives') may have on the interpretation and application of tax treaties. In determining such effect, this study focuses on the perspectives of public international law and the laws of the European Union.

## 1.2 BACKGROUND OF THIS STUDY

The subject of this study seems to have become more and more relevant.[1] This relevance can, first, be explained by the circumstance that the number of Directives has increased over time, as well as their overlap with distributive provisions of tax treaties concluded by the Member States.[2] The increase in overlap with distributive provisions can be illustrated as follows. As of 1 January 1992, the extent to which dividend payments may be taxed can be covered by the Parent-Subsidiary Directive,[3] as well as

1. *See*, *inter alia*, L. Hinnekens, EC Tax Review 1994/4, pp. 146 et seq., A.C.G.A.C. de Graaf, 2004, pp. 225 et seq., F. Avella, World Tax Journal 2012/6, O.C.R. Marres in: The KPMG Guide to the CCCTB, 2012, A. Pirlot in: European Tax Integration: Law, Policy and Politics (Pistone ed.), 2018, para. 14.2.2, P. Ariginelli in: The External Tax Strategy of the EU in a Post-BEPS Environment (Jiménez ed.), 2019, I.M. De Groot, Intertax 2019/8 & 9, F.A. Engelen, J. Vleggeert & T.M. Vergouwen, WFR 2019/257, Y. Brauner & G. Kofler in: Global Tax Treaty Commentaries, 2019, and I. Panzeri, European Taxation 2021/4.
2. Reference can, in addition to distributive provisions, also be made to the overlap between the Mutual Assitance Directive (77/799/EEC), (as been replaced by the Mutual Assistance Directive (2011/16/EU)) and Article 26 OECD Model (2017), as well as to the overlap between the Arbitration Directive ((EU) 2017/1852) and Article 25(5) OECD Model (2017).
3. Parent-Subsidiary Directive (90/435/EEC). This directive has subsequently been replaced by Parent-Subsidiary Directive (2011) and amended by Parent-Subsidiary Directive (2014) and Parent-Subsidiary Directive (2015).

Article 10 OECD Model.[4] In addition, as of 1 January 1992, the extent to which capital gains may be taxed can be covered by the Merger Directive,[5] as well as Article 13 OECD Model.[6] As of 1 January 2004, the extent to which interest and royalty payments may be taxed can be covered by the Interest and Royalty Directive,[7] as well as Articles 11 (for interest payments) and 12 (for royalty payments) OECD Model.[8] As of 1 January 2019, the extent to which business profits may be taxed can be covered by the Anti-Tax Avoidance Directive,[9] as well as Articles 7, 10(5) and 23 OECD Model.[10] Finally, the exit tax provision of ATAD1 may also apply to transactions covered by Article 13(5) OECD Model.[11]

As a second development illustrating the increasing relevance of the effect that the Directives may have on tax treaties, reference can be made to the changing nature of obligations arising from the Directives.[12] At the time of the adoption of the first Directives in 1990 (Parent-Subsidiary Directive and Merger Directive), the obligations imposed on the Member States were similar in nature to those arising under tax treaties in the sense that the Directives and tax treaties both provided for rules limiting the extent to which cross-border income could be taxed with a view to eliminating double taxation.[13] As of 2014, however, the duties arising under the Directives can be

---

4. TAXUD E1/FR DOC (05) 2306/A, pp. 6-7.
5. Merger Directive (90/434/EEC). This directive has subsequently been amended by Merger Directive (2005/19/EC) and has been replaced by Merger Directive (2009/133/EU).
6. *See* G.F. Boulogne, 2016 for various examples wherein the Merger Directive and Article 13 OECD Model would cover the same capital gain.
7. Interest and Royalty Directive.
8. TAXUD E1/FR DOC (05) 2306/A, pp. 7-8.
9. ATAD1 and ATAD2.
10. *See* I. Panzeri, European Taxation 2021/4, p. 1.2 who notes that the taxation of profits attributable to a permanent establishment can be covered by the controlled foreign company rules of ATAD1, as well as by Articles 7 and 23 OECD Model. *See* V. Chand, A. Turina & K. Romanovska, World Tax Journal 2022/2, p. 5 for the position that controlled foreign company rules, in general, can fall within the scope of Articles 7 and 10(5) OECD Model.
11. *See* K. Moser, Bulletin for International Taxation 2019/10, p. 542, as well as V. Chand, Bulletin for International Taxation 2013/4/5, para. 4.3.1.
12. *See* regarding the changing nature of the obligations arising from the Directives, F.P.G. Pötgens & T.M. Vergouwen in: Jubileumbundel 150 jaar WFR (Jansen & Stevens eds), 2022, para. 3.
13. The Directives adopted in 1990 – the Parent-Subsidiary Directive (90/435/EEC) and Merger Directive (90/434/EEC) – and 2003 – the Interest and Royalty Directive (2003/49/EC) – related to areas that were covered by tax treaties, but related to the same objective, i.e., avoiding international double taxation. With respect to the Parent-Subsidiary Directive (90/435/EEC), *see* M. Helminen in: Principles of Law: Function, Status and Impact in EU Tax Law (Brokelind ed.), 2017, para. 17.2 and A. Cordewener in: European Tax Law (Wattel, Marres & Vermeulen eds), 2018, p. 399. Regarding the objective of the Interest and Royalties Directive (2003/49/EC), *see* Joined Cases C-115/16, C-118/16, C-119/16 & C-299/16 (*N Luxembourg 1*), para. 90. Such objective is achieved – by the directives and tax treaties – by restricting the right of the source state (and, on occasion, the residence state) to tax dividend, interest, and royalty payments. Regarding the initial similarity of the obligations arising from the Directives and tax treaties, reference can also be made to Y. Brauner & G. Kofler in: Global Tax Treaty Commentaries 2019, para. 2.3.3.2 who note that 'treaty rules, such as articles 10 and 11 of the OECD Model, that would provide for reduced withholding taxes in the source Member State do not apply, as the domestic law that implemented the directives already provides for a zero withholding taxation', F.P.G. Pötgens & T.M. Vergouwen in: Jubileumbundel 150 jaar WFR (Jansen & Stevens eds), 2022, para. 3.1, D. Gutmann in: Building Global International Tax Law. Essays in Honour of Guglielmo Maisto (Pistone ed.), 2022, para. 18.1 who notes that these Directives provided for

incompatible with obligations arising under tax treaties.[14] This is due to Directives being able to, ever since 2014, impose an obligation to tax cross-border income (instead of merely imposing a duty to refrain from taxing cross-border income).[15] Such an obligation can be found in the Parent-Subsidiary Directive (2014/86/EU),[16] ATAD1 (2016/1164),[17] and ATAD2 (2017/952),[18] as well as in the on 31 October 2022 pending proposal for a directive on ensuring a global minimum level of taxation for multinational groups in the Union (hereinafter: the 'Pillar 2 Directive Proposal').[19] This duty to tax income may, contrary to the duty to refrain from taxing income, conflict with obligations arising under tax treaties if such treaties impose a duty to not tax that same income.[20] This could, for example, be the case where a tax treaty contains an exemption for income attributable to a permanent establishment without a switch-over

'the elimination of withholding taxes on a number of cross-border payments and make it possible to conduct restructurings of European groups without suffering adverse tax consequences', and L. de Broe in: Building Global International Tax Law: Essays in Honour of Guglielmo Maisto (Pistone ed.), 2022, para. 23.1 who states that the Directives have 'traditionally aimed at improving the effective functioning of the internal market by protecting corporate taxpayers against double taxation and providing for the equivalent tax treatment of domestic and cross-border transactions. The practical result of such legislation is that Member States relinquish certain taxing rights and that the taxpayer's situation is improved'.

14. *See* L. de Broe in: Building Global International Tax Law: Essays in Honour of Guglielmo Maisto (Pistone ed.), 2022, para. 23.1 noting that directives obliging Member States to include certain income items in the taxpayer's tax base that would otherwise go untaxed 'may impose obligations on Member States that conflict with their commitments under tax treaties'.
15. For the Parent-Subsidiary Directive, *see* recital (3) of Parent-Subsidiary Directive (2014) for the aim of avoiding double taxation and Article 1(1) for the obligation to tax certain dividend payments. For ATAD1, *see* recital (5) ATAD1 and Article 7 for the obligation to tax income of controlled foreign companies. For ATAD2, *see* recital (27) ATAD2 and Articles 9 and 9a for the obligation to tax income. *See also* F.A. Engelen, J. Vleggeert & T.M. Vergouwen, WFR 2019/257, p. 1553 and Y. Brauner & G. Kofler in: Global Tax Treaty Commentaries 2019, para. 2.3.3.3. Reference may also be made to W.C. Haslehner in: A Guide to the Anti-Tax Avoidance Directive (Haslehner, Pantazatou, Kofler & Rust eds), 2020, p. 32 who refers to ATAD as 'the first piece of major EU tax legislation that directly imposes a burden on corporate taxpayers'.
16. *See* Article 1(1) of Parent-Subsidiary Directive (2014) which provides that Member States are obliged to 'tax such profits to the extent that such profits are deductible by the subsidiary'.
17. *See* Article 5(1) ATAD1 as well as Article 7(2) ATAD1. Pursuant to Article 5(1), 'a taxpayer shall be subject to tax' over the difference between the market value less the value for tax purposes with respect to so defined 'transferred assets'. Moreover, Article 7(2) provides that Member States 'shall include in the tax base' certain categories of non-distributed income of controlled foreign companies.
18. *See* Articles 9(2)(b) and 9(5) ATAD2. Pursuant to Article 9(2) ATAD2, Member States are obliged to include income in the taxable base of its taxpayers in the event of a deduction without inclusion outcome whereas Article 9(5) imposes a duty to include income attributable to a disregarded permanent establishment in the taxable base as well.
19. Pillar 2 proposal (COM(2021) 823 final). Regarding the potential for a conflict between the Pillar 2 Directive Proposal and a tax treaty, *see* L. de Broe in: Building Global International Tax Law: Essays in Honour of Guglielmo Maisto (Pistone ed.), 2022, para. 23.2.2.
20. *See* F.A. Engelen, J. Vleggeert & T.M. Vergouwen, WFR 2019/257, p. 1553, Y. Brauner & G. Kofler in: Global Tax Treaty Commentaries 2019, para. 2.3.3.3, P. Ariginelli in: The External Tax Strategy of the EU in a Post-BEPS Environment (Jiménez ed.), 2019, para. 8.3.3, W.C. Haslehner in: A Guide to the Anti-Tax Avoidance Directive (Haslehner, Pantazatou, Kofler & Rust eds), 2020, p. 60, para. 2.66, I. Panzeri, European Taxation 2021/4, p. 147, and L. de Broe in: Building Global International Tax Law: Essays in Honour of Guglielmo Maisto (Pistone ed.), 2022, para. 23.1. Regarding the duty to deny benefits of a Directive and its overlap with tax treaties, *see* O.C.R. Marres & I. de Groot, European Taxation 2021/8, p. 339.

clause.[21] In the event that such income would qualify as non-distributed controlled foreign company income within the meaning of ATAD1 or as income attributable to a disregarded permanent establishment for the purposes of ATAD2, a Member State would be required to simultaneously tax the income attributable to the permanent establishment (under ATAD1 or ATAD 2) and to not tax that income under the relevant tax treaty.[22] The question that arises within this respect is whether the tax treaty can be affected in such a way, either under public international law or EU law, allowing for the taxation of such income in accordance with the provisions of ATAD1 and ATAD2. In addition to a conflict being able to arise between the duty to tax income in Directives and the duty to not tax income under tax treaties, the on 31 October 2022 pending ATAD3 Proposal may also give rise to a conflict with tax treaties given that it could require the Member States to disregard a tax treaty between the Member States.[23]

A third development relates to the judgment of the CJEU in the so-called *Danish Cases* of 2019. In these cases, the CJEU ruled that the general EU anti-abuse principle requires Member States to deny benefits of the Parent-Subsidiary Directive and Interest and Royalties Directive in fraudulent or abusive cases.[24] Denial of such benefits, i.e., an exemption of (source) taxation in respect of intra-group cross-border profit distributions, interest payments and royalty payments from a corporate taxpayer resident in one Member to a corporate taxpayer in another Member State, would entail a duty to not exempt such distributions and payments. A duty to not exempt would then seem to

21. *See*, regarding the relevance of a switch-over clause, I.M. de Groot, Intertax 2019/8 & 9, pp. 781-782.
22. The example regarding a controlled foreign company permanent establishment is also used by I.M. de Groot, Intertax 2019/8 & 9, pp. 781-782, F.A. Engelen, J. Vleggeert & T.M. Vergouwen, WFR 2019/257, p. 1553, Y. Brauner & G. Kofler in: Global Tax Treaty Commentaries 2019, para. 2.3.3.3, footnote 211, W.C. Haslehner in: A Guide to the Anti-Tax Avoidance Directive (Haslehner, Pantazatou, Kofler & Rust eds), 2020, p. 61, para. 2.66, A. Rust in: A Guide to the Anti-Tax Avoidance Directive (Haslehner, Pantazatou, Kofler & Rust eds), 2020, p. 182, para. 7.20, I. Panzeri, European Taxation 2021/4, p. 147, and L. de Broe in: Building Global International Tax Law: Essays in Honour of Guglielmo Maisto (Pistone ed.), 2022, para. 23.2.1. Reference made also be made, more generally, to P. Ariginelli in: The External Tax Strategy of the EU in a Post-BEPS Environment (Jiménez ed.), 2019, para. 8.3.2 who notes that the CFC rules of ATAD1 may conflict with tax treaties.

    S. Pancham in: The Implementation of Anti-BEPS Legislation in the European Union: A Comprehensive Study (Pistone & Weber eds), 2018, para. 19.4.6 and P. Ariginelli in: The External Tax Strategy of the EU in a Post-BEPS Environment (Jiménez ed.), 2019, para. 8.3.3 argue that the hybrid mismatch rules of ATAD2 with respect to disregarded permanent establishments may conflict with tax treaties, although not with respect to third states given the carve-out in Article 9(5) ATAD2. Ariginelli also notes in para. 8.3.3.3 that a conflict may arise between the obligation under Article 9(2)(b) ATAD2 to tax income with 'the tax treaties concluded by those states with third countries that oblige the relevant Member State to exempt the payments made by companies resident in the third country'. He also signals that no carve-out applies in this event. In addition, reference may also be made to C. Brokelind in: The External Tax Strategy of the EU in a Post-BEPS Environment (Jiménez ed.), 2019, para. 9.2.2.3 who notes that a conflict may arise between Article 9(5) ATAD2 and exemptions provided for by tax treaties.
23. *See* Article 11(1) ATAD3 Proposal (COM(2021) 565 final) which provides that a Member State 'shall disregard any agreements and conventions that provide for the elimination of double taxation of income, and where applicable, capital' if the conditions would be met.
24. Joined Cases C-115/16, C-118/16, C-119/16 & C-299/16 (*N Luxembourg 1*) and Joined Cases C-116/16 & C-117/16 (*T Danmark*).

entail a de facto obligation to tax. Such a de facto obligation to tax could then conflict with an obligation to not tax under a tax treaty. Hence, it has become apparent that as of 2019, a conflict may also arise in connection with Directives adopted before 2014 if the denial of their benefits is required under the general EU anti-abuse principle.

Finally, as a fourth development, it can be mentioned that there are relatively recent judgments of the CJEU concerning the interpretation of terms in Directives that resemble terms used in the OECD Model.[25] In *Berlioz*, the CJEU interpreted the term 'foreseeably relevant' in the Mutual Assistance Directive (2011/16/EU),[26] which term is also used in Article 26 OECD Model (2017). In the *Danish Cases*, the term 'beneficial owner' in the Interest and Royalty Directive (2003/49/EC)[27] was interpreted by the Court,[28] which term is also used in Articles 11 and 12 OECD Model (2017). These judgments, wherein the CJEU has interpreted terms that seem to have been 'borrowed' from the OECD Model, could raise the question as to whether national courts, when interpreting the 'original' OECD Model terms in tax treaties, must take the interpretation given by the CJEU to such terms into account.[29]

## 1.3 RESEARCH QUESTION

Against the background of the increasing overlap of Directives with provisions of tax treaties, the changing nature of obligations arising from, and in connection with, the Directives (and their potential for conflicts with tax treaties), and the CJEU interpreting Directive terms that are similar to those used in tax treaties, the present study is aimed at determining the effect that the Directives may have on tax treaties concluded by the Member States. Therefore, it seeks to answer the following research question:

> *To what extent do the Directives affect the interpretation and application of tax treaties concluded by the Member States?*

As follows from the research question, a distinction is drawn between the effect of the Directives on the interpretation and the application of tax treaties.[30] The reason for

25. *See* Case C-682/15 (*Berlioz*), para. 67 and Joined Cases C-115/16, C-118/16, C-119/16 & C-299/16 (*N Luxembourg 1*), para. 90. *See also* Y. Brauner & G. Kofler in: Global Tax Treaty Commentaries 2019, para. 2.3.3.5 who refer to this as 'the borrowing of treaty concepts'.
26. Article 1(1) of the Mutual Assistance Directive (2011/16/EU).
27. Article 1(1) of the Interest and Royalty Directive.
28. *See* Joined Cases C-115/16, C-118/16, C-119/16 & C-299/16 (*N Luxembourg 1*), paras 84-94.
29. *See* R.A. Bosman & F.P.G. Pötgens in: De toekomst van de vennootschapsbelasting (Van de Streek ed.), 2017, para. 13.4.2.3 and L. de Broe in: Current Tax Treaty Issues (Maisto ed.), 2019, para. 19.2. *See more generally*, F. Avella, World Tax Journal 2012/6, pp. 96 et seq. *See also* A.J. Martin Jiménez in: Global Tax Treaty Commentaries – Global Topics 2022, para. 5.7.2.4 highlighting that Spanish courts have, in fact, used the 'beneficial owner' interpretation of the CJEU in the so-called *Danish Cases*, i.e., Joined Cases C-115/16, C-118/16, C-119/16 & C-299/16 (*N Luxembourg 1*) and Joined Cases C-116/16 & C-117/16 (*T Danmark*).
30. It is thus not the purpose of the present thesis to determine the effect of the Directives on the 'conclusion' of tax treaties. With respect to such effect, it can nevertheless be mentioned here that, from the perspective of the laws of the EU, it can be derived from the so-called *Open Skies* judgments of the CJEU that the conclusion of tax treaty contrary to, at the time of conclusion, a Directive is not permitted because it would entail that the Member State(s) concerned failed to

drawing such a distinction between the effect on the 'interpretation' and 'application' of tax treaties is three-fold. First, it accurately reflects the basic rule that any application of a treaty is preceded by an interpretation, either consciously or subconsciously, of that treaty.[31] As such, 'interpretation' and 'application' of a treaty are two distinct steps in determining the effect of the Directives on tax treaties. The second reason is that this basic rule also seems to be recognised by the CJEU, considering that it has consistently held that 'the question [of] whether a national provision must be disapplied (...) arises only if no compatible interpretation of that provision proves possible'.[32] As such, before the application of a national provision can be affected by a Directive ('disapplied') under the laws of the EU, a national court must first determine whether the interpretation of such provision can be affected in such a way that it is compatible with a Directive ('compatible interpretation'). In addition, as a third reason, the VCLT 1969 also provides different sets of rules with respect to the interpretation of treaties (Part III, section 3 of the VCLT 1969) and the application of treaties (Part III, section 2 of the VCLT 1969). As such, drawing a distinction between the effect of the Directives on the interpretation and application of tax treaties would also seem justified under public international law.[33]

It also follows from the research question that the present study solely focuses on the effect of Directives on the interpretation and application of tax treaties. It is as such not the purpose of the present study to also determine the effect of other sources of EU law that are not linked to the Directives on the interpretation or application of tax treaties. The reasons for not addressing such other sources are as follows. First, the developments set out in section 1.2 demonstrate the increasing overlap of Directives

fulfil the obligations under Article 4 TEU (duty of Union loyalty) and Article 288 TFEU (*see, e.g.*, Case C-467/98 (*Open Skies (Denmark)*), para. 112). Hence, the effect of the Directives on the conclusion of tax treaties is that such treaties may not be concluded in a way that is incompatible with such Directives (from the perspective of the laws of the EU). *See*, in this respect, also F.P.G. Pötgens & T.M. Vergouwen in: Jubileumbundel 150 jaar WFR (Jansen & Stevens eds), 2022, para. 2.

The effect of the Directives on the 'conclusion' of tax treaties from the perspective of the laws of the EU should, however, also be compared with the public international law perspective. As such, the effect described in the previous paragraph of the present footnote represents only 'one side of the same coin'. The other side, the public international law side, should also be taken into account in this respect. This side is not discussed here (or elsewhere in the present thesis).

31. G. Schwarzenberger, Virginia Journal of International Law 1968/1, p. 8. This basic rule is also referred to by O. Dörr & K. Schmalenbach, 2018, p. 568, para. 14.
32. *See* Case C-585/19 (*Academia de Studii Economice din Bucureşti*), para. 68, Case C-308/19 (*Consiliul Concurenţei*), para. 63, Case C-122/17 (*Smith*), para. 41, Joined Cases C-569/16 & C-570/16 (*Wuppertal*), para. 25, Case C-306/12 (*Spedition Welter*), para. 28, Case C-97/11 (*Amia*), para. 27, and Case C-282/10 (*Dominguez*), para. 23.
33. This distinction between the effect of the Directives on the interpretation and application of tax treaties does not, however, detract from the fact that any effect that the Directives would have on the 'interpretation' would also affect the way in which a tax treaty is applied. As such, the reference in the research question to the effect of the Directives on the interpretation and application could also be understood as relating to the indirect (via the 'interpretation' question) and direct (via the 'application' question) of such Directives on the application of tax treaties.

and tax treaties.[34] As such, the effect of the Directives is most relevant.[35] Second, the effect that the Directives may have on the application of tax treaties from the perspective of the laws of the EU is fundamentally different from that of other sources such as the EU Treaties or regulations. This is due to the primacy of directly effective provisions of the EU Treaties and regulations being enforceable irrespective of the effect on taxpayers, whereas this is not the case for the Directives due to the prohibition of horizontal direct effect and reverse vertical direct effect.[36] As such, the effect of the Directives on the application of tax treaties is less clear-cut. Such effect essentially depends on whether relying on the primacy of a Directive, which could result in the setting aside of a tax treaty, would be beneficial or detrimental to a taxpayer. If one then takes into account that ATAD1 and ATAD2 seek to increase the tax burden of taxpayers, Directives may not be able to affect the application of tax treaties under the laws of the EU notwithstanding their primacy. This would have been different if

34. For these purposes, the obligation to deny the benefits of the Directives under the general EU anti-abuse rule is considered as linked to the Directives.

35. This does not mean, however, that the effect of the other sources of EU law on the interpretation and application of tax treaties would not be relevant. Such other sources would include the fundamental freedoms and state aid rules. Developments in the area of such freedoms and state aid rules may thus also be relevant for the interpretation and application of tax treaties. They are, however, less relevant at present in terms of the extent to which there have been developments over the period 2012-2022.

With respect to the relation between the fundamental freedoms and tax treaties, there does not seem to have been recent case law of the CJEU within the context of such freedoms that relates directly to the interpretation and application of tax treaties (most relevant would seem to be the so-called *Danish Cases*, but those are considered as being linked to the Directives). As such, the topic of the relation between the fundamental freedoms and tax treaties – in terms of recent case law of the CJEU – seems less relevant as compared to the topic of the effect of the Directives on tax treaties given the developments set out in section 1.2 (with respect to the academic debate regarding the relation between the fundamental freedoms and tax treaties, reference can be made in general to A.C.G.A.C. de Graaf, 2004. More specifically, i.e., with respect to limitation-on-benefits clauses, reference can also be made to Opinion Statement ECJ-TF 1/2018, p. 11, paras 52-54 where it is concluded that 'typical limitation-on-benefits clauses are likely to be incompatible with EU fundamental freedoms').

Moreover, with respect to the relation between tax treaties and state aid rules, the most relevant development would seem to be the state aid decision of the European Commission regarding alleged aid to McDonald's (SA.38945 (2015/NN – 2015/C) (reference can also be made to the investigation of the Commission into the limitations of benefits clause in the tax treaty between the Netherlands and Japan, as announced in the November Infringement Package, MEMO 15/6006. This investigation has not, however, resulted in a (formal) decision of the Commission). In its final decision of 26 July 2019, the Commission concluded, however, that the tax treaty between Luxembourg and the United States did not constitute aid. As such, the question as to whether such tax treaty would have been incompatible with the state aid rules has not been brought before the Courts of the EU. For that reason, there do not seem to have been concrete developments – in terms of state aid decisions of the European Commission or case law of the CJEU – within the area of the relation between tax treaties and state aid rules (with respect to the academic debate regarding such relation, reference can be made to R. Luja, European Taxation 2004/5, L. de Broe, EC Tax Review 2017/5, and Y. Brauner & G. Kofler in: Global Tax Treaty Commentaries 2019).

36. *See* S. Prechal, 2009, pp. 15-16. This prohibition does not apply with respect to the EU Treaties and regulations because they do not require transposition. For that reason, Member States cannot fail to implement obligations arising from such sources of EU law. This is different for Directives, considering that form and methods are left to the Member States to achieve the result of a Directive.

ATAD1 and ATAD2 had been adopted in the form of, for example, regulations because the enforceability of the primacy of regulations is not dependent on the effect on taxpayers. It thus follows that the nature of Directives is relevantly different from that of other sources of EU law.[37] As such, this study focuses on the effect of Directives only.

## 1.4 THREE PERSPECTIVES TOWARDS ANSWERING THE RESEARCH QUESTION

The effect that the Directives may have on tax treaties can be studied from the following three 'legal' perspectives: public international law, EU law, and Member State law. The interaction between these three perspectives can be illustrated as follows.

> Member State A has concluded a tax treaty with Member State B pursuant to which income attributable to a permanent establishment in Member State B must be exempt in Member State A. Under the constitution of Member State A, such a tax treaty takes precedence over any national legislation in the event that such legislation is incompatible with the tax treaty (which would not seem uncommon in the Member States, *see* section 1.4.3 below). Following the adoption of ATAD1, Member State A has amended its national legislation in such a way that certain categories of non-distributed income of a controlled foreign company permanent establishment in Member State B would be taxed. However, taking into account the superiority of tax treaties, it would seem that such national legislation aimed at implementing ATAD1 would have to be set aside by the tax treaty with Member State B entailing that Member State A has not been able to adequately implement ATAD1. At the same time, however, if such national legislation must be set aside by the tax treaty, the primacy of EU law might, in turn, require the setting aside of such tax treaty by Member State A (subject to the prohibition of reverse vertical direct effect).

From the Member State perspective, in this case, it follows that the application of its tax treaty with Member State B is, in principle, not affected by the national legislation aimed at implementing ATAD1. There may, however, also be Member States where tax treaties are not superior to national law. In such Member States, a domestic legislator would be able to effectively set aside tax treaties that would require an exemption with a view to ensuring that the result of the Directive is achieved. In such a way, a Directive could de facto be regarded as affecting the application of tax treaties. Such a 'treaty override' would not, however, have any effect on the binding nature of the obligation of such Member States to perform the obligations arising from a tax treaty in good faith. The extent to which the treaty obligation is affected is a matter of public international law and should therefore be studied from the public international law perspective.

37. This does not, however, entail that the findings of the present study are irrelevant for the effect of other sources of EU law on the interpretation and application of tax treaties. For example, the line of reasoning regarding the effect of the Directives on the interpretation and application of tax treaties under public international law may also be applied to the EU Treaties. The same applies to the arguments set out with respect to the EU law perspective, although one should bear in mind that the prohibition of reverse vertical direct effect only applies to directives.

The extent to which tax treaties are affected as a matter of public international law would be relevant for Member State A in the example above. This is because its national legislation aimed at implementing ATAD1 would only be set aside to the extent incompatible with a tax treaty. If such tax treaty would be affected by ATAD1 in such a way that it does not require an exemption of the income attributable to the permanent establishment in Member State B, the national legislation aimed at implementing ATAD1 would no longer be set aside by the tax treaty (because there is no longer any conflict), and the non-distributed income of the permanent establishment is taxed in accordance with ATAD1. Hence, it is relevant for Member State A to determine the extent to which its tax treaties would be affected by ATAD1 under public international law because this would have consequences, from its own (Member State) perspective, for the extent to which it has adequately implemented ATAD1.

If, however, the tax treaty with Member State B would not be affected in such a way under the rules of public international law that its application allows Member State A to tax controlled foreign company income attributable to a permanent establishment in Member State B, Member State A has not implemented the Directive correctly. If that were the case, the EU law perspective would be relevant because it provides for a conflict rule, i.e., the primacy of EU law, pursuant to which Member State courts must set aside tax treaties if they would stand in the way of complying with the obligations arising from the Directives (subject to the prohibition of reverse vertical direct effect). If set aside on the basis of such primacy, a tax treaty would be affected by a Directive under the EU law perspective.

The paragraphs above illustrate that tax treaties may be affected by a Directive under the national law of a Member State, under public international law, and under EU law. In addition, it demonstrates that the effect under EU law would, effectively, only be relevant after determining the effect of a Directive on tax treaties under the national laws of a Member State and public international law. This is due to the primacy of EU law being dependent upon a Member State not achieving the result of a Directive, which requires an assessment of the result achieved by a Member State bearing in mind the national laws of such a Member State and, if no treaty override is provided for, the public international law perspective. As such, in order to determine the effect of a Directive on (the interpretation and application of) tax treaties in a given situation, all three perspectives could, in principle, be relevant.

### 1.4.1 The Focus of the Present Thesis

While all three perspectives could be relevant, the present study focuses on only two: public international law and EU law. The reason for focusing on these two perspectives is that the effect of the Directives on the interpretation and application of tax treaties under public international law, at least to the extent that it concerns customary international law, and the laws of the European Union should be the same in all Member States. Thus, the findings of the present study should be relevant for all Member States. This would be different for the Member State perspective because the effect of national laws aimed at implementing a Directive on tax treaties may differ from one Member State to another. This would thus require a study of each individual Member State's legal order. This author is not able to perform such a study because he does not, for starters, have sufficient knowledge of the languages of each of the Member States to be able to perform a thorough study into the hierarchy of tax treaties within the legal order of each Member State. For that reason, the focus of the present thesis will be on the perspectives of the laws of public international law, to the extent reflecting customary international law, and EU law.

Whereas the focus is on these two perspectives, this author has performed a preliminary study into the priority of tax treaties in the Member States' legal orders in section 1.4.3. Such study aims to provide some insights into the extent to which national legislation, by means of which a Directive would have to be implemented, would seem to be able to override, and hence affect the application of, incompatible tax treaties.

### 1.4.2 The Public International Law and European Union Law Perspectives

As noted, the present study focuses on the effect of the Directives on the interpretation and application of tax treaties from the perspective of public international law and the perspective of EU law. As such, it seeks to essentially answer the following four questions:

(a) To what extent do the Directives affect the *interpretation* of tax treaties concluded by the Member States under *public international law*?
(b) To what extent do the Directives affect the *interpretation* of tax treaties concluded by the Member States under *the laws of the EU*?
(c) To what extent do the Directives affect the *application* of tax treaties concluded by the Member States under *public international law*?
(d) To what extent do the Directives affect the *application* of tax treaties concluded by the Member States under *the laws of the EU*?

The first and third questions, relating to the public international law perspective, are aimed at determining the effect that Directives can have, or are allowed to have, on tax treaties on the inter-state level (the public international legal order). The answer to this question is relevant for the Member States because it determines the extent to which giving effect to the Directives may be contrary to tax treaties. If, for example, a tax treaty would seem to be incompatible with a Directive but – following the application of the rules of public international law – would prove to be compatible with it, the effect of the Directive is achieved in a way that is consistent with such tax treaty (thereby avoiding any violation of tax treaty obligations). It is also relevant for those Member States wherein tax treaties have priority over national laws, including those implementing Directives, because it could prevent a conflict from arising between such laws and tax treaties. It is thus the purpose of the first and third questions to determine the extent to which Directives can affect tax treaties in such a way that conflicts with the Directives are avoided under public international law.

The second question and fourth questions have different purposes. Their purpose is to, essentially, determine the extent to which the Directives can have, or must have, an effect on the tax treaties concluded by the Member States. Their focus is on determining to what extent Member States would be obliged to ensure that the interpretation or application of their tax treaties is affected in order to achieve the result of a Directive. As such, these questions can be regarded as being aimed at determining the 'required' effect of the Directives on the interpretation and application of tax treaties whereas the first and third questions (i.e., the public international law questions) are more concerned with the 'allowed' effect of the Directives on the interpretation and application of tax treaties.

### 1.4.3 The Member State Law Perspective

In addition to the public international law and EU law perspective, the Member State law perspective (hereinafter: the 'Member State Perspective') would also be relevant for determining the effect that Directives may have on the interpretation of tax treaties in practice. With respect to such Member State Perspective, this section seeks to provide a preliminary insight into whether national law aimed at implementing a Directive may be able to override a tax treaty or may be overridden by such a tax treaty. This thus concerns the question regarding the hierarchy of (tax) treaties within the legal orders of the Member States vis-à-vis national laws.

The answer to this question is based on the information available on national legislation at https://e-justice.europa.eu (last accessed: 6 July 2022), an official website of the European Union providing 'information on justice systems and improving access to justice throughout the EU', as supplemented by publications of legal scholars in English. Based on the information on this website of the European Union, the following picture arises as a starting point:

(a) treaties are superior to national legislation, but not with respect to European Union Law and the constitution: Estonia, and Greece;
(b) treaties are superior to national legislation, except for the constitution: Cyprus, Lithuania, Portugal,[38] and Spain;[39]

38. *See* J.A. Fernandes & F. de Sousa da Camara in: IFA Cahiers 2010 – Volume 95A: Tax Treaties and Tax Avoidance: Application of Anti-avoidance Provisions 2010, para. summary ('the Portuguese Constitution has established a hierarchy where tax conventions prevail over domestic law if conflicts arise between a DAAR and a treaty, the DAAR will be deemed unlawful and hence inapplicable') and C.R. de Melo & T.C. Ramos in: IFA 2020, p. 672. ('Portugal adopts a monist system regarding international law and therefore the MLI and tax treaties are automatically applicable in Portuguese territory, after their entry into force, with no need to be incorporated or transformed into national law, prevailing over the latter. Therefore, domestic legislation will not be able to override the provisions brought forward by the MLI.')
39. *See* A. Ribes in: IFA 2020, p. 777 ('any kind of international treaty duly ratified by Congress, is considered legally superior to domestic law and must be implemented in accordance to this superior value over domestic legislation'.) and p. 778 ('Furthermore, Article 7(b) and (c) of the Spanish General Tax Act – the general framework of the Spanish taxation system and of all fiscal

(c) treaties are superior to national legislation (without clarifying the superiority with respect to the constitution): Belgium,[40] Bulgaria, Czech Republic, France,[41] Hungary,[42] Luxembourg,[43] Netherlands,[44] and Slovenia;
(d) the status of a treaty depends on the national measures by means of which it is given effect: Finland; and
(e) the status of treaties vis-à-vis national law is not clear because (i) the hierarchy of sources is not set out (Croatia, Denmark, Malta, Romania and Sweden), (ii) the hierarchical status of treaties is not explicitly addressed (Germany, Italy, Ireland and Slovakia), (iii) such hierarchical status is not explicitly confirmed (Latvia and Poland), or (iv) such hierarchical status is dependent on its content (Austria).

With respect to those Member States wherein the status of treaties is unclear, i.e., the Member States falling in category (e), the following can be noted based on publications of legal scholars. In Austria, Denmark, Germany, and Sweden, the domestic legislator seems to be able to override tax treaties by enacting subsequent legislation.[45] This seems to be different in Croatia, Ireland, Poland, Italy and Slovakia. In Croatia, Ireland, Poland, and Slovakia, treaties seem to take precedence over national law in the event of a conflict,[46] while this also seems to be the case in Italy

procedures – clearly regulates that international agreements take precedence over domestic laws and regulations on any tax issues.').

40. *See* E-J. Navez in: Taxation of Companies on Capital Gains on Shares under Domestic Law, EU Law and Tax Treaties (Maisto ed.), 2013, para. 12.8.1, C. Docclo, Fiscoloog 2017/406, and P. de Vos & C. Docclo in: IFA 2020, pp. 187-188 who note that tax treaties would also supersede the constitution.
41. *See* Report on Tax Treaty Override, p. 7, para. 15, N. Message in: Tax Treaties and Domestic Law (Maisto ed.), 2006, para. 8.2.1.1.2, and N. De Boynes in: IFA 2020, p. 362.
42. *See also* B. Kolozs & A. Koszegi in: IFA Cahiers 2010 – Volume 95A: Tax Treaties and Tax Avoidance: Application of Anti-avoidance Provisions 2010, para. 1.4.1.
43. O.R. Hoor & A. Medler in: IFA Cahiers 2020: Volume 105A – Reconstructing the Treaty Network 2020, p. 513 ('Luxembourg applies a monist theory according to which domestic law including the constitution must be amended or may be disregarded to the extent it is incompatible with international law (such as European primary and secondary law). International treaties (such as DTT or the MLI) first have to be ratified through the Luxembourg legislative procedure and transposed into domestic law. Therefore, such international treaties rank higher than domestic law and may not be overridden by contradictory Luxembourg legal provisions.').
44. *See* Report on Tax Treaty Override, p. 7, para. 15, F.G.F. Peters & A. Roelofsen in: IFA Cahiers 2010 – Volume 95A: Tax Treaties and Tax Avoidance: Application of Anti-avoidance Provisions 2010, para. 1.4, and D. Tiesinga & E. Nuku in: IFA 2020, p. 558.
45. D. Hohenwarter in: Tax Treaties and Domestic Law (Maisto ed.), 2006, para. 7.2.3 ('if it becomes evident in special treaty provision, this then is a case of treaty override which – at least from the point of view of the Austrian Constitution – has to be accepted'.), P.K. Schmidt in: IFA 2020, p. 335 (Denmark), A. Rust in: Tax Treaties and Domestic Law (Maisto ed.), 2006, para. 9.3.1 (Germany; *see also* Report on Tax Treaty Override, p. 8, para. 15 and A. Linn in: IFA Cahiers 2010 – Volume 95A: Tax Treaties and Tax Avoidance: Application of Anti-avoidance Provisions 2010, para. 1.5.1.2), and D. Edvinsson in: IFA Cahiers 2020: Volume 105A – Reconstructing the Treaty Network 2020, p. 793 (Sweden).
46. *See* S. Rodin, 55 1995, p. 797 (Croatia; 'legal force superior to ordinary laws'), D. Noone & A. Quinn in: IFA Cahiers 2010 – Volume 95A: Tax Treaties and Tax Avoidance: Application of Anti-avoidance Provisions 2010, para. 1.4.2 (Ireland; '[i]t is common case that if there is such a conflict [between domestic law and the double taxation treaty] it is the terms of the Convention

subject to the exception that a treaty might be inapplicable if domestic law would be more favourable.[47] The situation in Latvia seems less clear, but Mits argues that international law would be superior to national law except for the constitution.[48] Moreover, in Romania, the status of treaty seems to be linked to the status of the act of ratification,[49] which would seem similar to the Finnish system (*see* (d) above). Finally, the present author has not been able to ascertain the hierarchy of treaties within the national legal order of Malta, which seems to be in any event a dualist state.[50] Taking these considerations into account, a more complete overview can be provided:

(a) in 20 Member States, treaties are superior to non-constitutional national legislation;
(b) in 4 Member States, domestic legislators can override treaties by national legislation;
(c) in 2 Member States, the status of treaties is equal to that of the domestic act giving effect to such treaties; and
(d) in 1 Member State, the status of treaties could not be determined.

Based on this overview, it would seem that tax treaties may not necessarily be affected by national laws aimed at implementing Directives in 20 Member States. The key question with respect to such Member States would be whether the superiority of treaties also extends to national legislation aimed at implementing Directives as a matter of their (constitutional) laws. At least for one Member State, i.e., the Netherlands, this seems to be the case.[51]

---

that must prevail'), K. Lasiński-Sulecki & W. Morawski in: IFA 2020, p. 638 (Poland; 'precedence over statutes if such an agreement cannot be reconciled with the provisions of such statutes'), and A. Koronczióvá & M. Kacaljak, Economics and Social Issues Review 2017/3, p. 149 (Slovakia; reference is made to a constitutional provision that stipulates 'International treaties ... which were ratified and promulgated in the way laid down by a law shall have precedence over laws').

47. P. Bracco in: IFA Cahiers 2010 – Volume 95A: Tax Treaties and Tax Avoidance: Application of Anti-avoidance Provisions 2010, para. 1.4, and A. Zaimaj in: IFA 2020, p. 455.
48. M. Mits, 2016, The European Convention on Human Rights and Democratisation of Latvia, p. 5.
49. V. Vita, Germany Law Journal 2015/6, p. 1630.
50. *See* I. Mifsud, 2022, p. 50.
51. *See, e.g.*, Parliamentary Proceedings II 2020/2021, 25 087, no. 260, p. 28 where the Dutch State Secretary of Finance expressed the position that '[w]ithin the Dutch legal order treaties take precedence over national legislation based on Article 94 Dutch Constitution. In principle, this also applies if the applicable national legislation arises from the implementation of EU-directives' (unofficial translation by the present author). This also seems to have been the case, at least initially, in Belgium given that L. de Broe in: Building Global International Tax Law: Essays in Honour of Guglielmo Maisto (Pistone ed.), 2022, para. 23.2.1, footnote 8, notes that the 'Belgian legislator initially refused to include PEs in the CFC regulations on those grounds', i.e., because adopting 'CFC rules would force them to breach their existing tax treaties, leading to uncertainty for taxpayers'. De Broe also notes, in para. 23.4.3 that the Belgian legislator has subsequently adhered to the argument that 'since the Member States adopt these directives with unanimity, they simultaneously consent to amend their tax treaties and replace them with the provisions adopted under the directive'. Following such line of reasoning, Belgium should then be able to apply the domestic legislation aimed at giving effect to the CFC rules of ATAD1 to 'low-taxed PEs established in treaty countries'. The validity of this argument of the Belgian

If the superiority of treaties extends to national law aimed at implementing a Directive, the outcome under the Member State Perspective is that tax treaties are not affected by the Directives beyond the extent to which such treaties may be affected by such Directives under public international law. The effect of the Directives under the Member State Perspective would then, essentially, seem to be linked to that under the public international law perspective (which perspective is the focus of the present thesis). As such, the ability of such Member States to achieve the result of a Directive would essentially be dependent on the effect of the Directives on their tax treaties. If such effect does not go so far as allow the Member State concerned to achieve the result of a Directive, it would not achieve that result. It is in such a situation, i.e., a Member State cannot, or has not, (adequately) implement(ed) a Directive, that the tax treaty's interpretation or application may be required to be affected under the laws of the EU with a view to ensuring that the result of such Directive is achieved (notwithstanding the superiority of such a treaty from the Member State Perspective).[52] As such, EU law would then provide for a treaty override.[53]

If, however, the superiority of treaties does not extend to national legislation giving effect to the Directives, which would in any event seem to be the case in the six Member States wherein such treaties have no superiority over national laws, the result of the Directives can be achieved due to domestic law providing for the setting aside of incompatible tax treaties. As such, those Member States would be able to affect (the application of) tax treaties by means of their domestic legislation aimed at implementing a Directive in order to achieve the result of such Directive irrespective of the effect that the Directives would have on tax treaties under public international law. If tax treaties would be overridden by such domestic legislation, the result of the Directive would be achieved, and there would be no reason to (also) rely on the primacy of EU law to override a tax treaty. As such, for those Member States wherein a tax treaty can be overridden by national legislation, it would be less relevant what effect the Directives may have on tax treaties under public international law because they can achieve the result of such Directives irrespective of such effect. This does not, however, mean that the effect of the Directives on tax treaties under public international law would be irrelevant to them. If tax treaties are affected in such a way that they do not need to be performed to the extent incompatible with the result to be achieved by a Directive under public international law, the domestic treaty override would not violate obligations under such treaties. As such, no international responsibility would arise. By contrast, if tax treaties would not be affected under public international law, international responsibility would arise due to a treaty override by means of national legislation, which national legislation may not be invoked as a justification for a failure to perform a treaty under Article 27 VCLT 1969.[54]

legislator, which essentially assumes an effect of the Directives on tax treaties under public international law, is discussed in Chapter 6.

52. The extent to which such primacy may be applicable and enforceable is discussed in Chapter 7.
53. This question is addressed in Chapter 6 (application), as well as Chapter 3 (interpretation).
54. Article 27 VCLT 1969 reads as follows: 'A party may not invoke the provisions of its internal law as justification for its failure to perform a treaty. This rule is without prejudice to article 46.'

In sum, it follows from the previous paragraphs regarding the Member State perspective that 6 Member States seem to be able to override their tax treaties (and, hence, affect their application), while it seems questionable whether the national laws of the other 21 Member States would allow them to do so. With respect to 20 of them, it would seem to be the case that, as a starting point, national laws cannot override tax treaties. It is for those Member States that it may be impossible to implement Directives if their result would require them to set aside their tax treaties. If, however, such tax treaties would be affected in such a way, under the rules of public international law, that they are compatible with the Directives, the result of the Directives would also be achieved in those Member States notwithstanding the superiority of tax treaties vis-à-vis national legislation aimed at implementing a Directive.

## 1.5 EARLIER RESEARCH

The effect of Directives on tax treaties has, taking to account the developments set out in section 1.2, attracted a considerable amount of attention from legal scholars over the past years. Scholars have, for example, submitted that the Directives - or EU law in general - can have an effect on the interpretation of tax treaties from both the public international law[55] and the EU law perspectives.[56] In addition, the effect of the Directives on the application of tax treaties has also attracted the attention of legal scholars. Such scholars have mainly focused on such effect from the perspective of the laws of the EU,[57] i.e., the extent to which the Directives should take precedence over tax treaties under EU law. With respect to the effect of the Directives on the application of tax treaties under the public international law perspective, submissions have been made that Article 30 VCLT 1969 could affect the application of tax treaties (i.e., from the public international law perspective).[58] In-depth studies regarding the

55. F. Avella, World Tax Journal 2012/6 and L. de Broe in: Current Tax Treaty Issues (Maisto ed.), 2019, para. 16.2.

56. *See* R.A. Bosman & F.P.G. Pötgens in: De toekomst van de vennootschapsbelasting (Van de Streek ed.), 2017, para. 13.4.2.3 and L. de Broe in: Current Tax Treaty Issues (Maisto ed.), 2019, para. 16.2.3.

57. With respect to Directives, *see* F.A. Engelen, J. Vleggeert & T.M. Vergouwen, WFR 2019/257, I. Panzeri, European Taxation 2021/4, and L. de Broe in: Building Global International Tax Law: Essays in Honour of Guglielmo Maisto (Pistone ed.), 2022, para. 23.3 (De Broe also recognises that legal scholars have mainly focused on the EU perspective). In addition to these specific studies on the effect of the Directives - or EU law in general - on the application of tax treaties, other legal scholars have made submissions regarding such effect. *See*, in this respect, W.C. Haslehner in: A Guide to the Anti-Tax Avoidance Directive (Haslehner, Pantazatou, Kofler & Rust eds), 2020, pp. 59-63, P. Ariginelli in: The External Tax Strategy of the EU in a Post-BEPS Environment (Jiménez ed.), 2019, para. 8.3, and D.S. Smit in: European Tax Law (Wattel, Marres & Vermeulen eds), 2018, p. 490.

58. *See* O.C.R. Marres in: The KPMG Guide to the CCCTB 2012, p. 16, D.S. Smit in: European Tax Law (Wattel, Marres & Vermeulen eds), 2018, p. 490, footnote 19, I.M. de Groot, Intertax 2019/8 & 9, p. 782, and I. Panzeri, European Taxation 2021/4, pp. 148-149. *See also* TAXUD E1/FR DOC (05) 2306/A, p. 15 wherein the position is taken that Mutual Assistance Directive (2011/16/EU) would 'replace' tax treaties with more limited obligations in relation to the exchange of information or recovery of tax claims.

application of this provision of the VCLT 1969 to Directives and tax treaties do not, however, seem to have been performed to the present author's knowledge.

The present study is different from these previous studies for the following reasons. First, the present study focuses on both the public international law perspective and the perspective of the laws of the EU. In such a way, the present study is different from most of the previous studies because they generally focus on only one of the two perspectives.[59] By focusing on both perspectives, the present study seeks to determine the extent to which the public international law and EU law perspectives allow for the same outcome regarding the effect of the Directives on the interpretation and application of tax treaties. It thus aims to be able to provide an answer to the question as to what extent the 'required' effect of the Directives under the laws of the EU would overlap with the 'allowed' effect of such Directives on the interpretation and application of tax treaties under public international law.[60] Such a study aimed at determining such overlap has, to the knowledge of the present author, not been performed yet. The present study is also different from earlier studies because it addresses the preliminary question of what the status of the Directives is under public international law, which question is highly relevant, but often overlooked.[61] Third, the present study seeks to perform the, currently absent, study into the applicability of Article 30 VCLT 1969 to successive Directives and tax treaties. In that way, the present study is different from earlier publications wherein submissions have been made regarding the effect of the Directives under Article 30 VCLT 1969.

## 1.6 METHODOLOGY

With respect to the present study, the following methodologies are adopted. In answering the research question, the legal dogmatic methodology is adopted. Pursuant to this method, the relevant rules of public international law, to the extent reflecting customary international law, and rules of the EU as in force on 31 October 2022 will be analysed. Such an analysis will be based, mainly, on doctrines, literature, and case law (of the CJEU, ICJ and arbitral tribunals).[62] Based on the content of the rules in force up

59. The only exception seems to be, at present, L. de Broe in: Current Tax Treaty Issues (Maisto ed.), 2019, para. 16.2 who studies both the rules of interpretation of Article 3(2) OECD Model and Article 31 VCLT 1969, as well as the duty of consistent interpretation.
60. With respect to the reference to the 'required' effect of the Directives, it is noted that this relates to the effect that the Directives may be required to have under the duty of consistent interpretation or the primacy of EU law. As such, it does not reflect the 'required' effect of a Directive in terms of the result that must be achieved by it and the extent to which such result would 'require' tax treaties to be affected. For example, a Directive may require a result that is incompatible with a tax treaty. This could also be described as a 'required' effect in terms of the result that must be achieved. This is not, however, the meaning that is attributed to the term 'required' effect in the present thesis. In this thesis, the 'required' effect relates to the question to what extent the duty of consistent interpretation and primacy of EU law require the interpretation or application of a tax treaty to be affected in order to achieve the (required) result of a Directive (with respect to situations covered by tax treaties).
61. The only exception seems to be F. Avella, World Tax Journal 2012/6.
62. J. Vranken, Recht en Methode in onderzoek en onderwijs 2012/2, p. 43.

to and including 31 October 2022, the present author aims to determine the effect of the Directives on the interpretation and application of tax treaties.

In addition to this methodology, applied for the purposes of answering the research question, elements of the EU tax treaty network have also been empirically studied. The methodology adopted in that respect is set out in Annexes 1 and 2.

## 1.7 RELATIONS BETWEEN LEIDEN UNIVERSITY AND OTHER EMPLOYERS

Bearing in mind the academic debate in the Netherlands regarding legal scholars that work in academia and legal practice,[63] as well as the proposal of Vleggeert in his inaugural lecture 'Een burgerperspectief op belangenverstrengeling',[64] the author declares the following. During the period wherein the research regarding, and the drafting of, this thesis has been performed (between 1 September 2017 and 31 October 2022), the author has been employed by both Leiden University as a PhD-fellow (0,6 fte until 30 September 2022; 0,4 fte as of 1 October 2022) and De Brauw Blackstone Westbroek as a tax adviser (0,4 fte until 30 September 202; 0,6 fte as of 1 October 2022). Being aware of such dual employment relationship, the author and the supervisors declare that Leiden University has borne all salary costs associated with this thesis and that De Brauw Blackstone Westbroek has not been involved with the formation of this thesis. Moreover, the author declares that there has also not been any obligation vis-à-vis De Brauw Blackstone Westbroek to submit this thesis, or any drafts of it, to De Brauw Blackstone Westbroek for approval or otherwise. As such, this author declares, and the supervisors confirm, that this thesis has been written under the sole supervision of Leiden University and without any interference by De Brauw Blackstone Westbroek, either financially or otherwise.

## 1.8 STRUCTURE

This study is divided into four parts and has the following structure. In Part I, in addition to this introduction, the status of the Directives is discussed (Chapter 2). This discussion is key for the purposes of answering the research question.

In Part II, the effect of the Directives on the interpretation of tax treaties is discussed. Such effect is studied from the perspective of public international law first (Chapter 3) and, subsequently, from the perspective of the laws of the EU (Chapter 4). Part II ends with an assessment of the extent to which the Directives are simultaneously 'allowed' and 'required' to affect the interpretation of tax treaties (Chapter 5).

Having established the effect of the Directives on the interpretation of tax treaties, Part III addresses the effect of such Directives on the application of tax treaties. Such effect is first assessed from the perspective of public international law (Chapter 6), followed by the effect of such Directives under the laws of the EU (Chapter 7). Part III

63. *See, e.g.*, J. Vleggeert, 2020 and J. Vleggeert, 2022.
64. *See* J. Vleggeert, 2022, p. 7.

ends with an answer to the question regarding the extent to which the Directives are simultaneously 'allowed' and 'required' to affect the application of tax treaties (Chapter 8).

In the final part of the present thesis, Part IV, the answer to the research question is provided (Chapter 9). Based on such an answer, the final chapter provides recommendations aimed at aligning the 'allowed' and 'required' effect of the Directives on the tax treaties (Chapter 10).

CHAPTER 2

# The Nature of the Directives

## 2.1 INTRODUCTION

The present chapter aims to answer a simple, yet highly relevant, question: 'what is a Directive?' The answer to such question will be provided in two steps. First, the nature of the Directives from the perspective of the laws of the EU is addressed (section 2.2). This should provide an answer to the question, 'what is a Directive?' The second step is then, bearing such nature in mind, to determine the status of such Directives under the rules of public international law (section 2.3) and the laws of the EU (section 2.4). Such second step thus relates to the question: 'what source of law is a Directive?' This chapter ends with a conclusion regarding what a Directive is, both in terms of its nature and in terms of its status under the laws of public international law and the laws of the EU (section 2.5).

## 2.2 THE NATURE OF THE DIRECTIVES FROM THE PERSPECTIVE OF THE LAWS OF THE EU

In order to determine the nature of the directives adopted in the area of direct taxation (hereinafter: the '*Directives*') from the perspective of the laws of the EU, reference can first of all be made to Article 288(1) TFEU. This article, read in the context of its place in the TFEU, provides that directives, as legal acts of the Union, shall be adopted by the institutions to exercise the competences of the EU.[65] As such, directives are to be viewed as 'legal acts of the institutions of the EU' (aimed at exercising the competences of the EU).[66] Second, reference can be made to the definition of directives in

65. Article 288(1) TFEU also lists, in addition to directives, other legal acts that the institutions of the EU may adopt. Such additional acts, to the extent that they are binding, are regulations and decisions and, to the extent that they are non-binding, recommendations and opinions.
66. This characterisation is based on the circumstance that Article 288 TFEU is laid down in the section of the TFEU titled '[t]he legal acts of the Union' in conjunction with the provision itself providing that the institutions (of the EU) adopt directives.

Article 288(3) TFEU within the context of determining the nature of directives under the laws of the EU. Pursuant to this definition, directives are 'binding, as to the result to be achieved, upon each Member State to which it is addressed, but [leaving] to the national authorities the choice of form and methods.'[67] Bearing this definition in mind, the nature of the directives can then be more accurately described as 'binding legal acts of the institutions of the EU'.

Whereas it follows from Article 288 TFEU that directives are 'binding legal acts of the institutions of the EU', the adoption of a directive requires – ultimately – an agreement between (the representatives at the ministerial level of)[68] the Member States within the Council by, in principle, qualified majority (except where the Treaties provide otherwise).[69] Bearing in mind such requirement of agreement between the Member States, it would seem arguable that directives can be regarded as reflecting the agreement between the Member States as to a result that must be achieved. The question that may then be raised is whether a directive could be regarded as having the status of an international agreement between the Member States.

This question has been answered by the CJEU in *Commission v. Italy* (Case 91/79). In this case, the Italian government put forward the argument that a directive adopted on the basis of (now) Article 115 TFEU[70] was 'actually a convention drawn up in the form of a directive'.[71] In response to this argument, the CJEU ruled that a directive cannot be characterised as an 'international agreement'. The basis for such a ruling was twofold. First, directives based on (now) Article 115 TFEU are adopted within the context of the objectives of the European Union, i.e., the approximation of such laws, regulations or administrative provisions of the Member States that directly affect the establishment or functioning of the common market. As such, they are adopted with a view to achieving the objectives of the European Union.[72] Second, the institutional framework within which a directive is drawn up indicates that it is a legal act of the Council. Such institutional framework confers the power to adopt directives to the Council in its capacity as an institution of the European Union. As such, the institutional framework indicates that a Directive is a legal act of the Council and not an act of the Member States acting together.[73] Based on these two grounds, the CJEU

67. *See* F. Capotorti in: Making European Policies Work: The Implementation of Community Legislation in the Member States (Volume I) (Siedentopf & Ziller eds), 1988, p. 153, N. Blokker, Netherlands Yearbook of International Law 1999, p. 19, C.W.A. Timmermans, Common Market Law Review 1997/4, pp. 541-542, S. Prechal, 2009, p. 1, and R. Schütze, 2021, para. 5.3 who have all referred to (now) Article 288 TFEU as providing the (legal) definition of directives.
68. *See* Article 16(2) TEU.
69. Based on Article 16(3) TEU, the Council 'shall act by a qualified majority except where the Treaties provide otherwise'.
70. *See* preamble of Detergent Directive (73/404/EEC) which provides that '[h]aving regard to the Treaty establishing the European Economic Community, and in particular Article 100 thereof', Article 100 Treaty of Rome has been renumbered into Article 94 by means of the Treaty of Amsterdam (*see* Treaty of Amsterdam, p. 88), followed by a renumbering into, ultimately, Article 115 TFEU (*see* Treaty of Lisbon, C 306/213).
71. Case 91/79 (*Commission v. Italy*), para. 4.
72. *See* Case 91/79 (*Commission v. Italy*), para. 7 in conjunction with Case 91/79 (*Commission v. Italy*), para. 8.
73. *See* Case 91/79 (*Commission v. Italy*), para. 7 in conjunction with Case 91/79 (*Commission v. Italy*), para. 8.

ruled that a directive adopted on the basis of Article 115 TFEU cannot be described as an international agreement.[74]

Bearing in mind that the directives adopted in the area of direct taxation have been adopted on the basis of Article 115 TFEU, the judgment of the CJEU in *Commission v. Italy* (Case 91/79) would be applicable to them as well. Hence, the Directives cannot be regarded as having the status of an international agreement between the Member States from the perspective of the EU. As such, the circumstance that the Directives would reflect an (unanimous) agreement between the Member States does not affect their nature as 'binding legal acts of an institution of the EU'.

## 2.3 THE STATUS OF THE DIRECTIVES UNDER PUBLIC INTERNATIONAL LAW

The present section is aimed at determining the status of the Directives, as binding legal acts of the Council (an institution of the EU),[75] under the rules of public international law. The main question in this respect is whether the Directives, as binding legal acts of an institution of the EU, can be regarded as a source of public international law and, if so, as which source.[76]

### 2.3.1 The Directives as 'Sources' Within the Scope of Article 38 ICJ Statute

The starting point in determining the status of the Directives under public international law is Article 38 ICJ Statute, which provision is generally regarded as the most authoritative statement of the formal sources of public international law.[77] Based on Article 38(1) ICJ Statute, such sources comprise of (a) 'international conventions', (b)

74. *See* Case 91/79 (*Commission v. Italy*), para. 7 in conjunction with Case 91/79 (*Commission v. Italy*), para. 8.

75. In light of section 2.2, it is not further discussed whether a directive could be regarded as a treaty within the meaning of Article 2 VCLT 1969. Such a classification of a Directive has, in any event, been rejected by legal scholars. *See*, to that effect, L. de Broe in: Building Global International Tax Law: Essays in Honour of Guglielmo Maisto (Pistone ed.), 2022, para. 23.4.3 who notes that '[a]lthough the directive is inseparably linked with the TFEU and derives its effect from it, the directive does not have the status of a treaty under article 2 of the VCLT'. A similar position is adopted by F.P.G. Pötgens in: Building Global International Tax Law: Essays in Honour of Guglielmo Maisto (Pistone ed.), 2022, para. 20.3.2 who states that the 'EU Arbitration Directive and the Dutch Tax Arbitration Act cannot be regarded as bilateral or multilateral conventions', while referring to Case 38/69 (*Commission v. Italy*) and Case 91/79 (*Commission v. Italy*).

76. It can be noted, for completeness' sake, that it is not the purpose of this question to 'capture' the Directives in terms of other existing instruments of international law based on their nature (this would seem 'impossible' according to S. Prechal, 2009, p. 1). Instead, it is the purpose of the present section to determine their status under international law based on their nature irrespective of whether or not other instruments like the Directives would exist under international law.

77. J. Wouters, C. Ryngaert, T. Ruys & G. de Baere, 2019, p. 60. *See also* R. Jennings & A. Watts, 1992, p. 24, para. 9, F.A. Engelen, 2004, para. 2.1, and V. Lowe, 2007, p. 35. It is acknowledged that it does not follow explicitly from Article 38 ICJ Statute that it contains the formal sources of public international law, but this is usually inferred from the opening phrase wherein it is stated that it is the function of the ICJ to decide in accordance with international law. As a

'international custom', (c) 'the general principles of law recognized by civilized nations', and (d) 'judicial decisions and the teachings of the most highly qualified publicists of the various nations' (subject to the provisions of Article 59 ICJ Statute). Bearing in mind the nature of the Directives as 'binding legal acts of an institution of the EU', they do not fall within the scope of the sources of public international law as set out in Article 38 ICJ Statute.[78] Whereas the Directives may fall out of such scope, this is different for the treaty providing for the obligation to achieve the result of such Directives under Article 288 TFEU. Such obligation is laid down in Article 288 TFEU, which treaty has been concluded 'in the form of an international agreement'.[79] As such, the obligation to achieve the result of the Directives is, contrary to a Directive itself, laid down in a source of public international law within the meaning of Article 38 ICJ Statute.[80]

### 2.3.2 The Directives as 'Sources' Outside the Scope of Article 38 ICJ Statute

#### *2.3.2.1 The Non-exhaustive Nature of Article 38 ICJ Statute*

The circumstance that no reference is made to 'binding legal acts of an institution of the EU', or any similar term, in Article 38 ICJ Statute does not, however, entail that such acts are not among the sources of public international law. This is due to it being generally accepted that Article 38 ICJ Statute being incomplete.[81] Such incompleteness can be understood against the background that this provision has been drawn up in 1920 and that public international law has evolved over time.[82] As such, one of the

consequence, the sources listed in this provision of the ICJ Statute are the sources it will use to decide disputes in accordance with international law. *See*, in this respect, H. Thirlway, 2014, pp. 3-4.

78. In particular, it can be noted that the reference in Article 38(1)(a) ICJ Statute to 'international conventions' is commonly understood as including, in any event, 'treaties' within the meaning of Article 2(1)(a) VCLT 1969 (*see* J. Crawford in: Brownlie's Principles of Public International Law (Crawford ed.), 2019, p. 12), which defines the term 'treaty' as an 'international agreement concluded between States in written form and governed by international law'. Considering that the CJEU held that directives cannot be regarded as 'international agreements' or 'conventions in special form' (Case 91/79 (*Commission v. Italy*), para. 7), it follows from the nature of the directives under the laws of the EU that they cannot be regarded as treaties within the meaning of Article 2(1)(a) VCLT 1969 because the conditions of an 'international agreement' are not met. Furthermore, there are no reasons to assume that the Directives would fall within the scope of the sources of public international law referred to in Article 38(b) through (d) ICJ Statute.
79. Opinion 1/91 (*Draft agreement creation EEA*), para. 21 and Case C-357/19 (*Euro Box Promotion and Others*), para. 247.
80. *See*, in support of the characterisation of the EU Treaties as 'treaties', P. Nevill, Hungarian Yearbook of International Law and European Law 2013, pp. 281-282, B. de Witte in: European Union Law (Barnard & Peers eds), 2017, p. 177, C. Eckes & R.A. Wessel in: Oxford Principles of European Union Law: The European Union Legal Order (Vol. I) (Schütze & Tridimas eds), 2018, p. 81, and R.A. Wessel, Grotius Centre Working Paper Series No. 2018 2018/071 PIL, p. 4).
81. A. Pellet & D. Müller in: The Statute of the International Court of Justice: A Commentary (3rd Edition) (Zimmermann, Tams, Oellers-Frahm & Tomuschat eds), 2019, paras 76 and 90.
82. *See*, *e.g.*, H. Thirlway, 2014, pp. 19-20 who notes that '[t]he enumeration of formal sources in Article 38 ... was presumably then regarded as complete, or sufficiently complete for the

main criticisms of Article 38 ICJ Statute as a statement of the sources of public international law is its incompleteness.[83] Bearing in mind the incompleteness of Article 38 ICJ Statute, there are thus also other sources of public international law, which may resemble 'binding legal acts of an institution of the EU'. The most relevant other source of public international law, which is discussed in detail below, seem to be the category of 'decisions of an international organisation'.[84]

#### 2.3.2.2 *Decisions of International Organisations as 'Sources' of Public International Law*

With respect to the other, non-listed, sources of public international law, legal scholars have submitted that they include, in any event, decisions of international organisations.[85] Support for such inclusion can also be derived from the judgment of the ICJ in *Lockerbie*.[86] In this case, the ICJ ruled that a UN Security Council Resolution[87] prevailed over the obligations of Libya and the United Kingdom under an international agreement between them.[88] The ICJ thus seemed to recognise that, first, a UN Security Council Resolution was among the sources of international law and, second, that such a resolution could take precedence over an international agreement (a source of public international law within the meaning of Article 38 ICJ Statute).

With respect to the nature of a UN Security Council Resolutions, it is submitted that they are to be regarded as a decision of an international organisation on the following grounds. First, a UN Security Council Resolution is characterised in the UN Charter as a (binding) decision of the Security Council,[89] an organ of the UN.[90] Such a decision is then aimed at giving effect to the power granted to the UN Security Council to act under Chapter VII of the UN Charter ('Action with respect to threat to the peace, breaches of the peace, and acts of aggression').[91] Second, there seems to be

purposes of judicial settlement, which probably comes to the same thing. Whether or not it was so in 1920, it has since been questioned whether there may not be today other possible sources of international law'.

83. A. Pellet & D. Müller in: The Statute of the International Court of Justice: A Commentary (3rd Edition) (Zimmermann, Tams, Oellers-Frahm & Tomuschat eds), 2019, paras 76 and 90.
84. Regarding the relevance of 'decisions of international organisations', *see* I. Benzing in: Max Planck Encyclopedias of International Law, 2007, para. 2 who notes that characterising such decisions as a source of international law 'pays tribute to the fact that such secondary law plays an increasingly important role in the development of international law'.
85. *See* I. Benzing in: Max Planck Encyclopedias of International Law, 2007, paras 2 and 49 and A. Pellet & D. Müller in: The Statute of the International Court of Justice: A Commentary (3rd Edition) (Zimmermann, Tams, Oellers-Frahm & Tomuschat eds), 2019, para. 90.
86. ICJ 14 April 1992, Order, Provisional Measures (*Lockerbie*).
87. SC Resolution 748 (1992).
88. *See* ICJ.1992, Order, Provisional Measures (*Lockerbie*), p. 15, para. 39.
89. Regarding the binding nature, *see* Article 25 UN Charter.
90. *See* Article 7(1) UN Charter.
91. Regarding the characterisation of a UN Security Council Resolution as a 'decision', *see*, *inter alia*, Articles 25 and 27 UN Charter.

(unanimous) agreement that the United Nations qualifies as an international organisation.[92] As such, UN Security Council Resolution 748 (1992) can be regarded as a (binding) decision of an international organisation.[93] Such a decision could then be regarded, based on the ICJ taking such a decision into account in *Lockerbie*, as a source of public international law.[94] It thus follows that the ICJ considers decisions of international organisations as a source of international law when exercising its function to 'decide in accordance with international law such disputes as are submitted to it'.[95] This, in turn, provides support for the submission of legal scholars that decisions of international organisations are to be regarded as a source of public international law.

#### *2.3.2.3 The Directives as Decisions of the European Union as an International Organisation*

Having established that (binding) decisions of an international organisation constitute a source of public international law, the present section is aimed at determining whether the Directives, as 'binding legal acts of the Council (as an institution of the EU)', can be regarded as 'decisions of an international organisation'. In that respect, the preliminary question that must be answered is whether the European Union can be regarded as an 'international organisation'.

The starting point in answering this question is that there is no universally accepted definition of the term 'international organisation' in public international law.[96] Notwithstanding the absence of such a universally accepted definition, definitions that have been expressed do provide evidence of certain main characteristics that, if present with respect to a certain form of an inter-state organisation, would justify regarding such an organisation as an 'international organisation' under public

---

92. The characteristics of international organisations are discussed in detail in section 2.3.2.2. With respect to the characterisation of the UN as an 'international organisation', *see* J. Klabbers, 2015, para. 1.2 and J. Pauwelyn, 2003, p. 145 (implicitly).
93. *See* I. Benzing in: Max Planck Encyclopedias of International Law, 2007, para. 14 who notes that a UN Security Council is a textbook example for a binding act - i.e., a decision - of an international organisation.
94. Reference can also be made to the Advisory Opinion of the ICJ in Kosovo, wherein it held that it was necessary for the Court to 'interpret and apply the provisions of Security Council resolution 1244 (1999) in the course of answering the question put by the General Assembly', while also recognising that 'the Court, as the principal judicial organ of the United Nations, has also frequently been required to consider the interpretation and legal effects of such decisions' (*see* ICJ, 2010, Advisory Opinion (*Kosovo*), p. 430, para. 46. The ICJ refers, in this same paragraph, to various cases wherein it has done so).
95. *See*, in this respect, also A. Pellet & D. Müller in: The Statute of the International Court of Justice: A Commentary (3rd Edition) (Zimmermann, Tams, Oellers-Frahm & Tomuschat eds), 2019, paras 99-103.
96. *See, e.g.*, H.G. Schermers & N.M. Blokker, 2011, p. 36, at p. 32, J. Klabbers, 2015, para. 1.2, J. Klabbers in: A Companion to European Union Law and International Law (Patterson & Söderston eds), 2016, p. 4 ('no airtight definition'), and J. Wouters, C. Ryngaert, T. Ruys & G. de Baere, 2019, p. 26.

international law.[97] These main characteristics, reflecting 'regularly recurring elements',[98] are:

(a) the organisation is founded on an international agreement between states;
(b) the organisation has as least one organ with a will of its own (often referred to as the '*volonte distincte*'); and
(c) the organisation has been established under international law.[99]

In the absence of a universally accepted definition, it will be determined below whether the European Union would possess each of these three main characteristics of an international organisation.

#### *2.3.2.3.1 The European Union as Founded upon an International Agreement Between States*

International organisations are generally founded on a (multilateral) treaty concluded between more than two states.[100] Based on the TEU and TFEU as multilateral treaties, which has been recognised by the CJEU,[101] and as the foundation of the European Union,[102] the European Union possesses the first characteristic of an international organisation.

97. The reference to an 'inter-state organisation' seeks to encompass all forms of organisations set up by states. In setting up such organisations, it seems that states are not necessarily concerned with the exact legal qualification of such entity as an international organisation under public international law. Instead, their concern is to create an organisation that 'allows them to meet their ends, endow such entities with some characteristics they see fit (certain organs, certain powers), and then hope that their creation can do what they set it up to do' (*see* J. Klabbers, 2009, p. 6).
98. J. Klabbers, Melbourne Journal of International Law 2013/6, p. 5 who also notes that (p. 4) these elements are thus not to be regarded as 'hard and fast rules' or 'legal requirements' for determining whether an inter-state organisation qualifies as an 'international organisation'.
99. *See* J.E. Alvarez, 2005, para. 1.2, H.G. Schermers & N.M. Blokker, 2011, p. 37, para. 33, J. Klabbers in: A Companion to European Union Law and International Law (Patterson & Söderston eds), 2016, p. 4, and J. Klabbers, 2015, para. 1.2. Reference can also be made to J. Wouters, C. Ryngaert, T. Ruys & G. de Baere, 2019, pp. 256-257 who refer to (i) an association of subjects of international law, most often states, but sometimes also international organisations, (ii) established by a treaty or other instrument governed by international law, (iii) the pursuit of common objectives, and (iv) the existence of one or more organs which are able to generate an 'autonomous will' distinct from the organisation's members, are, in substance, the same.
100. *See* J. Klabbers, 2015, para. 1.2. There are, however, also exceptions. For example, the WTO – which is generally recognised as an international organisation – is founded upon a multilateral treaty to which the European Union is also a party.
101. *See* Opinion 1/91 (Draft agreement creation EEA), para. 21 and Case C-357/19 (*Euro Box Promotion and Others*), para. 247. In this respect, reference can also be made to Case C-284/16 (*Achmea*), para. 41 wherein the Court held that 'EU law ... must be regarded ... as deriving from an international agreement between the Member States'.
102. *See* Article 1(3) TEU which provides that the Union 'shall be founded on the present Treaty and on the Treaty on the Functioning of the European Union'.

#### 2.3.2.3.2 *The European Union with Organs with a Will of Their Own*

In addition to being founded upon a multilateral agreement between states, international organisations generally have one or more organs with a will distinct from the will of its Member States.[103] This characteristic can be regarded as the '*quintessential*' characteristic of international organisations that sets them apart from other forms of inter-state organisations.[104] In assessing whether the European Union has organs with such a will distinct from the Member States, Klabbers submits that two perspectives may be adopted: (i) a '*formalist*' perspective and (ii) a '*sociological*' perspective.[105]

Under the formalist perspective, an inter-state organisation can be said to have a will of its own (a '*volonte distincte*') if the organisation (by means of one or more of its organs) is able to tell its Member States what to do, even if those states would not agree.[106] It thus 'presupposes an organization which is, first, capable of taking decisions binding on the Member States and, second, capable of taking such decisions by majority vote'.[107] As such, inter-state organisations that cannot take binding decisions or only allow for such decisions to be taken after the consent of all of its Member States agree, would not have a will of its own under this view.[108] An example of an international organisation that is able to take such binding decisions against the will of their Member States is the United Nations.[109]

The European Union would seem to be another example. This can be illustrated as follows. First, the institutions of the EU are able to adopt binding legal acts, i.e., regulations, directives and decisions, without prior approval of all Member States. For example, the starting point for adopting such legal acts is that only a qualified majority is required in the Council,[110] an organ consisting of the representatives of each Member State at the ministerial level.[111] It is only when the TEU or the TFEU would provide otherwise, that voting may take place by unanimity.[112] Another example of an organ that is able to adopt binding legal acts without prior approval of the Member States is

103. It could thus be said that such a volonte distincte reflects the idea that an international organisation, although founded by its Member States, must possess a 'certain level of independence from those states' (J. Odermatt, EUI Working Papers 2016/7, p. 3). This also seems to be the view of the ICJ based on its judgment in ICJ. 1996, Advisory Opinion (*Legality of Nuclear Weapons in Armed Conflict*), p. 13, para. 18 wherein it ruled that the object of multilateral treaties establishing an international organisation is to 'create new subjects of law endowed with a certain autonomy'.
104. J. Klabbers, 2009, p. 12 and J. Klabbers in: A Companion to European Union Law and International Law (Patterson & Söderston eds), 2016, p. 4. *See also* J. Klabbers in: The Legitimacy of International Organizations (Coicaud & Heiskanen eds), 2001, p. 226.
105. J. Klabbers, 2015, para. 1.2.
106. J. Klabbers, 2015, para. 1.2.
107. J. Klabbers in: A Companion to European Union Law and International Law (Patterson & Söderston eds), 2016, p. 5.
108. According to Klabbers, there are 'precious few organisations that can take binding decisions against the will of one or more member states' (*see* J. Klabbers, 2015, para. 1.2).
109. J. Klabbers, 2015, para. 1.2, as well as J. Wouters, C. Ryngaert, T. Ruys & G. de Baere, 2019, p. 258.
110. *See* Article 16(2) TEU.
111. *See* Article 16(2) TEU.
112. *See* Article 16(3) and (4) TEU.

the Commission within the context of state aid decisions. State aid decisions adopted by the Commission, an institution of the EU that is independent of the Member States,[113] are binding upon the addressees of such decisions while the Member States are not able to vote for, or veto, such state aid decisions.[114] As such, the European Union has organs that can adopt legal acts that are binding on the Member States without the agreement of such Member States. It thus follows that the EU has at least two organs with a will distinct from the will of the Member States within the meaning of the formalist perspective.

In addition to determining the existence of a *volonte distincte* under the formalist perspective, such a determination can also be made under the (broader) sociological perspective. This latter perspective considers an inter-state organisation to have a will of its own based on a factual analysis. As such, whereas an organisation may not have a *volonte distincte* from a legal point of view, it may be the case that it is clear in practice that it does have such a will of its own. For example, 'the very idea of a secretariat proposing that an item be placed on the political agenda already suggests that the organisation does more than faithfully execute the common will of the member states, and thus can be deemed to have a distinct will'.[115] In such a sense, the European Union can also be said to have a will of its own due to, for example, the European Commission being able to propose directives to the Council. By issuing such directives, it is able to influence the political agenda. It thus follows that both under the '*formalist*' and '*sociological*', the European Union can be regarded as having will of its own or a *volonte distincte*.

### *2.3.2.3.3 The European Union as Established under International Law*

The final characteristic that must be assessed is whether the European Union can be regarded as having been established under international law. In this respect, it seems to follow from *Van Gend en Loos* that the European Union has been established under international law given that the CJEU ruled that that the Treaty of Rome had given rise to 'a new legal order of international law'.[116] It is acknowledged, in this context, that the reference 'of international law' has not been used in its subsequent case law.[117] Nevertheless, it still indicates that the CJEU considered the EU to have been established

113. *See* Article 17(3) TEU.
114. *See*, regarding the nature of state aid decisions under Article 108 TFEU as 'decisions' within the meaning of Article 288(4) TFEU, State Aid Notice (2019/C 247/01), p. 5, para. 30.
115. J. Klabbers, 2015, para. 1.2. Klabbers also recognised that it may also be the case that 'in practice it is often difficult for organisations to develop and maintain their own identity', 'even when from a legal point of view it is clear that an organisation has a will of its own'.
116. CJEU, 5 February 1963, Case 26/62 (*Van Gend en Loos*), p. 10.
117. Such reference may thus be regarded as having 'faded away' (*see* F.C. Mayer in: The Past and Future of EU Law: The Classics of EU Law Revisited on the 50th Anniversary of the Rome Treaty (Maduro & Azoulai eds), 2010, p. 21). Other scholars noting that the 'qualification' was dropped in its subsequent case law are H.G. Krenzler & O. Landweher in: From Bilateralism to Community Interest: Essays in Honour of Bruno Simma (Fastenrath, Geiger, Khan, Paulus, Schorlemer & Vedder eds), 2011, pp. 1004-1005, B. de Witte in: The Worlds of European Constitutionalism (De Búrca & Weiler eds), 2012, pp. 38-39 and K. Lenaerts, Post AISDUE 2019/I, p. 2.

under international law.[118] Support for such a view can also be derived from the relatively recent judgment of the CJEU in *Achmea* wherein the Court held that EU law 'must be regarded ... as deriving from an international agreement between the Member States'.[119] As deriving from an international agreement between the Member States, it thus seems that the CJEU recognises that the EU – as was already ruled in *Van Gend en Loos* – has been established under international law. The international law basis of the European Union has also been recognised by the ECtHR in *Matthews*,[120] as well as by the ICSID in *Electrabel* considering that it held that 'EU law is based on international treaties: EU law is international law because it is rooted in international law'.[121] As such, the European Union would also possess this third characteristic that is common for international organisations.

#### *2.3.2.3.4 Conclusion Regarding the European Union as an 'International Organisation'*

It follows from the preceding sections that the European Union, as an example of an inter-state organisation, *'ticks all the boxes'* in the sense that it possesses the three main characteristics of an 'international organisation': it was created by an international agreement between states (section 2.3.2.3.1), it possesses organs (*'institutions'*) with a will distinct from the will of the Member States (section 2.3.2.3.2), and it was established under international law (section 2.3.2.3.3).[122] As such, it is concluded that

118. *See*, to that effect, B. de Witte in: European Union Law (Barnard & Peers eds), 2017, p. 177 and T. Molnar, 2021, p. 15 ('[t]he CJEU first has to emancipate EU law from international law'), as well as T.C. Hartley, British Yearbook of International Law 2001, p. 12. Hartley does note that the reference, at the same time, indicates the separateness of the EU legal order from international law.
119. Case C-284/16 (*Achmea*), para. 41. *See* L. Gasbarri, 2018, Regime Interactions and the Dual Legality of EU Law: The Case of Slovak Republic v. Achmea, The Global (https://theglobal.blog/2018/04/26/regime-interactions-and-the-dual-legality-of-eu-law-the-case-of-slovak-republic-v-achmea/) who notes that the 'Achmea decision reminds us that the international origin of EU law is not abandoned'.
120. *See* ECtHR, Application No. 24833/94 (*Matthews v. United Kingdom*), para. 32. According to C. Binder & J.A. Hofbauer, European Yearbook of International Economic Law 2017, p. 29 the ECtHR 'clearly perceived [the EU] as a "classic" international organization'. Reference may also be made to ECtHR, Application No. 45036/98 (*Bosphorus*), para. 154, which has been interpreted by C. Eckes, Europe and the World: A Law Review 2020/1, p. 14 as indicating that the ECtHR regards the EU as an international organisation.
121. ICSID 25 November 2015, Case No. ARB/07/19 (*Electrabel v. Hungary*), para. 4.120, which position has also been adopted in ICSID, Case No. ARB/12/12 (*Vattenfall*), para. 146. *See*, in support of the characterisation of the EU Treaties as 'treaties', also H.G. Krenzler & O. Landwehr in: From Bilateralism to Community Interest: Essays in Honour of Bruno Simma (Fastenrath, Geiger, Khan, Paulus, Schorlemer & Vedder eds), 2011, p. 1005, P. Nevill, Hungarian Yearbook of International Law and European Law 2013, pp. 281-282, B. de Witte in: European Union Law (Barnard & Peers eds), 2017, p. 177, C. Eckes & R.A. Wessel in: Oxford Principles of European Union Law: The European Union Legal Order (Vol. I) (Schütze & Tridimas eds), 2018, p. 81, and R.A. Wessel, Grotius Centre Working Paper Series No. 2018 2018/071 PIL, p. 4.
122. *See* for the conclusion that the EU 'ticks all the boxes', B. de Witte in: European Union Law (Barnard & Peers eds), 2016, pp. 178-179. Other legal scholars who consider the EU as an 'international organisation' are P. Eeckhout, 2011, p. 323, J. Klabbers, 2015, para. 1.2, J.

the European Union must be regarded as an 'international organisation' for the purposes of this thesis. Such conclusion would seem aligned with the view of the CJEU considering that it has ruled that an agreement concluded between the European Union and a third state fell 'squarely' within the definition of an agreement within the meaning of Article 2(1)(a)(i) VCLT 1986 ('an international agreement governed by international law concluded in written form: (i) between one or more States and one or more international organisations').[123] As such, the CJEU seems to regard the European Union as an international organisation as well.[124]

#### *2.3.2.3.5 Conclusion Regarding the Directives as Decisions of an International Organisation*

Based on sections 2.3.2.3.1 through 2.3.2.3.4, the European Union is regarded as an international organisation for the purposes of this thesis. This would entail that directives such as the Directives can be described as 'binding legal acts of an institution of an international organisation'. Based on such description, also taking into account that the ICJ considered a binding decision (Security Council Resolution) of an organ (the UN Security Council) of another international organisation (the UN) as a source of

Klabbers in: A Companion to European Union Law and International Law (Patterson & Söderstron eds), 2016, pp. 8-9 ('it meets the requirements of international law'), and C. Eckes & R.A. Wessel in: Oxford Principles of European Union Law: The European Union Legal Order (Vol. I) (Schütze & Tridimas eds), 2018, p. 99. Reference may also be made to C. Binder & J.A. Hofbauer, European Yearbook of International Economic Law 2017, p. 4 who note that from an international law perspective, the EU is most commonly 'classified as a (supranational) international organization, i.e. an international organization which is embedded in international law by virtue of its founding instruments', while adding that it is in many aspects 'more advanced or different than other international organizations'.

123. Case C-327/91 (*Commission v. France*), para. 25. A similar characterisation of the European Union under the VCLT 1986 has been (implicitly) adopted by the CJEU in Case C-386/08 (*Brita*), para. 41 and Case C-613/12 (*Helm*), para. 37 regarding agreements concluded by the European Union and Israel (Brita) and Egypt (Helm).

124. It furthermore seems to be aligned with the view of the European Commission. *See* to that effect the submission of the Commission in ECtHR, Application No. 45036/98 (*Bosphorus*), para. 122 (the Member States had 'ceded powers to an international organisation', or Brief of the European Commission on behalf of the European Union as Amicus Curiae in support of neither party (*United States v. Microsoft*), p. 1 (the European Union is a 'treaty-based international organization with the competence to develop and enforce Union-wide legislation in specified areas and policy'. These submissions lead C. Binder & J.A. Hofbauer, European Yearbook of International Economic Law 2017, p. 9 to submit that the 'the EU represents itself as an international organization albeit with special features'. Reference can furthermore be made to the submission of the Commission in Comments and observations received from Governments and international organisations, A/CN.4/556, p. 31 ('In particular, the European Community is an international organization with special features as envisaged in the founding treaties.').

It is acknowledged that there are legal scholars who disagree with characterising the European Union, at present, as an international organisation. *See, e.g.*, S. Douglas-Scott, 2002, p. 260 who notes that 'even if the EEC did conform to the status of international organizations in its early days (which is unlikely) it has not moved well beyond that' and R. Schütze, Common Market Law Review 2009/4, p. 1088 who states that the EU's 'formation was clearly international and its amendment still is. ... The fact remains that the European legal order has adopted the "originality hypothesis" and cut the umbilical cord with the international legal order'.

international law,[125] it can be concluded that that the Directives, as binding legal acts of an organ of the European Union as an international organisation, would be among the sources of international law as 'decisions of an international organisation'.[126]

Whereas the arguments underlying this conclusion seem aligned with the positions of the CJEU,[127] i.e., directives are legal acts of an institution of the European Union, and the European Union is an 'international organisation', there are legal scholars who assert that the European Union and its laws are detached from public international law.[128] Support for such detachment is often derived from the 'autonomy' of the EU legal order vis-à-vis international law.[129] Pursuant to such autonomy, the laws of the European Union are not affected by external laws, such as those of public international law and national law, unless EU law allows it.[130] In *Kadi*, for example, the CJEU ruled that 'an international agreement cannot affect (...) the autonomy of the Community legal system'.[131] Therefore, international agreements cannot, for example, affect the constitutional principles of the EU Treaties[132] or the exclusive competence of the CJEU to rule on the interpretation of EU law.[133] The autonomy of EU law thus serves to 'protect' the EU legal order from external influences such as international law.[134] Such autonomy does not, however, entail that the EU must be regarded as detached from public international law or that the CJEU has 'cut the umbilical cord' with public international law.[135] Whereas the case law of the CJEU might be interpreted by legal scholars as the EU and its laws being detached from public international law, this author disagrees with such a view. The reason for such disagreement is that the CJEU

125. *See* section 2.3.2.2.
126. In support of such a conclusion *see, inter alia,* I. Benzing, in: Max Planck Encyclopedias of International Law, 2007, para. 3 who notes that the law produced by the organs – or institutions – of the European Union is one of 'the most prominent examples of secondary law of international organizations'.
127. In particular, reference can be made to the characterisation of directives as legal acts of the Council (and not as international agreements) in Case 91/79 (*Commission v. Italy*) and the EU Treaties as international agreements reflecting international law (*see* Case C-284/16 (*Achmea*)), as well as to the CJEU regarding international agreements concluded by the European Union with states as concluded between such states and an international organisation (*see* Case C-386/08 (*Brita*) and Case C-613/12 (*Helm*)).
128. *See, e.g.*, R. Schütze, 2021, Chapter 3, Introduction, who notes that the CJEU has '*expressly cut the umbilical cord with classic international law by insisting that the European legal order was a "new legal order"*', while adding that '*with a stroke of the pen, the Court confirmed the independence of the European legal order from classic international law*'.
129. *See, e.g.*, R. Schütze, 2021, Chapter 3, Introduction. Regarding the autonomy vis-à-vis international law, *see* K. Lenaerts, Post AISDUE 2019/I, p. 2.
130. *See* J. Odermatt, EUI Working Papers 2016/7, p. 11, K. Lenaerts, Post AISDUE 2019/I, p. 6, M.-L.Öberg, European Public Law 2020/3, p. 712, and C. Eckes, Europe and the World: A Law Review 2020/1, p. 4. *See also* Opinion of Advocate General Maduro in: Joined Cases C-402/05 P & C-415/05 P (*Kadi*), para. 23 where it is noted that 'in the final analysis, the Community Courts determine the effect of international obligations within the Community legal order by reference to conditions set by Community law'.
131. Joined Cases C-402/05 P & C-415/05 P (*Kadi and Al Barakaat*), para. 282.
132. Joined Cases C-402/05 P & C-415/05 P (*Kadi and Al Barakaat*), para. 285. *See also* C. Eckes, Europe and the World: A Law Review 2020/1, p. 3.
133. Case C-284/16 (*Achmea*), paras 58-60.
134. *See* M.-L.Öberg, European Public Law 2020/3, p. 712.
135. *See* regarding such detachment, R. Schütze, 2021, Chapter 3, Introduction.

has merely ruled that the EU legal order is 'autonomous'. Based on its dictionary meaning, being 'autonomous' entails that the EU would have 'the freedom to govern itself or control its own affairs' (Oxford Dictionary) and that an organisation would be 'independent' in the sense of having 'the freedom to govern itself' (Cambridge Dictionary). As such, the reference to the EU legal order being 'autonomous' would seem to indicate that the EU can determine how it functions, irrespective of external sources of law. It does not, by contrast, seem to indicate that such legal order would also be completely separate from, for example, the international legal order. The 'autonomy' of the EU legal order, based on the dictionary meaning of 'autonomous', can thus be understood as merely indicating the independence of the EU when it comes to how the EU legal order is shaped and how it functions. It cannot, however, be understood as meaning that the EU is detached from international law. This also seems to be view of Lenaerts who states that the 'emphasis that the Court of Justice places on autonomy cannot be read as an attempt to cut the EU loose from its international law origins entirely; autonomy must not be confused with complete detachment'.[136] The case law of the CJEU wherein it held that the EU legal order is 'autonomous' is thus understood as meaning that such legal order cannot be affected by external sources of law, such as public international law unless this is provided for by the EU legal order itself. It is not, however, understood as referring to the European Union being isolated or detached from public international law.[137] Based on this understanding, the conclusion that the Directives can be regarded as a source of public international law is not incompatible with (the autonomy of) the EU.

### 2.3.3 Conclusion Regarding the Status of the Directives under Public International Law

With respect to the status of the Directives under public international law, it follows from section 2.3.2 that they are among the sources of public international law as decisions of the European Union as an international organisation. Moreover, it follows from section 2.3.1 that the general obligation to achieve the result of the directives is also laid down in a source of public international law. As such, both the Directives and the obligation to achieve their result are part of the sources of public international and, for that reason, must be regarded as having the status of international law for the purposes of the present thesis.

136. K. Lenaerts, Post AISDUE 2019/I, p. 5. *See also* M.-L.Öberg, European Public Law 2020/3, p. 717 who notes that the case law of the CJEU 'illustrates well the perception of the EU as an autonomous legal order (...) yet not as one completely isolated from the international legal regime'. *See also* B. de Witte, Netherlands Yearbook of International Law 1994, p. 300, B. de Witte in: The Worlds of European Constitutionalism (De Búrca & Weiler eds), 2012, p. 39, and C. Binder & J.A. Hofbauer, European Yearbook of International Economic Law 2017, p. 2.2.2.

137. Support for this position may also be derived from Case C-284/16 (*Achmea*), para. 41 where the CJEU held that EU law stems from an international agreement.

## 2.4 THE STATUS OF THE DIRECTIVES THE LAWS OF THE EU

In addition to analysing the status of the Directives under public international law, their status can also be analysed from the perspective of the laws of the EU. The starting point for the purposes of such an analysis is the statement of the CJEU in *Achmea* that 'given the nature and characteristics of EU law (...), that law must be regarded both as forming part of the law in force in every Member State and as deriving from an international agreement between the Member States'.[138] This statement indicates that EU law, comprising of both the EU Treaties and legal acts of the institutions, must be regarded as having a 'dual nature':[139] EU law has the status of both the 'laws in force in every Member State', i.e., essentially as domestic law, as well as 'international law'.

### 2.4.1 The Directives as 'Part of the Laws in Force in Every Member State'

The status of directives as 'part of the laws in force in every Member State' can be traced back to the judgment of the CJEU in *Costa/ENEL* wherein it held that the EEC Treaty had created its 'own legal system which, on the entry into force of the Treaty, became an integral part of the legal systems of the Member States and which their courts are bound to apply'.[140] This reference has been subsequently interpreted as indicating that 'the whole body of [EU] law (including directives, which are components of this law) is as such incorporated within the national legal orders, without measures or transformation, incorporation – or whatever else the terminology might be – being necessary'.[141] As such, directives are 'integrated' in the national legal system of the Member States from the moment of their entry into force.

Such 'integration', in practice, entails that directives are 'part of the laws in force in every Member State' and that individuals can rely on them before national courts.[142]

138. Case C-284/16 (*Achmea*), para. 41. *See also* Opinion AG Szpunar, Case C-741/19 (*Komstroy*), para. 75.
139. *See* L. Gasbarri, 2018, The Global, S. Hindelang, European Law Review 2019/3, p. 8, C. Glinksi, Legal Studies Research Paper Series, Paper No. 2019/70, p. 13, and T. Molnar, 2021, p. 15 ('the dual character of EU law, both as a self-standing and self-integrating sui generis legal order and as a legal order of international origin, not hermetically closed and thus not having completely cut its ties from international law'). Reference can also be made to Opinion AG Szpunar, Case C-741/19 (*Komstroy*), para. 75, as interpreted by J. Odermatt, European Papers 2021/3, p. 1266 ('According to the AG, EU law has a dual character.').

    The rationale for referring to the EU Treaties as deriving from an international agreement can be found in Article 8 Netherlands-Slovakia BIT. Pursuant to this provision, an arbitral tribunal would decide on the basis of the law, taking into account in particular, the law in force of the contracting party concerned and other relevant agreements between the contracting states (*see also* Case C-284/16 (*Achmea*), para. 40). By concluding that the EU Treaties had to be regarded as deriving from an international agreement, as well as forming part of the laws in force of the Member States, the CJEU essentially ruled that the arbitral tribunal may be called upon to interpret the laws of the EU (Case C-284/16 (*Achmea*), para. 42).
140. CJEU, 15 July 1964, Case 6/64 (*Costa v. ENEL*), p. 593.
141. S. Prechal, 2009, p. 92, as well as C.W.A. Timmermans, Common Market Law Review 1997/4, p. 534.
142. *See*, in general, C.W.A. Timmermans, Common Market Law Review 1997/4, pp. 534-535 who distinguishes four ways in which directives may be relied upon by individuals before a court.

Such reliance can take, for example, the form of Member State courts being under a duty to interpret national laws, as far as possible, in light of the wording and the purpose of a directive (duty of consistent interpretation).[143] In addition, Member State courts are required to set aside national law that conflicts with the result to be achieved by a Directive if such a directive (provision) has direct effect.[144] As such, the Directives are part of the laws of the Member States on which individuals can rely, irrespective of the forms and methods chosen by a Member State to transpose such Directives into its laws.[145]

### 2.4.2 The Directives as 'Deriving from an International Agreement Between the Member States'

Whereas the status of the laws of the EU as 'part of the laws of the Member States' can be traced back to the judgment of the CJEU in *Costa/ENEL* in 1964, the status of such laws as 'deriving from an international agreement' has only been explicitly confirmed as of 2018 by the judgment of the Court in *Achmea*. The background of such confirmation is a request for a preliminary ruling from the German *Bundesgerichtshof* (Federal Court of Justice) regarding the compatibility of Article 8 of the bilateral investment treaty, pursuant to which arbitration proceedings had been commenced against Slovakia,[146] concluded between the Netherlands and Slovakia with Articles 267 and 344 TFEU.[147] In determining such compatibility, the CJEU noted that it first had to ascertain whether the arbitral tribunal would be called on to resolve disputes relating to 'the interpretation or application of EU law'.[148] In that respect, the CJEU referred to Article 8(6) Netherlands-Slovakia BIT. Pursuant to this provision, an arbitral tribunal 'shall decide on the basis of the law, taking into account in particular though not exclusively: the law in force of the Contracting Party concerned [and] the provisions of this Agreement, and other relevant Agreements between the Contracting Parties'.[149] Based on such provision, an arbitral tribunal may thus be called upon to interpret or

143. *See*, regarding such duty, Chapter 4.
144. *See*, regarding direct effect, section 7.3.2. With respect to such direct effect, it is noted that individuals are generally not able to (effectively) rely on directly effective directive provisions against another private party (the directives cannot, as such, have 'horizontal direct effect'). *See*, in this respect, Case 152/84 (*Marshall*), para. 48 and Case C-91/92 (*Faccini Dori*), paras 22-25. Scholars who have published about such 'horizontal direct effect' include S. Prechal, 2009, pp. 261 et seq., K. Lenaerts & P. van Nuffel, 2017, p. 597, para. 781, and R. Schütze, 2021, para. 5.3.aa.
145. *See* S. Prechal, 2009, p. 93 who notes that the requirement of transposition in Article 288 TFEU 'does not, however, alter the fact that directives are part of the body of law which is valid within the national legal order and may as such produce various kinds of effect'.
146. *See* Case C-284/16 (*Achmea*), para. 9.
147. Article 8(1) Netherlands-Slovakia BIT provides that '[a]ll disputes between one Contracting Party and an investor of the other Contracting Party concerning an investment of the latter shall if possible, be settled amicably'. Article 267 TFEU relates to the jurisdiction of the CJEU, while Article 334 TFEU provides that 'Member States undertake not to submit a dispute concerning the interpretation of application of the Treaties to any method of settlement other than those provided for therein'.
148. *See* Case C-284/16 (*Achmea*), para. 38.
149. *See* Case C-284/16 (*Achmea*), para. 39.

apply EU law if EU law would qualify as either 'law in force of the Contracting Party' or as 'other relevant Agreements between the Contracting Parties'. Based on the ruling of the CJEU that EU law has a dual nature, i.e., as part of the laws in force in the Member States and as deriving from an international agreement between the Member States, the CJEU was able to rule that the 'arbitral tribunal ... may be called on to interpret or indeed to apply EU law'.[150] Based on such ruling, Article 8 of the Netherlands-Slovakia BIT was found to be incompatible with Articles 267 and 344 TFEU.

### 2.4.3 Conclusion Regarding the Legal Status of the Directives

Based on sections 2.4.1 and 2.4.2, Directives must be regarded as having a dual nature under the laws of the EU. They enjoy the status of both 'laws in every Member State' and 'as deriving from an international agreement between the Member States'.

## 2.5 CONCLUSION

It has been the purpose of this chapter to determine the nature and status of the Directives under the laws of public international law and the laws of the EU. In that respect, the following is concluded for the purposes of the present thesis:

(a) *The nature of the Directives*: binding legal acts of the Council, an institution of the European Union, aimed at giving effect to the objective of the EU to approximate such laws, regulations or administrative provisions of the Member States which directly affect the establishment or functioning of the internal market (section 2.2).
(b) *Status of the Directives under public international law*: a source of public international law as (binding) decisions of an institution, i.e., the Council, of the European Union as an international organisation (section 2.3).
(c) *Status of the Directives under the laws of the EU*: a source of both the laws of the Member States and as deriving from an international agreement between states (section 2.4).

150. *See* Case C-284/16 (*Achmea*), paras 41-42.

PART II

# The Effect of the Directives on the Interpretation of Tax Treaties

In this second part of the present thesis, it will be assessed to what extent the Directives may affect the interpretation of tax treaties concluded by the Member States. Such assessment is made by addressing the effect of the Directives on the interpretation of tax treaties from the perspective of public international law (Chapter 3) and from the perspective of the laws of the EU (Chapter 4). Based on the outcomes regarding the effect of the Directives on the interpretation of tax treaties under both perspectives, it will then be assessed in Chapter 5 to what extent such effect overlaps, i.e., to what extent is the 'allowed' effect (under public international law) equal to the 'required' effect (under the laws of the EU). The approach of this part is as follows. This Part II seeks to determine the effect that Directives may have on the interpretation of tax treaties (i) by means of Directives containing terminology that is similar to that used in tax treaties and (ii) by the result that a Directive requires to be achieved by the Member States. With respect to the effect of terminology of Directives that is similar to that used in tax treaties on the interpretation of such tax treaties, the relevant questions under the public international law perspective that are addressed in this Part II are whether, when interpreting, for example, the undefined 'beneficial owner' term in such tax treaties, (i) the definition of the term 'beneficial owner' in the Interest and Royalties Directive, as interpreted by the CJEU in the *Danish Cases*,[151] may be taken into account under the rules governing the interpretation of tax treaties, i.e., Article 3(2) OECD Model (2017) and Articles 31-33 VVCLT 1969 and, if so, (ii), how much weight would have to be attributed to such definition. Additionally, under the perspective of the laws of the EU, the relevant question would be to what extent a Member State court would be obliged to interpret the term 'beneficial owner' in a tax treaty in the same way as such term has been defined in the Interest and Royalties Directive (and interpreted by the CJEU in the *Danish Cases*). Based on the answers under both perspectives, it can

151. Joined Cases C-115/16, C-118/16, C-119/16 & C-299/16 (*N Luxembourg 1*), paras 84-94.

then be assessed to what extent the effect of the 'beneficial owner' term in the Interest and Royalties Directive on the interpretation of a tax treaty under the rules of public international law would be equal to the effect that such term should have on the interpretation of tax treaties under the laws of the EU.

In addition to assessing the effect that terms in Directives may have on the interpretation of tax treaties, it will also be determined to what extent the result to be achieved under a Directive would be able to affect the interpretation of tax treaties under either perspective. The relevant question under public international law would then be whether, first, the result that a Directive requires to be achieved, may be taken into account under the rules of interpretation of tax treaties and, second, how much weight would have to be attributed to such a result when interpreting a tax treaty. In addition, under the perspective of the laws of the EU the question would be to what extent a Member State court would be obliged to interpret a tax treaty in a way that its application is consistent with the result to be achieved by a Directive.

# CHAPTER 3
# The Effect of the Directives on the Interpretation of Tax Treaties from the Perspective of Public International Law

## 3.1 INTRODUCTION

This chapter addresses the question to what extent the Directives affect the interpretation of tax treaties under the rules of public international law. In answering this question, a distinction shall be drawn between the 'direct' effect and the 'indirect' effect of such Directives on the interpretation of tax treaties. Directives would be considered as directly affecting the interpretation of tax treaties if terms used in a Directive are taken into account when interpreting a tax treaty. By means of example, a Directive would be considered as 'directly' affecting the interpretation of a tax treaty if, when interpreting the term 'beneficial owner' in a tax treaty, the definition of such term in the Interest of Royalties Directive would be taken into account under the rules of public international law. In addition to such a direct effect of the Directives, it is also conceivable that a Directive may affect the interpretation of tax treaties in a more indirect way by means of the result that must be achieved by the Member States. Such an indirect effect would arise if taking into account the result to be achieved by a Directive (provision) when interpreting a tax treaty would entail that, in the event of two conceivable interpretations of a tax treaty of which only one is compatible with such result, the interpreter would be directed towards the interpretation that is compatible with the result that must be achieved pursuant to a Directive provision by reason of taking into account such a result. In such case, it is not the terminology of a Directive that affects the interpretation of a tax treaty, but rather the result to be achieved by that Directive (provision).

In answering the question of the present chapter, the specific interpretation provision of Article 3(2) OECD Model (section 3.2) is addressed first, followed by a discussion of Article 2(2) MLI (section 3.3). Subsequently, the customary rules of interpretation of treaties as codified in Articles 31 through 33 VCLT 1969 (section 3.4) are set out.[152] The rationale for discussing Articles 3(2) OECD Model and Article 2(2) MLI first is that these provisions are generally considered as the *lex specialis* vis-à-vis the provisions of the VCLT 1969 (as the *lex generalis*).[153] As such, when interpreting a tax treaty, or the MLI, the starting point would generally be either Article 3(2) OECD Model or Article 2(2) MLI. The relationship between these specific interpretation provisions and the general interpretation provisions of the VCLT 1969 is discussed in more detail in section 3.5. This chapter ends with an answer to the question (section 3.6).

## 3.2 THE EFFECT OF THE DIRECTIVES LAW UNDER ARTICLE 3(2) OECD MODEL (2017)

> Article 3 OECD Model (2017)
>
> 2. As regards the application of the Convention at any time by a Contracting State, any term not defined therein shall, unless the context otherwise requires or the competent authorities agree to a different meaning pursuant to the provisions of Article 25, have the meaning that it has at that time under the law of that State for the purposes of the taxes to which the Convention applies, any meaning under the applicable tax laws of that State prevailing over a meaning given to the term under other laws of that State.

### 3.2.1 Introduction

This section is aimed at answering the question to what extent the Directives affect the interpretation of tax treaties under the interpretative rule of Article 3(2) OECD Model. This interpretative rule stipulates that an undefined term in a tax treaty shall have the meaning it has under the law of the state applying the treaty subject to the context requiring otherwise.[154] In order to determine the effect of the Directives under this rule, it shall first be addressed whether the Directives fall within the scope of the reference to the laws of the state applying the treaty (section 3.2.2). Second, in section 3.2.3, the role played by the Directives, if falling within such scope, within the interpretation rule of Article 3(2) OECD Model is assessed. Such assessment includes determining whether the Directives may be regarded as part of the 'context' within the meaning of

152. Regarding the customary nature, *see, inter alia*, P. Ariginelli, 2015, para. 1.1.2 and O. Dörr & K. Schmalenbach, 2018, pp. 561-564, paras 6-7.
153. This seems to be the prevailing opinion. *See*, to this effect, J.F. Avery Jones, C.J. Berg, H. Depret, M. Ellis, P. Fontaneau, R. Lenz, T. Miyatake, S.I. Roberts, C. Sandels & J. Strobl, British Tax Review 1984/1, pp. 477-478, F.A. Engelen, 2004, para. 10.10.2, and J. Bossuyt, 2021, para. 8.2.2.1. For the MLI, *see* R.A. Bosman, MBB 2017/4, pp. 127-128.
154. As of the 2017 update to the OECD Model, the meaning under the 'laws of that State' is also subject to 'the competent authorities agree to a different meaning pursuant to the provisions of Article 25' (*see*, to that effect, 2017 Update to the OECD Model p. 15, para. 16). The role of this phrase, however, is not further discussed in the present thesis.

Article 3(2) OECD Model and, if so, to what extent they may require otherwise. This section ends with an answer to the question to what extent the Directives may affect the interpretation of tax treaties under Article 3(2) OECD model (section 3.2.4).

### 3.2.2 Directives Providing the Meaning a Term Has under the Law of That (Member) State

Pursuant to Article 3(2) OECD Model, the starting point in interpreting an undefined treaty term is that such term shall have the meaning it has under the laws of the contracting state applying the treaty. The rationale for the reference to the laws of the state applying the treaty, which may give rise to diverging meanings of the same treaty term depending on which contracting state applies the treaty, is that a tax treaty imposes limitations on the right to tax certain categories of income by the contracting states. Such function can, as has been submitted by legal scholars, be best fulfilled if the meanings of a term in domestic law and a tax treaty correspond.[155] As such, the starting point for an interpretation in accordance with Article 3(2) OECD Model is that undefined treaty terms shall have the meaning under the laws of the contracting state applying the tax treaty.

The relevant question that arises bearing in mind such starting point, is whether a Directive qualifies as 'law of that State' within the meaning of Article 3(2) OECD Model.[156] If that were the case, it would be conceivable that undefined treaty terms shall be given the meaning such terms have in the Directives. An example of where this may be relevant would concern the interpretation of the term 'beneficial owner' in Article 11 OECD Model. Such term is not defined in the OECD Model (and, for that matter, in tax treaties based on the OECD Model). As such, reference can be made to Article 3(2) OECD Model. If the Interest and Royalties Directive would then be part of the law of a Member State applying such tax treaty, the meaning of the term 'beneficial owner' in Article 1(4) of such Directive (as interpreted by the CJEU) could be used to give meaning to the undefined treaty term in Article 11 OECD Model. As such, if the Directives would be part of the 'law of that State' within the meaning of Article 3(2)

155. *See* A.P. Dourado, G. Kofler, E. Reimer, A. Rust, R. Ismer & J. Ruß in: Klaus Vogel on Double Taxation Conventions (Reimer & Rust eds), 2022, pp. 229-230, para. 116 and J.F. Avery Jones & J. Hattingh, 2021, para. 4.3.1. Although this may be best for performing the function of tax treaties, the consequences is that two contracting states may interpret the same treaty term or provision in different ways. Such a result is, however, acceptable under Article 3(2) OECD Model in light of the circumstance that such diverging interpretations still avoid double taxation and double non-taxation in nearly all instances. *See*, to this effect, A.P. Dourado, G. Kofler, E. Reimer, A. Rust, R. Ismer & J. Ruß in: Klaus Vogel on Double Taxation Conventions (Reimer & Rust eds), 2022, p. 230, para. 117.

156. It is recalled, in this respect, that this question relates to whether the Directives themselves may be regarded as part of the 'law of that State'. It is not concerned with the question whether the Directives could be regarded as part of such law after their transposition in the national laws of a Member State. According to the present author, relying on such national laws aimed at transposing a Directive should be regarded as using national law to give meaning to undefined treaty terms and not the Directives themselves.

OECD Model, they would be able to affect the interpretation of undefined tax treaty terms when interpreting such terms on the basis of Article 3(2) OECD Model.[157]

#### 3.2.2.1 *The Meaning of the Term 'Law of That (Member) State'*

It follows from the previous section that it is relevant whether a Directive qualifies as part of the 'law of that State' within the meaning of Article 3(2) OECD Model. Whether this is the case, depends, essentially, on the meaning of the term 'law of that State' in Article 3(2) OECD Model (section 3.2.2.2). In determining such meaning, the starting point is that this term should be interpreted on the basis of Articles 31 through 33 VCLT 1969.[158]

In that respect, the starting point would seem to be the ordinary meaning of the 'law of that State'. Such wording is often referred to by legal scholars, as well as by the OECD,[159] as a reference to 'domestic law'.[160] Regarding the term 'law of that State' as meaning 'domestic law' is, however, not very helpful as it would merely shift the question towards whether the Directives can be regarded as 'domestic law', which, in turn, requires an interpretation of the term 'domestic law'. If viewed as a reference to 'domestic law', however, it would seem conceivable that the Directives would not qualify as such. This is due to, for example, the CJEU distinguishing domestic law from EU law within the context of the duty of consistent interpretation.[161] As such, regarding the reference to the 'law of that State' as meaning 'domestic law' may entail that the Directives cannot be used to give meaning to undefined treaty terms.

This would especially be the case when 'domestic law' is understood as meaning those laws enacted by a domestic legislator. Whether such an understanding accurately reflects the term 'the law of that State' in Article 3(2) OECD Model may, however, be questioned. It is, in any event, relevant whether the reference to the 'law of that State' is limited to domestic law enacted by a domestic legislator, i.e., 'national law', only or whether it would, for example, also include other laws applicable within a Member State (such as the Directives irrespective of their transposition into domestic law). An

---

157. Within the reference to the 'law of that State', the result to be achieved of a Directive does not seem relevant. This is because Article 3(2) OECD Model refers to the meaning an undefined treaty term has 'under the law' of the state applying the tax treaty (*see* J. Bossuyt, 2021, para. 8.2.2.4). It seems likely that such meaning must be derived from the provisions of a Directive, such as definitions like 'beneficial owner' or 'permanent establishment'. The objective of a Directive, by contrast, does not contain definitions or meanings of terms, but rather a result to be achieved. For that reason, reference is only made to the provisions of the Directives here only.
158. J.F. Avery Jones & J. Hattingh, 2021, para. 4.2.
159. Commentaries to Article 3(2) OECD Model Tax Convention on Income and on Capital (2017), para. 12 ('paragraph 2 specifies that the domestic law meaning ...'), as well as para. 13.1 ('may be ascertained by reference to the meaning it has for the purpose of any relevant provision of the domestic law of a Contracting State').
160. *See, inter alia*, F.A. Engelen, 2004, para. 10.10.4, A.P. Dourado, G. Kofler, E. Reimer, A. Rust, R. Ismer & J. Ruß in: Klaus Vogel on Double Taxation Conventions (Reimer & Rust eds), 2022, p. 229, para. 115, R.A. Bosman, 2015, para. 3.3.1, J.F. Avery Jones & J. Hattingh, 2021, para. 4.4.1, and J. Bossuyt, 2021, para. 8.2.2.4.
161. *See, e.g.*, Case C-573/17 (*Poplawski*), paras 77-78 regarding the duty to interpret 'domestic law in conformity with EU law'.

example of when this would be relevant seems to be the 'beneficial owner' and 'permanent establishment' definitions of the Interest and Royalties Directive. Based on a report of the Commission regarding the implementation of such Directive, 'some MS have chosen not to transpose the Article 1(4) definition at all, others have relied on domestic definitions, and yet another group of MS have transposed it with deviations. As regards PEs, some MS have chosen either not to transpose Article 1(5) at all, or to transpose it with national variations'.[162] As such, if the 'law of that State' would be understood as only referring to 'domestic law' or 'national law', the 'beneficial owner' and 'permanent establishment' definitions of the Interest and Royalties Directive would not be part of the 'laws of that state' for those Member States that have not correctly transposed such definitions. Only for those Member States that would have correctly transposed such definition could the Directives be relevant, but only *through* the national law by means of which such definitions are transposed. By contrast, if the 'law of that State' would have to be understood as including the Directives themselves it is irrelevant whether a Member State has correctly transposed the definitions of a Directive because such definitions are – irrespective of such transposition – already part of the 'law of that State' and could, therefore, be used to give meaning to the treaty terms 'beneficial owner' and 'permanent establishment'.[163]

In the present author's view, the wording of Article 3(2) OECD Model indicates a wider meaning than only those laws of a Member State that have been enacted by a domestic legislator. Such wording indicates a reference to those laws that are in force (or applicable) within a state, irrespective of whether they have been enacted by a domestic legislator. This understanding of the meaning of the 'law of that State' also seems aligned with the position of legal scholars that (non-transposed) EU law, without elaborating on the meaning to be given to the term 'law of that State', can be regarded as 'law of that State'.[164] Taking these positions into account, as well as the (broad) wording of Article 3(2) OECD Model, the present author adopts the view that the

162. Report from the Commission to the Council in accordance with Article 8 of Council Directive 2003/49/EC on a common system of taxation applicable to interest and royalty payments made between associated companies of different Member States p. 4.

163. Regarding the difference between EU law as 'national law' and as 'laws of that State', *see* J.P. Warner, The Law Quarterly Review 1977/93, p. 351 who states that '[i]t is not quite true to say, as is sometimes said, that Community law "has become part of English law" ... though it would be true to say that it has become part of the law applicable in England'.

164. A.P. Dourado, G. Kofler, E. Reimer, A. Rust, R. Ismer & J. Ruß in: Klaus Vogel on Double Taxation Conventions (Reimer & Rust eds), 2022, p. 231, para. 120, for example, state that the reference to domestic law in Article 3(2) OECD Model includes primary and secondary EU law for Member States (this position was also adopted in the fourth edition of Klaus Vogel on Double Taxation Conventions (*see*, to that effect, E. Reimer & A. Rust, 2015, p. 208, para. 113)). A similar opinion is expressed by De Broe who states that 'EU law is part of the law of EU Member States and EU directives in the field of income tax are part of the income tax laws of the Member States. ... EU law should therefore be considered when applying a tax treaty where a Member State construes a term which is undefined in that treaty if EU law provides a meaning of that term' (L. de Broe in: Current Tax Treaty Issues (Maisto ed.), 2019, para. 16.2.2). Other authors, expressing their conclusion in more cautious terms, state that the reference in Article 3(2) OECD Model to domestic law seems to be broad enough to include EU law (F. Avella, World Tax Journal 2012/6, p. 113), should be regarded as including EU law (F. Avella, World Tax Journal 2012/6, p. 113), or that it is, in principle, 'difficult to see' why it should not be, as EU law becomes domestic law (J.F. Avery Jones & J. Hattingh, 2021, para. 4.5.4).

reference to 'laws of that State' in Article 3(2) OECD Model should be understood as 'laws in force in that State' or 'laws applicable in that State' and not merely 'national law' only.

#### 3.2.2.2 *The Directives as Part of the Law of That State for the Purposes of the Taxes to Which the Convention Applies*

Based on the view that the term 'laws of that State' must be understood as being broader than only enacted (domestic) law, the question arises whether the Directives can be regarded as forming part of the law of the (Member) State applying the treaty.[165] The starting point in this respect is that, according to the CJEU, the EU Treaties have created their own legal system which has become 'an integral part of the legal systems of the Member States'[166] entailing that the laws of the EU form 'part of the law in force in every Member State'.[167] As such, the Directives, as laws of the EU, must be regarded as part of the laws in force in the Member States.[168] This entails that the Directives, under a broader understanding of the 'law of that State', form part of the 'law of that state' and that they may thus be used to give meaning to undefined tax treaty terms.

Based on this conclusion, the Directives may be resorted to for the purposes of giving meaning to undefined treaty terms under Article 3(2) OECD Model.[169] As such,

165. *See also* F. Avella, World Tax Journal 2012/6, p. 113 who states that the reference to the state which applies the tax treaty 'seems to be broad enough to include law which is not "national"'.
166. CJEU, 15 July 1964, Case 6/64 (*Costa v. ENEL*), p. 593. *See also* Case 14/68 (*Walt Wilhelm and Others*), para. 6, Joined Cases C-6/90 & C-9/90 (*Francovich*), para. 31, and Case C-453/99 (*Courage and Crehan*), para. 19.
167. Case C-284/16 (*Achmea*), para. 41.
168. This position regarding the status of EU law as forming part of the legal order of the Member States has also been recognised in ICSID 25 November 2015, Case No. ARB/07/19 (*Electrabel v. Hungary*), para. 4.119.
169. It is noted that Article 3(2) OECD Model (2017) does not require identical terms, but similar terms (*see*, to that effect, F.A. Engelen, 2004, para. 10.10.4.5). Hence, the circumstance that the Parent-Subsidiary Directive (2011) does not use the term 'dividends', as used in Article 10 OECD Model, but the terms 'distributed profits' (Article 4(1)) or 'profits which a subsidiary distributes' (Article 5) would not necessarily entail that these terms of the Parent-Subsidiary Directive (2011) are not relevant for the purposes of Article 3(2) OECD Model (2017). An interpretation in good faith, according to Engelen, entails that it would be 'only reasonable to assume that it also applies to the terms of a tax treaty that have the same content and meaning as similar but not identical terms of domestic law' (*see* F.A. Engelen, 2004, para. 10.10.4.5). Reference may also be made to F. Avella, World Tax Journal 2012/6, pp. 110-111, who refers to the example of Article 13(1) OECD Model referring to 'alienation' being interpreted by using the meaning of very similar terms such as 'disposal' or 'sale' under the laws of the contracting state applying the treaty. In addition to such an approach being in line with good faith, it has also been argued that requiring (sufficiently) similar terms instead of identical terms is aligned with the principle of effectiveness (which is linked to good faith). If, for example, the term 'alienation' in Article 13(1) OECD Model is not part of the laws of the state applying the treaty, while those laws do include the term 'disposal' for taxing the capital gain in respect of an alienation of immovable property, it is conceivable that not using the meaning of the domestic term 'disposal' may result in a situation where Article 13(1) OECD Model is not applicable to the case at hand because the term 'alienation' is interpreted by applying the VCLT 1969 rules for the sole reason that the domestic laws of the contracting state do not include the term 'alienation'. For reasons of effectiveness, it would seem reasonable to assume that similar, but

it is conceivable that the undefined 'beneficial owner' tax treaty term can be interpreted by reference to the defined 'beneficial owner' term in Article 1(4) Interest and Royalties Directive provided that such term would be part of the law for the purposes of the taxes to which the tax treaty applies.[170] This latter condition would seem to be fulfilled with respect to the Directives because they generally relate to (non-)taxation of income falling within the scope of tax treaties. If fulfilled, the 'beneficial owner' definition of the Interest and Royalties Directive may be used to give meaning to the undefined 'beneficial owner' term in Articles 11 (interest) and 12 (royalty's) of tax treaties that are applied by Member States.[171] As such, it is concluded that the Directives can be part of the law of that State for the purposes to which a tax treaty applies and may be used to give meaning to undefined treaty terms.

---

not identical, terms of domestic laws may be used when interpreting a tax treaty term in accordance with Article 3(2) OECD Model (*see* R.A. Bosman, 2015, para. 3.3.2).

170. This thus appears to exclude, for example, reliance on the meaning of undefined treaty terms under private law or a tax law that is not covered by the tax treaty (assuming that such tax law meaning is not applied (by analogy) to taxes covered by the tax treaty) (*see*, to that effect, K. Vogel & R.G. Prokisch in: Interpretation of Double Taxation Conventions 1993, p. 80, F.A. Engelen, 2004, para. 10.10.4.3, and R.A. Bosman, 2015, para. 3.3.2). In this respect, the OECD Commentaries express the position that 'the meaning of an undefined treaty term may be ascertained by reference to the meaning it has for the purpose of any relevant provision of the domestic law of a contracting state, whether or not it is a tax law' (*see* para. 13.1 OECD Commentaries (2017) to Article 3). It seems to follow from the reference to any 'relevant' provisions, the criterion to be applied is not necessarily whether the source of the domestic law meaning is to be classified as, for example, private, public or tax law. Instead, what is relevant is whether such meaning, regardless of its classification, is used for the purpose of the law of a tax covered by the tax treaty (F.A. Engelen, 2004, para. 10.10.4.3 and J.F. Avery Jones & J. Hattingh, 2021, para. 4.4.1). If it would be determined that there is a relevant provision of domestic law, such meaning shall be applied; if it would be established that the meaning is not used for the purpose of the law of a tax covered by the treaty, such meaning cannot be used for the purposes of Article 3(2) OECD Model (J.F. Avery Jones & J. Hattingh, 2021, para. 4.4.1). One may challenge this position that the domestic law meaning must be used for tax laws to which the treaty applies, based on the reference in Article 3(2) OECD Model that 'any meaning under the applicable tax laws of that State prevailing over a meaning given to the term under other laws of that State'. According to Engelen, this reference would seem to have no purpose or effect if it is concluded that 'the meaning of a term may not be ascertained by reference to the meaning it has under ... other laws, if it is not also adopted under the applicable tax laws'. This leads him to conclude, based on the principle of effectiveness, that it is 'reasonable to assume that ... the meaning of any term not defined in a tax treaty may be ascertained by reference to the meaning that it has for the purposes of any relevant provision of domestic law of a contracting state' (F.A. Engelen, 2004, para. 10.10.4.3).

171. It is acknowledged that Article 10 OECD Model also contains the undefined 'beneficial owner' term. It is conceivable that the 'beneficial owner' definition of the Interest and Royalties Directive would also be of use in that respect, but the link seems less strong than would be the case with respect to Articles 11 and 12 OECD Model considering that such articles relate to the same payments as the Interest and Royalties Directive. Nevertheless, the reference in Article 3(2) OECD Model to the 'meaning that it has ... under the law of that State for the purposes of the taxes to which the Convention applies' might be broad enough to also allow for the Interest and Royalties Directive's definition to be used for Article 10 OECD Model given that it only refers to the taxes to which the Convention applies as a whole. As such, if the definition of the Directive may be used for one provision, it would seem to qualify as among such taxes, it would seem that it may also be used for other provisions such as Article 10 OECD Model.

#### 3.2.2.3 *At Any Time ... at That Time*

Having established that the Directives may be used to give meaning to undefined tax treaty terms, a question that needs answering is whether the reference to the meaning of a term under the law of a state is that which is current at the date of conclusion of the treaty ('static') or that which is in force at the time of application of such treaty ('ambulatory' or 'dynamic').[172] The relevance of this question can be illustrated as follows:

> Under a static approach, the Directives can only be used to give meaning to undefined treaty terms if they would have been adopted before the conclusion of a tax treaty. Based on Annex 1, this would entail that the Directives would only be of use with respect to approximately 2.9% (ATAD2) to 38.4% (Interest and Royalties Directive) of the tax treaties concluded by the Member States.[173] By contrast, if a dynamic approach is adopted, the Directives may be resorted to for the purposes of all tax treaties concluded by the Member States.

In determining whether the reference to the 'law of that State' is to be understood as either static or dynamic, the starting point is that this question had not been resolved by the OECD Commentaries until 1992. As of the 1992 and 1995 amendments to the OECD Model and its Commentaries, the OECD made it explicitly clear that Article 3(2) OECD Model should be applied dynamically.[174] Such a dynamic understanding of the reference to the 'law of that State' could, however, already be implicitly derived from the wording of Article 3(2) OECD Model before such amendments. As such, it is concluded that the dynamic approach should also apply with respect to tax treaties concluded before 1992/1995.[175]

Based on this conclusion, the date of adoption of such Directive is not, in principle, relevant. It is only 'in principle' not relevant because an interpretation on the basis of the (earlier or later) laws of a state applying the treaty is subject to the context requiring otherwise.[176] The context may, for example, require a meaning based on a (later) Directive (as part of the laws of the Member State applying the tax treaty) to be rejected if such state, by using a later Directive to give meaning to an undefined treaty

172. J.F. Avery Jones, C.J. Berg, H. Depret, M. Ellis, P. Fontaneau, R. Lenz, T. Miyatake, S.I. Roberts, C. Sandels & J. Strobl, British Tax Review 1984/1, p. 25.
173. Annex 1, para. 3.4.2 in connection with para. 3.4.3. ATAD1would be earlier with respect to 53 out of 1,849 tax treaties concluded by the Member States (6 Intra-EU Treaties and 47 (Extra-EU Treaties)) (2.7%) whereas the Interest and Royalties Directive would be earlier with respect to 692 tax treaties (270 Intra-EU Treaties and 441 Extra-EU Treaties) (38.4% of the total 1,849 tax treaties).
174. This dynamic approach is reflected in the added references in Article 3(2) OECD Model as of 1995 to 'at any time' in connection with 'at that time'. *See* F.A. Engelen, 2004, para. 10.10.4.6 and D.O. Corredor Velásquez, Intertax 2016/12, p. 966.
175. *See* para. 11 OECD Commentaries (2017) to Article 3.
176. A.P. Dourado, G. Kofler, E. Reimer, A. Rust, R. Ismer & J. Ruß in: Klaus Vogel on Double Taxation Conventions (Reimer & Rust eds), 2022, p. 229, para. 115, R.A. Bosman, 2015, para. 3.3.5, and J.F. Avery Jones & J. Hattingh, 2021, para. 4.6. This principle is also reflected in para. 13 of the OECD Commentaries where it is stated that 'a State should not be allowed to make a convention partially inoperative by amending afterwards in its domestic law the scope of terms not defined in the Convention'.

term, erodes or evades its treaty obligations under the guise of an interpretation in accordance with Article 3(2) OECD Model.[177]

In sum, Article 3(2) OECD Model should be applied dynamically. As such, reference can be made to the laws of a contracting state at the time of application of the tax treaty. Therefore, the Directives - irrespective of their date of adoption - can be made reference to as the 'law of that State' for the purposes of giving meaning to undefined treaty terms. The date of adoption of a Directive, as compared to the date of conclusion of a tax treaty, may, however, be relevant in determining whether the context requires otherwise (section 3.2.3.2).

### 3.2.3 The Operation of Article 3(2) OECD Model (2017)

It follows from the preceding sections that the Directives may be used to give meaning to undefined treaty terms under Article 3(2) OECD Model as part of the 'law of that State'. If an undefined tax treaty term is interpreted by reference to the meaning such term has under a Directive, the interpretation of a tax treaty would be affected by such a Directive. It is, however, to be borne in mind that such a meaning based on a Directive as part of the 'law of that State' is subject to the context not otherwise requiring.[178] As such, the 'context' within the meaning of Article 3(2) OECD Model can limit the extent to which a Directive as part of 'the law of that state' may be able to affect the interpretation of undefined tax treaty terms. The meaning of the term 'context' (section 3.2.3.1), as well as under what circumstances such context may require otherwise (section 3.2.3.2), is thus relevant in determining the effect of the Directives on the interpretation of undefined tax treaty terms pursuant to Article 3(2) OECD Model.

#### *3.2.3.1 The Context Within the Meaning of Article 3(2) OECD Model (2017)*

Given that the context within the meaning of Article 3(2) OECD Model may limit the extent to which undefined treaty terms may have a meaning based on a Directive as part of the laws of a Member State applying a tax treaty, the meaning of the term 'context' in Article 3(2) OECD Model must be ascertained. With respect to ascertaining such meaning, it is acknowledged at the outset that there does not seem to be consensus among legal scholars, which may be partially due to the absence of a definition in the OECD Model or in the Commentaries to Article 3(2) OECD Model.[179] Given the absence of consensus and a definition in the OECD Model, various interpretations of the term 'context' have been put forward, which can be categorised as follows:

177. *See*, with respect to the use of later 'law of that State' in general: F.A. Engelen, 2004, para. 10.10.4.6.
178. A.P. Dourado, G. Kofler, E. Reimer, A. Rust, R. Ismer & J. Ruß in: Klaus Vogel on Double Taxation Conventions (Reimer & Rust eds), 2022, p. 229, para. 115.
179. The OECD Commentaries only provide a partial explanation of what could be considered context.

(a) The context as the text immediately preceding and following the term in question (the narrowest sense).[180]
(b) The context as the text of the treaty as a whole, including preambles and annexes, as well as its object and purpose (the narrow sense).[181] Such an interpretation of the term 'context' could be based on the ordinary meaning to be given to the words '*unless the context otherwise requires*' in their context and would resemble the meaning of the term 'context' laid down in Article 31(2) VCLT 1969.[182]
(c) The context also including extraneous elements and instruments that have some connection with the tax treaty (the broader sense).[183] In this sense, the text of the treaty as a whole, its object and purpose, but also subsequent agreements, subsequent practices or relevant rules of international law having a link to the treaty being interpreted would be part of the context.[184]
(d) The context, for all practical purposes, as referring to all means of interpretation that may be used under the interpretative rules of the VCLT 1969, i.e., Articles 31 and 32 VCLT 1969 (the wide sense).[185]
(e) In its widest sense, the term 'context' could be interpreted as 'all items which may generally be taken into account or to which one may have recourse in interpreting'.[186] In this sense, the term 'context' encompasses any relevant material that throws light on whether or not a meaning based on the laws of the state applying the treaty should be used.[187] As such, it would follow that internal and external instruments and elements qualify as 'context',[188] while 'the relevant provisions of the two national legal systems' may also be regarded as part of such context.[189]

180. E. van der Bruggen, European Taxation 2003/5, p. 143 and R.A. Bosman, 2015, para. 3.3.3.
181. *See* J. Bossuyt, 2021, para. 8.2.2.6, E. van der Bruggen, European Taxation 2003/5, p. 143, and R.A. Bosman, 2015, para. 3.3.3 also refer to this view of the context being adopted by legal scholars.
182. This narrow understanding seems to be the position of J. Bossuyt, 2021, para. 8.2.2.6.
183. R.A. Bosman, 2015, para. 3.3.3.
184. For these purposes, it is insufficient that subject matters may be similar. It is required that there would be a link between the treaty being interpreted and, for example, a Directive. In general terms, Directives – with, perhaps, the exception of the Arbitration Directive – and the EU Treaties do not seem to have a clear link with tax treaties concluded by the Member States.
185. This would seem to be the position of Van der Bruggen who argues that 'unless the context otherwise requires' may just as well be read as 'unless the Vienna Convention [1969] otherwise requires' (*see* E. van der Bruggen, European Taxation 2003/5, p. 155). Lang also seems to adopt this view by stating that the concept of 'context' should comprise all of the interpretation materials set out in Articles 31 et seq. VCLT 1969 (M. Lang, 2016, p. 117, as well as M. Lang, Bulletin for International Taxation 2020/11, para. 7).
186. Wording derived from R.A. Bosman, 2015, para. 3.3.3. An advocate of such a widest sense seems to be J.F. Avery Jones, Bulletin for International Taxation 2020/11, para. 1 who notes that it 'could comprise anything that could be used for treaty interpretation'.
187. J.F. Avery Jones & J. Hattingh, 2021, para. 5.1.1.
188. R.A. Bosman, 2015, para. 3.3.3.
189. A.P. Dourado, G. Kofler, E. Reimer, A. Rust, R. Ismer & J. Ruß in: Klaus Vogel on Double Taxation Conventions (Reimer & Rust eds), 2022, pp. 235-236, para. 130. *See also* para. 12 OECD Commentaries (2017) to Article 33 ('The context is determined in particular by the intention of the Contracting States when signing the Convention as well as the meaning given to the term in question in the legislation of the other Contracting State.').

While there may not be consensus among legal scholars as to the correct view of the term 'context',[190] the meaning to be given to the term 'context' is relevant for present purposes. If, for example, the term 'context' would be interpreted in its wide sense, this entails that the Directives as well as the EU Treaties, as (relevant) rules of international law applicable in the relations between the parties within the meaning of Article 31(3)(c) VCLT 1969 (*see* section 3.4.2.2), would be part of the context with respect to Intra-EU Treaties.[191] Moreover, if the widest sense would be adopted, the Directives and EU Treaties may even be regarded as forming part of the context with respect to tax treaties concluded with third states, i.e., Extra-EU Treaties, as part of the laws of the EU Member State.[192] By contrast, if the broader, narrow, or narrowest view would be adopted, the Directives and the EU Treaties would not form part of the context for the purposes of Article 3(2) OECD Model and would not be able to have any 'contextual' effect on the interpretation of tax treaties.

As noted above, there is no consensus regarding the meaning of the term 'context' for the purposes of Article 3(2) OECD Model. As such, adopting any position regarding the meaning of the 'context' would seem to be arbitrary and subject to debate. Nevertheless, the present author will determine below whether the Directives would qualify as 'context' based on the OECD Commentaries (2017). Such Commentaries are, based on the Introduction to the OECD Model (2017), 'regularly taken into account when interpreting and applying tax treaties based on the OECD Model, by tax administrations, taxpayers and courts alike.'[193] As such, if the Directives would qualify as 'context' within the meaning of such Commentaries, it would be likely that they would be able to have a 'contextual' effect on the interpretation of tax treaties, especially when it would concern the interpretation of a tax treaty concluded between two OECD member countries.[194]

Based on the OECD Commentaries (2017), the 'context' for the purposes of Article 3(2) OECD Model should be determined in particular by the intention of the contracting states 'when signing the Convention as well as the meaning given to the term in question in the legislation of the other Contracting State (an implicit reference

190. This was already the case in 1984. *See*, to that extent, J.F. Avery Jones, C.J. Berg, H. Depret, M. Ellis, P. Fontaneau, R. Lenz, T. Miyatake, S.I. Roberts, C. Sandels & J. Strobl, British Tax Review 1984/2, p. 105 where it is noted that the authors are unable to draw any conclusion regarding the correct approach to the term 'context'. More recently, diverging views have been expressed by J. Bossuyt, 2021, para. 8.2.2.6 (narrow sense), J.F. Avery Jones & J. Hattingh, 2021, para. 5.1.1 (widest sense), J.F. Avery Jones, Bulletin for International Taxation 2020/11, para. 1 (widest sense) and M. Lang, Bulletin for International Taxation 2020/11, para. 7 (wide sense).

191. L. de Broe in: Current Tax Treaty Issues (Maisto ed.), 2019, para. 16.2.2 seems to take this position considering that he states that '[i]t is submitted that for treaties concluded by EU Member States, EU law is part of the context in which article 3(2) operates'.

192. *See* Case C-284/16 (*Achmea*), para. 41 where the CJEU notes that 'EU law ... must be regarded as forming both part of the law in force in every Member State and as deriving from an international agreement between the Member States.'

193. Paragraph 29 of the Introduction to the OECD Model (2017).

194. *See*, to this effect, X.R. Resch, 2020, pp. 210-211. It is noted, in this respect, that not all Member States are also OECD member countries (i.e., Bulgaria, Croatia, Cyprus, Malta and Romania are not also OECD member countries).

to the principle of reciprocity on which the Convention is based)'.[195] The reference to the intention of the parties when signing the tax treaty would seem to indicate that the context should be construed in a narrow sense. As such, the context would comprise of the means of interpretation referred to in Article 31(1) and (2) VCLT 1969. The means of interpretation referred to in Article 31(3) VCLT 1969 would, at first glance, be excluded from its scope because, at least to the extent that it concerns a subsequent agreement or a subsequent practice, they do not shed light on the intentions of the contracting states when signing a tax treaty.

Whether the relevant rules of international law referred to in Article 31(3)(c) VCLT would also be excluded is less clear-cut. To the extent that such rules of international law were in force at the time a tax treaty was signed, it follows from the principle of good faith that the contracting states are presumed to not have intended to conclude a treaty contrary to such earlier rules of international law.[196] The presumption against conflict entails that, to the extent that a Directive would be in force at the time of conclusion of an Intra-EU Treaty, a presumed intention against conflict with such a Directive could be part of the 'context'. Such a presumed intention could, however, only be part of the context with respect to Intra-EU Treaties because the Directives are not applicable in the relations with third states and, for that reason, cannot reflect a (presumed) common intention between a Member State and a third state. Furthermore, this presumption would only be applicable to post-accession Intra-EU Treaties that also postdate a Directive (representing, at best, 21.1% of the Intra-EU Treaties).[197] With respect to pre-accession Intra-EU Treaties and post-accession, yet pre-Directive Intra-EU Treaties, a presumed common intention against conflict following from the principle of good faith would, however, not apply.

> An interesting question would nevertheless be whether, with respect to post-accession, pre-Directive Intra-EU Treaties, a presumed common intention against conflict with EU law may be inferred at the time of conclusion that also extends to later Directives. Such a common intention could, for example, be based on the duty of Union loyalty that is to be observed by both Member States when concluding tax treaties after their accession to the EU. The idea would then be that when concluding a post-accession Intra-EU Treaty, both Member States would be presumed to have a general intention to not jeopardise their compliance with present and future obligations under the EU Treaties.[198] With respect to this Union loyalty based general presumption against conflict with – earlier and later – EU law, it is acknowledged that there is no judicial or academic support. Nevertheless, the present author considers it conceivable in light of the obligations that arise from the duty of Union loyalty. If such a general presumption against conflict with

195. Paragraph 12 of the Commentaries to Article 3(2) OECD Model (2017).
196. *See* section 3.4.3.1.1.
197. *See* Annex 1, para. 3.4.1 regarding the Interest and Royalties Directive (2003/49/EC). Considering that this presumption needs to be applied at the time of signing of an Intra-EU Treaty, it would be required that the relevant Directive was adopted at that time. The earliest of such Directives as currently in force is the Interest and Royalties Directive (2003/49/EC). This Directive is, however, 'later' as compared to 270 Intra-EU Treaties (78.9%) and, conversely, 'earlier' compared to 72 Intra-EU Treaties (21.1%). To the extent 'earlier', the Member States may have been aware of its adoption at the time of conclusion of such treaties.
198. *See*, to this effect, Case C-307/97 (*Saint Gobain*), paras 56-57.

> EU would exist, its importance should not be overstated. It would merely concern a presumption, which could, of course, be rebutted. In the event that it would not be rebutted, the consequence of a general presumption against conflict with EU law would be that it would have to be presumed that the Member States, when concluding a post-accession Intra-EU Treaty, intended such a treaty to be consistent with existing and future EU law. Such a general presumption against conflict with - present and future - EU law would then apply with respect to each post-accession Intra-EU Treaty (and not only to those Intra-EU Treaties that have been concluded after accession of both Member States and after the adoption of a Directive).

In addition to referring to the common intentions at the time of signing, which common intentions may include a presumption against conflict with (earlier) Directives, the OECD Commentaries (2017) also provide support for considering the Directives as part of the context of Article 3(2) OECD Model with respect to in Intra-EU Treaties as part of the laws of the other contracting state.[199] Such support can be derived from the reference in such Commentaries to the legislation of the other contracting state and the principle of reciprocity on which the OECD Model is based. Considering that the Directives must be regarded as part of the laws of each EU Member State, irrespective of their transposition into domestic law (section 3.2.2.2), the laws of the Member States - to the extent that they comprise of the Directives - would be identical. As such, with respect to Intra-EU Treaties, reference may also be made to the Directives as part of the context based on the nature of Directives as part of the legislation in the other contracting (Member) State. It would seem irrelevant, in this respect, whether it concerns the legislation of the other contracting state at the time of conclusion of a tax treaty. As such, the Directives, as part of the legislation of the contracting (Member) States, would be part of the context with respect to all Intra-EU Treaties and not merely those concluded after accession to the EU (via a conceivable presumption against conflict with EU law) or the adoption of a Directive (via a presumption against conflict with obligations under public International law). The Directives would not, however, be part of the 'context' in their capacity as law of the other contracting state with respect to Extra-EU Treaties because they are not part of the laws of third states.

Based on the OECD Commentaries (2017), the Directives can be regarded as part of the context for the purposes of Article 3(2) OECD Model to the extent that it concerns the interpretation of Intra-EU Treaties. Such Directives would be part of such 'context' as either reflecting the common intentions of the Member States at the time of conclusion of such a treaty or as part of the legislation of the other contracting state. As such, the present author concludes that the Directives are part of the context for the purposes of Article 3(2) OECD Model with respect to the interpretation of Intra-EU Treaties if the OECD Commentaries (2017) would be adhered to when determining the elements that are part of the 'context' within the meaning of such provision.

199. Regarding the dual nature of the Directives, *see* Case C-284/16 (*Achmea*), para. 41 and section 2.4.

### *3.2.3.2 When the Context Requires Otherwise*

If the Directives would be part of the 'context' of Article 3(2) OECD Model, they could affect the interpretation of tax treaties in their capacity as context (in addition to their effect as part of the 'law of that State'). This is due to the context being able to require a meaning based on the 'law of that State' to be rejected. As such, the Directives might be able to 'require otherwise' within the meaning of Article 3(2) OECD Model when interpreting an Intra-EU Treaty. Taking into account the possibility of such a 'contextual' effect, the relevant question that needs to be addressed is when the context, which may include a Directive when interpreting an Intra-EU Treaty, could require a meaning other than that based on the 'law of that State'. In answering such question, the starting point is that – as was also the case with respect to the meaning of the term 'context' – legal scholars have not reached consensus regarding the question when the context otherwise requires. These diverging views can be summarised as follows:

> The first group of authors considers that, should treaty definitions be missing, one must initially refer to the meaning of a term in the respective domestic law, unless the context requires otherwise. The second group of authors prefers to reach a common interpretation among Contracting States by any means possible and is of the opinion that, should convention definitions be missing, one has to initially try and identify the meaning within the context of the convention. Only if this should not be possible should a subsidiary reference be made to domestic law.[200]

The present author concurs with the first group of authors for the following reasons. First, the wording of Article 3(2) OECD Model does not indicate a systematic preference for a contextual interpretation.[201] Article 3(2) reads 'unless the context otherwise requires' and not 'if the context does not lead to a different interpretation'[202] or 'unless the context yields no other, or absolutely no other, interpretation'.[203] In addition, the word 'requires' seems to indicate that 'not every apparently convincing interpretation from the context should give rise to a divergence from the rule of Article 3(2) [OECD Model]'.[204] The word 'requires' has, by its nature, 'some force'[205] and indicates that the

200. K. Vogel & R.G. Prokisch in: Interpretation of Double Taxation Conventions 1993, p. 81. For recent publications, reflecting that the two groups of authors still exist, reference can be made to J.F. Avery Jones, Bulletin for International Taxation 2020/11, M. Lang, Bulletin for International Taxation 2020/11, and J. Bossuyt, 2021, para. 8.2.2.6.
201. K. Vogel & R.G. Prokisch in: Interpretation of Double Taxation Conventions 1993, p. 81. *See also* J. Bossuyt, 2021, para. 8.2.2.6.
202. K. Vogel & R.G. Prokisch in: Interpretation of Double Taxation Conventions 1993, p. 81.
203. A.P. Dourado, G. Kofler, E. Reimer, A. Rust, R. Ismer & J. Ruß in: Klaus Vogel on Double Taxation Conventions (Reimer & Rust eds), 2022, p. 235, para. 129. *See also* K. Vogel, Berkeley Journal of International Law 1986/1, p. 73.
204. A.P. Dourado, G. Kofler, E. Reimer, A. Rust, R. Ismer & J. Ruß in: Klaus Vogel on Double Taxation Conventions (Reimer & Rust eds), 2022, p. 235, para. 129. *See also* K. Vogel, Berkeley Journal of International Law 1986/1, p. 73 and K. Vogel & R.G. Prokisch in: Interpretation of Double Taxation Conventions 1993, p. 81.
205. J.F. Avery Jones, C.J. Berg, H. Depret, M. Ellis, P. Fontaneau, R. Lenz, T. Miyatake, S.I. Roberts, C. Sandels & J. Strobl, British Tax Review 1984/2, p. 108, D.A. Ward, J.F. Avery Jones, L. de Broe, M.J. Ellis, S.H. Goldberg, J. Killius, J-P. Le Gall, G. Maisto, T. Miyatake, H. Torrione, C. van Raad & B. Wiman, 2005, p. 31, J.F. Avery Jones in: Tax Treaties and Domestic Law (Maisto ed.), 2006, p. 99, and R.A. Bosman, 2015, para. 3.3.3.

indications of the context must be 'reasonably strong'.[206] As such, only convincing arguments that would be relatively strong should be able to result in the context setting aside the meaning based on the law of the contracting state applying the tax treaty.[207] Second, the history and development of Article 3(2) OECD Model also indicate that 'an interpretation contrary to the meaning a term has under domestic law must constitute an exception'.[208] Based on these arguments, it is concluded that the context should only require otherwise if strong arguments follow from such context against adopting a meaning based on the laws of the state applying the relevant tax treaty.

Whether the context, including the Directives, would provide such strong arguments cannot be answered in the abstract and can, therefore, only be answered on a case-by-case basis.[209] It can, however, be noted in general that the strength of a contextual argument seems linked to the extent to which it reflects a common intention of the contracting states. If it appears that adopting a meaning based on the laws of the contracting state applying (and interpreting) the tax treaty is contrary to such 'contextual' common intention, this could indicate that the context requires otherwise.[210] If such 'law of that State' based interpretation is aligned with the 'contextual' common intention of the parties, it would seem less likely that the context requires otherwise. This approach towards the extent to which the context may require otherwise is relevant for present purposes. It entails, in any event, that the Directives are unlikely to require otherwise if regarded as context in the widest sense with respect to Extra-EU Treaties because they would only be able to reflect an intention of the Member State, but not that of the third state. As such, it would not be able to reflect any common intention between the Member States and the third state. At the same time, with respect to Intra-EU Treaties, the Directives could reflect a common intention between the parties if regarded as part of such context pursuant to, for example, an OECD Commentaries (2017) based understanding of the context (section 3.2.3.1).

Such a Directive based common intention can, for example, be based on the result that must be achieved by a Directive. The line of reasoning in that respect could be as follows. The Member States, as represented by their ministers in the Council, have agreed to achieve the result of a Directive and have voted in favour of its adoption by the Council. Following its adoption, Member States are obliged, under Article 288 TFEU, to achieve the result of such a Directive in respect of which they have voted in favour. If such result would be that certain income must be taxed, it would seem reasonable to presume a common intention between the Member States towards that

206. J.F. Avery Jones & J. Hattingh, 2021, para. 5.1.1.
207. R.A. Bosman, 2015, para. 3.3.3. *See also* J.F. Avery Jones, C.J. Berg, H. Depret, M. Ellis, P. Fontaneau, R. Lenz, T. Miyatake, S.I. Roberts, C. Sandels & J. Strobl, British Tax Review 1984/2, p. 108.
208. K. Vogel, Berkeley Journal of International Law 1986/1, p. 73, A.P. Dourado, G. Kofler, E. Reimer, A. Rust, R. Ismer & J. Ruß in: Klaus Vogel on Double Taxation Conventions (Reimer & Rust eds), 2022, pp. 235-236, para. 130. *See also* F.A. Engelen, 2004, para. 10.10.2 who derives the exceptional nature of the context displacing the domestic law meaning from the words of Article 3(2) OECD Model.
209. J.F. Avery Jones, C.J. Berg, H. Depret, M. Ellis, P. Fontaneau, R. Lenz, T. Miyatake, S.I. Roberts, C. Sandels & J. Strobl, British Tax Review 1984/2, p. 108.
210. *See, e.g.*, J.F. Avery Jones & J. Hattingh, 2021, para. 5.1.1.

end. The role of such a presumed common intention, as part of the context within the meaning of Article 3(2) OECD Model, can then be illustrated as follows. Pursuant to ATAD1, Member States may be required to tax certain non-distributed income of controlled foreign company subsidiaries.[211] As such, a presumed common intention would apply pursuant to which the Member States intend to tax such non-distributed income. The compatibility of such a controlled foreign company rule with, for example, Article 7 OECD Model has - especially prior to the 2003 update to the OECD Commentaries and the 2017 update to the OECD Model - been subject to debate.[212] In *Schneider Electric*, for example, the French Supreme Court ruled that the French-controlled foreign company rules were incompatible with Article 7(1) of the French-Swiss tax treaty.[213] Such incompatibility followed from an interpretation of the term 'profits' in Article 7(1) of such tax treaty in accordance with Article 3(2) based on the laws of France (as the law of the state applying the tax treaty). In *Schneider Electric*, it followed from such laws that the profits within the meaning of Article 7(1) of the French-Swiss tax treaty did not include profits of a Swiss resident subsidiary. As such, Article 7(1) did not allow for the application of the French-controlled foreign company rules. In concluding that Article 7(1) of the French-Swiss tax treaty precluded taxing income of the Swiss-controlled foreign company, the French Supreme Court applied Article 3(2) OECD Model and interpreted the term 'profits' in Article 7(1) on the basis of the national law meaning of such term, while also concluding that the context did not require otherwise. The interesting question after the adoption of ATAD1 would be whether the French Supreme Court would, with respect to an Intra-EU Treaty, again rule that the context, comprising of the presumed common intention of the Member States, as derived from ATAD1, to tax income of a controlled foreign company, would not require otherwise. With respect to an Intra-EU Treaty, it would seem conceivable that the context within the meaning of Article 3(2) OECD Model could provide a strong argument for rejecting the earlier interpretation of the term 'profits' in *Schneider Electric* so as to allow France to comply with its obligations ATAD1 (and, hence, to act in accordance with the common intention of France and the other Member State as reflected by the adoption of ATAD1).

Whereas this example illustrates how the Directives, as context, may affect the interpretation of tax treaties, this effect should not be overestimated. First the contextual effect of the Directives is limited to Intra-EU Treaties only considering that no common intention to achieve the result of a Directive would seem to exist in the case of tax treaties concluded with third states (i.e., Extra-EU Treaties). Second, it is to be borne in mind that the context for the purposes of Article 3(2) OECD Model may consist of various elements in addition to the Directives. With respect to such other elements, it cannot be excluded that they may, for example, provide (strong) indications of a common intention contrary to the result to be achieved by a Directive. In the event of contradicting strong contextual arguments, Article 3(2) OECD Model does not tell an

211. *See* Article 7(2) ATAD1.
212. *See*, to this effect, P. Ariginelli in: The External Tax Strategy of the EU in a Post-BEPS Environment (Jiménez ed.), 2019, para. 8.3.2.
213. Conseil d'État, no. 232 276 (*Schneider Electric*).

interpreter how to determine which contextual argument must be regarded as decisive. It merely refers to the 'context', not 'contexts' or 'a contextual argument'. It would therefore seem reasonable to assume that the 'context', similar to the 'rule of interpretation' (singular) in Article 31 VCLT 1969, can only produce one single outcome.[214] Hence, in the event of contradicting contextual arguments, a decision would have to be made, in good faith,[215] which contextual argument is decisive for determining whether the context otherwise requires. Such a decision would then seem to depend on which contextual argument would be the best reflection of the common intention of the parties with respect to the tax treaty being interpreted. As a consequence, there would in any event not be an *a priori* preference for rejecting contextual arguments that would, if given effect to, result in a non-Directive consistent outcome.

It follows from the above that a Directive as part of the context within the meaning of Article 3(2) OECD Model can, by means of a (presumed) common intention between Member States to achieve the result of such a Directive, provide strong contextual arguments for rejecting or confirming a meaning based on the laws of the contracting state applying an Intra-EU Treaty. While potentially providing strong arguments, the contextual effect of a Directive should not be overestimated because the context might also provide strong arguments against a Directive consistent meaning. In the event that such non-Directive consistent arguments would be found to be stronger than the arguments deriving from a Directive as part of the context, i.e., more closely reflecting the common intentions of the contracting states to an Intra-EU Treaty, it would seem reasonable to assume that the context requires a meaning to be adopted that is contrary to the Directives, even if the meaning of the undefined treaty term would have been determined on the basis of a Directive as part of the law of the contracting (Member) State applying the tax treaty. This is due to such a Directive-based meaning being no different from any other meaning based on the law of such contracting state from the perspective of Article 3(2) OECD Model.

### 3.2.4 Conclusion

Based on the previous sections, the following conclusions can be drawn with respect to the effect that the Directives may have on the interpretation of tax treaties under Article 3(2) OECD Model:

(a) The Directives, irrespective of their transposition into domestic law, are part of the 'law of that State' within the meaning of Article 3(2) OECD Model for the Member States. This entails that reference may be made to the meaning of terms in the Directives for the purposes of giving meaning to undefined tax treaty terms (section 3.2.2.1).

(b) Both earlier and later Directives (as compared to the date of conclusion of the tax treaty being interpreted) are part of the 'law of that State' following a

214. *See* section 3.4.3.1.

215. This is based on the general understanding that Article 3(2) OECD Model must, itself, be interpreted in accordance with Articles 31 et seq. VCLT 1969.

dynamic application of Article 3(2) OECD Model. Whether a Directive is later in time may, however, still be relevant for the purposes of determining whether the context requires otherwise (section 3.2.2.3).

(c) Any meaning based on the 'law of that State', including a meaning based on the Directives as part of such law, is subject to the context otherwise requiring.

(d) Whereas there does not seem to exist consensus regarding the meaning of the term 'context' in Article 3(2) OECD Model, an understanding based on the OECD Commentaries (2017) would entail that the Directives can be considered part of the context of Intra-EU Treaties as:

  (i) providing evidence of a (presumed) common intention at the time of signing of such a treaty against a conflict with such Directives. In such capacity, the Directives could be regarded as 'context' with respect to (part of) the post-accession Intra-EU Treaties; and

  (ii) as domestic law of the other contracting state at the time of application of a tax treaty. In such capacity, the Directives would be part of the 'context' of all Intra-EU Treaties (section 3.2.3.1).

  With respect to Extra-EU Treaties, the Directives cannot be considered part of the 'context' within the meaning of Article 3(2) OECD Model when a Member State would apply such a tax treaty. This is due to a Directive not being able to reflect a common intention between a Member State and a third state while also not being part of the legislation of the other contracting, third, state.

(e) In its capacity as 'context' of Intra-EU Treaties, a Directive can provide strong arguments for adopting a Directive consistent meaning. As such, a Directive may (via the presumption against conflict (with EU law) or as part of the laws of the other contracting state) be able to have a 'contextual effect' on the interpretation of an Intra-EU Treaty by providing a strong argument for adopting or rejecting a meaning based on the laws of the Member State applying an Intra-EU Treaty (depending on whether such meaning is (in)consistent with (the result of) the relevant Directive) (section 3.2.3.2).

(f) With respect to the 'contextual effect' of a Directive, it does need to be borne in mind that (a presumed common intention derived from) a Directive is not necessarily the only element of the context within the meaning of Article 3(2) OECD Model. As such, it cannot be excluded that other contextual elements would provide strong arguments for adopting an interpretive outcome that would be inconsistent with the result laid down in a Directive. If this were the case, it would have to be assessed which contextual argument(s) must be regarded as decisive given that it seems reasonable to assume that the 'context' (singular) must be understood as providing one single outcome regarding the question of whether it requires otherwise. In assessing the decisive contextual argument, it would seem that this must be done in good faith and that there would be no *a priori* preference for a Directive consistent outcome (section 3.2.3.2).

## 3.3 THE EFFECT OF THE DIRECTIVES UNDER ARTICLE 2(2) MLI

> Article 2 MLI
>
> 2. As regards the application of this Convention at any time by a Party, any term not defined herein shall, unless the context otherwise requires, have the meaning that it has at that time under the relevant Covered Tax Agreement.

Whereas the previous section was aimed at determining the effect of the Directives on the interpretation of bilateral tax treaties under Article 3(2) OECD Model, the present section seeks to answer the question of to what extent the Directives may be able to affect the interpretation of provisions of the MLI under the interpretative rule of Article 2(2) MLI. The structure of this interpretative rule is, at first glance, comparable to the rule of Article 3(2) OECD Model. The starting point is that the scope of Article 2(2) MLI is limited to terms that are not defined in the (in this case: multilateral) treaty. With respect to such undefined terms, Article 2(2) MLI refers to an external source of law (in this case: the bilateral tax treaty whose application the MLI seeks to affect). Moreover, any meaning based on such an external source is, again, subject to the context of the MLI otherwise requiring.

As reference is made to the meaning of undefined MLI terms under the relevant covered tax treaty, the interpretative rules of, and the effect of the Directives on the interpretation of a tax treaty under, Article 3(2) OECD Model and 31 VCLT 1969 would seem relevant. For example, if the undefined MLI term is included in a covered tax agreement (CTA) (which may also be referred to as a covered tax treaty), but not defined therein, Article 3(2) Model would seem to be the starting point in determining the meaning of the undefined CTA term. In such event, the effect of the Directives under Article 3(2) OECD Model as set out in section 3.2 would be relevant. If a Directive would affect the interpretation of the undefined term of the CTA, such effect would then also extend to the interpretation of the undefined MLI term under Article 2(2) MLI. Similarly, if the CTA includes the undefined MLI term and would be interpreted in accordance with Article 31 VCLT 1969, any effect of such a Directive, as discussed in section 3.4, on the interpretation of such a (covered) tax treaty would then also be able to affect the interpretation of undefined MLI terms given the reference in Article 2(2) MLI to the meaning that undefined MLI terms have under the relevant CTA.

If a Directive would affect the interpretation of an undefined MLI term via the reference in Article 2(2) MLI to the meaning such term has under a CTA, it follows from the wording of Article 2(2) MLI that such effect would still be subject to the context of the MLI otherwise requiring. With respect to such MLI context, it can be noted that it seems conceivable that it is different from that of Article 3(2) OECD Model due to the MLI having, *inter alia*, a different object and purpose and different character.[216] As such, the conclusion that (the common intention to achieve the result of) a Directive

216. D.W. Blum, Bulletin for International Taxation 2018/3 and W.C. Haslehner, Bulletin for International Taxation 2020/4 & 5, p. 227.

can be part of the context of Article 3(2) OECD Model in Intra-EU Treaties does not necessarily entail that such a Directive would also be part of the context within the meaning of Article 2(2) MLI. With respect to the question of whether such (common intention derived from a) Directive can be considered part of the context within the meaning of Article 2(2) MLI seems to be dependent on whether the MLI is to be regarded as a bilateral, multilateral or hybrid treaty.[217]

If, or to the extent that, the MLI would be regarded as a bilateral treaty, (the common intentions as derived from) the Directives may be part of the context to the extent that the MLI would affect an Intra-EU Treaty. The considerations regarding the weight of a Directive as part of the context with respect to Article 3(2) OECD Model would then apply mutatis mutandis to a Directive as part of the context in Article 2(2) MLI. If, or to the extent that, the MLI would have to be viewed as a multilateral treaty, however, the MLI is to be regarded essentially as an Extra-EU Treaty because not all parties to the MLI are Member States. The consequence of regarding the MLI as a multilateral Extra-EU Treaty would be that a Directive cannot reflect a common intention between all parties to the treaty while such a Directive would also not be applicable in the relations between all the parties to the MLI. For these reasons, the Directives should not be part of the context of the MLI if, and to the extent that, it is regarded as a multilateral treaty.

## 3.4 THE EFFECT OF THE DIRECTIVES UNDER THE RULES OF INTERPRETATION OF THE VCLT 1969

### 3.4.1 Introduction

Having established the effect of the Directives on the interpretation of tax treaties by means of Articles 3(2) OECD Model and 2(2) MLI, this section addresses the question to what extent the Directives may affect the interpretation of tax treaties under the rules of interpretation of the VCLT 1969. In determining such effect, the focus will be on the general rule of interpretation of the VCLT 1969, which is laid down in Article 31 VCLT and reflects customary international law.[218] The article reads as follows:

217. D.W. Blum, Bulletin for International Taxation 2018/3, paras 2.2 and 3.2.

218. In support of regarding Article 31 VCLT 196 as reflecting customary international law, *see, inter alia*, D.O. Corredor Velásquez, Intertax 2016/12, pp. 962-963, R.A. Bosman, 2015, para. 3.2.1, and O. Dörr & K. Schmalenbach, 2018, p. 561, para. 6. The customary international law status of Article 31 VCLT 1969 is also recognised by the CJEU. *See* to that effect, Case C-15/17 (*Bosphorus Queen Shipping*), para. 67 and Case C-266/16 (*Western Sahara Campaign*), para. 58.

The circumstance that Article 31 VCLT 1969 reflects customary international law is relevant because not all Member States are parties to the VCLT 1969 (i.e., France and Romania are not parties to such treaty (*see*, to that effect https://treaties.un.org/Pages/ViewDetailsIII.aspx?src=TREATY&mtdsg_no=XXIII-1&chapter=23&Temp=mtdsg3&clang=_en (date accessed: 1 July 2022)). The customary status of Article 31 VCLT 1969 thus entails that it would also apply with respect to the interpretation of tax treaties concluded by those states that are not parties to the VCLT 1969.

Article 31 VCLT

General rule of interpretation

1. A treaty shall be interpreted in good faith in accordance with the ordinary meaning to be given to the terms of the treaty in their context and in the light of its object and purpose.
2. The context for the purpose of the interpretation of a treaty shall comprise, in addition to the text, including its preamble and annexes:
   (a) any agreement relating to the treaty which was made between all the parties in connection with the conclusion of the treaty;
   (b) any instrument which was made by one or more parties in connection with the conclusion of the treaty and accepted by the other parties as an instrument related to the treaty.
3. There shall be taken into account, together with the context:
   (a) any subsequent agreement between the parties regarding the interpretation of the treaty or the application of its provisions;
   (b) any subsequent practice in the application of the treaty which establishes the agreement of the parties regarding its interpretation;
   (c) any relevant rules of international law applicable in the relations between the parties.
4. A special meaning shall be given to a term if it is established that the parties so intended.

In determining the effect of the Directives on the interpretation of tax treaties under Article 31 VCLT 1969, it will first be determined whether the Directives, as well as the obligation under the EU Treaties to achieve the result of such Directives, can be regarded as means of interpretation under Article 31 VCLT 1969 (3.4.2). Based on the hypothesis that (the obligation to achieve the result of) a Directive can be regarded as such means,[219] its role within the interpretative process of the rules of the VCLT 1969 is set out (section 3.4.3). This section ends with an answer regarding the effect of the Directives on the interpretation of tax treaties under the VCLT 1969 in section 3.4.4.

The focus on Article 31 VCLT 1969 entails that the interpretive rules of Articles 32 and 33 will not be further discussed. With respect to Article 32 VCLT 1969, it suffices to note here that it can be interpreted as allowing for the taking into account of any relevant evidence or indications of the intention of the parties.[220] As such, if a Directive would provide such evidence or indications, which would seem conceivable with respect to Intra-EU Treaties and inconceivable within the context of interpreting an Extra-EU Treaty, it can be regarded as a 'supplementary means' within the meaning of Article 32 VCLT 1969. The role of a Directive as a supplementary means of interpretation would, however, seem to be rather limited considering that it would in principle be confined to confirming an interpretation based on the general rule of interpretation of Article 31 VCLT 1969. Only if application of such general rule of interpretation would result in an ambiguous or obscure meaning or would lead to a result which is

219. Such hypothesis would, *inter alia*, be based on F. Avella, World Tax Journal 2012/6, pp. 96-109.

220. *See*, to that effect, F.A. Engelen, 2004, para. 7.4. It is, however, acknowledged that there does not seem to exist consensus about the scope of the reference to supplementary means in Article 32 VCLT 1969 (*see* O. Dörr & K. Schmalenbach, 2018, p. 626, para. 25).

manifestly absurd or unreasonable could a Directive, as a supplementary means of interpretation, determine the meaning of a treaty term. Article 33 VCLT 1969 is also not further addressed because this provision does not refer to any means of interpretation external to the treaty, which implies that the Directives cannot be of any use when applying such provision.

### 3.4.2 The Directives as a Means of Interpretation Within the Meaning of Article 31 of the VCLT 1969

#### *3.4.2.1 General*

Article 31 VCLT 1969 provides the general rule of interpretation pursuant to which an interpreter *must* take into account the following means of interpretation when interpreting a (tax) treaty: good faith, the ordinary (or special) meaning of the term being interpreted, the object and purpose (of the treaty) and the internal (paragraph 2) and external (paragraph 3) context.[221] In determining whether the Directives are among such means, it becomes evident that, given that they are not part of the treaty itself or connected to it, the focus should be on whether they could be considered part of the external context within the meaning of Article 31(3) VCLT 1969. More specifically, the focus in the present section will be on determining whether the Directives could qualify as relevant rules of international law applicable in the relations between the parties referred to in Article 31(3)(c) VCLT 1969. As such, the question whether the Directives may be regarded as giving rise to a subsequent agreement within the meaning of Article 31(3)(a) VCLT 1969,[222] or a subsequent practice referred to in Article 31(3)(b) VCLT 1969, is not further discussed in this thesis.[223]

---

221. The term 'internal context' is used because the 'context' in Article 31(2) has an intrinsic element, i.e., in connection with the conclusion of the treaty, whereas the 'external context' of Article 31(3) is extrinsic in the sense that the material referred to does not relate to the conclusion of the treaty (*see* I. Sinclair, 1984, pp. 118-119). J.-M. Sorel & V.B. Eveno in: The Vienna Convention on the Law of Treaties (Corten & Klein eds), 2011, pp. 38 et seq. also refer to the means of Article 31(2) and (3) as 'internal' and 'external' context.
222. With respect to directives as 'any subsequent agreement between the parties regarding the interpretation of the treaty or the application of its provisions' it would seem unlikely that this view should be adopted. The first argument against such a view would be that the CJEU has explicitly ruled that directives are acts of an institution of the EU and not international agreements (*see*, to that effect, Case 91/79 (*Commission v. Italy*), para. 7 where it was held that 'a measure which has the features of a decision when viewed in the light of its objective and the institutional framework within which it has been drawn up, cannot be described as an "international agreement". The same considerations apply where a Council directive is concerned'.). Another argument within this context would be that the Directives do not reflect an explicit interpretive agreement regarding Intra-EU Treaties. However, it would seem conceivable that the ATAD3 Proposal (COM(2021) 565 final) could be construed as reflecting an intention to de facto change the application of Intra-EU Treaties. Nevertheless, the issue remains that directives are – according to the CJEU – not to be regarded as agreements between the Member States, while – as would become apparent with respect to Article 31(3)(c) VCLT 1969 – such directive would already be taken into account when interpreting an Intra-EU Treaty.
223. The present author is not aware of any indications that reflect that the Member States have – generally – adopted a practice in the application of their tax treaties reflecting an agreement

### 3.4.2.2 *The Directives as Relevant Rules of International Law Applicable in the Relations Between the Parties Within the Meaning of Article 31(3)(c) of the VCLT 1969*

Article 31(3)(c) VCLT 1969 reflects customary international law and provides that relevant rules of international law applicable in the relations between the parties 'shall be taken into account'.[224] It should therefore be assessed, in order to establish the extent to which the Directives may affect the interpretation of tax treaties under Article 31 VCLT 1969, whether the Directives qualify as such relevant rules of international law applicable in the relations between the parties. The starting point for answering such question is that the Directives are, as concluded in Chapter 2, to be regarded as a source of international law. As such, they provide rules of international law within the meaning of Article 31 (3)(c) VCLT 1969.[225] Bearing this in mind, the present section is aimed at determining whether the following two conditions are met by the Directives: the Directives must be 'relevant' (section 3.4.2.2.1) and the Directives would have to be 'applicable in the relations between the parties' (section 3.4.2.2.2).[226]

#### *3.4.2.2.1 The Directives as 'Relevant' Rules of International Law*

The requirement that rules of international law must be 'relevant' is, it has been submitted, among the interpretive difficulties of Article 31(3)(c) VCLT 1969.[227] Such difficulties may, partially, be due to the lack of clear guidance in the drafting history of Article 31(3)(c) VCLT 1969 regarding the meaning of such term. The only guidance that may be derived from such history is that 'the relevance of rules of international law for the interpretation of treaties in any given case was dependent on the intentions of the parties'.[228]

---

regarding its interpretation. Moreover, in light of the conclusion with respect to Article 31(c) VCLT 1969, the Directives may already be used under Article 31(3)(c) VCLT 1969.

224. *See*, to this effect, ICJ, 1999, Judgment (*Kasikili/Sedudu Island (Botswana/Namibia)*), p. 1075, para. 48 and ICJ, 2008, Judgment (*Certain Questions of Mutual Assistance in Criminal Matters (Djibouti v. France)*), p. 219, para. 112.
225. Support for such view can be derived from the consensus among legal scholars that the reference to 'relevant rules of international law' should be understood as referring to all (recognised) sources of public international law. *See* to that effect O. Dörr & K. Schmalenbach, 2018, pp. 604-605, para. 95. This was also the opinion of the ILC, *see* Report of the ILC (A/CN.4/L.682), p. 215, para. 426. For a similar view *see*, *inter alia*, N. Matz-Lück, Finnish Yearbook of International Law 2006, p. 44, U. Linderfalk, Netherlands International Law Review 2008/3, pp. 344-345, D.M. Broekhuijsen, Bulletin for International Taxation 2013/9, para. 3.2, and D.M. Broekhuijsen, 2018, p. 161. Furthermore, support for the use of decisions of an international organisation within the context of Article 31(3)(c) VCLT 1969 may also be derived from the judgment of the ECtHR in Application No. 15318/89 (*Loizidou v. Turkey*), paras 42-47 wherein it referred to UN Security Council Resolutions after stating that account is to be taken of 'any relevant rules of international law applicable in the relations between the parties'.
226. *See*, in this respect, also the approach adopted in SCC Arbitration V (2016/135) (*Jurisdictional Award Green Power Partners*), para. 389.
227. I. Van Damme, Finnish Yearbook of International Law 2006, p. 25.
228. YBILC 1966, Volume II, p. 222, para. 16.

Notwithstanding the absence of clear guidance from the drafting history of Article 31(3)(c) VCLT 1969, it seems that legal scholars agree that the term 'relevant' should be interpreted in a broad sense. Scholars have, for example, expressed the view that rules of international law qualify as 'relevant' 'whenever a rule of international law may have a bearing on the treaty and is potentially relevant for its interpretation',[229] as well as whenever such rules would in any way affect the interpretation of the treaty being interpreted.[230] Applied to the case of the Directives, they may be considered relevant if it can be demonstrated that they govern – or touch upon – the same subject matter as the treaty being interpreted.[231] Such sameness of subject matter may, in practice, be deemed to exist if, for example, the rules of a Directive would apply to the same set of facts as the treaty being interpreted.[232] Whereas the sameness subject matter test could be applied for the purposes of determining whether rules of international law would be relevant, it is not necessarily the only way.[233] Bossuyt, for example, submits a broader view pursuant to which 'all rules of international law could fall within the scope of Article 31(3)(c) of the VCLT insofar as they may assist in interpreting the treaty, irrespective of their subject matter or their clarifying nature.'[234] This broader view is also the view of the present author given that the mere relevance of rules of international law for the purposes of Article 31(3)(c) VCLT 1969 does not entail that such rules would also be decisive for the interpretation of a treaty (*see*, to that effect, section 3.4.3.2).[235] As such, there would be no reason not to account for all rules of international law that may assist in interpreting the treaty.

Pursuant to the broader view, a Directive could be considered 'relevant' for the purposes of Article 31(3)(c) VCLT 1969 if it could be of any assistance in interpreting a tax treaty. This may, for example, be the case if the Directive contains a meaning that

229. P. Ariginelli, 2015, para. 6.2.3.3.4.
230. F. Avella, World Tax Journal 2012/6, p. 99 and R.K. Gardiner, 2015, p. 3.2.1.
231. F.A. Engelen, 2004, p. 254. *See also* P. Sands, Yale Human Rights and Development Law Journal 1998/1, p. 102 ('"Relevance" refers to subject matter: It should be related in some way to the treaty norm being interpreted'), P. Merkouris, 2010, p. 16, and F. Avella, World Tax Journal 2012/6, p. 99. The line of reasoning would then be that if the rules of international law touch upon the same subject matter, it would seem reasonable to assume that such rules must have a bearing on – or affect – the treaty being interpreted (*see*, in this respect, J. Pauwelyn, 2003, p. 263).
232. F.A. Engelen, 2004, pp. 253-254.
233. P. Merkouris, 2010, p. 16. *See also* B. Simma & T. Kill in: International Investment Law for the 21st Century: Essays in Honour of Christoph Schreuer (Binder, Kriebaum, Reinisch & Wittich eds), 2009, p. 696 ('the drafters chose to use the term "relevant", a term whose ordinary meaning is broader than "addressing the same subject matter"'.).
234. J. Bossuyt, 2021, para. 8.1.2.5.2.
235. *See*, in this respect, also B. Simma & T. Kill in: International Investment Law for the 21st Century: Essays in Honour of Christoph Schreuer (Binder, Kriebaum, Reinisch & Wittich eds), 2009, p. 697 who note that '[a]lmost any rule of international law will be "relevant" when considered with the proper degree of abstraction. If this degree of abstraction is high, however, then the impact of the rule on the interpretation of the treaty in dispute should be low. If, however, the rules do provide "operational guidance" for the determination of the meaning of a treaty's terms as argued by either party, then it is appropriate for that rule to play a greater role in informing the interpreter's understanding of the treaty'.

is similar to that of a tax treaty term being interpreted[236] or if a Directive applies to the same factual situation.[237]

### *3.4.2.2.2 The Directives as 'Applicable in the Relations Between the Parties'*

If it is concluded that a Directive is 'relevant', this does not, in and of itself, entail that such a Directive must be taken into account when interpreting a tax treaty pursuant to Article 31 VCLT 1969. This would only be the case if a Directive would also be 'applicable in the relations between the parties'. With respect to this requirement, the following three distinct relevant elements can be recognised:

(a) the relevant rule of international law, i.e., (the obligation to achieve the result of) the Directive, must be 'applicable';
(b) 'in the relations between the parties'; and
(c) the timing of the relevant rule of international law as compared to the date of conclusion of the tax treaty (the so-called inter-temporal element).[238]

#### i The Directives as 'Applicable'

The first relevant element, i.e., the relevant rules must be 'applicable', is commonly understood as referring to instruments of international law that are 'in force' or 'legally binding' upon the parties.[239] With respect to the Directives, as well as the obligation to achieve their result under Article 288 TFEU, it follows from Chapter 2 that they are - as a matter of public international law - legally binding. For that reason, a Directive is to

236. *See*, in this respect, F. Avella, World Tax Journal 2012/6, p. 118 who refers to the term 'beneficial owner'.
237. *See*, in this respect, F. Avella, World Tax Journal 2012/6, p. 108 who notes that when treaty 'provisions affecting taxes on income are at issue, rules of EU law dealing with income tax should be considered to be "relevant"'.
238. *See* B. Simma & T. Kill in: International Investment Law for the 21st Century: Essays in Honour of Christoph Schreuer (Binder, Kriebaum, Reinisch & Wittich eds), 2009, p. 697 who note that the question of whether a rule is applicable in the relations between the parties can be separated into 'three categories of inquiry'.
239. P. Sands, Yale Human Rights and Development Law Journal 1998/1, p. 102, M.E. Villiger, 2009, p. 433, para. 25, and F. Avella, World Tax Journal 2012/6, p. 99. It has been noted that this seems to exclude non-binding rules between the parties (*see* M.E. Villiger, 2009, p. 433, para. 25 who argues that the term 'applicable' leaves no room for doubt that non-binding rules cannot be relied upon), while there are also scholars who suggest that this would be open for debate (*see* D.M. Broekhuijsen, Bulletin for International Taxation 2013/9, para. 3.3.1, as well as B. Simma & T. Kill in: International Investment Law for the 21st Century: Essays in Honour of Christoph Schreuer (Binder, Kriebaum, Reinisch & Wittich eds), 2009, p. 698 who express the view that non-binding rules can be considered under Article 31(3)(c) VCLT 1969 if, although not legally binding, it is 'at least implicitly accepted or tolerated' by the parties to the treaty being interpreted').

be regarded as 'applicable' for the purposes of Article 31(3)(c) VCLT 1969 once it has entered into force.[240]

ii 'In the Relations Between the Parties'

Based on the second relevant element, a Directive must be applicable 'in the relations between the parties' in order to qualify as a means of interpretation within the meaning of Article 31(3)(c) VCLT 1969. It follows from this element that a distinction must be drawn between Intra-EU Treaties and Extra-EU Treaties. With respect to Intra-EU Treaties, it would be clear that the Directives, as well as any obligations arising from the EU Treaties with respect to such Directives, are applicable in the relations between the Member States (i.e., the parties to the 342 Intra-EU Treaty).[241] At the same time, it is clear that such Directives or obligations relating to such Directives are not applicable in the relations between a Member State and a third state (i.e., the parties to an Extra-EU Treaties). As such, (the obligation to achieve the result of) the Directives can only qualify as 'applicable in the relations between the parties' when interpreting an Intra-EU Treaty.

While it may be easy in practice to determine whether (the obligation to achieve the result of) a Directive is applicable in the relations between the parties to a bilateral tax treaty, this may be more problematic with respect to the MLI. At first glance, one might presume that (the obligations relating to) the Directives are not applicable in the relations between the parties to the MLI because the parties to the MLI also include non-Member States. It would, as such, seem to resemble an Extra-EU Treaty. Be that as it may, there is a school of thought regarding the meaning of the term 'the parties' in Article 31(3)(c) VCLT 1969 that would provide support for regarding the Directives as applicable in the relations between the parties to the MLI in the event of a dispute between two Member States.[242] At the same time, however, there are also scholars who adopt the view that the reference to 'the parties' must be interpreted as meaning 'all the parties to the treaty'. At the date of the present thesis, both views seem defensible, and

240. *See*, for a different opinion, J. Bossuyt, 2021, para. 8.1.2.5.2 who considers it 'questionable whether a Court of Justice of the European Union (ECJ) interpretation of term in an EU Directive could be considered as falling within the scope of Article 31(3)(c) of the VCLT, as such interpretation could only be considered "binding" with respect to the term in the relevant EU Directive'. The same author does, however, recognise that '[n]othing in article 31(3)(c) of the VCLT prevents an interpreter from taking into account rules of international law arising from sources other than those mentioned in article 38(1) of the Statute of the ICJ, provided that consensus could be reached on whether this is possible'. Based conclusion in the present thesis that Directives are to be regarded as decisions of the EU as an international organisation and, as such, as among the sources of public international law, the present author would take the view that Bossuyt would agree that directives – if qualifying as among the sources of public international law – do qualify as 'applicable'.
241. *See* Annex 1, para. 3.1.
242. *See* R.K. Gardiner, 2015, p. 3.3. *See also* U. Linderfalk, Netherlands International Law Review 2008/3, p. 345.

no consensus seems to have been reached between legal scholars regarding the meaning of the term 'the parties' in Article 31(3)(c) VCLT 1969.[243]

Whether the narrow interpretation ('all the parties to the treaty') or broader interpretation ('all the parties to the dispute') is adopted is relevant for present purposes because only under the broader interpretation would it be conceivable that (the obligation to achieve the result of) a Directive can be regarded as being applicable in the relations between the parties of the MLI for the purposes of Article 31(3)(c) VCLT 1969. Under the narrow interpretation, the Directives are clearly not applicable in the relations between the parties to the MLI because not all such parties are also Member States. Given the importance of the interpretation of the term 'the parties' for the effect of the Directives on the interpretation of the MLI, an overview is provided of the arguments based on the means of interpretation of Article 31 VCLT 1969, for both the narrow and broader interpretation.

*- The ordinary meaning of 'the parties'*

With respect to the ordinary meaning of 'the parties', legal scholars have expressed diverging views.[244] It has, for example, been submitted that the ordinary meaning of the parties referred to in Article 31(3)(c) VCLT 1969 - by applying the existing rules of pragmatics - is perfectly clear and means 'all parties to the interpreted treaty, and nothing else'.[245] At the same time, however, it has also been argued that a dictionary meaning, reflecting the ordinary meaning, does not exclude either the narrow or broad interpretation because it defines the term 'party' as either a party to an agreement or legal transaction or the party to a legal dispute.[246] As such, the ordinary meaning could provide support for either interpretation.

*- The contextual meaning of 'the parties'*

Under Article 31(1) VCLT 1969, the ordinary meaning of a treaty term must be interpreted in light of its context. In ascertaining such contextual meaning, reference can be made to the use of the term 'the parties' or 'parties' in other provisions of the VCLT 1969. Such other provisions include, for example, the definition of the term 'party' in Article 2(1)(g) VCLT 1969. This provision defines the term 'party' as 'a State which has consented to be bound by the treaty and for which the treaty is in force.' Although shedding light on the meaning of the term 'party', it does not conclusively resolve the issue as to whether the reference to 'the parties' in Article 31(3)(c) of the VCLT 1969 refers to all parties or merely the parties to a dispute.[247] Support for this inconclusiveness can be derived from the circumstance that explicit references can be

243. P. Merkouris, 2010, p. 17. *See also* M. Samson, Leiden Journal of International Law 2011/3, p. 704 who states that there 'is some debate in the literature as to whether the term "the parties" mentioned in Article 31(3)(c) refers to all the parties to the treaty under interpretation or only those who are in dispute'.
244. R.K. Gardiner, 2015, p. 3.3.
245. U. Linderfalk, Netherlands International Law Review 2008/3, p. 351.
246. P. Merkouris, 2010, p. 17 and footnote 71.
247. R.K. Gardiner, 2015, p. 3.3 and O. Dörr & K. Schmalenbach, 2018, p. 610, para. 103.

found in the VCLT 1969 to 'all the parties'[248] or 'any one of the parties to a dispute'.[249] As such, the definition of 'party' for the purposes of the VCLT 1969 does not provide an argument in favour of either the narrow or broader interpretation.

Reference can furthermore be made to the immediate context of Article 31(3)(c) VCLT 1969. In Article 31(2), for example, reference is made to 'all the parties' instead of merely to 'the parties'. The absence of 'all' in Article 31(3)(c) VCLT 1969 would seem to indicate that the drafters intended a broader interpretation.[250] At the same time, however, it should be acknowledged that there are also provisions in the VCLT where reference is made to 'the parties' while it is clear that such reference is to be understood as meaning 'all of the parties' even though the word 'all' is omitted.[251] See, in this respect, for example, the references to 'the parties' in Article 31(3)(a) and (b) which are commonly understood as meaning 'all the parties'.[252] As such, the omission of the word 'all' before 'the parties', based on the context of Article 31(3)(c) VCLT 1969, does not provide conclusive support for a broader interpretation.

*– The meaning of 'the parties' based on the object and purpose of Article 31 VCLT1969*

The meaning of the term 'the parties' may also be derived from the object and purpose of Article 31 VCLT 1969. With respect to such purpose, it can be noted that the general rule of interpretation aims to give effect to the common intention of the parties to a treaty.[253] This focus on the common intention seems to provide support for adopting the narrow interpretation; if the broader interpretation was adopted, it would, in principle, allow rules which would reflect the common intention of some of the parties to affect the rules with respect to all of the parties. The broader interpretation would thus seem contrary to the overarching purpose of Article 31 VCLT 1969 to give effect to the common intentions of all the parties to a treaty.[254] Moreover, the broader interpretation would also seem contrary to the principle of pacta tertiis pursuant to which 'a state cannot be held by a treaty it did not agree to, nor can it see the interpretation of a treaty to which it is bound affected by a treaty it refused to sign'.[255] Taking these considerations into account, it follows that the purpose of Article 31 VCLT

248. *See, inter alia,* Article 15(c), Article 20(2), Article 30(3), Article 30(4), Article 31(2), Article 40(2), Article 54(b), Article 57, Article 59 and Article 60(2)(a)(ii).
249. Article 66. *See also* P. Merkouris, 2010, p. 18.
250. U. Linderfalk, Netherlands International Law Review 2008/3, p. 353.
251. R.K. Gardiner, 2015, p. 3.3. *See also* U. Linderfalk, Netherlands International Law Review 2008/3, p. 353.
252. R.K. Gardiner, 2015, p. 3.3, who notes that these references are 'clearly to states which have some relationship to the treaty in question rather than to those which have some question between them as to the treaty's meaning'. *See also* U. Linderfalk, Netherlands International Law Review 2008/3, p. 355 and P. Ariginelli, 2015, para. 6.2.3.3.4.
253. *See* WTO Appellate Body Report of 5 June 1998, European Communities – Customs Classification of Certain Computer Equipment, WT/DS62/AB/R, WT/DS67/AB/R, WT/DS/68/AB/R, para. 84.
254. *See* M. Samson, Leiden Journal of International Law 2011/3, p. 705.
255. J. Pauwelyn, 2003, p. 257.

1969 seems to provide a strong argument for rejecting the broader interpretation and adopting the narrow interpretation.[256]

With respect to the strength of such a purpose-based argument, it can be noted that such argument is especially relevant when interpreting a multilateral treaty that is multilateral in nature. If, by contrast, a multilateral treaty, by its nature, provides obligations that are more bilateral in nature, the argument is less strong. This is because the interpretation of one 'bilateral' provision of a multilateral treaty, applicable between states A-B, should not have consequences for the interpretation of that same 'bilateral' provision with respect to the other treaty relations of state A. As such, in the case of 'bilateral' aspects of multilateral treaties, the argument against adopting a broader interpretation of the term 'the parties' would seem less strong. It is therefore unsurprising that legal scholars have adopted the view that 'bilateral' multilateral treaties, to the extent a provision would be bilateral, 'may very well be considered in light of other obligations applying bilaterally between two parties only'.[257] The idea of drawing a distinction between 'multilateral' and 'bilateral' multilateral treaties for the purposes of the reference to 'the parties' in Article 31(3)(c) VCLT 1969 has also been advanced by the ILC in its Fragmentation Report (2006).[258] Such an idea would, according to the ILC, ensure the coherence and consistency of a 'multilateral' multilateral treaty,[259] while also acknowledging that no risk regarding the coherence and consistency would arise with respect to 'bilateral' multilateral treaties. It follows that if a multilateral treaty between two or more Member States and one or more third state(s) would be, at least to some extent, 'bilateral', then (the obligations regarding) the Directives could be considered as applicable in the relations between the parties to the extent that a bilateral relationship of such a multilateral treaty would concern two Member States.

Drawing a distinction between 'bilateral' and 'multilateral' multilateral treaties, or treaty provisions, seems relevant for the purposes of determining the effect of the Directives on the interpretation of the MLI under Article 31 VCLT 1969. This is because the MLI can be characterised as a 'hybrid' multilateral treaty.[260] 'Hybrid' in the sense that it contains both 'bilateral' and 'multilateral' multilateral treaty provisions. Its provisions can be regarded as bilateral to the extent that they seek to modify the application of (covered) tax treaties.[261] Such bilateral nature can be derived from the

256. This interpretation is also adopted by WTO Appellate Body Report of 5 June 1998, European Communities - Customs Classification of Certain Computer Equipment, WT/DS62/AB/R, WT/DS67/AB/R, WT/DS/68/AB/R, para. 84.
257. O. Dörr & K. Schmalenbach, 2018, pp. 610-611, para. 103.
258. It should be noted that the ILC itself regards interpreting the reference to 'the parties' as the 'parties in dispute' as the 'better solution'. Fragmentation Report, A/CN.4/L.682, p. 238, para. 472.
259. Fragmentation Report, A/CN.4/L.682, p. 239, para. 472.
260. D.M. Broekhuijsen, FED 2018/65, para. 5, D.W. Blum, Bulletin for International Taxation 2018/3, paras 2.2 and 3.2, and W.C. Haslehner, Bulletin for International Taxation 2020/4 & 5, p. 222. *See also* R. Szudoczky & D. Blum in: International and EU Tax Multilateralism: Challenges Raised by the MLI (Dourado ed.), 2020, para. 5.4.
261. *See*, to that effect, also P. Baker, Bulletin for International Taxation 2021/11 & 12, p. 602 who notes that the part of the MLI that modifies covered tax treaties reflects bilateralism triumphing over multilateralism.

circumstances in which the parties to the MLI themselves determine how treaties are affected and to what extent.[262] At the same time, however, there are also provisions of the MLI that do not seek to affect the application of bilateral (covered) tax treaties, but that relate to the operation of the MLI itself, i.e., the process for making reservations, the notifications and the final provisions. These obligations would seem to be of a multilateral nature as they concern the relations between all the parties to the MLI. Based on the hybrid nature of the MLI, (the obligations relating to) the Directives may thus be considered applicable in the relations between 'the parties' to the extent the relevant MLI provision is of a bilateral nature and seeks to affect the application of an Intra-EU Treaty.[263]

*– The meaning of 'the parties' for the purposes of the present thesis*

It follows from the previous paragraphs that the ordinary and contextual meaning of the reference to 'the parties' provide arguments for both a narrow and a broader interpretation, whereas its purpose provides a strong argument for adopting a narrow interpretation. In light of the purpose-based argument, a narrow interpretation is adopted for the purposes of the present thesis. As such, (the obligation to achieve the result of) a Directive is, in principle, not applicable in the relations between the parties to the MLI because not all parties to the MLI are also parties to the EU Treaties (and hence bound by the Directives). This is, however, different for those provisions of the MLI that are essentially of a bilateral nature. With respect to 'bilateral' provisions of the MLI, the strong argument against adopting a broader interpretation no longer applies because the rights and obligations of third states would not be affected by an interpretation that takes into account the Directives as such interpretation only applies to the bilateral relations regulated by the MLI between two Member States. For that reason, the present author concludes that (the obligation to achieve the result of) a Directive is applicable in the relations between the parties to the MLI to the extent that the MLI is of a bilateral nature affecting Intra-EU Treaties. To the extent that the MLI is of a multilateral nature, as well as with respect to Extra-EU Treaties that are affected by the MLI, (the obligation to achieve the result of) a Directive is not applicable in the relations between the parties.

### iii The Inter-temporal Question

Having established that the Directives can qualify as 'relevant rules of international law applicable in the relations between the parties' in the event of the interpretation of an Intra-EU Treaty or a 'bilateral' MLI provision affecting an Intra-EU Treaty, one final question remains: should the reference to 'applicable in the relations between the parties' be understood as the applicable rules 'at the time of the conclusion of the

262. D.M. Broekhuijsen, FED 2018/65, para. 5 and P. Baker, Bulletin for International Taxation 2021/11 & 12, p. 602.
263. For completeness' sake, it is noted that (the obligations relating to) the Directives would still not be applicable in the relations with third states because they are only applicable between Member States.

treaty' (the static approach) or 'at the time of the interpretation of the treaty' (the dynamic approach) (the inter-temporal question)?[264] Based on the analysis of the EU tax treaty network (*see* Annex 1), this question is highly relevant.

> Assume that ATAD2 would be relevant for the interpretation of an Intra-EU Treaty because it would apply to the same factual circumstances as such a tax treaty (*see* section 3.4.2.2.1). If a static approach to the reference 'applicable in the relations between the parties' is adopted, it follows that ATAD2 is, first of all, not applicable in the relations between the parties to the 233 pre-accession Intra-EU Treaties because any EU obligation postdates the conclusion of such a tax treaty.[265] Furthermore, with respect to the 109 post-accession Intra-EU Treaties, ATAD2 has been adopted after the conclusion of 103 of such treaties.[266] Hence, under a static approach, ATAD2 would only be applicable in the relations between the parties with respect to 6 of the 342 Intra-EU Treaties (1.8%).[267] Under a dynamic approach, by contrast, the date of accession to the EU or adoption of ATAD2 would, in principle, not be relevant. Hence, ATAD2 would be applicable in the relations between the parties to all 342 Intra-EU Treaties (100%).

With respect to determining whether a static or dynamic approach is to be adopted, the Commentaries to the VCLT 1969 provide that the relevance of rules of international law 'for the interpretation in any given case was dependent on the intentions of the parties' and that the correct application of the temporal element 'would normally be indicated by interpretation of the term in good faith'.[268] As such, it would have to be determined based on the common intention of the parties whether a static or dynamic approach would have to be adopted. Such an intention-based approach is also reflected in the case law of the ICJ.[269]

In determining the intentions of the parties regarding a static or dynamic approach, the rules of interpretation laid down in Articles 31 and 32 VCLT 1969 apply.[270] It should thus be ascertained in good faith, by reference to the (internal and external) context and the object and purpose of the treaty,[271] whether the parties intended a treaty term to be interpreted statically or dynamically. With respect to ascertaining this intention, there may be a presumption that the parties intended a treaty term's interpretation to have a dynamic approach if the parties have used generic terms, the meaning of which necessarily evolves over time.[272] This would, for example, be the case where the 'concept is one which implies taking into account subsequent technical, economic or legal developments', 'the concept sets up an obligation for

264. P. Merkouris, 2010, p. 121. *See also* J. Pauwelyn, 2003, pp. 267-268. Moreover, P. Ariginelli, 2015, para. 6.2.2.3.4 refers to this 'inter-temporal question' as one of the 'fundamental issues' of Article 31(3)(c) VCLT 1969.
265. Annex 1, para. 3.2.
266. Annex 1, para. 3.3. The number of '103' is based on the number of Intra-EU Treaties (342) minus the number of such tax treaties with respect to which ATAD2 ((EU) 2017/952) is 'earlier' (336).
267. Annex 1, paras 3.4.1 and 3.4.2, based on 100% minus 98.2%.
268. YBILC 1966, Volume II, p. 222, para. 16.
269. F.A. Engelen, 2004, pp. 285 et seq. *See*, more recently, also F. Avella, World Tax Journal 2012/6, p. 100 who, in addition to case law of the ICJ, also refers to case law from the ECtHR.
270. F.A. Engelen, 2004, p. 285.
271. F.A. Engelen, 2004, p. 285.
272. O. Dörr & K. Schmalenbach, 2018, p. 612, para. 108. *See also* P. Merkouris, 2010, pp. 97-98.

further progressive developments for the parties', or 'the concept has a very general nature or is expressed in such general terms that is must take into account changing circumstances'.[273] With respect to tax treaties, in general, it has been submitted that the law at the time the tax treaty is applied must be taken into account because it concerns a very technical field of law.[274] It is, however, conceivable that there may also be cases wherein a dynamic approach would have to be rejected because this would, for example, be contrary to the principle of good faith. This could, for example, be the case in which taking into account a later rule of international law would change the application of a tax treaty in such a way that cannot reasonably be assumed to be in line with the common intentions of the parties to the tax treaty. As such, it would have to be assessed on a case-by-case basis whether the contracting states to a tax treaty have had, or may be presumed to have had, a dynamic or static intention with respect to the interpretation of a treaty term.

##### *3.4.2.2.3 Conclusion*

The central question in this section 3.4.2.2 has been whether (the obligation to achieve the result of) the Directives can qualify as relevant rules of international law applicable in the relations between the parties within the meaning of Article 31(3)(c) VCLT 1969. This question can, based on the preceding sections, be answered in the affirmative. Such answer is based on the following considerations with respect to each of the conditions of Article 31(3)(c) VCLT 1969:

(a) *Rules of international law:* the Directives, as decisions of the EU as an international organization, as well as the obligation to achieve the result of such Directives, laid down in Article 288 TFEU, are rules of international law (section 3.4.2.2);
(b) *Relevance:* whether (the obligation to achieve the result of) a Directive is 'relevant' depends on whether such (obligation relating to) a Directive may be of any assistance in interpreting a tax treaty provision. This may, for example, be the case if a Directive contains a similar term to that being interpreted, or if a Directive applies to the same factual situation (section 3.4.2.2.1).
(c) Applicable in the relations between the parties:
    (i) the Directives, as well as the obligation to achieve their result, are only applicable in the relations between the Member States. Hence, the Directives may only qualify as a means of interpretation within the meaning of Article 31(3)(c) VCLT 1969 with respect to the 342 Intra-EU Treaties (section 3.4.2.2.2, under b));

273. ILC, Fragmentation Report (2006), No. 10 (A/61/10), pp. 415-416, para. 23.
274. F. Avella, World Tax Journal 2012/6, p. 108.

(ii) whether (the obligation to achieve the result of) the Directives should, in a given situation, be regarded as applicable in the relations between the parties within the meaning of Article 31(3)(c) VCLT 1969 depends on whether such (obligations relating to the) Directives predate the relevant Intra-EU Treaty. If this is the case, (the obligations relating to) the Directives are applicable in the relations between the contracting (EU Member) states. To the extent that this is not the case, it would depend on whether the contracting (EU Member) states intended the treaty provision or term being interpreted to have a static or a dynamic meaning (section 3.4.2.2.2, under c));

(iii) with respect to the MLI, whether (the obligations relating to) the Directives are applicable in the relations between the parties depends on whether the relevant provision is of a 'bilateral' nature affecting an Intra-EU Treaty. If that is the case, (the obligations relating to) the Directives can be regarded as applicable in the relations between the parties to the MLI. If that is not the case, i.e., the relevant provision is of a 'multilateral' nature or would affect the application of an Extra-EU Treaty, (the obligations relating to) the Directives are not applicable in the relations between the parties (section 3.4.2.2.2, under c)).

### 3.4.3 The Role of the Directives Within the General Rule of Interpretation

It follows from section 3.4.2 that (the obligation to achieve the result of) a Directive can qualify as a relevant rule of international law applicable In the relations between the parties within the meaning of Article 31(3)(c) VCLT 1969 when interpreting Intra-EU Treaties and 'bilateral' provisions of the MLI affecting (covered) Intra-EU Treaties. If qualifying as such, it follows from Article 31(3) VCLT that an interpreter would be required to take (the obligation to achieve the result of) a Directive into account when interpreting a treaty provision in accordance with the general rule of interpretation of Article 31 VCLT 1969 ('shall be taken into account'). The mere obligation to '*take into account*' does not, however, indicate how much weight should be attributed to, in this case, (the obligations relating to) a Directive (the 'weight question'). This weight question is addressed in this section.

The answer to the weight question will be based on an assessment of the operation of the general rule of interpretation of Article 31 VCLT 1969. Such an assessment should provide an understanding of the weight to be attributed to each mean of interpretation referred to in Article 31 VCLT, including (the obligations relating to) the Directives. This operation is set out by assessing the purpose of the general rule of interpretation (section 3.4.3.1) followed by an analysis of the operation of the various means of interpretation within the context of the general rule, including – in particular – the role of relevant rules of international law (section 3.4.3.2).

### *3.4.3.1 The Purpose of the General Rule of Interpretation*

Article 31 VCLT 1969 contains the 'general rule of interpretation' (singular). As such, it contains one single rule, requiring one single combined operation,[275] and requiring one single, i.e., the one and only, (ordinary or special) meaning of a term of a treaty as an outcome.[276] The operation of this rule of interpretation may be illustrated by the metaphor of a crucible:

> [t]he interpreter has to determine all potentially relevant means to construe the specific treaty, in light of the circumstances of the case, and throw them into the crucible of interpretation: a proper construction of the treaty will come out of such crucible.[277]

The metaphor of the crucible reflects the principle that the proper construction of a treaty term 'should be reached only after all relevant elements and means of interpretation have been taken into account and duly weighted in light of the whole analysis carried out'.[278] In determining the weight to be duly attributed to the various means of interpretation, the starting point is that there does not exist an *a priori* preference for one element over another.[279] Instead, the guiding principle that would determine the weight to be attached to the various means of interpretation is that the more a mean of interpretation reflects the common intentions of the parties with respect to the treaty being interpreted, the more weight would have to be attached to such a mean.[280]

With respect to determining such a common intention-based single outcome, it is to be borne in mind, however, that it must be based *'above all'* on the text of the treaty.[281] This 'textual' limitation applies because the general rule of interpretation is based on the premise that the text of a treaty reflects the 'best evidence of the finally

275. YBILC 1966, Volume II, p. 219, para. 8. This position seems to be accepted by legal scholarship. *See, inter alia*, A. Aust, 2013, p. 206 ('one rule'), P. Ariginelli, 2015, para. 6.2.2 ('single operation'), and J.F. Avery Jones & J. Hattingh, 2021, para. 3.4.1 ('single rule of interpretation').
276. *See* Separate opinion of Judge Torres Bernárdez, Land, Island and Maritime Frontier Dispute, para. 195 who states that he does 'not consider that ... a "true" interpretation is provided by applying each of the recognised interpretative principles and elements independently of each other in a selective way. The "integrated whole" criterion is ... paramount and should prevail.' *See also* A. Orakhelashvili, 2008, p. 317.
277. P. Ariginelli, 2015, para. 6.2.2 who refers to YBILC 1966, Volume II, p. 95, para. 4 and pp. 219-220, para. 8, as well as R.K. Gardiner, 2015, pp. 9-10.
278. P. Ariginelli, 2015, para. 6.2.2. YBILC 1966, Volume II, p. 220, para. 9.
279. YBILC 1966, Volume II, p. 220, para. 9 and P. Ariginelli, 2015, para. 6.2.2. Such a preference can, in any event, not be derived from the order in which the various means of interpretation have been set out in Article 31 VCLT 1969; the order was made on the basis of logic rather than any considerations of hierarchy (*see*, to this effect, YBILC 1966, Volume II, p. 220, para. 9. *See also* A. Aust, 2013, p. 206 who states that the view that a priori greater weight should be attributed to, for example, the text of the treaty to the detriment of the object and purpose of the treaty can be found in the circumstance that such an approach would have been contrary to the jurisprudence of the ICJ).
280. McNair, 1961, p. 365, P. Ariginelli, 2015, para. 6.2.3.2 and para. 6.3, and O. Dörr & K. Schmalenbach, 2018, p. 560, para. 3.
281. ICJ.1992, Order, Provisional Measures (*Lockerbie*), para. 41.

agreed intent of the parties'.[282] As such, the general rule of interpretation aims to give effect to the objectified common intention of the parties.[283] The importance of the text should, however, also not be overestimated. The single interpretive outcome should only be 'based on' the text. As such, the ordinary meaning of the text might be the starting point (*see also* section 3.4.3.1.2), but it does not necessarily have to be the point of arrival of the single combined operation of Article 31 VCLT.[284] This is due to Article 31 VCLT 1969 clarifying that the single interpretive outcome must be based on the ordinary (textual) meaning as interpreted in good faith, in its (internal and external) context and in light of its object and purpose.[285] As such, if good faith, the (internal or external) context and the object and purpose would indicate that the parties intended a treaty term to have a meaning different from the (initial) interpretation derived from the text, such different meaning should be adopted (provided that it can be said to be based on such text). A textual interpretation of a term may thus be the point of departure, but not necessarily the point of arrival after having considered (the role of) the other means of interpretation referred to in Article 31 VCLT 1969. These means of interpretation are discussed in sections 3.4.3.1.1 through 3.4.3.1.5 below.

#### *3.4.3.1.1 The Role of Good Faith*

It follows from the wording of Article 31 VCLT 1969 that a treaty must be interpreted in good faith. Whereas there is no universally agreed definition of 'good faith', there does seem to be consensus among legal scholars that it requires a treaty term to be interpreted in a reasonable, fair and honest way.[286] Good faith thus 'sets the tone and directs the undertaking as a whole'.[287] The tone set by it is that, when examining the other means of interpretation of Article 31 VCLT 1969, the appreciation of such means and their weight as compared to the other means must be made in a reasonable, fair and honest way.[288] The principle of good faith, therefore, provides 'fundamental

282. R.K. Gardiner, 2015, p. 164, who refers to YBILC 1966, Volume II, p. 220, para. 11. *See also* I. Sinclair, 1984, p. 115, and O. Dörr & K. Schmalenbach, 2018, p. 560, para. 3. Support for this premise can also be derived from case law of the ICJ. *See* ICJ, 1994, Judgment, Territorial Dispute (*Libya/Chad*), p. 22, para. 41, as well as ICJ, 2004, Preliminary Objections, Legality of Use of Force (*Serbia and Montenegro v. Belgium*), p. 318, para. 100.
283. This can be contrasted with basing the common intention on (less reliable) subjective sources. *See* in that respect, Interpretation and Implied (Tacit) Modification of Treaties – Comments on Articles 27, 28, 29 and 38 of the ILC's 1966 Draft Articles on the Law of Treaties, p. 496, O. Dörr & K. Schmalenbach, 2018, pp. 560-561, para. 3, and R.K. Gardiner, 2015, p. 6.
284. R. Kolb, 2016, p. 136.
285. *See* A. Orakhelashvili, 2008, p. 312.
286. *See* M.E. Villiger, 2009, p. 425, para. 7, P. Ariginelli, 2015, para. 6.2.3.2, J.F. Avery Jones & J. Hattingh, 2021, para. 3.3, and J. Bossuyt, 2021, para. 6.3.5.1. *See also* ICJ, 1997, Judgment (*Gabcikovo-Nagymaros*), p. 7, para. 142 ('The principle of good faith obliges the Parties to apply it in a reasonable way and in such a manner that its purposes can be realised.').
287. O. Dörr & K. Schmalenbach, 2018, p. 587, para. 59. *See also* P. Ariginelli, 2015, para. 6.2.3.2 who notes that it 'directs the way in which such legal rules must be interpreted'.
288. O. Dörr & K. Schmalenbach, 2018, p. 587, para. 59.

guidance for the interpretation' of tax treaties.[289] It essentially safeguards that a treaty should be interpreted 'in accordance with its spirit rather than too strictly according to the letter'.[290]

As such, good faith seeks to prevent a treaty from being interpreted in such a way that treaty obligations are evaded,[291] that the object and purpose of a treaty are frustrated,[292] or, more generally, that the interpretation would be contrary to the common intention of the parties.[293] The principle of good faith thus essentially precludes adopting an interpretation that would misrepresent the 'genuine content of what [the contracting states] have undertaken through the treaty'.[294] In addition to clarifying what interpretation should not be adopted, good faith also directs 'the interpreter towards the most reasonable construction'.[295] Such most reasonable construction requires the interpretive outcome to reflect the common, real understanding of the terms of a treaty.[296] In the event of two possible interpretations – 'one of which results in an unreasonable or absurd outcome' – good faith could thus direct an interpreter to adopt the interpretation that produces the reasonable outcome.[297] Adopting such reasonable outcome would then have to be presumed as reflecting the common intention of the parties. In determining the 'reasonable' outcome, the object and purpose of the tax treaty being interpreted may be relevant given that it is mentioned in the ILC Commentaries that '[w]hen a treaty is open to two interpretations one of which does and the other does not enable the treaty to have appropriate effects, good faith and the objects and purposes of the treaty demand that the former should be adopted'.[298] Together with the object and purpose, good faith thus 'leads to an interpretive approach highly focused on establishing the intention of the parties starting from text'.[299] In addition to guiding an interpreter to adopt a meaning that gives effect to the object and purpose of a treaty, good faith may also guide an interpreter towards adopting a meaning that is consistent with earlier rules of public international law via the presumption against conflict (*see* section 3.4.3.2.2).[300] As such, good faith may guide an interpreter, when facing two possible interpretations, one of which is consistent with the result to be achieved by a Directive while the other is not, to adopt the interpretation that is consistent with such a Directive.[301]

289. P. Ariginelli, 2015, para. 6.2.3.2.
290. *See* Verdross in ILC, Summary record of 772nd meeting, 1964 (Vol. I), p. 326, para. 3.
291. F.A. Engelen, 2004, para. 2.5.
292. *See also* R.A. Bosman, 2015, para. 3.2.2 and P. Ariginelli, 2015, para. 6.2.3.2.
293. F.A. Engelen, 2004, para. 2.5. This preventive effect of good faith may be described as its negative aspect. *See* R. Kolb, 2016, pp. 148-149. *See also* P. Ariginelli, 2015, para. 6.2.3.2 who refers to good faith precluding an abuse of rights under a treaty.
294. A. Orakhelashvili, 2008, p. 398.
295. R. Kolb, 2016, pp. 148-149.
296. E. Van der Bruggen, British Tax Review 2003/1, para. 3.1.
297. *See* J. Bossuyt, 2021, para. 8.1.2.2.
298. *See* YBILC 1966, Volume II, p. 219, para. 6. *See also* ICJ, 1997, Judgment (*Gabcikovo-Nagymaros*), p. 7, para. 142.
299. P. Ariginelli, 2015, para. 6.2.3.2.
300. *See*, to this effect, also J. Bossuyt, 2021, para. 6.8.4.2.
301. *See*, to this effect, F.A. Engelen, 2004, para. 10.7 who notes that 'when a tax treaty is open to two constructions one of which does and the other does not conflict with the obligations of the contracting States under EC law, good faith demands that the latter construction be adopted'.

### *3.4.3.1.2 The Role of the Ordinary Meaning*

Under the general rule of interpretation of Article 31 VCLT 1969, the text of the treaty must be the starting point for the purposes of determining the meaning of a treaty term (*see* section 3.4.3.1). This is also reflected by the reference to the 'ordinary meaning' in Article 31 VCLT 1969.[302] The rationale for taking the ordinary meaning as the starting point is that 'the parties are to be presumed to have that intention which appears from the ordinary meaning of the terms used by them'.[303] Such terms have been 'carefully negotiated' by the parties and can thus be seen as an authentic expression of their intentions.[304] As such, the interpretation of a treaty term, in order to give effect to the intentions of the parties, must be based, above all, upon the text of the treaty.[305]

In determining the ordinary meaning of a treaty term, the linguistic or grammatical analysis of the text of the treaty would seem useful as a starting point.[306] In such an analysis, the interpreter looks for the meaning of a term that is 'regular, normal or customary'.[307] Such a 'regular, normal or customary' meaning is, however, not necessarily the point of arrival for establishing the ordinary meaning under Article 31(1) VCLT 1969.[308] This is because 'there is no such thing as an abstract ordinary meaning of a phrase, divorced from the place which that phrase occupies in the text to be interpreted'.[309] As such, it must be accepted that there will not be a single common 'ordinary meaning' that is determined in the abstract by adhering to a purely grammatical analysis of the text of the treaty.[310] Establishing the ordinary meaning thus

302. R. Kolb, 2016, p. 135.
303. YBILC 1966, Volume II, p. 221, para. 12. *See also* P. Ariginelli, 2015, para. 6.2.3.3.
304. R. Kolb, 2016, p. 135. *See also* A. Aust, 2013, p. 209 and P. Ariginelli, 2015, para. 6.2.3.3.
305. O. Dörr & K. Schmalenbach, 2018, pp. 560-561, para. 3. *See also* ICJ, 1994, Judgment, Territorial Dispute (*Libya/Chad*), p. 22, para. 41 and ICJ, 2004, Preliminary Objections, Legality of Use of Force (*Serbia and Montenegro v. Belgium*), p. 318, para. 100.
306. O. Dörr & K. Schmalenbach, 2018, p. 581, para. 40. *See also* J. Bossuyt, 2021, para. 6.3.5.1 who notes that 'a grammatical and too literal interpretation is not appropriate, but that should not prevent an interpreter from initiating the process of interpretation by having recourse to a grammatical interpretation – as one must start somewhere – thereby resorting to dictionaries, both ordinary and of a professional nature'.
307. O. Dörr & K. Schmalenbach, 2018, p. 581, para. 40. Other scholars expressing similar views are R.A. Bosman, 2015, para. 3.2.5 and M.E. Villiger, 2009, p. 427, para. 9.
308. YBILC 1966, Volume II, p. 220, para. 12. *See also* ICJ, 1952, Judgment (*Anglo-Iranian Oil Company (United Kingdom v. Iran)*), p. 104 ('the Court cannot base itself on a purely grammatical interpretation of the text. It must seek the interpretation which is in harmony with a natural and reasonable way of reading the text'), ICJ, 1961, Preliminary Objections, Judgment (*Temple of Preah Vihear (Cambodia v. Thailand)*), p. 32 ('the principle of ordinary meaning does not entail that words and phrases are always interpreted in a purely literal way'), as well as Separate opinion of Judge Torres Bernárdez, Land, Island and Maritime Frontier Dispute, para. 190. Reference can also be made to F.A. Engelen, 2004, para. 6.4.1 and R.A. Bosman, 2015, para. 3.2.5.
309. I. Sinclair, 1984, p. 121. *See also* R. Gardiner in: The Oxford Guide to Treaties (Hollis ed.), 2012, p. 3 480, para. II.A, D.O. Corredor Velásquez, Intertax 2016/12, p. 964, J. Bossuyt, 2021, para. 6.3.5.1, and J.F. Avery Jones & J. Hattingh, 2021, para. 3.4.4.
310. F.A. Engelen, 2004, para. 6.4.4. *See also* Sir Humprey Waldock in United Nations Conference on the Law of Treaties, A/CONF.39/C.1/SR.33, p. 184, para. 69 who states that 'nothing could have been further from the Commission's intention than to suggest that words had a "dictionary" or intrinsic meaning in themselves. The provisions of article [31], paragraph 1, clearly indicated that a treaty must be interpreted "in good faith" in accordance with the

requires supplementary criteria,[311] which criteria are listed – for the purposes of the general rule of interpretation – in Article 31 VCLT 1969[312] (and, to some extent, Article 32 VCLT 1969).[313] Only after taking these elements into consideration, as well as the principle of good faith,[314] would one be able to establish the ordinary meaning of the terms being interpreted.[315] Therefore, the reference to the 'ordinary meaning' is to be understood as an ordinary meaning that is qualified by all interpretative elements referred to in Article(s) 31 (and 32) VCLT 1969.[316]

#### *3.4.3.1.3 The Role of the Object and Purpose*

In addition to good faith and the ordinary meaning, Article 31 VCLT 1969 requires an interpreter to also take into account the object and purpose of a treaty.[317] As such, the object and purpose 'are among the elements to be thrown in the crucible when giving the terms of the treaty their ordinary meaning'.[318] Within such crucible, the object and purpose function as a 'qualifier of the ordinary meaning to be attributed to treaty

---

ordinary meaning of the words "in their context". The Commission had been very insistent that the ordinary meaning of terms emerged in the context in which they were used, in the context of the treaty as a whole, and in the light of the object and purpose of the treaty'. According to P. Ariginelli, 2015, para. 6.2.3.3 this position of Sir Humprey Waldock is 'semantically supported by the use of the expression "the ordinary meaning to be given to the terms" in article 31(1) of the [Vienna Convention 1969], which indicates that the ordinary meaning is not intrinsic to the terms but must be attributed by the interpreter by choosing among the various possible meanings according to the specific circumstances of the case'. *See also* R. Gardiner in: The Oxford Guide to Treaties (Hollis ed.), 2012, p. 3 and A. Aust, 2013, p. 209. Reference may furthermore be made to ICJ, 1978, Judgment (*Aegean Sea Continental Shelf*), paras 52 et seq. for an example wherein the ICJ did not rely on a purely grammatical interpretation advanced by Greece, as well as to Separate opinion of Judge Torres Bernárdez, Land, Island and Maritime Frontier Dispute, pp. 719-720, paras 191-192.

311. M. Herdegen in: Max Planck Encyclopedias of International Law (Wolfrum ed.), 2013, para. B.3.a and P. Ariginelli, 2015, para. 6.2.3.3 who notes that the adjective 'ordinary' is 'qualified by the subsequent specifications encompassed in article 31 of the VCLT'. *See also* J. Bossuyt, 2021, para. 8.1.2.3.
312. Separate opinion of Judge Torres Bernárdez, Land, Island and Maritime Frontier Dispute, para. 190. *See also* F.A. Engelen, 2004, para. 6.4.4 and J.F. Avery Jones & J. Hattingh, 2021, para. 3.4.4.
313. P. Ariginelli, 2015, para. 6.2.3.3.
314. *See, e.g.*, R. Kolb, 2016, p. 137 and P. Ariginelli, 2015, para. 6.2.3.3 who argue that good faith requires the ordinary meaning to be determined within a certain field of law and not in the abstract.
315. D.O. Corredor Velásquez, Intertax 2016/12, p. 964.
316. P. Ariginelli, 2015, para. 6.2.3.3. *See also* Separate opinion of Judge Torres Bernárdez, Land, Island and Maritime Frontier Dispute, para. 190. Reference can furthermore be made to also J. Bossuyt, 2021, para. 6.3.5.1 who concludes that 'there can be little doubt that the ordinary meaning ex article 31(1) of the VCLT can only be established based on a weighted analysis of all permissible means of interpretation set forth in articles 31 and 32 of the VCLT'.
317. It is acknowledged that, whereas Article 31(1) VCLT 1969 refers to 'object and purpose' in the singular, it seems that, in practice, in the event of multiple objects and purposes of a treaty, these may also be taken into account (*see* O. Dörr & K. Schmalenbach, 2018, p. 585, para. 54, as well as P. Ariginelli, 2015, para. 6.2.3.3.1).
318. F.A. Engelen, 2004, para. 6.6.2.5. *See also*, regarding the requirement to take the object and purpose into account, Separate opinion of Judge Torres Bernárdez, Land, Island and Maritime Frontier Dispute, para. 206.

terms'.[319] As a qualifier, it can provide indications of the 'dividing line between acceptable and non-acceptable interpretations',[320] especially when the principle of effectiveness is taken into account pursuant to which treaty terms should be interpreted 'so as to give them, as far as possible, an effect consistent with the object and purpose of a treaty'.[321]

While the object and purpose mean of interpretation would thus seem important under Article 31(1) VCLT 1969, its importance should not be overestimated.[322] This is because the object and purpose are 'relative to the text' in the sense that it can shed 'light' on the treaty terms being interpreted.[323] It cannot, by contrast, be used to provide an autonomous meaning that does not find its basis in the text.[324] As such, object and purpose cannot result in a meaning to be attributed to a term that would go beyond 'what is expressed or necessarily implied in the actual terms of the treaty so as to give effect to its object and purpose' because this would not be 'in accordance with the textual approach to treaty interpretation underlying article 31 [VCLT 1969]'.[325] As such, the main function of the object and purpose would seem to be to determine which (potential) interpretive outcomes are acceptable or not (especially in conjunction with the principle of good faith).

#### *3.4.3.1.4 The Role of the (Internal) Context*

It follows from Article 31(1) VCLT 1969 that the ordinary meaning of a term must be determined in its context (as well as in the light of its object and purpose).[326] It is thus the purpose of this context, as defined in Article 31(2) VCLT 1969,[327] to guide an interpreter to the ordinary meaning of the terms of the treaty.[328] Such purpose can be fulfilled by either confirming the 'prima facie ordinary meaning' or by aiding in 'ascertaining the proper meaning insofar as that prima facie ordinary meaning would be vague or ambiguous'.[329] As such, the context helps an interpreter, together with the

319. P. Ariginelli, 2015, para. 6.2.3.3.1.
320. Reference can, for example, be made to the statement of the ILC that 'when a treaty is open to two interpretations, one of which does and the other does not enable the treaty to have appropriate effects, good faith and the objects and purposes of the treaty demand that the former interpretation should be adopted' (*see* YBILC 1966, Volume II, p. 219, para. 6). *See also* P. Ariginelli, 2015, para. 6.2.3.3.1.
321. P. Ariginelli, 2015, para. 6.2.3.3.1.
322. *See* J. Bossuyt, 2021, para. 8.1.2.6.3.
323. F.A. Engelen, 2004, para. 6.6.2.5, P. Ariginelli, 2015, para. 6.2.3.3.1, and R.A. Bosman, 2015, para. 3.2.3. *See* for the risk, I. Sinclair, 1984, p. 131 who states that there is 'the risk that the placing of an undue emphasis on the "object and purpose" of a treaty will encourage teleological methods of interpretation. The teleological approach, in some of its more extreme forms, will even deny the relevance of the intentions of the parties'.
324. *See* J. Bossuyt, 2021, para. 8.1.2.6.3 who notes that object and purpose 'must remain within the textual contours of the treaty terms'.
325. F.A. Engelen, 2004, para. 6.6.2.5 and P. Ariginelli, 2015, para. 6.2.3.3.1.
326. F.A. Engelen, 2004, para. 6.1. *See also* R.A. Bosman, 2015, para. 3.2.6.
327. F.A. Engelen, 2004, para. 6.7.1 and R.A. Bosman, 2015, para. 3.2.6.
328. YBILC 1966, Volume II, p. 221, para. 13.
329. J. Bossuyt, 2021, para. 8.1.2.4.

object and purpose and good faith, 'to draw the borders of what may be considered an acceptable interpretation'.[330]

Regarding the elements on the context within the meaning of Article 31 (2) VCLT 1969, it follows that such elements comprise three distinct elements,[331] but is not limited to such elements.[332] The decisive criterion for qualifying a potential mean of interpretation as context within the meaning of Article 31 (2) VCLT 1969 is whether it (i) reflects the agreement of the contracting states (ii) at the time of the conclusion of the treaty.[333] It follows from this criterion that unilateral statements made during negotiations – or laid down in the *travaux préparatoires* – are not considered to be part of such context because they do not necessarily reflect the final agreement reached by the parties in connection with the conclusion of the treaty.[334] Non-listed bilateral text-based material and unilateral instruments agreed by other parties in connection with the conclusion of the treaty do, however, qualify as context within the meaning of Article 31 (2) VCLT 1969.[335]

#### *3.4.3.1.5 The Role of a Special Meaning*

Article 31 (1) VCLT 1969 is based on the presumption that the ordinary meaning reflects the intention of the parties.[336] This presumption is, however, rebuttable taking into account that it follows from Article 31 (4) VCLT 1969 that a special meaning should be given to a term if it is established that the parties so intended.[337] Such a special meaning is 'special' as compared to the ordinary meaning because it would go 'beyond, and no

330. P. Ariginelli, 2015, para. 6.2.3.3.2.
331. The first element, derived from the opening sentence of Article 31 (2) VCLT 1969, is the text of the treaty, which includes the preamble and the annexes, if any (*see* R.A. Bosman, 2015, para. 3.2.6 and J.F. Avery Jones & J. Hattingh, 2021, para. 3.4.5.2). The second element, laid down in subparagraph (a), makes it clear that, in addition to the text of the treaty, the context comprises of any agreements relating to the treaty, 'to the extent that these were agreed upon by all contracting states and made in connection with the conclusion of the treaty'. Examples of such agreements would be protocols, memoranda of understanding, and notes and letters exchanged during the signing of a treaty (*see* R.A. Bosman, 2015, para. 3.2.6). The third and final element, laid down in subparagraph (b), stipulates that the context also comprises of other unilateral instruments relating to the treaty made by one or more contracting state(s) and accepted by the other contracting state(s). Examples of this element would be certain declarations of policy and reservations of policy and reservations made upon the signing of the treaty (*see* R.A. Bosman, 2015, para. 3.2.6).
332. R.A. Bosman, 2015, para. 3.2.6 and D.O. Corredor Velásquez, Intertax 2016/12, p. 964.
333. P. Ariginelli, 2015, para. 6.2.3.3.2.
334. J.F. Avery Jones & J. Hattingh, 2021, para. 3.4.5.2. This does not mean, however, that they are of no relevance for the purpose of interpreting treaties. Such material 'can still be considered, but only as supplementary means of interpretation within article 32 of the Vienna Convention (1969)'.
335. D.O. Corredor Velásquez, Intertax 2016/12, p. 965. *See also* J.F. Avery Jones & J. Hattingh, 2021, para. 3.4.5.2 who states that all components have a 'bilateral element'.
336. F.A. Engelen, 2004, para. 6.1. *See also* section 3.4.3.1.2.
337. F.A. Engelen, 2004, para. 6.1, P. Ariginelli, 2015, para. 6.2.3.3.2, and J. Bossuyt, 2021, para. 8.1.2.3. In this respect, the burden of proof lies with the party asserting a special meaning instead of an ordinary meaning.

longer corresponds with, the apparent ordinary meanings of the term'.[338] Considering that the special meaning must be distinct from the ordinary meaning, it follows that such special meaning operates as an alternative to, and takes precedence over,[339] the ordinary meaning.[340]

In the event that it would be so established that the parties to a treaty intended a term to have a special meaning, the content of such meaning should be established in good faith and in its (internal and external) context and in light of its object and purpose.[341] Taking into consideration that thus both the ordinary and special meaning must be determined in the same manner under Article 31 VCLT 1969, the interpretive process and the role of the ordinary or special meaning do not seem to be different.[342]

#### *3.4.3.2 The Role of the Directives Within the General Rule of Interpretation*

Having set out the role of the means of interpretation referred to in Article 31(1) and (2) VCLT 1969, the present section focuses on the role of the Directives, as well as the obligation to achieve the result of such Directives under Article 288 TFEU, as relevant rules of international law applicable in the relations between the parties within the meaning of Article 31(3)(c) VCLT 1969. With respect to determining to such effect, it is, first of all, recalled that the Directives are of equal rank as compared to any other relevant rule of international law applicable in the relations between the parties and must, for that reason, be given the same weight as any such other rule.[343] Second, it is recalled that Article 31 VCLT 1969 provides a single combined operation aimed at giving effect to the common intentions of the parties with respect to the treaty being interpreted (section 3.4.3.1). Such intentions are to be determined by taking into account the relevant rules of international law applicable in the relations between the parties, including (the obligations relating to) the Directives, together with the (other elements of the) context, object and purpose and the ordinary (or special) meaning of a treaty in order to determine the single meaning of a treaty term.[344] In determining the role of (the obligations relating to) the Directives, it is furthermore to be borne in mind that the single outcome under Article 31 VCLT 1969 should, above all, be based on the text of the treaty. This thus limits the effect of (the obligations relating to) the Directives in the sense that they cannot rewrite the treaty being interpreted or substitute a plain

338. M.E. Villiger, 2009, pp. 434-435, para. 26. *See also* P. Ariginelli, 2015, para. 6.2.3.4 and O. Dörr & K. Schmalenbach, 2018, p. 613, para. 109.
339. R.A. Bosman, 2015, para. 3.2.8.
340. J.F. Avery Jones & J. Hattingh, 2021, para. 3.4.11.
341. F.A. Engelen, 2004, para. 6.2.5. *See also* R.A. Bosman, 2015, para. 3.2.8 and J.F. Avery Jones & J. Hattingh, 2021, para. 3.4.11.
342. *See*, to this effect, F.A. Engelen, 2004, para. 6.5.7.
343. *See* M. Prost in: The Oxford Handbook of the Sources of International Law (Besson & d'Aspremont eds), 2018, para. I who notes that the lack of hierarchy among sources of international law is considered by most legal scholars as a 'central fact of international law and the starting point for theorizing about international law'.
344. C. McLachlan, International and Comparative Law Quarterly 2005/2, p. 311 who notes that 'it is always essential to keep in mind that Article 31(3)(c) is only part of a larger interpretation process, in which the interpreter must first consider the plain meaning of the words in their context and in the light of the object and purpose of the provision'.

reading of a treaty provision contradicting its wording.[345] Taking into consideration these general comments regarding the weight to be attributed to relevant rules of international law applicable in the relations between the parties within the context of Article 31 VCLT 1969, it will be assessed in the sections below to what extent the Directives may reflect common intentions between the Member States with respect to their Intra-EU Treaties.

#### *3.4.3.2.1 The Role of the Directives as Relevant Rules of International Law Applicable in the Relations Between the Parties*

With respect to the role that Directives may play as relevant rules of international law applicable in the relations between the parties, Directives would seem able to provide evidence of a common intention with respect to tax treaties in two ways. They can provide explicit evidence by means of reference to tax treaties in their preamble or in their provisions (section 3.4.3.2.2) or implicit evidence by covering situations that are similar to those covered by tax treaties or by using terminology that is similar to that used in tax treaties (section 3.4.3.2.3). In determining whether a Directive reflects a common intention of the Member States with respect to their Intra-EU Treaties, an assessment of the individual Directives reveals that the extent to which such an intention may be derived from them differs. Most of the Directives currently in force do not contain language reflecting evidence of an explicit common intention regarding their effect on, or relation with, the application (or interpretation) of tax treaties concluded by the Member States.

#### *3.4.3.2.2 Directives Providing Explicit Evidence of a Common Intention*

Only ATAD2 and the Arbitration Directive provide explicit indications of their envisaged effect on tax treaties concluded by the Member States. In ATAD2, for example, two references can be found regarding the effect of such Directive on tax treaties concluded by the Member States. First, in recital (11) of the preamble to ATAD2, it is noted that any adjustments resulting from the application of ATAD2 should not, 'in principle', affect the allocation of taxing rights under (apparently, both Intra-EU and Extra-EU) tax treaties.[346] Second, Article 9(5) ATAD2 provides evidence of an intention that its rule should not affect tax treaties with Extra-EU Treaties that would not allow for the taxation of profits attributable to a so-called disregarded permanent establishment. Both references thus reflect an intention of the effect that ATAD2 should not have on tax treaties. They do not, however, reflect an intention as to what effect ATAD2 should have on such treaties. This is different from the Arbitration Directive. It follows clearly from Article 16(5) of such Directive that the submission of a complaint

345. *See*, to this effect, ICSID, Case No. ARB/12/12 (*Vattenfall*), para. 154. This position has also been adopted by the ICSID, Case No. ARB/15/50 (*Eskosol S.p.a. v. Italian Republic*), para. 126 and has also been recognised in SCC Arbitration V (2016/135) (*Jurisdictional Award Green Power Partners*), para. 395.

346. *See* recital (11) of the preamble to ATAD2.

on the basis of Article 3 of the Arbitration Directive 'shall put an end to any other ongoing proceedings under the mutual agreement procedure or dispute resolution procedure under an agreement or convention that is being interpreted or applied in relation to the relevant question in dispute'. As such, it would seem that the Arbitration Directive contains evidence of a common intention between the Member States with respect to the effect that such a Directive should have on their Intra-EU Treaties.

> Such evidence of a common intention regarding Intra-EU Treaties can also be derived from the 2011 proposal for a CCCTB. Article 8 of such proposal, titled 'Directive overrides agreements between Member States', provided that the provisions of the CCCTB 'shall apply notwithstanding any provision to the contrary in any agreement concluded between Member States'.[347] Similarly, the explanatory memorandum of the proposal for a Significant Digital Presence Directive (2018) indicated that its provisions should apply to 'cross border digital activities within the Union, even if the applicable double taxation treaties between Member States have not been modified accordingly'.[348] Finally, Article 11 of the, on 31 October 2022, pending, ATAD3 Proposal provides that Intra-EU Treaties would have to be 'disregarded', which would also seem to reflect evidence of a common intention between the Member States as regards the effect of such a Directive on their Intra-EU Treaties.[349]

In the other Directives, no references are made regarding the effect that they should have on tax treaties. This does not, however, entail that they do not refer to such tax treaties. In the Parent-Subsidiary Directive and Merger Directive, for example, reference is made to Extra-EU Treaties within the context of the definition of a 'company of a Member State'.[350] Such references seek to ensure that the benefits of those Directives are not granted to companies that are, under such Extra-EU Treaties, resident of third states. As such, these references do not reflect a common intention regarding the effect of the Directives with respect to such treaties but rather reflect an intention that their application is dependent on the application of (the residence provision of) Extra-EU Treaties. The same applies to the reference in Article 9b of ATAD2 to an Intra-EU Treaty. Pursuant to such provision relating to tax residency mismatches, the Member State where the taxpayer 'is not deemed to be a resident according to the double taxation treaty between two Member States concerned shall deny the deduction'. It follows from this provision that the Member State that is required to deny a deduction is dependent on the application of an Intra-EU Treaty. Moreover, the reference in the exit taxation provision of ATAD1 to a Member State no longer having 'the right to tax the transferred assets'[351] can also be categorised as reflecting an intention that the

347. *See* Proposal for a Council Directive on a Common Consolidated Corporate Tax Base (CCCTB) (COM(2011) 121).
348. *See* Significant Digital Presence Proposal (COM(2018) 147 final), p. 3.
349. *See* ATAD3 Proposal (COM(2021) 565 final).
350. *See* Article 2(b)(ii) Interest and Royalties Directive, Article 3(b) Merger Directive (2009), Article 2(a)(ii) Parent-Subsidiary Directive (2011).
351. *See* Article 5(1)(a), (b) and (d) ATAD1.

application of a Directive is dependent on tax treaties.[352] In addition to such references that indicate a link between the application of a Directive and a tax treaty, reference may also be made to tax treaties in Directives with a view to confirming that a Directive shall not affect the application of domestic or agreement-based provisions that are designed to eliminate or lessen economic double taxation,[353] to prevent fraud or abuse,[354] to enter into wider cooperation in the field of taxation,[355] or to safeguard a higher level of protection for domestic corporate tax bases.[356] Such references also do not reflect a common intention regarding the effect of the Directives with respect to tax treaties. These provisions merely confirm that the relevant Directives do not stand in the way of tax treaties being concluded for the purposes referred to in such Directives.

Given the purpose of Article 31 VCLT 1969 to give effect to the common intentions of the parties with respect to the treaty being interpreted, it would seem that the more a Directive reflects such a common intention, the more weight it may be attributed. As such, the weight to be attributed to ATAD2 and the Arbitration Directive within the general rule of interpretation of Article 31 VCLT 1969 seems likely to exceed, as a general rule of thumb, the weight that may be attributed to the other Directives reflecting less explicit common intentions between the Member States regarding their tax treaties.

#### *3.4.3.2.3 Directives Providing Implicit Evidence of a Common Intention*

In addition to the Directives providing explicit evidence of a common intention between the Member States regarding their effect on Intra-EU Treaties, the Directives may also provide implicit evidence of a common intention with respect to Intra-EU Treaties. Such an implicit common intent may, for example, be derived from terminology in Directives terms being similar to those used in Intra-EU Treaties.[357] As such, when interpreting the term 'beneficial owner' in Article 11 of an Intra-EU Treaty based on the OECD Model (2017), it cannot be excluded that an interpreter would consider the definition of the same term in the Interest and Royalties Directive as relevant and applicable in the relations between the parties.[358] Such relevance of the 'beneficial

352. *See*, to this effect, recital (10) of the preamble to ATAD1 which provides that the right to tax must be determined at the national level. This seems to imply that the application of the exit taxation provision is dependent on tax treaties because such treaties may restrict the right to tax assets.
353. Article 7(2) Parent-Subsidiary Directive (2011). *See also* Article 9 Interest and Royalties Directive.
354. Article 5(1) Interest and Royalties Directive.
355. Recital (21) of the Mutual Assistance Directive (2011/16/EU), as well as Article 1(3) of this Directive.
356. Article 3 ATAD1.
357. *See*, for an example, ICJ, 2 February 2017, Preliminary Objections (*Maritime Delimitation in the Indian Ocean (Somalia v. Kenya)*, Judgment, p. 38, para. 91 where the ICJ held that 'in line with Article 31, paragraph 3 (c), of the Vienna Convention, and particularly given the similarity in wording between the sixth paragraph of the MOU and Article 83, paragraph 1, of UNCLOS, the Court considers it reasonable to read the former in light of the latter'.
358. *See*, to this effect, for example L. de Broe in: Current Tax Treaty Issues (Maisto ed.), 2019, para. 16.2.1.

owner' definition in the Interest and Royalties Directive may be based on (i) the Directive and the tax treaty dealing with the same subject matter ('i.e. the exemption or reduction of withholding tax in the state of source where interest or royalties are paid to a non-resident of that state') and (ii) their similarity in terms of objectives ('i.e. ensuring that that exemption or reduction of withholding tax is enjoyed by the person who benefits from the income and that it is not wrongfully obtained by an interposed intermediary who passes on the benefit of the income to some other person').[359] Moreover, given the sameness of such subject matter, the 'beneficial owner' definition in the Interest and Royalties Directive may also be referred to 'as part of the quest for the appropriate ordinary meaning'.[360] As such, notwithstanding the absence of a clear common general intention regarding the application (or interpretation) of Intra-EU Treaties, the effect of the Interest and Royalties Directive may still be considered relevant and, for that reason, such Directive may still affect the interpretation of such treaties.

In both situations, i.e., similarity between situations covered or terminology used, the effect of the Directives would, essentially, be based on presumed common intentions. Such presumed common intentions would either be derived from the required result by a Directive in a given situation that is also addressed by an Intra-EU Treaty or from the similarities between a Directive's term and the terminology used in an Intra-EU Treaty. Whereas presumed common intentions may affect the interpretation of an Intra-EU Treaty, it should be stressed that presumptions may be rebutted. As such, the mere circumstance that a Directive could reflect a common implicit intention does not mean that effect must be given to such an intention.

#### *3.4.3.2.4 The Role of the Directives via Presumptions of Common Intent*

The previous section focused on the extent to which the Directives themselves could affect the interpretation of Intra-EU Treaties. Within that context, it has been considered conceivable that they can affect the interpretation of such treaties by reason of such Directives containing explicit evidence of a common intention with respect to Intra-EU Treaties, or due to them containing terminology that is similar to that used in such treaties. The present section is aimed at addressing the role that the result of a Directive may play within the general rule of interpretation.

The starting point in this respect is that the principle of good faith requires an interpreter to take the principle of systemic integration into account when interpreting a treaty.[361] Under this principle, treaties are to be interpreted against the background of their normative environment (the international law 'system'),[362] which background

359. *See* L. de Broe in: Current Tax Treaty Issues (Maisto ed.), 2019, para. 16.2.1.
360. L. de Broe in: Current Tax Treaty Issues (Maisto ed.), 2019, para. 16.2.1 who refers to R.K. Gardiner, 2015, p. 325. It would seem that other terms used in the Interest and Royalties Directive that could shed a light on the ordinary meaning of tax treaty terms would be 'interest', 'royalties', and 'permanent establishment'.
361. Fragmentation Report, A/CN.4/L.682, p. 208, para. 413.
362. Fragmentation Report, A/CN.4/L.682, p. 208, para. 413. The rationale for such principle is that '[a]ll treaty provisions receive their force and validity from general law and set up rights and

includes all relevant rules of international law applicable in the relations between the parties. Hence, the Directives could also affect the interpretation of Intra-EU Treaties by reason of being part of the normative environment within which such treaties have been concluded.

In their capacity of normative environment, a Directive may especially play a role in the interpretation of an Intra-EU Treaty if a tax treaty conflicts with the result to be achieved by such a Directive. This is due to the common intention as reflected by one source of public international law, i.e., the Directive, conflicting with an expression of another common intention laid down in another source of public international law, i.e., an Intra-EU Treaty. Within the context of such a conflict, an interpreter can make reference to the widely accepted presumption against conflict.[363]

Pursuant to this presumption, which is to be taken into account as part of the principle of good faith,[364] contracting states are presumed to have had an intention not to derogate from their (earlier) obligations under public international law when concluding a subsequent treaty.[365] The idea of such a presumption is that 'when States negotiate and implement their various international obligations, they are aware of the ramifications of their commitment and want them to remain coherent in order to achieve sustainable development and world peace'.[366] As such, states are not to be presumed to have 'changed their minds' in the absence of explicit language.[367] Such presumption thus seeks to avoid conflict and ensure the unity of public international law.[368] As such, a presumption against conflict with the result of the Directives provides a presumed common intention-based argument within the crucible of the general rule of interpretation for arriving at an interpretive outcome of an Intra-EU Treaty that is consistent with the result of a Directive.

The effect of such Directive-based presumed common intentions of the parties to an Intra-EU Treaty should, however, not be overstated and be taken to reflect a 'panacea to the issue of norm conflict'.[369] First of all, with respect to Intra-EU Treaties, this is due to the limited number of treaties affected by this presumption. As the presumption against conflict with the result of the Directives only applies if the Intra-EU Treaty is concluded after (i) accession of both contracting states to the EU and (ii) the adoption of the relevant Directive(s), the number of treaties with respect to which the presumption may be relevant ranges from 6 (ATAD2 and the Arbitration Directive) to 72 (Interest and Royalties Directive) (representing 1.8% to 21.1% of the

obligations that exist alongside rights and obligations established by other treaty provisions and rules of customary international law' (*see* para. 414).

363. Fragmentation Report, A/CN.4/L.682, p. 26, para. 38. It has also been recognised by the ICJ in ICJ. 1957, Judgment (Right of passage (Preliminary Objections)), p. 142.

364. C.W. Jenks, Yearbook of British International Law 1953, p. 428 and G. Marceau, Finnish Yearbook of International Law 2006, p. 18.

365. Fragmentation Report, A/CN.4/L.682, p. 26, para. 38. *See also* J. Pauwelyn, 2003, p. 907 and M. Samson, Leiden Journal of International Law 2011/3, p. 712.

366. G. Marceau, Finnish Yearbook of International Law 2006, p. 18.

367. *See* J. Pauwelyn, 2003, p. 240.

368. P. Merkouris, 2010, p. 179.

369. P. Merkouris, 2010, p. 125.

total number of Intra-EU Treaties).[370] As such, the majority of the Intra-EU Treaties would not be affected by the presumption against conflict with (obligations relating to) the Directives.

The second reason for not overstating the relevance of the effect of (the obligations relating to) the Directives via the presumption against conflict is that such presumption is, ultimately, only one of the means of interpretation that shall be taken into account and may be rebutted. It must thus be weighed against - and be assessed in light of - the other means of interpretation. If such other means would provide clear evidence of an intention to deviate from earlier rules of international law, the presumption against conflict is rebutted and cannot override the common (subsequent) intention.[371] In addition, even in the absence of such clear evidence, the presumption must be weighed against the other means of interpretation providing evidence of the common intentions of the parties. If, for example, giving effect to the presumption against conflict would frustrate the object and purpose of a treaty, it would be likely that such presumption should not be decisive in determining the single outcome of the general rule of interpretation of Article 31 VCLT 1969.[372] The same applies with respect to the presumption against conflict being incompatible with the text of a treaty. In such case, the presumption cannot have an overriding effect.[373] As such, the presumption against conflict may provide an argument for interpreting an Intra-EU Treaty in conformity with (the obligations relating to) the Directives, but such presumption does not function as an overriding principle.[374] If, however, an interpretation would be open to two interpretations, having taken all means of interpretation into account, the presumption against conflict may nevertheless be found to be decisive and require an interpreter to adopt a Directive consistent outcome.[375]

370. *See* Annex 1, para. 3.4.1.
371. C.W. Jenks, Yearbook of British International Law 1953, p. 429. For example, in ECtHR, Application No. 10593/09 (*Nada v. Switzerland*), para. 172 the ECtHR ruled that the presumption against conflict with earlier international law was rebutted in light of the 'clear and explicit language, imposing an obligation to take measures capable of breaching human rights, that was used in that [Security Council] resolution'.
372. C.W. Jenks, Yearbook of British International Law 1953, p. 429.
373. C.W. Jenks, Yearbook of British International Law 1953, p. 429.
374. C.W. Jenks, Yearbook of British International Law 1953, p. 429. *See also* D.M. Broekhuijsen, 2018, p. 173. *See also* ICSID, Case No. ARB/12/12 (*Vattenfall*), para. 154 where it noted that '[i]t is not the proper role of Article 31(3)(c) VCLT to rewrite the treaty being interpreted, or to substitute a plain reading of a treaty provision with other rules of international law, external to the treaty being interpreted, which would contradict the ordinary meaning of its terms'. Reference may also be made to Concurring opinion of Judge Wojtyczek in ECtHR, Application No. 31045/10 (*National Union of Rail, Maritime and Transport Workers*), para. 2 who notes that Article 31(3)(c) VCLT 1969 '*is* mainly a tool for clarifying the meaning of ambiguous or obscure terms and phrases and not for extending the scope of treaty obligations irrespective of its wording. Article 31(3)(c) may not be understood as an entitlement to align the meaning of a treaty with the content of international law'. *See also* Fragmentation Report, A/CN.4/L.682, p. 239, para. 473 where it is noted that the 'importance of those rights and obligations does not reside in their overriding character. As we have seen, this function is reserved by international law to jus cogens.'
375. *See*, in general, J. Pauwelyn, 2003, pp. 242-243. *See also* F.A. Engelen, 2004, para. 10.7. Engelen writes, in this respect, more generally, that 'in the relation between EU Member States, for example, the rules of primary and secondary EC law may assume particular importance within the context of article 31(3)(c). Indeed, when a treaty is open to two constructions one of which

###### *3.4.3.2.5 The Role of the Result of the Directives via the Duty of Union Loyalty*

In the previous section, the role of the result of the Directives as reflecting evidence of a presumed common intention within the general rule of interpretation has been discussed. In that respect, reference has been made to the widely recognised presumption against conflict. The question that is addressed in this section is whether, when interpreting an Intra-EU Treaty, a presumed common intention against conflict with (earlier) obligations under the laws of the EU may be derived from the duty of Union loyalty laid down in Article 4(3) TEU.

Support for such a presumed intention based on the duty of Union loyalty may be derived from the *Open Skies* cases wherein the CJEU held that the Member States are required to ensure fulfilment of their EU law obligations when concluding new (tax) treaties.[376] As such, it would seem reasonable to assume, in light of the duty of Union loyalty, that Member States can be presumed to have had a common intention to only conclude Intra-EU Treaties that are consistent with, and do not conflict with, their EU law obligations, including, at the time of conclusion of an Intra-EU Treaty, already existing obligations relating to the Directives. If such a presumption against conflict with earlier EU law obligations can be derived from the duty of Union loyalty, this presumed common intention would be similar to that of the presumption against conflict which also assumes that Member States would not have intended to derogate from earlier obligations under the EU Treaties.

Whereas a presumption against conflict with earlier EU law may be derived from the duty of Union loyalty, the more interesting question would seem to be whether a presumption against conflict with, at the time of conclusion of the Intra-EU Treaty, not yet existing EU law may also be derived from the duty of Union loyalty. It would seem support that for such a general presumption against conflict with EU law may be derived from the case law of the CJEU. In *Saint Gobain*, the CJEU ruled that the Member States must exercise their taxation powers, including the application of their tax treaties, consistently with EU law.[377] Moreover, it follows from *Gottardo* that when giving effect to international agreements either between the Member States or between a Member State and a third state, the Member States are required to comply with the

does and the other does not conflict with the obligations of the contracting states under EC law, good faith demands that the latter construction be adopted'.

An example wherein EU law was decisive would be the SCC Arbitration V (2016/135) (*Jurisdictional Award Green Power Partners*) wherein the tribunal ruled that 'interpreting Article 26 ECT without resorting to EU law is inconclusive in the circumstances of this case' (para. 412). An analysis of the relevant EU case law lead the tribunal to recognise the primacy of EU law and such primacy precluding 'the unilateral offer to arbitrate in Article 26 ECT' (para. 476). As such, Article 26 ECT precluded the tribunal to interpret and apply the EU Treaties (para. 477). This, in turn, entailed that the offer to arbitrate was found invalid (para. 477). As such, it follows that the tribunal interpreted Article 26 ECT 'as rendering the Respondent's offer to arbitrate invalid in the sense of "to be disapplied"' (para. 412 in conjunction with para. 477). The SCC Arbitration V (2016/135) (*Jurisdictional Award Green Power Partners*) thus provides an example wherein EU law, taken into account as a relevant rule of international law applicable in the relations between the parties, was decisive under Article 31 VCLT 1969.

376. *See*, to this effect, Case C-467/98 (*Open Skies (Denmark)*), para. 112.

377. Case C-307/97 (*Saint Gobain*), paras 57-58.

obligations that EU law imposes on them.[378] As such, when two Member States conclude an Intra-EU Treaty after both have acceded to the EU, they are aware that (i) their taxation powers must be exercised in a way that is compatible with present and future Directives and (ii) that the obligations under EU law must be respected when giving effect to international agreements, including Intra-EU Treaties. From the two cases referred to above, it can thus be derived that both Member States of an Intra-EU Treaty are, essentially, required to apply their Intra-EU Treaty in a way that is compatible with the obligations arising from the laws of the EU, including Directives. Taking this into account, the Member States to an Intra-EU Treaty may thus be presumed to have had a similar intention, at the time of conclusion of the Intra-EU Treaty, with respect to the way in which such treaty would have to be applied if it would conflict with such obligations. Support for such a presumption against conflict with EU law when interpreting Intra-EU Treaties may also be derived from case law of the CJEU pursuant to which a Member State court 'must presume that the [Member] State had the intention of fulfilling entirely the obligations arising from the directive concerned'.[379] As such, it would seem conceivable - or arguable - that a presumption against conflict with present and future EU law, including the Directives, could be derived from the laws of the EU with respect to post-accession Intra-EU Treaties. Such a presumption would then have a broader scope than the presumption against conflict of the previous section because the relevant criterion would not be whether the Directive predates the relevant Intra-EU Treaty but rather whether accession predates such treaty. In such a way, a presumption against conflict with EU law would apply with respect to all post-accession Intra-EU Treaties (i.e., 31.9% instead of 1.8% to 22.1% of the Intra-EU Treaties under the presumption against conflict).[380] With respect to pre-accession Intra-EU Treaties, such a presumption would not apply because one or both contracting state(s) were not yet Member States. As such, there would seem to be no basis for presuming any common intention, at the time of conclusion of such an Intra-EU Treaty, with respect to (future) EU law obligations.

Whereas such a presumed intention cannot have been present at the time of conclusion of a pre-accession Intra-EU Treaty, one could wonder whether accession to the EU by both states can be regarded as reflecting an expression of a later common intention between such states from which it can be derived that they intent their previously concluded tax treaties to be applied in a way that is consistent with their commitments under EU law. The idea underlying such a presumed intention would be that by concluding an accession treaty, the contracting states would enter into a treaty that would no longer allow them to exercise their taxation powers in a way that is inconsistent with such treaty. In such a way, the entry into of an accession treaty would reflect a later intention to merely apply Intra-EU Treaties to the extent compatible with the obligations under the EU Treaties (and the Directives).

378. Case C-55/00 (*Gottardo*), para. 33.
379. *See* Case C-334/92 (*Wagner Miret*), para. 20, as well as Joined Cases C-397/01 to C-403/01 (*Pfeiffer and Others*), para. 112.
380. *See* Annex 1, para. 3.2.

### 3.4.3.3 *Conclusion Regarding the Weight to Be Attributed to (the Obligations Relating to) the Directives Within the General Rule of Interpretation*

Based on sections 3.4.3.1 and 3.4.3.2, an answer can be provided to the question regarding the role of, and the weight to be attached to, the Directives when interpreting tax treaties concluded by the Member States under the general rule of interpretation of Article 31 VCLT 1969.

(a) *Type of treaties affected:* the Directives, either directly or by means of the result to be achieved, shall only be taken into account, if relevant when interpreting Intra-EU Treaties. They cannot be taken into account when interpreting Extra-EU Treaties because such Directives are not applicable in the relations between a Member State and a third state (section 3.4.2.2.2). As a consequence, the Directives do not affect the interpretation of most of the tax treaties concluded by the Member States, i.e., the Extra-EU Treaties, under the general rule of interpretation of Article 31 VCLT 1969 (81.5% of the total number of treaties concluded by the Member States).[381]

(b) *The different ways the interpretation may be affected by the Directives:* the interpretation of Intra-EU Treaties may be affected by (the obligations relating to) the Directives in one of the following ways:
   (i) *Via common intentions regarding tax treaties in the Directives:* Directives can contain explicit language regarding the effect that they are intended to have on Intra-EU Treaties. Most clear in this respect would be the ATAD3 Proposal that provides that such treaties shall be 'disregarded'. If such a common intention is laid down in a Directive, such common intention regarding such treaties may guide an interpreter towards an interpretation that is consistent with a Directive (section 3.4.3.2.2).
   (ii) *Via terminology in the Directives that is similar to that used in tax treaties:* If a Directive has the same subject matter as a tax treaty and uses terms that are similar to those being interpreted, such as for example the term 'beneficial owner' in the Interest and Royalties Directive, the terms of a Directive may be used to guide an interpreter towards the ordinary meaning of a treaty term that is being interpreted (section 3.4.3.2.3).
   (iii) *Via presumed common intentions based on the result of a Directive:* When interpreting Intra-EU Treaties, it follows from the principle of good faith that Member States are presumed have intended not to derogate from obligations under public international law entered into before the conclusion of their Intra-EU Treaties. As such, a presumption

381. *See* Annex 1, para. 3.1.

against conflict with earlier obligations relating to the Directives applies. Via such presumption, the result of the Directives may thus affect the interpretation of Intra-EU Treaties. It is, however, to be borne in mind that the result of the Directives only affects a small number of Intra-EU Treaties via the presumption against conflict (at best, 21.1% of the Intra-EU Treaties) (section 3.4.3.2.4).

(iv) *Via the duty of Union loyalty*: It follows from the duty of Union loyalty that Member States are obliged to comply with their obligations under EU law when concluding and applying their tax treaties. As such, it seems arguable - or conceivable - that a presumption against conflict with EU law could be construed. Such a presumption would then apply with respect to, in any event, post-Directive Intra-EU Treaties (similar to the presumption against conflict based on good faith). In addition, bearing in mind the case law of the CJEU, it also seems conceivable that such a presumption applies with respect to post-accession, yet pre-Directive Intra-EU Treaties based on the presumption that Member States, when concluding a treaty, would share a common intention not to act inconsistently with present or future obligations under EU law. Finally, a presumption against conflict with EU law may also be deemed conceivable with respect to pre-accession Intra-EU Treaties by means of an accession treaty reflecting an intention between the contracting states to apply their (pre-accession) tax treaties in a way that is consistent with their EU law obligations after accession (including the obligations relating to the Directives). Such later intention, given that it was not present at the time of conclusion of an Intra-EU Treaty, would seem to carry less weight than the presumption against conflict with post-accession, pre-Directive Intra-EU Treaties (section 3.4.3.2.5).

(c) *The weight to be attributed to (the obligations relating to) the Directives*: with respect to each of the ways in which (the obligations relating to) the Directives may affect the interpretation of an Intra-EU Treaty, it is to be recalled that it is the purpose of Article 31 VCLT 1969 to give effect to the common intention of the parties regarding the tax treaty being interpreted. As such, the more a Directive provides evidence of such a common intention with respect to such a treaty, the more likely it is that such a Directive may be able to affect the outcome of the single combined operation of Article 31 VCLT 1969. It is, however, to be borne in mind that an interpretation under Article 31 VCLT 1969 must at all times be based on the text of the treaty, while good faith also requires that it is interpreted in a reasonable, honest and fair way and in line with its object and purpose. Hence, the evidence of a common intention as derived from (the obligations relating to) a Directive must be balanced with the other material evidencing a (perhaps different) common intention with respect to the treaty being interpreted. It thus follows that the weight of (the obligations relating to) the Directives depends on the extent to which they (can be presumed to) reflect common intentions of the Member States with respect to an Intra-EU Treaty on the one hand, and on the other, on the evidence of the common intentions between the Member States that appear from the other elements of interpretation referred to in Article 31 VCLT 1969 (section 3.4.3.2).

### 3.4.4 Conclusion

In this section 3.4, the central question has been if, and to what extent, the Directives affect the interpretation of tax treaties concluded by the Member States under Article 31 VCLT 1969. In this respect, it has been concluded that the Directives have to be taken into account when interpreting tax treaties pursuant to Article 31(3)(c) VCLT 1969 if they qualify as relevant (section 3.4.2.2.1) and as applicable in the relations between the parties (section 3.4.2.2.2). It follows from this conclusion that the Directives can only be taken into account when they would potentially have bearing, i.e., they would be relevant, on the interpretation of Intra-EU Treaties (because the Directives are not applicable in the relations between a Member State and a third state).

If the Directives are to be taken into account under Article 31(3)(c) VCLT 1969, they may affect the interpretation of an Intra-EU Treaty. This may either be due to the Directives providing evidence of a common intention between the Member States regarding such a treaty, due to similarity of terminology used, or via a presumed common intention against conflict with such Directives.

It is, however, to be acknowledged that, irrespective of the way in which Directives may affect the interpretation of an Intra-EU Treaty, the common intentions as derived from (the result of) the Directives must be duly weighed against any evidence of (different) common intentions as derived from the other means of interpretation that must also be taken into account under the general rule of interpretation (section 3.4.3.2). With respect to such weighing, it is concluded that the effect of (the obligations relating to) the Directives cannot go as far as requiring an interpretation that is (i) contrary to the wording of the treaty provision being interpreted, (ii) contrary to good faith, or (iii) contrary to the object and purpose of the relevant treaty (section 3.4.3.2). It thus follows that the effect of the Directives under the general rule of interpretation of Article 31 VCLT 1969 on a given Intra-EU Treaty provision cannot be determined in the abstract. The effect of such Directives on the interpretation of an Intra-EU Treaty depends on the indications regarding the meaning of such a treaty based on the other means of interpretation.

## 3.5 THE INTERACTION BETWEEN ARTICLE 3(2) OECD MODEL, ARTICLE 2(2) MLI AND ARTICLES 31 VCLT 1969

It follows from sections 3.2 through 3.4 that the Directives may affect the interpretation of tax treaties under Articles 3(2) OECD Model, 2(2) MLI and 31 VCLT 1969. The extent to which a Directive may affect such an interpretation of a tax treaty differs from one provision to another. Under Article 3(2) OECD Model and Article 2(2) MLI, a Directive may be the starting point in determining the meaning of an undefined term in a tax treaty. By contrast, under Article 31 VCLT 1969, the starting point in interpreting a treaty term is the ordinary meaning of the wording of a treaty term (which ordinary meaning may be determined by taking into account a Directive term that is similar). In addition, there is a difference in terms of the treaties affected. With respect to Article 3(2) OECD Model and Article 2(2) MLI, undefined treaty terms in both Intra-EU and Extra-EU Treaties may be given the meaning they have under the Directives. Under Article 31 VCLT 1969, however, the Directives may only affect the interpretation of treaty terms in Intra-EU Treaties because such Directives are not applicable in the relations with third states. Taking these differences into consideration, the interaction and relationship between these rules of interpretation is discussed below.

As has been indicated in section 3.1, Article 3(2) OECD Model operates as a *lex specialis* to Article 31 VCLT 1969.[382] This means that application of Article 31 VCLT 1969 is subject to Article 3(2) OECD Model not being applicable with respect to the interpretation of a tax treaty. In order to determine the extent to which Article 31 VCLT 1969 guides the interpretation of a tax treaty, it should thus be assessed when Article 3(2) OECD Model would not be applicable. Based on the wording of Article 3(2) OECD Model, this would be the case if (i) the relevant treaty is not being applied within the meaning of Article 3(2) OECD Model,[383] (ii) the term being interpreted is defined in the treaty, or (iii) the laws of the state applying the treaty do not provide a relevant meaning for the undefined treaty term.[384] In each of these situations under (i) through (iii), a tax treaty provision or term cannot be interpreted by reference to Article 3(2) OECD Model. As such, it should then be interpreted by reference to Article 31 VCLT 1969.

With respect to the relationship between Article 2(2) MLI and Article 31 VCLT 1969, the *lex specialis* nature of Article 2(2) MLI implies that it must first be assessed whether an undefined term of the MLI can be interpreted based on Article 2(2) MLI,

382. *See*, to that effect, F.A. Engelen, 2004, para. 10.10.2, R.A. Bosman, 2015, para. 3.3.1, A.P. Dourado, G. Kofler, E. Reimer, A. Rust, R. Ismer & J. Ruß in: Klaus Vogel on Double Taxation Conventions (Reimer & Rust eds), 2022, p. 235, para. 129, and J. Bossuyt, 2021, para. 8.2.2.1.

383. With respect to the 'application' of a treaty for the purposes of Article 3(2) OECD Model, it can be noted that its meaning is subject to debate among legal scholars. *See* D.O. Corredor Velásquez, Intertax 2016/12, p. 970. Vogel, for example, considers the term 'application' to mean 'each decision of a fiscal authority or a court concerning a tax question in which the treaty is referred to (or should be referred to)' (*see* K. Vogel, Berkeley Journal of International Law 1986/1, p. 71). Avery Jones adopts a different view pursuant to which a treaty would only be 'applied' if it limits the contracting state in its application of its domestic law (J.F. Avery Jones, C.J. Berg, H. Depret, M. Ellis, P. Fontaneau, R. Lenz, T. Miyatake, S.I. Roberts, C. Sandels & J. Strobl, British Tax Review 1984/1, p. 50). Support for this view could be derived from the opening words of Article 3(2), which stipulates that it provides a 'general rule of interpretation for the purpose of the application of the treaty by a contracting state' (F.A. Engelen, 2004, para. 10.10.4.1). The consequence of adopting the position of Avery Jones would be that the residence state is bound by the qualification - and interpretations - to the source state and, as such, no longer needs to interpret the treaty in question. In this respect, reference may also be made to F.A. Engelen, 2004, para. 10.10.4.1 who notes that 'the better view is that a treaty is also applied when an item of income is taxed in accordance with its provisions'. R.A. Bosman, 2015, para. 3.3.4 seems to agree with this position. According to him, this approach of Engelen 'seems to be in accordance with the ordinary meaning of the term application'.

384. *See* D.O. Corredor Velásquez, Intertax 2016/12, p. 970.

before an interpretation may be based on Article 31 VCLT 1969. Only if it would be established that (i) the MLI is not 'applied' in the sense of Article 2(2) MLI, (ii) the term being interpreted is defined in the MLI, or (iii) the relevant tax treaty that is covered by the MLI does not provide a meaning of an undefined MLI term, should a treaty term in the MLI be interpreted on the basis of Article 31 VCLT 1969.

## 3.6 CONCLUSION

It has been the purpose of the present chapter to determine the extent to which the Directives affect the interpretation of tax treaties under the rules of public international law. In determining this effect, a distinction has been made between the different rules of interpretation that may be resorted to when interpreting a tax treaty. Based on an assessment of the effect of (the result of) the Directives under Article 3(2) OECD Model (section 3.2), Article 2(2) MLI (section 3.3) and Article 31 VCLT 1969 (section 3.4), it follows that such effect depends on the relevant rule of interpretation governing the interpretation of a tax treaty (term). As such, the answer to the question regarding the effect of the Directives on the interpretation of tax treaties under the rules of public international law depends on which rule of interpretation would have to be resorted to for the purposes of such an interpretation.

### 3.6.1 Article 3(2) OECD Model

Under Article 3(2) OECD Model, the Directives can affect the interpretation of undefined tax treaty terms as part of the laws the state applying the tax treaty if it is a Member State that applies a tax treaty (irrespective of whether such tax treaty has been concluded with another Member State or a third state). As part of the law of a Member State applying a tax treaty, the 'beneficial owner' definition in the Interest and Royalties Directive may be used to give meaning to the undefined 'beneficial owner' term in, for example, Articles 11 and 12 OECD Model. It should, however, be borne in mind that such a meaning based on the laws of a Member State is subject to the context otherwise requiring. As such, the effect of the Directives as part of the laws of the Member States is dependent on the context within the meaning of Article 3(2) OECD Model.

With respect to the context otherwise requiring, it has been concluded that – based on the OECD Commentaries (2017) – (the result of) the Directives can be part of such context with respect to Intra-EU Treaties, whereas it is not part of such context when interpreting Extra-EU Treaties. Considering the Directives as context within the meaning of Article 3(2) OECD Model with respect to Intra-EU Treaties can, first of all, be based on the reference in such Commentaries to the context being determined in particular by the common intentions of the contracting states at the time a tax treaty is signed. Based on the presumption against conflict and the duty of Union loyalty, Member States can be presumed to have had a common intention to conclude a tax treaty that would be consistent with their obligations under EU law, including those relating to the Directives, at the time of the conclusion of such a treaty. Additionally, the Directives may also be considered part of the context based on the reference in the OECD Commentaries (2017) to the laws of the other contracting state, which laws - in the event of an Intra-EU Treaty - would include such Directives.

As part of the context, (the result of) a Directive can require a meaning based on the laws of the Member State applying the tax treaty to be adopted (if consistent with the result to be achieved under the Directive) or to be rejected (if inconsistent with the result to be achieved under the Directive). Such a contextual effect of a Directive should not, however, be overestimated. This is because Article 3(2) OECD Model refers to the 'context' (singular). As such, the context within the meaning of Article 3(2) OECD Model may comprise of elements other than (obligations relating to) a Directive such as, for example, the principle of good faith. Therefore, if the context as a whole provides indications that the parties to an Intra-EU Treaty intended an undefined treaty term to have a meaning that would be inconsistent with the meaning of such term under a Directive or the result of such a Directive, the context may require such a meaning to be adopted notwithstanding the circumstance that the Directive would also be part of such context. As such, the mere circumstance that (the result of) the Directives would be part of the context does not warrant the conclusion that the interpretation of Intra-EU Treaties by means of Article 3(2) OECD Model will always result in the adoption of a meaning based on the meaning of a term in a Directive or a meaning that is consistent with the result required to be achieved by a Directive. Similarly, taking into consideration that (the result of) the Directives are not part of the context of Extra-EU Treaties, the context may also require a meaning that is inconsistent with a Directive to be adopted (or rejected) with respect to such Extra-EU Treaties.

### 3.6.2 Article 2(2) MLI

Based on the reference in Article 2(2) MLI to the meaning that an undefined MLI term has under a (covered) Intra-EU Treaty, the Directives may affect the interpretation of such an undefined term. This can, for example, be due to the term also not being defined in the relevant (covered) Intra-EU Treaty as well, in which case reference should, in principle, be made to Article 3(2) OECD Model. The effect of the Directives with respect to this provision of the OECD Model, as set out in sections 3.2 and 3.6.1, can then indirectly affect the interpretation of undefined MLI terms under Article 2(2) MLI (subject to the context of the MLI requiring otherwise). Moreover, it would also be conceivable that the effect of a Directive under Article 31 VCLT 1969 on the interpretation of an undefined MLI term in a(n) (covered) Intra-EU Treaty (section 3.4 and section 3.6.3), would also extend to the MLI under Article 2(2) MLI (subject to the context of the MLI requiring otherwise) (section 3.3).

With respect to the context of the MLI, it has been submitted that (the result to be achieved pursuant to) the Directives can be part of such context to the extent that the provision of the MLI that is being interpreted is of a 'bilateral' nature and affecting a(n) (covered) Intra-EU Treaty. To the extent that the MLI would be 'multilateral', or affecting an Extra-EU Treaty, the Directives are not part of such context because they cannot reflect any common intention of the contracting states. In addition, similar to

Article 3(2) OECD Model, whether such (obligations relating to) Directives as context within the meaning of Article 2(2) MLI would require a Directive consistent meaning to be adopted with respect to a (covered) Intra-EU Treaty depends on an assessment of the context as a whole.

### 3.6.3 Article 31 VCLT 1969

With respect to the effect of the Directives on the interpretation of tax treaties under Article 31 VCLT 1969, the starting point is that this general rule of interpretation only applies, as the *lex generalis*, if Article 3(2) OECD Model is not applicable, as *lex specialis* (section 3.5). If Article 31 VCLT 1969 is applicable, a distinction needs to be drawn between Intra-EU Treaties and Extra-EU Treaties. Directives, as well as the result to be achieved pursuant to them, can only affect the interpretation of Intra-EU Treaties as relevant rules of international law applicable in the relations between the parties (in the sense of Article 31(3)(c) VCLT 1969). They cannot have any effect on the interpretation of Extra-EU Treaties under Article 31 VCLT 1969, which represent the majority of the tax treaties concluded by the Member States (81.5 %),[385] because the Directives are not applicable in the relations between the Member States and third states (section 3.4.2.2.2).[386]

In determining the effect that (the result to be achieved under) the Directives may have on the interpretation of Intra-EU Treaties, the first step is to establish that a Directive is relevant and that the relevant treaty (provision), if concluded before the adoption of such Directive, was intended to be interpreted dynamically:

(a) whether a rule of EU law would be relevant depends on it (potentially) having bearing on the interpretation of the treaty concerned, which could be the case if, for example, the Directive covers the same factual situation as the tax treaty or includes a term that is similar to the tax treaty term being interpreted (section 3.4.2.2.1);
(b) whether a treaty (provision) is to be interpreted dynamically, depends on the (presumed) common intention of the Member States with respect to such treaty (provision) and cannot be determined in the abstract (section 3.4.2.2.2).

If it would be established that a Directive is relevant (and the relevant treaty (provision) is to be interpreted dynamically in the event that such treaty (provision) is earlier as compared to such Directive), it follows from Article 31(3)(c) VCLT 1969 that

385. Annex 1, para. 3.1.
386. The same applies with respect to the MLI. First, to the extent that the MLI is a 'multilateral' multilateral treaty, the Directives are not applicable in the relations between (all) the parties. Second, to the extent that the MLI is a 'bilateral' multilateral treaty, a distinction can be drawn between Intra-EU Treaties and Extra-EU Treaties whose application is modified by the MLI. Only when the application of an Intra-EU Treaty would be affected by a 'bilateral' MLI provision can the Directives affect the interpretation of the MLI under Article 31(3)(c) VCLT 1969.

such a Directive '*shall be taken into account*' when interpreting an Intra-EU Treaty in accordance with Article 31 VCLT 1969.

If a Directive is to be taken into account, the weight that needs to be attributed to (the obligations relating to) such a Directive would have to be determined. With respect to determining such weight, the starting point in interpreting an Intra-EU Treaty under Article 31 VCLT 1969 is formed by the ordinary (or special) meaning of the text of the treaty. Such ordinary (or special) meaning is then to be interpreted in good faith and in its (internal and external) context, including (the obligations relating to) the Directive that is to be taken into account, and in light of its object and purpose. The (obligations relating to the) Directive thus function as one of the means of interpretation that contribute to establishing the ordinary (or special) meaning of a treaty term.

In determining the weight to be attributed to a Directive as one of the means of interpretation that shall be taken into account, the overarching purpose of Article 31 VCLT 1969 to give effect to the common intentions of the parties with respect to their treaty seems to be an important factor. The more closely (obligations relating to) a Directive reflect(s) such a common intention with respect to an Intra-EU Treaty, the more effect such a Directive may have on the interpretation of an Intra-EU Treaty (section 3.4.3.1). With respect to the extent to which (the obligations relating to) a Directive may reflect(s) such common intentions, a distinction has been drawn between the Directives as relevant rules of international law and the obligation to achieve the result of the Directives as relevant rules of international law:

(a) With respect to the Directives themselves, it follows that they may contain explicit (ATAD2 and the Arbitration Directive) evidence of a common intention with respect to the Intra-EU Treaties. In addition, Directives may contain implicit evidence of a common intention with respect to the meaning of treaty terms by means of, for example, the use of similar terms in Directives governing the same subject matter (such as, for example, the 'beneficial owner' definition in the Interest and Royalties Directive) (section 3.4.3.2.1).
(b) With respect to the result to be achieved under a Directive, a common intention against conflict with such a result may be presumed to exist with respect to post-Directive Intra-EU Treaties based on the presumption against conflict that is part of the good faith that must be taken into account under Article 31 VCLT 1969 (section 3.4.3.2.4). In addition, it is considered 'arguable' – or 'conceivable' – that such a presumption can also be based on the duty of Union loyalty. Pursuant to such duty, Member States are obliged to conclude (tax) treaties that are consistent with their obligations under EU law. Moreover, it has been considered arguable that Member States may be presumed to have a common intention not to act contrary to present or future laws of the EU if they are Member States at the time of conclusion of an Intra-EU Treaty. Such presumed common intention could then also provide a basis for a Directive affecting the interpretation of an Intra-EU Treaty. Additionally, it may also be conceivable that accession to the EU, with respect to pre-accession Intra-EU Treaties, could be regarded as reflecting a later common intention against conflict with EU law because the acceding state

agrees to adhere to the case law of the CJEU pursuant to which it must exercise its competences under tax treaties in a way that is compatible with the Directives (section 3.4.3.2.5).

If a Directive, or the result to be achieved, is taken into account under Article 31(3)(c) VCLT 1969 and such a Directive (or result) provides evidence of a common intention with respect to a tax treaty, the question arises as to how much weight would have to be attributed to such a Directive. In that respect, the starting point is that this question cannot be determined in the abstract. There is no *a priori* preference for a Directive-based, or a Directive-consistent, meaning under Article 31 VCLT 1969. The role of Directives is the same as any other relevant rule of international law and must be regarded as being part of the search for the (objectified) common intention of the parties to a tax treaty. As such, the evidence of a common intention based on the Directives (or their result) must be weighed against the indications of the common intentions between the parties as derived from the other means of interpretation that must also be taken into account under Article 31 VCLT 1969. With respect to this weighing, it has been concluded that a Directive cannot, in any event, require a (Directive-based or Directive-compliant) interpretation of a tax treaty that would (i) be contrary to the ordinary (or special) meaning of the wording of such treaty, (ii) result in an interpretation that is contrary to the principle of good faith, or (iii) frustrate the object and purpose of such treaty (section 3.4.3.2). It may thus be the case that, notwithstanding the taking into account of the Directives, Article 31 VCLT 1969 would result in a meaning that conflicts with (the result to be achieved under) a Directive. Therefore, it is concluded that (the result to be achieved under) a Directive may affect the interpretation of Intra-EU Treaties if taken into account, but the mere taking into account of such Directives does not entail that a Directive-consistent meaning must be adopted under Article 31 VCLT 1969 that ensures that the result of a Directive is achieved.

CHAPTER 4

# The Effect of the Directives on the Interpretation of Tax Treaties from the perspective of the EU

## 4.1 INTRODUCTION

In the previous chapter, the effect of (the result to be achieved under) the Directives on the interpretation of tax treaties under the rules of public international law has been assessed. In the present chapter, the effect that the Directives should have on the interpretation of tax treaties under the rules of EU law will be addressed. As such, the present chapter is aimed at answering the question to what extent the interpretation of tax treaties should be affected by the Directives from the perspective of the laws of the EU.

With respect to answering the central question of the present chapter, the starting point is that Member State courts are under a general obligation to interpret all national law in a way that is consistent with both primary and secondary EU law (the duty of consistent interpretation).[387] Such duty of consistent interpretation is, according to case law of the CJEU, based on the obligation of the Member States under Article 288

387. *See* K. Lenaerts & P. van Nuffel, 2011, p. 757 where reference is made, in footnote 13, to Case C-106/89 (*Marleasing*), para. 8 (with respect to directives), Case C-267/97 (*Engelbrecht*), para. 39 (reference is made to '*Community law*'), and Case C-60/02 (*X*), para. 59 (reference is made to 'the Community rule'). *See also* D. Gutmann in: Building Global International Tax Law: Essays in Honour of Guglielmo Maisto (Pistone ed.), 2022, para. 18.2.1.1 who notes that the CJEU has held that 'the reference to the directives for the interpretation of national law is not only an option for the national judge, but also an obligation', while also concluding in para. 18.4 that consistent interpretation of 'any legal norm (either of a domestic or conventional character) that is subordinated to EU law' has a 'compulsory character', i.e., there is a 'duty' of consistent interpretation.

TFEU to achieve the result envisaged by a directive and the general duty under Article 4(3) TEU to take all appropriate measures, whether general or particular.[388]

To determine the extent to which such starting point (or duty) also applies with respect to the interpretation of tax treaties, the legal basis of the duty of consistent interpretation is set out first (section 4.2). This is followed by an assessment of the scope of such duty (section 4.3) as well as its limitations (section 4.4). This chapter ends with an answer to the question to what extent the Directives should affect the interpretation of tax treaties concluded by the Member States (section 4.5).

## 4.2 LEGAL BASIS OF THE DUTY OF CONSISTENT INTERPRETATION

The duty of consistent interpretation within the context of directives in general is, based on the judgment of the CJEU in *Von Colson*, founded upon the obligation of the Member States under Article 288 TFEU to achieve the result envisaged by a directive, as well as upon the general duty under Article 4(3) TEU to take all appropriate measures, whether general or particular, to ensure the fulfilment of that obligation.[389] In subsequent case law, the CJEU has also held that the duty of consistent interpretation follows from 'the system of the Treaty, since it permits the national court, for matters within its jurisdiction, to ensure the full effectiveness of [EU] law when it determines the dispute before it'.[390] Additionally, the CJEU has also ruled that the duty of consistent interpretation follows from the primacy of EU law.[391]

## 4.3 THE APPLICATION OF THE DUTY OF CONSISTENT INTERPRETATION TO (TAX) TREATIES

Having established the legal basis of the duty of consistent interpretation, the present section seeks to determine the extent to which the interpretation of tax treaties concluded by the Member States falls within the scope of the duty of consistent interpretation. In that respect, it will first be assessed to what extent Intra-EU and Extra-EU Treaties fall within such scope (section 4.3.1), after which it will be determined under what circumstances the duty of consistent interpretation may apply (section 4.3.2).

---

388. *See* Case 14/83 (*Von Colson*), para. 26. *See also* S. Prechal, 2009, pp. 180-181 and G. Conway, 2015, p. 229. It is acknowledged that the CJEU has subsequently held that the duty of consistent interpretation also follows from 'the system of the Treaty, since it permits the national court, for matters within its jurisdiction, to ensure the full effectiveness of [EU] law when it determines the dispute before it' (Joined Cases C-397/01 to C-403/01 (*Pfeiffer and Others*), para. 114) and that it follows from the primacy of the laws of the EU (Case C-573/17 (*Poplawski*), para. 57).
389. *See* Case 14/83 (*Von Colson*), para. 26. *See also* S. Prechal, 2009, pp. 180-181 and G. Conway, 2015, p. 229.
390. Joined Cases C-397/01 to C-403/01 (*Pfeiffer and Others*), para. 114. *See also* S. Prechal, 2009, p. 181, P. Craig, European Law Review 2009/3, p. 357, and S. Haket, Review of European Administrative Law 2015/2, p. 218. The legal basis of this duty may, also, be taken to be the duty of Union loyalty (*see*, to that effect, Case 14/83 (*Von Colson*), para. 26).
391. Case C-573/17 (*Poplawski*), para. 57.

### 4.3.1 The Application of the Duty of Consistent Interpretation to Tax Treaties

With respect to determining the extent to which the duty of consistent interpretation applies to tax treaties, the starting point is that the CJEU does not seem to have explicitly confirmed the application of such duty with respect to all treaties entered into by the Member States. Nevertheless, there are indications in the case law of the CJEU that the duty of consistent interpretation applies with respect to treaties as well.[392]

First of all, reference can be made to the judgment of the Court in *Commune de Mesquer* wherein the CJEU ruled that a national court - or Member State court - is required to interpret national law, irrespective of 'whether the provisions in question ... derive from international agreements entered into by the Member State', so far as possible, in light of the wording and purpose of the relevant directive, in order to achieve the result of that directive.[393] This ruling has been interpreted by De Broe as evidence of the applicability of a duty of consistent interpretation with respect to treaties concluded by the Member States.[394] In support of this conclusion, he notes that, within the EU legal order, 'international treaties have - like unilateral acts of Member States - the status of national legislation'.[395]

In addition to (this interpretation of) the judgment of the CJEU in *Commune de Mesquer*, reference can also be made to *Budějovický Budvar* (C-216/01). In this case, the Court expressly confirmed the application of the duty of consistent interpretation with respect to treaties falling within the scope of Article 351 TFEU, i.e., treaties concluded between a Member State and a third state before accession of such Member State (*see*, regarding the scope of Article 351 TFEU, section 7.2.2 below).[396] In ruling that such duty applied to pre-accession Extra-EU Treaties, the CJEU referred to the obligation of the Member States under the second paragraph of Article 351 TFEU to 'take all appropriate steps to eliminate the incompatibilities between an agreement concluded before a Member State's accession and the TFEU'.[397] The reference to this second paragraph is of particular relevance for the purposes of the present section because such paragraph can be regarded as a 'specific illustration' or 'application' of the general duty of Union loyalty.[398] Pursuant to such general duty of Union loyalty, Member States are required to follow 'any appropriate measures ... to ensure fulfilment

392. Legal scholars have also adopted the position that (tax) treaties are subject to the duty of consistent interpretation. *See*, to that effect, D. Gutmann in: Building Global International Tax Law: Essays in Honour of Guglielmo Maisto (Pistone ed.), 2022, para. 18.2.2 who notes that '[t]he norms that are subject to consistent interpretation include domestic law and some tax treaties, as well as a combination of both'.
393. *See* Case C-188/08 (*Commune de Mesquer*), para. 84.
394. L. de Broe in: Current Tax Treaty Issues (Maisto ed.), 2019, para. 16.2.3.
395. L. de Broe in: Current Tax Treaty Issues (Maisto ed.), 2019, para. 16.2.3.
396. Case C-216/01 (*Budějovický Budvar*), para. 169 and Joined Cases C-720/18 & C-721/18 (*Ferrari*), para. 68.
397. *See* Case C-216/01 (*Budějovický Budvar*), para. 168, as well as Joined Cases C-720/18 & C-721/18 (*Ferrari*), para. 67.
398. P. Koutrakos, 2006, p. 304 who considers it a 'specific illustration' and M. Klamert, 2014, p. 16 who states that it can be deemed an application of the general duty of cooperation (i.e., the duty of Union loyalty). Reference can also be made to Opinion of Advocate General Tizzano in:

of the obligations arising out of the Treaties or resulting from the acts of the institutions of the Union'.[399] Based on a comparison of the wording of Article 351(2) TFEU and 4(3) TEU, it follows that both provisions impose a duty on the Member States to ensure that the obligations arising from the EU Treaties (and secondary EU law) are fulfilled. As such, it would seem reasonable to assume that the duty of consistent interpretation also applies with respect to treaties falling outside the scope of Article 351 TFEU, i.e., Intra-EU Treaties and post-accession Extra-EU Treaties, based on the duty of Union loyalty.[400]

### 4.3.2 The Circumstances under Which a Duty of Consistent Interpretation Applies

Having established that all treaties concluded by the Member States fall within the scope of the duty of consistent interpretation, the next step for the purpose of this chapter would be to determine under what circumstances a Member State court would become obliged to interpret – or could be required to interpret – a tax treaty in a way that is consistent with (the result to be achieved under) a Directive. In this respect, the starting point would be that the deadline for implementation of a Directive must have passed.[401] Until such deadline has passed, there is, in principle, no obligation under the laws of the EU pursuant to which a Member State court would be required to (attempt to) interpret a tax treaty in a way that is consistent with (the result of) a Directive. Within this context, it should, however, be acknowledged that during the period laid down for transposition of a Directive, Member States are obliged to refrain from adopting measures liable to seriously compromise the result to be achieved by a Directive.[402] As such, there seems to exist a de facto duty against non-consistent interpretation during the period between adoption of a Directive and the deadline for its transposition.

Taking the above into account, it follows that the duty of consistent interpretation is applicable after the deadline for transposition of a Directive has passed, while it may be de facto applicable during the period for transposition. If applicable, the question that needs to be answered is to what extent a Member State courts would be obliged to interpret tax treaties in a way that is consistent with (the result of) a Directive. In that

---

Joined Cases C-466/98, C-467/98, C-468/98, C-471/98, C-472/98, C-475/98 & C-476/98 (*Open Skies*), para. 38 who states that, in a way, Article 351(2) TFEU can be seen as an application of the general duty of cooperation.

399. *See* Article 4(3) TEU.

400. It would seem irrelevant, based on the case law of the CJEU with respect to the duty of consistent interpretation within the context of national laws, whether the treaty has been concluded before or after the relevant Directive (*see*, to that effect, Case C-106/89 (*Marleasing*), para. 8 and Joined Cases C-397/01 to C-403/01 (*Pfeiffer and Others*), para. 108).

401. Joined Cases C-397/01 to C-403/01 (*Pfeiffer and Others*), para. 115. This is not to say that courts shall be free to interpret in any way they want; Member States, including their courts, are under a duty to refrain from taking any measures that are liable to seriously compromise the result prescribed in a directive during the period for transposition. *See*, to that effect, Case C-129/96 (*Inter Environment Wallonie*), para. 45.

402. *See*, to that effect, Case C-129/96 (*Inter Environment Wallonie*), para. 45.

respect, the starting point would be that it follows from case law of the CJEU that Member State courts are obliged to interpret all (inter)national law 'so far as possible' in a way that is consistent with the obligations arising from a Directive. The scope of the phrase 'so far as possible' is further discussed in the next section.

## 4.4 LIMITS TO THE DUTY OF CONSISTENT INTERPRETATION

### 4.4.1 General

Based on section 4.3, the duty of consistent interpretation applies with respect to all tax treaties concluded by the Member States. As such, Member State courts are, in principle, obliged to interpret each tax treaty in a way that is consistent with the obligations arising from a Directive. This obligation to interpret a tax treaty in a way that is consistent with a Directive does not, however, entail that such a treaty must, at all times, be interpreted in a way that it is consistent with such a Directive. Such obligation only applies 'so far as possible'. It is the purpose of this section to address the scope of the phrase 'so far as possible' with a view to determining the limits of the duty of consistent interpretation: how far are Member State courts required to go, when interpreting a tax treaty, to ensure that a Directive consistent interpretation is achieved, i.e., to what extent does the duty of consistent interpretation require Member State courts to interpret tax treaties in a way that is consistent with (the result of) a Directive?

In determining the scope of the duty of consistent interpretation, the starting point would seem to be that it follows from case law of the CJEU that the words 'so far as possible' entail that a Member State court is not required to interpret national law in a way that is consistent with a Directive if such an interpretative result would be contrary to general principles of law, which include 'in particular those of legal certainty and non-retroactivity' while the duty of consistent interpretation can also not 'serve as the basis for an interpretation of national law contra legem'.[403] It also follows from the CJEU's case law that a Directive consistent interpretation is only required to the extent that this would be possible by application of the interpretive methods recognised by domestic laws.[404] Moreover, with respect to those (pre-accession) tax treaties that fall within the scope of Article 351 TFEU, it has been held by the CJEU that

403. *See* Case C-212/04 (*Adeneler and Others*), para. 110. The words 'in particular' have been taken to clearly suggest that other principles may also come into play. In that respect, Prechal refers to, by way of example, principles of unjust enrichment, equity, equality and proportionality (S. Prechal, 2009, pp. 204-205). In addition, in Case C-282/10 (*Dominguez*), para. 93 it is indicated that it appears that the ECJ has 'opted not to undertake a precise classification of general principles to retain the flexibility it needs in order to decide on substantive matters which arise regardless of terminological discrepancies'. *See* for a discussion of potential additional principles paras 94-96 of the judgment.

404. Case 14/83 (*Von Colson*), para. 26, which became settled case law after Joined Cases C-397/01 to C-403/01 (*Pfeiffer and Others*), para. 116. For recent examples wherein the CJEU referred to the principle of consistent interpretation Case C-573/17 (*Poplawski*), paras 73 and 77, as well as Case C-579/15 (*Poplawski*), para. 35.

the duty of consistent interpretation requires a Member State court to remain compliant with international law.[405]

While each of the above-mentioned limitations would be relevant for the purposes of determining whether, in a given situation, a Member State court would be required to interpret a tax treaty in a way that is consistent with (the result of) a Directive, the sections below focus on the limitations of the duty of consistent interpretation relating to application of 'the interpretive methods recognised by domestic laws' (section 4.4.2) and 'compliance with international law' (section 4.4.3). The rationale for focusing particularly on these two limitations is that they can be analysed in more general terms than the limitations relating to general principles such as 'legal certainty', 'non-retroactivity' and '*contra legem*', which require a more case-by-case analysis. Whether a given interpretation would be contra legem, for example, is difficult to determine in the abstract.[406] The interpretive methods recognised by domestic law, especially within the context of treaty interpretation, as well as compliance with international law, can, by contrast, be determined in a more general way that transcends a case-by-case analysis.

### 4.4.2 Interpretive Methods Recognised by Domestic Law

Whereas the interpretative methods recognised by national law may differ from one Member State to another,[407] it is recalled that the interpretative methods recognised by *international law* regarding the interpretation of tax treaties do not, or at least should not, differ from one Member State to another. This is due to the interpretation of each tax treaty being governed by the same rules of interpretation: Articles 31 through 33 VCLT 1969,[408] reflecting customary international law,[409] and the more specific

405. Case C-216/01 (*Budějovický Budvar*), para. 169.

406. With respect to the contra legem limitation within the context of the duty of consistent interpretation, the CJEU's case law indicates that it is up to national courts to determine whether a consistent interpretation would be *contra legem* (*see*, to this effect, Case C-579/15 (*Poplawski*), para. 39 and Case C-414/16 (*Egenberger*), paras 73-75). It does, however, follow from case law of the CJEU that the Court may 'provide guidance, based on the file in the main proceedings and on the observations which have been submitted to it, in order to enable the national court to give judgment' (*see*, to this effect, Case C-183/18 (*Bank BGZ BNP Paribas*), para. 73).

Within the context of determining whether an interpretation would be contra legem, the CJEU has ruled that a national court may be obliged to 'to change its established case-law, where necessary, if it is based on an interpretation of national law that is incompatible with the objectives of a directive' (Case C-441/14 (*Dansk Industri*), para. 34, as well as C-414/16 (*Egenberger*), para. 73 and Case C-573/17 (*Poplawski*), para. 78), to deviate from 'any contrary interpretation which may arise from the *travaux preparatoires* for the national rule' (Case C-371/02 (*Björnekulla Fruktindustrier*), para. 13), and to set aside positions expressed by academics regarding the interpretation of a national law (*see*, to this effect, Case C-183/18 (*Bank BGZ BNP Paribas*), paras 68-69).

407. *See*, to this effect, for example, S. Prechal, Common Market Law Review 2005/5, p. 1459 who notes that the 'reliance on the interpretative methods existing under national law will inevitably lead to differences in outcome. Arguably, what is still possible in one legal system is not necessarily also possible in another one'.

408. *See* section 3.1.

409. Regarding the customary nature, *see*, *inter alia*, P. Ariginelli, 2015, para. 1.1.2 and O. Dörr & K. Schmalenbach, 2018, pp. 561-564, paras 6-7.

interpretative provisions of Article 3(2) OECD Model (or Article 2(2) MLI). It would thus seem that the interpretative methods to be applied by each Member State court when interpreting tax treaties are identical: such court needs to apply (and comply with) either Article 3(2) OECD Model (or Article 2(2) MLI) or Articles 31 through 33 VCLT 1969. As such, within the context of this thesis, the limitation relating to the interpretative methods recognised by national law is understood as entailing that the duty of consistent interpretation only requires an interpretation that is consistent with the result of a Directive if such a result can be achieved by a national court applying the interpretative methods recognised by *international law*. It follows that national courts would only be required to interpret tax treaties in a way that is consistent with the result of the Directives to the extent that this would be allowed for under the interpretative methods recognised by international law (as set out in Chapter 3).[410]

### 4.4.3 The Limitation Relating to Compliance with International Law

In addition to a consistent interpretation only being required to the extent this would be allowed for by the rules of public international law regarding the interpretation of treaties, the CJEU has explicitly ruled that treaties concluded by Member States before, essentially, their accession to the EU with third states should be interpreted in a way that is consistent with EU law only if this is '*in compliance with international law*' (*see*, in more detail regarding the scope of Article 351 TFEU, section 7.2.2). With respect to such pre-accession Extra-EU Treaties, the CJEU has thus explicitly confirmed that the interpretative methods of public international law must be adhered to (as otherwise an interpretation would not compliant with international law):

> In *Budejovicky Budvar* (Case C-216/01) and *Ferrari* (Joined Cases C-720/18 & C-721/18), the CJEU held that a 'court must ascertain whether a possible incompatibility between [EU law] and the ... convention can be avoided by interpreting that convention, to the extent possible and in compliance with international law, in such a way that it is consistent with [EU] law'.[411]

The public international law limitation formulated by the CJEU regarding the duty of consistent interpretation in *Budějovický Budvar* (Case C-216/01) and *Ferrari* (Joined Cases C-720/18 & C-721/18) can be understood against the background of Article 351 TFEU. This provision is aimed at protecting the rights of, and obligations towards, third states under treaties that Member States have entered into before they acceded to the EU.[412] As such, the limitation that the duty of consistent interpretation only applies '*in*

410. With respect to the extent to which such international interpretative methods allow domestic courts to take such Directives into account has been discussed in Chapter 3 and is not further discussed here.

411. Case C-216/01 (*Budějovický Budvar*), para. 169 and Joined Cases C-720/18 & C-721/18 (*Ferrari*), para. 68. It can be noted that the CJEU uses the wording 'to the extent possible' in these two cases as opposed to 'so far as possible' in, for example, Joined Cases C-397/01 to C-403/01 (*Pfeiffer and Others*), para. 113. A comparison of the Dutch versions of these cases indicates, however, that the reference to 'to the extent possible' (in Dutch: 'zo veel mogelijk') is not different from 'so far as possible' (in Dutch: 'zoveel mogelijk').

412. *See* section 7.2.2 for a discussion of Article 351 TFEU.

*compliance with international law'* can be regarded as the logical consequence of the general principle of Article 351 TFEU that the Member States must respect rights of, and obligations towards, at all times, including the situation where a national court would be interpreting a (pre-accession) Extra-EU Treaty falling within the scope of such provision.

## 4.5 THE CONSEQUENCES (OF THE DUTY) OF CONSISTENT INTERPRETATION

If it would be established that the interpretative methods under international law would allow for two different interpretations of a treaty term, one inconsistent with (the result of) the Directives and the other consistent with such (result of the) Directives, the duty of consistent interpretation would require a domestic court to adopt the consistent interpretation,[413] even if the result would be detrimental to a taxpayer.[414] It may, however, also be conceivable that the duty of consistent interpretation does not require a Member State court to choose between two interpretations. This would be the case where two different, yet possible, interpretations of a treaty would both be consistent with the result to be achieved by a Directive. If such a situation arises, the duty of consistent interpretation would not oblige a Member State court to choose one interpretation over the other because both would already be consistent with its result to be achieved. As such, if the interpretative methods under international law would allow for two interpretations of the term 'beneficial owner' in Article 12 OECD Model, one similar to the meaning given to such term by the CJEU and one different from such meaning, the duty of consistent interpretation would not require a domestic court to adopt the CJEU's meaning if both meanings would be consistent with the result to be achieved by, for example, the Interest and Royalties Directive.

> An example of a situation wherein it would not follow from the duty of consistent interpretation that one interpretation should be chosen over another would seem to be as follows. Pursuant to Article 1(1) Interest and Royalties Directive, royalty payments arising in one Member State shall be exempt from source taxes provided that the beneficial owner of such royalties is resident in another Member State. The result to be achieved pursuant to this provision is thus exemption of source taxation. Tax treaties would not seem capable of providing for obligations that are incompatible with this result given that they do not impose obligations on the contracting states to tax income. On the contrary, tax treaties merely impose limitations with respect to the extent to which cross-border income may be taxed. Within the context of royalty payments within the meaning of Article 12 OECD Model, such limitation takes the form of a limitation of the right of the source state,

413. *See*, by analogy, Joined Cases C-397/01 to C-403/01 (*Pfeiffer and Others*), para. 116 (as well as the interpretation accorded to this paragraph by S. Prechal, 2009, p. 199 and S. Haket, Review of European Administrative Law 2015/2, p. 220). *See also* K. Sawyer, Statute Law Review 2007/3, p. 171, as well as 31 who notes that the duty of consistent interpretation obliges national courts 'to give preference to the one [interpretation] that enables the result envisaged by the directive to be achieved'.
414. *See* S. Prechal, 2009, p. 213.

either by means of an exemption or by maximising the right to tax a royalty payments up to a certain percentage of the gross amount, if the royalties are beneficially owned by a resident of the other state. As such, if royalties are beneficially owned by a resident of one contracting state, Article 12 OECD Model would oblige the source state to limit the extent to which it may tax a royalty payment without imposing a duty to tax such payments. In the absence of imposing a duty to tax a royalty payment, it would seem that a tax treaty cannot conflict with the obligation under Article 1(1) Interest and Royalty Directive to exempt royalty payments. This is due to the circumstance that it is ultimately up to the contracting states as to whether they tax a royalty payment if such taxation (up to a certain percentage) would be allowed for by a tax treaty. Taking this into account, it would seem difficult to envisage a situation wherein one interpretation of the term 'beneficial owner' in Article 12 OECD Model would give rise to a situation wherein obligations are imposed on a Member State that are incompatible with the obligation arising from Article 1(1) Interest and Royalties Directive to exempt a royalty payment. As such, any interpretation of the term 'beneficial owner' in Article 12 OECD Model would not seem capable of giving rise to a result that is inconsistent with the result required by Article 1(1) Interest and Royalties Directive. In that situation, the duty of consistent interpretation would not seem to require one interpretation to be chosen over another as both interpretations would be consistent with the result to be achieved by such Directive.

In this example, the duty of consistent interpretation would thus not impose any obligations on the Member State court and, as such, would not affect the interpretation of the term 'beneficial owner'. At the same time, however, if an interpretation of the term 'beneficial owner' that differs from the CJEU's interpretation would result in the treaty becoming inconsistent with the obligations arising from, or with respect to, a Directive, the Member State court would be required to reject such an interpretation and adopt the meaning that is consistent with such Directive.

An example of a situation wherein an interpretation of the term 'beneficial owner' in a tax treaty may be incompatible with a Directive could be as follows. Assume that Article 1 of the Interest and Royalties Directive would require royalty payments to be taxed at source if the recipient of such royalties does not qualify as the beneficial owner of the royalties. In this situation, the result to be achieved would be taxation of royalties if the owner of such royalties does not qualify as a beneficial owner within the meaning of this Directive. Assume, at the same time, that Article 12 OECD Model provides for an exemption at source of royalty payments that are beneficially owned by a resident of one of the contracting states. If in this situation, the interpretative methods under international law would allow for two different interpretations of a treaty term, one ensuring that the exemption of Article 12 OECD Model is inapplicable if Article 1 of the Interest and Royalties Directive requires taxation of the royalty payments and one that results in the exemption of royalty payments that must be taxed. In accordance with Article 1 of such Directive, the duty of consistent interpretation would require the meaning to be adopted that is consistent with the result to be achieved by the Interest and Royalties Directive, i.e., the result that allows for the taxation of the royalty payments that are not beneficially owned within the meaning of such Directive.

With respect to this latter example, it needs to be stressed that the duty of consistent interpretation would require a Member State to adopt an interpretation that ensures the achievement of the result of the Interest and Royalties Directive. It does not, as such, require the adoption of the CJEU's interpretation of the term 'beneficial owner' in the *Danish Cases*.[415] In ensuring that such result is achieved, a Member State court may be inclined to interpret the term 'beneficial owner' in the tax treaty in the same way as the CJEU has interpreted such term in the *Danish Cases*. Such court may, however, also achieve such result by other means. It could, for example, adopt a meaning that deviates from such term, but that does allow for the result of a Directive to be achieved. Alternatively, a Member State court may also attempt to achieve the result of a Directive by, for example, interpreting the Principal Purpose Test, if part of a tax treaty, in such a way so as to ensure that the result of the Directive is achieved. From the perspective of the laws of the EU, there would not seem to be a preference for a consistent interpretation of either the 'beneficial owner' term or Principal Purpose Test, provided that the result of the Directive is achieved.

It follows that a Member State court is only under a duty to interpret a tax treaty in a way that is consistent with the result of a Directive (and not under a duty to interpret tax treaty terms in the same way as terms in a Directive for the sole reason of such terms being similar or identical). The way in which such a consistent interpretation is reached, is left to the discretion of Member State courts. Such courts may (attempt to) achieve this by means of a Directive-based interpretation of, for example, the 'beneficial owner' term, but they may also achieve this by other means (such as an interpretation of the Principal Purpose Test that ensures achievement of the result of a Directive).

## 4.6 CONCLUSION

In this chapter, the central question has been to what extent the Directives should affect the interpretation of tax treaties under the laws of the EU. The answer to this question is that the Member State courts are, in principle, obliged to interpret tax treaties in a way that is consistent with (the result of) the Directives. This obligation does not, however, require domestic courts to interpret a treaty in a way that is inconsistent with general principles of law or, within the context of the interpretation of tax treaties, the interpretative methods recognised by international law (as well as, with respect to pre-accession Extra-EU Treaties, international law in general). If, however, it would be consistent with the interpretative methods of international law to interpret a tax treaty in a way that is consistent with a Directive, the duty of consistent interpretation would require a Member State court to adopt such interpretation.

415. Joined Cases C-115/16, C-118/16, C-119/16 & C-299/16 (*N Luxembourg 1*) and Joined Cases C-116/16 & C-117/16 (*T Danmark*).

CHAPTER 5

# The Effect of the Directives on the Interpretation of Tax Treaties: Bringing the Public International Law and EU Law Perspective Together

It has been the purpose of Part II of this thesis to answer the question to what extent the Directives - directly or indirectly (via the result to be achieved under such Directives) - may affect the interpretation of tax treaties concluded by the Member States. In providing an answer to such question, it has been determined to what extent the Directives can have, or are 'allowed' to have, an effect on the interpretation of tax treaties under the rules of public international law (Chapter 3), as well as to what extent a Member State court is obliged to ensure that such Directives affect the interpretation of tax treaties under the laws of the EU with a view to ensure that such treaties are interpreted in a way that is consistent with the result to be achieved by a Directive, i.e., the 'required' effect (Chapter 4). Chapter 5 seeks to combine the findings of the previous two chapters.

In that respect, the first item to note is that the duty of consistent interpretation does not require an interpretation consistent with a Directive if such an interpretation would not be allowed under the interpretative methods of public international law (section 4.4.2). Such methods for the purposes of tax treaties concluded by the Member States have been discussed in Chapter 3. Considering that it has been the purpose of such chapter to determine the extent to which the Directives may - directly or indirectly - affect the interpretation of tax treaties, it follows that Chapter 3 essentially determines the answer to the central question of Part II of the present thesis. This is due to the circumstance that going beyond the limits identified in that chapter would mean going beyond the interpretative methods of international law, which a Member State court cannot be required to do under the duty of consistent interpretation.

Bearing this in mind, the sections below reflect on the extent to which the Directives are 'allowed' and 'required' to affect the interpretation of tax treaties. In that respect, a distinction is drawn between (i) the type of treaty being interpreted, i.e., an Intra-EU Treaty or an Extra-EU Treaty, and (ii) the interpretative provision used to interpret such treaty, i.e., Article 3(2) OECD Model, Article 2(2) MLI, or Article 31 VCLT 1969.[416]

## 5.1 THE EFFECT OF THE DIRECTIVES ON THE INTERPRETATION OF INTRA-EU TREATIES

### 5.1.1 The Effect of the Directives on the Interpretation of Intra-EU Treaties under Article 3(2) OECD Model

With respect to the interpretation of Intra-EU Treaties under Article 3(2) OECD Model, the Directives can, first of all, affect the interpretation of undefined tax treaty terms in their capacity as part of the law of the Member State applying the tax treaty (section 3.2.2.2). Second, (the result of) the Directives can also, based on the OECD Commentaries (2017), affect the interpretation of Intra-EU Treaties as context within the meaning of Article 3(2) OECD Model in their capacity as either part of the relevant rules of international law at the time of conclusion (bearing in mind the presumption against conflict) of such tax treaty or as part of the laws of the other contracting state (section 3.2.3.1). The contextual effect of (the result of) a Directive can be as follows:

(a) providing strong arguments for adopting the meaning of an undefined treaty term based on the laws of the Member State applying the Intra-EU Treaty, which laws may include Directives, if such meaning is consistent with, for example, the result of a Directive;
(b) in a case where more than one relevant meaning can be derived from the laws of the Member State applying an Intra-EU Treaty, (the result of) a Directive could provide a strong argument in favour of adopting the meaning that avoids a conflict with such Directive;
(c) providing strong arguments against adopting a meaning based on the laws of the Member States applying the Intra-EU Treaty, if the outcome of adopting such a meaning would be inconsistent with the result to be achieved under a Directive (3.2.3.2).

As part of the context, (the result of) the Directives may thus provide strong arguments for interpreting an Intra-EU Treaty in such a way that is consistent with (the result to be achieved pursuant to) a Directive. In a way, the contextual effect of (the result of) the Directives may be perceived as reflecting the duty of consistent interpretation in the sense that Directives as part of the context could require an undefined tax treaty term to have a meaning that is consistent with the result of a Directive. An important difference with such duty is nevertheless that the context can comprise of

416. For these purposes, the MLI is considered an Extra-EU Treaty considering that not all parties to the MLI are also parties to the EU Treaties.

more than (the result of) the Directives. As such, if other contextual material would provide strong arguments against adopting a Directive-consistent meaning, it may be that, based on an assessment of all material forming part of the context (including the result of the Directives) for the purposes of Article 3(2) OECD Model, the context requires a meaning that is inconsistent with a Directive to be adopted (or a Directive-consistent meaning to be rejected). Given that the duty of consistent interpretation applies only to the extent consistent with the interpretative methods under international law, such duty would respect such a non-Directive-consistent outcome resulting from an application of the rules of interpretation of international law provided for by Article 3(2) OECD Model.

### 5.1.2 The Effect of the Directives on the Interpretation of Intra-EU Treaties under Article 31 VCLT 1969

When interpreting an Intra-EU Treaty on the basis of Article 31 VCLT 1969, (the result of) the Directives can affect the interpretation of an Intra-EU Treaty as relevant rules of international law applicable in the relations between the parties (section 3.4.2.2). With respect to their effect, the starting point is that Article 31 VCLT 1969 seeks to give effect to the common intentions of the parties with respect to the treaty being interpreted (section 3.4.3.1). This entails that the extent to which a Directive would provide evidence of such a common intention affects the extent to which it can have an effect on the interpretative outcome under Article 31 VCLT 1969. With respect to providing evidence of a common intention, it has been concluded that this can be derived from the Directives in one of the following ways:

(a) Explicit language in (the preamble or (a) provision(s) of) a Directive addressing its relationship with tax treaties concluded by the Member States (section 3.4.3.2.2).
(b) Similarities in terminology may provide evidence of an implicit common intention regarding the ordinary meaning of terms in Intra-EU Treaties (section 3.4.3.2.3).
(c) In the event of a conflict between a Directive that was in force at the time of conclusion of a post-accession Intra-EU Treaty, a common intention against conflict with such (earlier) Directive may be presumed (the presumption against conflict) (section 3.4.3.2.4).
(d) In the event of a conflict between a Directive and any Intra-EU Treaty, it is conceivable that a common intention between the Member States in favour of applying their tax treaties in a way that is consistent with the result to be achieved by a Directive may be presumed on the basis of case law of the CJEU (Article 4(3) TEU) (the presumption against conflict with EU law) (section 3.4.3.2.5).

Whereas the Directives may – directly or indirectly via the presumption against conflict (with EU law) – provide evidence of a common intention pursuant to which they may be able to affect the interpretation of Intra-EU Treaties under Article 31 VCLT 1969, it should be borne in mind that Article 31 VCLT 1969 refers to more than just the relevant rules of international law applicable in the relations between the parties. As such, the ordinary (or special) meaning, (internal and other elements of the) external context, object and purpose and the principle of good faith are also to be considered. The extent to which the Directives may affect the interpretation of an Intra-EU Treaty thus depends on the indications of a common intention provided by such other means.

With respect to the effect of the Directives, it is further recalled that an interpretation pursuant to Article 31 VCLT can only result in one (single) outcome, which outcome is aimed at reflecting the common intention of the parties with respect to the treaty being interpreted. Hence, if the other means of interpretation referred to in Article 31 VCLT 1969 provide proof of a common intention that would be contrary to the intention that may be derived from (the result of) the Directives, an interpreter would have to determine which common intention most accurately reflects the common intention of the Member States with respect to the Intra-EU Treaty being interpreted. In making such determination, the effect that the Directives may have on the interpretation of an Intra-EU Treaty under Article 31 VCLT 1969 is, in any event, limited by (i) the wording of the treaty (provision) being interpreted, (ii) the object and purpose of such treaty (provision), and (iii) the principle of good faith pursuant to which the interpretation must be reasonable, fair and honest (section 3.4.4). Based on the respect of the duty of consistent interpretation for (the interpretative methods laid down in) Article 31 VCLT 1969, Member State courts would not be required to go beyond such limits. As such, if Article 31 VCLT 1969 results in an ordinary (or special) meaning that is not consistent with the result of a Directive, this is respected by the duty of consistent interpretation in the sense that such duty does not require a Member State court to change the interpretative outcome reached by application of the general rule of interpretation of Article 31 VCLT 1969.

## 5.2 THE EFFECT OF DIRECTIVES ON THE INTERPRETATION OF EXTRA-EU TREATIES

### 5.2.1 The Effect of the Directives on the Interpretation of Extra-EU Treaties under Article 3(2) OECD Model

Similar to the interpretation of Intra-EU Treaties under Article 3(2) OECD Model, the Directives can be used as part of the laws of the Member State applying an Extra-EU Treaty for the purposes of giving meaning to undefined treaty terms. In such a way, there is no difference between the effect of the Directives on the interpretation of Intra-EU and Extra-EU Treaties via Article 3(2) OECD Model.

This conclusion does not, however, entail that such Directives have the same effect on an interpretation of Extra-EU Treaties under Article 3(2) OECD Model. This is because (the result of) the Directives do(es) not reflect any common intention between a Member State and a third state because third states are not bound by such Directives while the Directives are also not part of the laws of such third states. As such, (the result of) the Directives would not be part of the context within the meaning of Article 3(2) OECD Model and, hence, would not be able to affect the interpretation of Extra-EU Treaties as context within the meaning of Article 3(2) OECD Model in the ways referred to in section 5.1.1. Considering that the rejection of the Directives as part of the context follows from Article 3(2) OECD Model, such rejection would not be contrary to the duty of consistent interpretation. In addition, similar to what has been concluded in section 5.1.1 with respect to Intra-EU Treaties, the context - not comprising of (the result of) the Directives - may require a non-Directive-consistent meaning to be adopted under Article 3(2) OECD Model. Such an outcome would, again, not raise any issues from the EU law perspective because the duty of consistent interpretation respects the operation of Article 3(2) OECD Model as an interpretative method under international law.

### 5.2.2 The Effect of the Directives on the Interpretation of Extra-EU Treaties under Article 31 VCLT 1969

Directives can have no effect on the interpretation of Extra-EU Treaties under Article 31 VCLT 1969 because they are not applicable in the relations between the parties.[417] Considering that taking them into account would be contrary to the interpretative method of Article 31 VCLT 1969, the duty of consistent interpretation does not apply, in practice, when interpreting an Extra-EU Treaty in accordance with such provision.

### 5.2.3 The Effect of the Directives on the Interpretation of the MLI under Article 2(2) MLI

Directives may affect the interpretation of undefined MLI terms via the reference in Article 2(2) MLI to the meaning of such terms in the covered bilateral tax treaty. If the interpretation of such a bilateral tax treaty would have been affected by a Directive, for example, via Article 3(2) OECD Model, such a Directive would indirectly also be able to have an effect on the meaning of the same term in the MLI. It should, however, be noted that using the meaning of undefined MLI terms based on the covered bilateral tax treaty is subject to the context of the MLI requiring otherwise. Depending on the nature of the relevant MLI provision (as bilateral or multilateral), such context can include (the obligations relating to) the Directives, but their effect should not be overstated (*see* section 5.1.1 for Intra-EU Treaties affected by bilateral provisions of the MLI and section 5.2.1 with respect to Extra-EU Treaties affected by bilateral provisions of the MLI, which considerations also apply to multilateral MLI provisions).

With respect to the effect of the Directives on the MLI under Article 31 VCLT 1969, the preliminary question to be answered is whether the relevant MLI provision is

417. It may nevertheless be conceivable that the Directives could be resorted to as supplementary means of interpretation (*see* section 3.4.1), but their effect should be very limited considering that they would only reflect the unilateral intention of an EU Member State. Given the purpose of Article 31 VCLT 1969 to give effect to the common intention of the parties to a treaty, such unilateral intention would, in any event, have very little (if none at all) effect on the interpretation of an Extra-EU Treaty.

of a bilateral nature and affecting an Intra-EU or Extra-EU Treaty. If it concerns a bilateral MLI provision affecting an Intra-EU Treaty, the conclusions set out in section 5.1.2 apply. With respect to multilateral MLI provisions, as well as bilateral MLI provisions affecting Extra-EU Treaties, the conclusions of section 5.2.2 apply.

# Part III

# The Effect of the Directives on the Application of Tax Treaties

In this part III, the central question will be to what extent the Directives may affect the application, in the sense of 'applicability' of tax treaties concluded by the Member States (after such treaties would have been interpreted). To answer this question, a structure similar to that used in part II is adhered to. As such, the extent to which the Directives may affect the application (meaning: applicability) of tax treaties under the rules of public international law is discussed first (Chapter 6), followed by a discussion of the effect of such Directives under the laws of the EU (Chapter 7). The reason for adopting such a similar structure is that the rules of EU law that may result in a Directive affecting the application of tax treaties are, essentially, dependent on the relevant tax treaty being applicable within the internal legal order of a Member State. As such, it should first be determined whether the application of a tax treaty would be affected by a Directive under the rules of public international law. If so, especially for Member States wherein tax treaties would be superior to national law, there may no longer be a duty to (also) affect such application from the perspective of the laws of the EU because the treaty would no longer be applicable (in a way incompatible with (the national rules aimed at implementing) a Directive).[418] The effect that a Directive may have on the application of tax treaties under the rules of the EU is thus essentially dependent on such application not already having been affected by such a Directive under the rules of public international law (or under the laws of a Member State). This justifies addressing the public international law perspective in Chapter 6 before the EU law perspective in Chapter 7. Part III ends with a discussion regarding the extent to

418. *See* section 1.4.3.

which the effect of Directives on the application of tax treaties under public international is similar, or different, to the effect of such Directives under the laws of the EU (Chapter 8).[419]

419. To the extent that one would question the relevance of addressing the public international law perspective given the primacy of the Directives, reference is made to the lack of enforceability of such primacy in the event that reliance on the primacy of a (directly effective) Directive would be detrimental for a taxpayer (*see* section 7.3.3).

Chapter 6

# The Effect of the Directives on the Application of Tax Treaties under Public International Law

## 6.1 INTRODUCTION

In this chapter, the question of to what extent the Directives may affect the application of tax treaties concluded by the Member States under the rules of public international law is addressed. In determining such effect, two relevant fundamental principles of public international law - *pacta sunt servanda* and *pacta tertiis nocent nec prosunt* - are discussed first (sections 6.2. and 6.3). Afterwards, the *lex posterior* and *lex specialis* conflict rules of public international law are set out (section 6.4). Based on sections 6.2 through 6.4, an answer to the question regarding the extent to which the Directives may affect the application of tax treaties is provided in section 6.5. This chapter ends with observations with respect to those cases wherein such conflict rules do not result in the Directives affecting the application of tax treaties (section 6.6).

For the purposes of answering the question of the present chapter, the following starting points apply:

(a) the Directives are decisions of the EU as an international organisation;
(b) the EU Treaties are treaties within the meaning of Article 2(1)(a) VCLT 1969;
(c) the tax treaties are treaties within the meaning of Article 2(1)(a) VCLT 1969.[420]

420. *See* Chapter 2 for the line of reasoning regarding each of these starting points.

## 6.2 *PACTA SUNT SERVANDA* (ARTICLE 26 VCLT 1969)

> Article 26
>
> 'Pacta Sunt Servanda'
>
> Every treaty in force is binding upon the parties to it and must be performed by them in good faith.

The principle of *pacta sunt servanda*, codified in Article 26 VCLT 1969 provides that each treaty in force has an obligatory character for the parties,[421] that each treaty must be performed by them, and that such performance must be done in good faith. The principle essentially confirms the mandatory character of treaties: the parties to a treaty must perform each of their obligations entered into.[422] As such, the principle of *pacta sunt servanda* entails that tax treaties concluded by the Member States must be performed by them in good faith, i.e., 'in a reasonable way and in such a manner that its purpose can be realised', irrespective of any (contrary) obligations arising from the EU Treaties, including the obligation to achieve the result of the Directives, and the Directives themselves.[423] The same applies with respect to the EU Treaties, including the obligation to achieve the result of a Directive under Article 288 TFEU. These treaties must also be performed by the Member States in good faith notwithstanding any other (conflicting) obligations under their tax treaties.

It thus follows from the *pacta sunt servanda* principle that each treaty in force is binding upon the parties to it and must be performed by them. Member States will be able to comply with this principle of public international law to the extent that the application of a tax treaty is consistent with, *inter alia*, the obligation to achieve the result of the Directives as laid down in Article 288 TFEU (also a treaty). This can be illustrated by means of the following example.

> Assume Company X, resident in Member State A, makes a profit distribution to its 100% parent, Company Y, resident in Member State B. With respect to such a dividend distribution, it follows from the Parent-Subsidiary Directive that Member State A must exempt such a profit distribution (Article 5). At the same time, the tax treaty between Member States A and B – based on the OECD Model (2017) – stipulates that such profit distribution may be taxed by Member State A up to 5% of the gross amount of the dividend distribution (Article 10(2)(a)). Member State A thus faces two obligations in respect of the same profit distribution: first, an obligation to exempt the distribution and then also an obligation to not tax such distribution at a rate of more than 5% of the gross amount. If Member State A complies with the Parent-Subsidiary Directive, it does not tax the profit distribution. By refraining from taxing the profit distribution, it would seem that this does not affect any obligations towards or rights of Member State B because this would only have been so if Member State A had taxed the profit distribution for an

421. J. Salmon in: The Vienna Conventions on the Law of Treaties (Vol. I) (Corten & Klein eds), 2011, para. 33.
422. *See* S.A. Sadat-Akhavi, 2003, p. 211.
423. ICJ, 1997, Judgment (*Gabcikovo-Nagymaros*), pp. 78-79, para. 142.

amount exceeding 5% of the gross distribution. It thus follows that Member State A can perform its obligations under both treaties at the same time.

In the event that the application of a tax treaty would be inconsistent with obligations arising from the EU Treaties or a Directive, compliance with the principle of *pacta sunt servanda* becomes impossible. This can be illustrated as follows.

Assume Company A, resident in Member State Y, has a permanent establishment in Member State Z. Assume further that the permanent establishment must be treated as a controlled foreign company within the meaning of Article 7 ATAD1. As the permanent establishment is to be treated as a controlled foreign company, Article 8 ATAD1 obliges Member State Y to include in the taxable base (qualifying) income of the permanent establishment situated in Member State Z. At the same time, the tax treaty between Member States Y and Z stipulates that such profits attributable to a permanent establishment must be exempt. In such an event, Member State Y faces two – mutually exclusive – obligations: (i) tax the income of the permanent establishment situated in Member State Z (and comply with the obligation to achieve the result required by Article 8 ATAD1) and (ii) exempt the income of such permanent establishment (and comply with the obligation under the tax treaty with Member State Z).

With respect to such a situation wherein performance of one treaty would result in non-performance of another, the principle of *pacta sunt servanda* will be violated if either treaty is performed.[424] If violated, a Member State would incur international responsibility because such responsibility arises as soon as a state fails to fulfil a treaty obligation (*see* section 6.6).

## 6.3 *PACTA TERTIIS NOCENT NEC PROSUNT* (ARTICLE 34 VCLT 1969)

Article 34

General rule regarding third states

A treaty does not create either obligations or rights for a third State without its consent.

The principle of *pacta tertiis nec nocent nec prosunt* is, similar to the principle of *pacta sunt servanda*, well established under public international and considered customary international law.[425] Pursuant to this principle, which has been codified in Article 34

424. *See* J. Pauwelyn, 2003, p. 426 who provides the example of State A being bound by a norm with State B, while also being bound by a – contradictory – norm to State C. In such case, both treaties are binding upon State A pursuant to *pacta sunt servanda*. *See also* A.C.G.A.C. de Graaf, 2004, p. 235, footnote 35 who notes that a treaty override violates the principle of *pacta sunt servanda*.

425. *See*, to this effect, E. David in: The Vienna Convention on the Law of Treaties (Corten & Klein eds), 2011, para. 4. It has also been applied in ICJ, 1952, Judgment (Anglo-Iranian Oil Company (*United Kingdom v. Iran*)), p. 109 while the CJEU considered the *pacta tertiis* principle as customary international law in Case C386/08 (*Brita*), paras 42-44.

VCLT 1969,[426] a treaty does not create obligations or rights for third states.[427] As such, it confirms the relative effect of treaties under international law: treaties only create rights and obligations for the states that are parties to them (and, as such, have consented to be bound by them).[428] Within this context, rights and obligations can be understood as 'either a subjective legitimate interest or prerogative recognized by law (here, international law), or an obligation similarly established and defined by a rule of international law'.[429,430] For the purposes of this chapter, it follows from Article 34 VCLT 1969 that the principle of pacta *tertiis* entails that the Directives (and EU Treaties):

(a) can create rights and obligations for the Member States, as states that have consented to the rights and obligations arising from the Directives (and EU Treaties);[431] and
(b) cannot, as '*res inter alios actas*' (things between others), affect the rights of, or obligations towards, third states.[432]

## 6.4 THE CONFLICT RULES OF PUBLIC INTERNATIONAL LAW

### 6.4.1 Introduction

It follows from sections 6.2 and 6.3 that the Directives do not, in principle, affect the application of Intra-EU Treaties, as well as Extra-EU Treaties. Such tax treaties remain binding and must be performed in good faith under the principle of *pacta sunt servanda*. As follows from section 6.2 it may, however, become impossible, in practice, to perform the obligations under both a Directive and a tax treaty. It is with respect to such a situation that the conflict rules of public international law, as discussed in this section 6.4, would be relevant.

426. The codification of the *pacta tertiis* principle in Article 34 VCLT has been recognised by, *inter alia*, Case C386/08 (*Brita*), para. 52. Moreover, the *pacta tertiis* principle is also reflected by Article 30(4)(b) VCLT 1969. *See*, to that effect, A. Orakhelashvili in: The Vienna Conventions on the Law of Treaties (Corten & Klein eds), 2011, para. 22 and O. Dörr & K. Schmalenbach, 2018, pp. 542-543, para. 9.
427. M.E. Villiger, 2009, p. 469, para. 4.
428. E. David in: The Vienna Convention on the Law of Treaties (Corten & Klein eds), 2011, para. 1. *See also* O. Dörr & K. Schmalenbach, 2018, p. 655, para. 1 and L.F. Oppenheim, 2012, p. 563. *See* furthermore M.E. Villiger, 2009, p. 470, para. 7 who notes that Article 34 is formulated in such a way as to make it clear 'what a treaty cannot achieve'. It can also be noted that in such a way the principle of *pacta tertiis* reflects the 'negative facet of the principle of pacta sunt servanda' in the sense that it confirms that a treaty is not in force for a state (*see* O. Dörr & K. Schmalenbach, 2018, p. 655, para. 1).
429. E. David in: The Vienna Convention on the Law of Treaties (Corten & Klein eds), 2011, para. 12.
430. J. Pauwelyn, 2003, p. 257.
431. *See* Article 2(1)(g) VCLT 1969 which defines a party as a state which has consented to be bound by a treaty and for which the treaty is in force.
432. E. David in: The Vienna Convention on the Law of Treaties (Corten & Klein eds), 2011, para. 1, as well as O. Dörr & K. Schmalenbach, 2018, p. 655, para. 1.

If it follows from such conflict rules that a tax treaty would no longer be applicable if it conflicts with a Directive, a Member State would no longer be obliged to perform its obligations under such a treaty and, as such, would no longer face two conflicting obligations. Instead, such Member State would only face the obligation to achieve the result of the Directive, which obligation could then be adhered to without violating an incompatible obligation under a tax treaty (and, as such, without giving rise to state responsibility). It follows that it is thus relevant to determine the effect that Directives may have on the application of tax treaties under the conflict rules of public international law. In that respect, the following conflict rules of public international law may be distinguished:

(a) the *lex superior derogat de legi inferiori* rule: a norm of a higher rank prevails over a norm of a lower rank.[433]

433. Notwithstanding the horizontal nature of the sources of public international law, the *lex superior* rule applies in the event of a conflict between a norm of public international law and (i) *ius cogens* or (ii) Article 103 UN Charter (*see*, regarding both as *lex superior*, W. Czaplinski & G.M. Danilenko, Netherlands Yearbook of International Law 2009, p. 42 who write that 'the lex superior is not applicable – perhaps with two possible exceptions: jus cogens, which is, however, de lega lata more a theoretical concept rather than a practical regulation, and the priority clause of Article 103 of the UN Charter which is, in fact, often infringed'). In support of the superiority of *ius cogens, see* A.C.G.A.C. de Graaf, 2004, pp. 240-242, E. Vranes, Zeitschrift für ausländisches öffentliches Recht und Völkerrecht 2005/2, p. 402, footnote 48, Fragmentation Report, A/CN.4/L.682, pp. 181-192, and J. Wouters, C. Ryngaert, T. Ruys & G. de Baere, 2019, p. 168). With respect to the superiority that arises as a result of Article 103 UN Charter, *see* ICJ, 1992, Order, Provisional Measures (*Lockerbie*), p. 15, paras 39-40, and E. Vranes, Zeitschrift für ausländisches öffentliches Recht und Völkerrecht 2005/2, p. 402, footnote 48. Moreover, in more general terms, the *lex superior* rule has also been recognised by P. Niemelä, 2017, p. 27 as a conflict rule of general international law and by M. Prost in: The Oxford Handbook of the Sources of International Law (Besson & d'Aspremont eds), 2018, para. II as a 'conflict resolution principle'. Moreover, H.M. Pit, 2017, p. 6.5.4.2, footnote 571, also recognises the *lex superior* rule as a conflict rule of (customary) public international law.

Within the context of conflicts between the laws of the EU and treaties concluded between the Member States and the *lex superior* conflict rule, it has been submitted by Member States before arbitral tribunals that a *lex superior* conflict rule can be derived from Declaration 17 to the Treaty of Lisbon (*see* ICSID, Intra-EU Jurisdictional Objection, Case No. ARB/15/45 (*Landesbank Baden-Württemberg and others v. Kingdom of Spain*), para. 189). Declaration 17 provides that '[t]he Conference recalls that, in accordance with settled case law of the Court of Justice of the European Union, the Treaties and the law adopted by the Union on the basis of the Treaties have primacy over the law of Member States, under the conditions laid down by the said case law'. In ICSID, Intra-EU Jurisdictional Objection, Case No. ARB/15/45 (*Landesbank Baden-Württemberg and others v. Kingdom of Spain*), para. 191, the tribunal concludes, however, that this declaration 'appears to be a recognition by all EU Member States that EU law takes priority over the agreements they have concluded insofar as those agreements take effect in national law'. As such, Declaration 17 was regarded as not relating to the effect that EU law has under public international law (paras 189-192). Similar conclusions regarding the effect of Declaration 17 have been adopted in ICSID, Intra-EU Jurisdictional Objection and Merits, Case No. ARB/16/18 (*Infracapital F1 S.à r.l. and Infracapital Solar B.V. v. Kingdom of Spain*), para. 101 under 306 ('at best, they make an interpretation as to the effect under EU law, and not public international law'). Hence, under public international law Declaration 17 should not be regarded as implying that the laws of the EU are *lex superior* vis-à-vis other rules of public international law (from the perspective of public international law). Hence, the laws of the EU and other sources of public international law are – as a matter of public international law – to be regarded as of the same rank (*see*, to this effect, ICSID 25 November 2015, Case No.

(b) the *lex prior in tempore, potior in jure* rule: an earlier norm prevails over a later norm;[434]

(c) the *lex posterior derogat de lege priori* rule: a later norm prevails over an earlier norm;[435] and

(d) the *lex specialis derogat generali* rule: a special norm prevails over a general norm.[436]

---

ARB/07/19 (*Electrabel v. Hungary*), para. 4.126, ICSID, Case No. ARB/13/30 (*RREEF*), para. 87, ICSID, Case No. ARB/12/12 (*Vattenfall*), para. 131, and ICSID, Case No. ARB/15/50 (*Eskosol S.p.a. v. Italian Republic*), para. 186. It is acknowledged that a different conclusion was reached in SCC Arbitration V (2016/135) (*Jurisdictional Award Green Power Partners*), para. 469). This ruling has, however, been criticised (*see*, to this extent, N. Lavranos, 2022, Lex superior: How EU law trumps investment law (28 June 2022), Thomson Reuters. Practical Law. Arbitration Blog (http://arbitrationblog.practicallaw.com/lex-superior-how-eu-law-trumps-investment-law/) and D. Müller, 2022, EU Law and Arbitration under International Investment Instruments: The Surprising Award in Green Power v. Spain (28 June 2022), Jus Mundi (https://blog.jusmundi.com/eu-law-and-arbitration-under-international-investment-instruments-the-surprising-award-in-green-power-v-spain/)) and deviates from earlier decisions of arbitral tribunals. Hence, it is concluded that the Green Power Partners judgment cannot – in the absence of subsequent judgments also confirming the supremacy of the laws of the EU under public international law – be understood as implying that as a rule of public international law the laws of the EU must be regarded as *lex superior* under public international law.

434. This principle is recognised by J. Pauwelyn, 2003, p. 424, Fragmentation Report, A/CN.4/L.682, pp. 122-125, paras 236-242, M.E. Villiger, 2009, pp. 399-400, para. 1, N. Matz-Lück in: The Max Planck Encyclopedias of Public International Law (Wolfrum ed.), 2010, para. 14, J. Klabbers in: The Law of Treaties Beyond the Vienna Convention (Cannizzaro ed.), 2011, p. 197, para. 3, C.J. Borgen in: The Oxford Guide to Treaties (Hollis ed.), 2012, para. 2, and P. Niemelä, 2017, p. 27.

435. This conflict rule is codified in Article 30 VCLT 1969 and is generally recognised by legal scholars. *See*, to that effect, I. Sinclair, 1984, pp. 10-21, A.C.G.A.C. de Graaf, 2004, p. 239, C.J. Borgen, 2005, p. 603, Fragmentation Report, A/CN.4/L.682, p. 129, para. 252, E. Vranes, European Journal of International Law 2006/2, p. 396 (established conflict principle), M.E. Villiger, 2009, p. 410, para. 21, P. Merkouris, 2010, p. 131 (either customary international law or as general principle), P. Niemelä, 2017, p. 27 (conflict rule of general international law), O. Dörr & K. Schmalenbach, 2018, pp. 542-543, para. 9, and H.M. Pit, 2017, p. 6.5.4.2.

436. The *lex specialis* conflict rule is 'widely accepted' by legal scholars according to Fragmentation Report, A/CN.4/L.682, p. 34, para. 56. *See*, in support of this position, I. Sinclair, 1984, p. 96 ('widely supported in doctrine'), E. Vranes, European Journal of International Law 2006/2, p. 396 (established conflict principle), P. Merkouris, 2010, p. 131 (either customary international law or as general principle), J. Finke in: Research Handbook on the Law of Treaties (Tams, Tzanakopoulos & Zimmermann eds), 2014, p. 422 ('scholars and tribunals have referred to and applied it regularly over the course of a century in the context of conflicts between treaties'), P. Niemelä, 2017, p. 27 (conflict rule of general international law), and D.M. Broekhuijsen, 2018, p. 174 ('widely supported in doctrine as relevant to treaty conflict'). An example wherein a tribunal recognised the *lex specialis* conflict rule is ICSID, Case No. ARB/15/50 (*Eskosol S.p.a. v. Italian Republic*), para. 142 wherein it was ruled that the *lex specialis* conflict rule is '*widely accepted*' in public international law and has an '*independent role to play*' as a conflict rule.

*See*, regarding this list of conflict rules under public international law, H.M. Pit, 2017, p. 6.5.4.2 and M. Prost in: The Oxford Handbook of the Sources of International Law (Besson & d'Aspremont eds), 2018, para. II. M.E. Villiger, 2009, pp. 399-400, para. 1 also refers to the *lex prior in tempore, potior in jure* conflict rule, while acknowledging that this *lex prior* rule is unlikely to 'attract the required general State practice' to reflect customary international law. P. Niemelä, 2017, p. 27 also refers to these three conflict rules, as well as to the *lex prior* rule as conflict rules of international law.

For these purposes, the *lex specialis derogat generali* rule is understood as also including the *lex posterior non derogat legi priori speciali* rule: a later general norm does not prevail over

In this section 6.4, the effect of the Directives on the application of tax treaties under the *lex posterior derogat de lege priori* rule, as codified in Article 30 VCLT 1969 (section 6.4.2), and the *lex specialis derogat generali* rule (section 6.4.3), will be discussed. The rationale for focusing on these two conflict rules is that they are generally accepted as conflict rules that may be resorted to under public international law (in the absence of conflict clauses).[437, 438]

This is different from the other two conflict rules. First, the *lex superior derogat legi inferiori* rule, although widely recognised, would only be relevant if there would be a hierarchy under public international law between the Directives (or the EU Treaties) and tax treaties. This is, however, not the case. Tax treaties, the EU Treaties, and the Directives, as decisions of the European Union as an international organisation, are of equal rank under public international law.[439] Consequently, the *lex superior* conflict

an earlier specific norm. This conflict rule is, for example, mentioned by N. Kontou, 1994, p. 20 who notes that 'opinions differ as to whether a prior but special treaty will prevail over a new but more general custom. It is sometimes said that the treaty will always prevail by virtue of the principles lex posterior generalis non derogat legi priori speciali'. Similarly, within the context of conflicts between treaties and customary law, Moreover, J. Wouters, C. Ryngaert, T. Ruys & G. de Baere, 2019, p. 168 note that 'a later general rule does not prevail over a specific earlier rule: lex posterior generalis non derogat legi priori speciali. For example, a specific bilateral treaty will not be changed by later general custom'. Based on p. 170, however, these authors seem to consider the *lex posterior generalis non derogat legi priori speciali* as more generally functioning as an exception to the *lex posterior* rule. Reference can furthermore be made to M.E. Villiger, 2009, p. 400, para. 1 who refers to the rule *lex specialis derogat legi generali* having been developed by authors into *lex posterior generalis non derogat legi priori speciali*.

437. *See*, regarding the residual nature of these conflict rules, H. van Asselt, New York University Journal of International Law and Politics 2012/4, p. 1250 and C.J. Borgen in: The Oxford Guide to Treaties (Hollis ed.), 2012, para. 24. Regarding the position that the *lex posterior* and *lex specialis* conflict rules apply in the event of a conflict between sources of public international law, *see* L. Hinnekens, EC Tax Review 1994/4, p. 160, Pauwelyn, 2003, W. Czaplinski & G.M. Danilenko, Netherlands Yearbook of International Law 2009, p. 42, P. Merkouris, 2010, p. 133, and D.M. Broekhuijsen, 2018, p. 173.

438. The *lex posterior* rule can be resorted to because it has been codified in Article 30 VCLT 1969, thereby resembling customary international law (O. Dörr & K. Schmalenbach, 2018, pp. 542-543, para. 9 who note that the *lex posterior* rule is among the 'well established principles of customary international law'. Furthermore, M.E. Villiger, 2009, p. 410, para. 21 refers to the *lex posterior* rule certainly predating the VCLT 1969. Also, I. Sinclair, 1984, pp. 10-21 considers Article 30 VCLT 1969 as a codification of customary international law, which would thus include the *lex posterior* rule. Regarding the codification of the *lex posterior* rule, reference can furthermore be made to C.J. Borgen, 2005, p. 603 and Fragmentation Report, A/CN.4/L.682, p. 129, para. 252. *See also* A.C.G.A.C. de Graaf, 2004, p. 239 and H.M. Pit, 2017, p. 6.5.4.2), whereas the *lex specialis* rule, notwithstanding its non-codification, has been widely recognised as a conflict-resolution rule under public international law (authors recognising both the *lex posterior* and *lex specialis* as conflict rules in public international law include L. Hinnekens, EC Tax Review 1994/4, p. 160 (referring to both rules as 'international legal principles'), M.E. Villiger, 2009, p. 209, para. 19, P. Merkouris, 2010, p. 131 ('considered by all as either customary international law or as general principles'), H. van Asselt, New York University Journal of International Law and Politics 2012/4, p. 1250 (referring to both rules as 'conflict resolution rules'), D.M. Broekhuijsen, 2018, p. 173 ('conflict rules')). As such, there seems sufficient support for resorting to these two conflict rules.

439. The absence of a hierarchical relationship, under public international law, between EU law and treaties has been consistently recognised by ICSID tribunals. *See*, to this effect, ICSID 25 November 2015, Case No. ARB/07/19 (*Electrabel v. Hungary*), para. 4.126 ('in the Tribunal's view, there is no fundamental difference in nature between international law and EU law that could justify treating EU law, unlike other international rules, differently in an international

rule is not relevant with respect to the resolution of conflicts between tax treaties and the EU Treaties or the Directives under public international law. Moreover, the *lex prior in tempore, potior in jure* will, to some extent, be discussed within the context of the codified *lex posterior* rule of Article 30(4) VCLT 1969. It is not, however, discussed separately. This is due to this conflict rule mainly being relevant within the context of conflicts between sources of public international law with respect to which the parties are not identical.[440] Such conflicts are covered by Article 30(4) VCLT 1969. If, however, the parties are identical, the *lex posterior* and *lex specialis* conflict rules should be applied instead of the *lex prior* rule.[441] For that reason, the *lex prior* rule is thus not separately discussed.

arbitration requiring the application of relevant rules and principles of international law'), ICSID, Case No. ARB/13/30 (*RREEF*), para. 87 ('EU law does not and cannot "trump" public international law'), ICSID, Case No. ARB/12/12 (*Vattenfall*), para. 131 ('Respondent identifies no principle of public international law, or even EU law, which would permit the Tribunal to interpret the words of the ECT, being its foundational jurisdictional instrument, so as to give priority to external treaties (the TFEU and TEU), and a court judgment interpreting those treaties'), and ICSID, Case No. ARB/15/50 (*Eskosol S.p.a. v. Italian Republic*), para. 186 ('The Tribunal is required to operate in the international legal framework of the ECT and the ICSID Convention, outside the EU and the dictates of EU law.').

It is, however, acknowledged, that the SCC Arbitration V (2016/135) (*Jurisdictional Award Green Power Partners*), para. 469 ruled that the 'primacy of EU law in the relations between EU Member States, such as Denmark and Spain, is not a matter of lex specialis or of lex posterior, but one of lex superior'. This ruling of the Arbitration Institute of the Stockholm Chamber of Commerce regarding the superiority of EU law has, however, been criticised. N. Lavranos, 2022, Thomson Reuters. Practical Law. Arbitration Blog, for example, notes that it is 'questionable whether from the perspective of public international law, which ought to be the perspective of an international arbitral tribunal established on the basis of an international treaty (such as the ECT), a legal hierarchy between the ECT and EU treaties actually exists', while adding that the reasoning of tribunal is 'kind of circular ... since it presupposes that EU law is lex superior as regards the ECT in the first place, which is very questionable'. The *lex superior* qualification of EU law is further criticised by D. Müller, 2022, Jus Mundi who notes that 'there is no (partial) international law in which the EU treaties enjoy primacy over all other rules of international law'. Bearing in mind this criticism, as well as the consistent line of case law of the ICSID tribunals, the finding of the SCC that EU law would be a *lex superior* vis-à-vis the ECT, a treaty, cannot, at present, be taken to indicate that such law must be considered as a *lex superior* that would trump all treaties concluded between the Member States in the event of a conflict.

440. This principle is recognised by J. Pauwelyn, 2003, p. 424, M.E. Villiger, 2009, pp. 399-400, para. 1, and C.J. Borgen in: The Oxford Guide to Treaties (Hollis ed.), 2012, para. 2. Pauwelyn refers to this principle within the context of 'the earlier AB norm prevail[s] over the later conflicting AC norm (lex prior principle or prior in tempore potior in jus)'). Moreover, Villiger writes that the principle of *lex prior in tempore, potior in jure* is among the principles serving to resolve conflicts between successive treaties. According to him, the lex prior principle is aimed 'in particular at conflicting treaties with diverging membership'. Finally, Borgen considers the *lex priori* principle 'most likely to be used when there is no commonality between the two treaties (eg AB:AC) or where there may be partial commonality overall (eg ABCD:ABEF) but no commonality among the specific counterparties to the conflict (eg comparing A's obligations to C or D to its obligations to E or F)'.

441. *See*, in particular, C.J. Borgen in: The Oxford Guide to Treaties (Hollis ed.), 2012, para. 4 who notes that, regarding the relation of the *lex prior* and *lex posterior* and *lex specialis* rules that such latter rules should most likely apply in the event of states that are parties to both treaties, whereas the *lex prior* would then be applicable with respect to conflicts where there is no unity of the parties.

### 6.4.2 The *Lex Posterior* Rule

As set out in section 6.4.1, the *lex posterior* rule, as codified in Article 30 VCLT 1969, is one of the main conflict rules of public international law.[442] Pursuant to this codified conflict rule, a later treaty would take priority over an earlier treaty in the event of a conflict. The rationale underlying this precedence of the later treaty is that such treaty must be presumed to reflect the latest, and thereby present, (legislative) intent of the parties with respect to a given situation. Such latest (legislative) intent should then prevail over earlier (legislative) intent between the same parties.[443] In codified form, the *lex posterior* rule reads as follows:

> Article 30
>
> Application of successive treaties relating to the same subject matter
> 1. Subject to Article 103 of the Charter of the United Nations, the rights and obligations of States Parties to successive treaties relating to the same subject matter shall be determined in accordance with the following paragraphs.
> 2. When a treaty specifies that it is subject to, or that it is not to be considered as incompatible with, an earlier or later treaty, the provisions of that other treaty prevail.
> 3. When all the parties to the earlier treaty are parties also to the later treaty but the earlier treaty is not terminated or suspended in operation under article 59, the earlier treaty applies only to the extent that its provisions are compatible with those of the later treaty.
> 4. When the parties to the later treaty do not include all the parties to the earlier one:
>    (a) as between States Parties to both treaties the same rule applies as in paragraph 3;
>    (b) as between a State party to both treaties and a State party to only one of the treaties, the treaty to which both States are parties governs their mutual rights and obligations.
> 5. Paragraph 4 is without prejudice to article 41, or to any question of the termination or suspension of the operation of a treaty under article 60 or to any question of responsibility which may arise for a State from the conclusion or application of a treaty the provisions of which are incompatible with its obligations towards another State under another treaty.

---

442. It can be recharacterised as customary international law (I. Sinclair, 1984, pp. 10-21, M.E. Villiger, 2009, p. 410, para. 21, and O. Dörr & K. Schmalenbach, 2018, pp. 542-543, para. 9) and as a general principle of international law (*see* L. Hinnekens, EC Tax Review 1994/4, p. 160 (referring to both rules as 'international legal principles'). *See also* P. Merkouris, 2010, p. 131 who considers this a way of classifying the *lex posterior* rule).
443. ILC, A/CONF.39/C.1/SR.91253, para. 39 where Expert Consultant Sir Humphrey Waldock confirmed that the '[t]he notion behind it was that, when the second treaty was adopted, there was a new legislative intention; that intention, as expressed in the later instrument, should therefore be taken as intended to prevail over the intention expressed in the earlier instrument'. *See also* J. Pauwelyn, 2003, p. 368 who notes that - in the event of identical parties - the idea of legislative intent may make sense.

This provision, given the absence of a codification of other conflict rules, is the central provision of the VCLT 1969 for resolving conflicts between treaties.[444] It has even been described as the rule of first resort for the purposes of resolving conflicts under public international law.[445] As such, it seems relevant to determine the effect that the Directives may have on the application of tax treaties under Article 30 VCLT 1969 before resorting to the *lex specialis* conflict rule.

Below, the provisions of Article 30 VCLT 1969 are discussed in detail with a view to determining the extent to which the *lex posterior* rule of this provision may result in the Directives affecting the application of tax treaties concluded by the Member States. In answering this question, the scope and applicability of Article 30 VCLT 1969 are discussed first (section 6.4.2.1). Based on the assumption that conflicts between (the obligation to give effect to) the Directives and tax treaties fall within such scope,[446] the consequences of applying the *lex posterior* conflict rule of Article 30 VCLT 1969 to such conflicts are set out (sections 6.4.2.2). The answer to the question regarding the effect of the Directives on the application of tax treaties under Article 30 VCLT 1969 is provided in section 6.4.2.4.

#### *6.4.2.1 Scope and Applicability of the Codified* **Lex Posterior** *Rule (Article 30(1) VCLT 1969)*

Article 30(1) VCLT 1969 provides that the conflict rules of Article 30 VCLT 1969, laid down in paragraphs 2 through 5 of that provision, shall only apply if it is established

444. N. Matz-Lück in: The Max Planck Encyclopedias of International Law (Wolfrum ed.), 2010, para. 11. *See also* J. Finke in: Research Handbook on the Law of Treaties (Tams, Tzanakopoulos & Zimmermann eds), 2014, p. 421 who notes that the 'most prominent provision dealing with the relationship of conflicting treaties or obligations is Article 30 VCLT'. Reference may also be made to C.J. Borgen in: The Oxford Guide to Treaties (Hollis ed.), 2012, para. C noting that 'article 30 contains the main treaty conflict rules, but Article 26 (pacta sunt servanda), 31 (Interpretation), and 41 (inter se agreements) are also useful in addressing normative conflicts'. *See also* ILC, Fragmentation Report (2006), No. 10 (A/61/10)118, para. 226 where it is noted that '[t]he question of conflicts between earlier and later treaties is today covered by articles 30 and 41 VCLT'. Article 41 is discussed, within the context of addressing the application of Article 30 VCLT 1969.

445. J. Pauwelyn, 2003, p. 409. Legal scholars have also submitted that Article 30 VCLT 1969 applies to, and could resolve, conflicts between a Directive and a tax treaties (*see* O.C.R. Marres in: The KPMG Guide to the CCCTB 2012, p. 16, D.S. Smit in: European Tax Law (Wattel, Marres & Vermeulen eds), 2018, p. 490, footnote 19, I.M. de Groot, Intertax 2019/8 & 9, p. 782, and I. Panzeri, European Taxation 2021/4, pp. 148-149).

446. Such hypothesis is based on the submissions of various legal scholars. It has, for example, been submitted that a conflict between a directive and a tax treaty may be regarded 'as a treaty conflict, since [a directive] is binding on the Member States on the basis of the TFEU and is therefore inextricably linked to the TFEU' (O.C.R. Marres in: The KPMG Guide to the CCCTB 2012, p. 16) and that, as such, Article 30 VCLT 1969 'comes into play' (O.C.R. Marres in: The KPMG Guide to the CCCTB 2012, p. 16. *See also* I.M. de Groot, Intertax 2019/8 & 9, p. 782 and I. Panzeri, European Taxation 2021/4, pp. 148-149). As regards the application of the *lex posterior* rule, it has furthermore been submitted that one should look at the dates of – adoption (O.C.R. Marres in: The KPMG Guide to the CCCTB 2012, p. 16) or entry into force (I.M. de Groot, Intertax 2019/8 & 9, p. 782) of – a directive, on the one hand, and the date of conclusion of a tax treaty on the other (*see* I. Panzeri, European Taxation 2021/4, p. 149 who does not express a preference for adoption or entry into force).

that there are (i) two treaties (section 6.4.2.1.1) (ii) that are successive (section 6.4.2.1.2) and (iii) relating to the same subject-matter (section 6.4.2.1.3).[447]

### *6.4.2.1.1 The Requirement of Two 'Treaties'*

It follows from the wording of Article 30 VCLT 1969 that its application is limited to successive *treaties* only. Therefore, the (codified) *lex posterior* rule only applies in the event that there are two treaties within the meaning of Article 2(1)(a) VCLT 1969.[448] *Given that the Directives are not regarded as 'treaties' within the meaning of the VCLT 1969*,[449] the *lex posterior* conflict rule of Article 30 VCLT 1969 is not applicable to conflicts between Directives and tax treaties.[450] As such, the qualification of the Directives as decisions of an international organisation entails that they cannot affect the application of tax treaties under Article 30 VCLT 1969.[451]

Whereas the Directives cannot affect the application of tax treaties under the *lex posterior* rule of Article 30 VCLT 1969, it should be recalled that the duty to achieve the result of the Directives is laid down in Article 288 TFEU. The TFEU, contrary to the Directives, is a treaty within the meaning of Article 2(1)(a) VCLT 1969. As such, the condition of two treaties under Article 30 VCLT 1969 would be met if a conflict between a Directive and a tax treaty is regarded as a conflict between Article 288 TFEU and a tax treaty.[452]

---

447. It is noted that reference is also made to Article 103 UN Charter. Article 103 UN Charter provides that '[i]n the event of a conflict between the obligations of the Member States of the United Nations under the present Charter and their obligations under any other international agreement, their obligations under the present Charter shall prevail'. The present thesis concerns the (directives adopted on the basis of the) EU Treaties and tax treaties and, as such, not the UN Charter. For that reason, the reference to Article 103 UN Charter is not further discussed.

448. It is noted that the reference to '*treaties*' is very general, and that no distinction is drawn between bilateral or multilateral treaties, nor is a distinction drawn based on the content or nature of treaties. *See* in this respect M. Villiger, 2009, p. 409, para. 20 and O. Dörr & K. Schmalenbach, 2018, p. 543, para. 10. Moreover, it follows from Article 2(1) that, for the purposes of the VCLT 1969, the term 'treaty' means a treaty as defined in Article 2(1)(a) VCLT 1969.

449. *See* Chapter 2, as well as L. de Broe in: Building Global International Tax Law: Essays in Honour of Guglielmo Maisto (Pistone ed.), 2022, para. 23.4.3 (to whom reference is made in Chapter 2).

450. *See* J. Pauwelyn, 2003, p. 384 who notes that Article 30 VCLT 1969 only applies to 'treaty norms'.

451. This would be contrary to the earlier submissions of legal scholars who have asserted that such a conflict does fall within the scope of Article 30 VCLT 1969. *See*, to that effect, O.C.R. Marres in: The KPMG Guide to the CCCTB 2012, p. 16, I.M. de Groot, Intertax 2019/8 & 9, p. 782, and I. Panzeri, European Taxation 2021/4, pp. 148-149.

452. *See* O. Dörr & K. Schmalenbach, 2018, p. 543, para. 10, who note that the rules laid in Article 30 VCLT 1969 also apply to charters of international organisations and that this 'is valid even for the TFEU'. Reference can also be made to J. Klabbers, 2008, p. 195 who recognises such possibility as he notes that under 'the classic international organisations model, EC instruments are indeed best regarded as emanations from the original EC Treaty: a regulation gives rise to obligations under the EC Treaty, albeit in an indirect manner. Those obligations derive, ultimately, from the effect the EC Treaty attaches to Regulations, and thus, one could plausibly argue, they are extensions of the EC Treaty. Without the EC Treaty, there would be no regulations; without the EC Treaty, regulations would be devoid of any legal effect'.

### *6.4.2.1.2 The Requirement of 'Successive' Treaties*

Based on the wording of Article 30(1) VCLT 1969, its provisions containing the conflict rule only apply when there would be two 'successive' treaties. As such, it would have to be established that there is an earlier and a later, successive, treaty.[453] Within the context of a conflict between a Directive and a tax treaty, the relevant treaties, bearing in mind the conclusions of section 6.4.2.1.1, would be the EU treaty containing Article 288 TFEU and a tax treaty.

With respect to determining the order of such treaties, there is consensus among legal scholars that the date of conclusion of the treaties is decisive.[454] The starting point in that respect is that a treaty is 'concluded' once both states have expressed their intention to be bound by such treaty. The rationale for adhering to the date of conclusion - and not, for example, the date of entry into force - is that the conclusion of a (new) treaty marks the expression of (new) legislative intent by states,[455] whereas the application of the *lex posterior* rule of Article 30 VCLT 1969 is based on the idea that later legislative intent should prevail over earlier legislative intent.[456] In order to determine whether the tax treaty is successive to the TFEU or vice versa, it should thus be determined when such treaties have been concluded.

#### i Article 288 TFEU and Bilateral Tax Treaties as 'Successive' Treaties

Determining the order of conclusion of the treaty containing Article 288 TFEU and a bilateral tax treaty is relatively straightforward. This is because this can be established by comparing the date that such a tax treaty was signed with the date upon which an

453. *See* O. Dörr & K. Schmalenbach, 2018, p. 543, para. 11.
454. I. Sinclair, 1984, p. 98, J.B. Mus, Netherlands International Law Review 1998/2, pp. 221-222, M.E. Villiger, 2009, p. 402, para. 5 and O. Dörr & K. Schmalenbach, 2018, pp. 543-544, para. 11. *See also* C.J. Borgen, 2005, p. 602, and C.J. Borgen in: The Oxford Guide to Treaties (Hollis ed.), 2012, para. III.C writes that 'States now generally agree that determining the timing of the earlier treaty's conclusion is based on the date of adoption, not entry into force.' There are, however, also authors who take the position that the entry into force of a treaty should be decisive. *See*, in this respect, E.W. Vierdag, British Yearbook of International Law 1989, p. 96 and W. Czaplinski & G.M. Danilenko, Netherlands Yearbook of International Law 2009, p. 19. This seems, however, to reflect only a minority opinion. *See*, to that effect, Fragmentation Report, A/CN.4/L.682, p. 120, para. 232 where it is noted that 'Many authors, including the expert-consultant at the Vienna Conference, Humphrey Waldock, argue that the critical date for the determination of the time-point (earlier/subsequent) is that of the date of the adoption of a the treaty and not, for example, its ratification or entry into force, at least unless nothing else appears from the context. A minority opinion supports the date of the entry into force or drawing this from the intention of the parties.'
455. J. Pauwelyn, 2003, p. 371. The date of this expression can generally be found at the end of a treaty where it is mentioned when the treaty has been 'done'.
456. ILC, A/CONF.39/C.1/SR.91253, para. 39 where Expert Consultant Sir Humphrey Waldock confirmed that the '[t]he notion behind it was that, when the second treaty was adopted, there was a new legislative intention; that intention, as expressed in the later instrument, should therefore be taken as intended to prevail over the intention expressed in the earlier instrument'. *See also* J. Pauwelyn, 2003, p. 368 who notes that - in the event of identical parties - the idea of legislative intent may make sense.

accession treaty or the Treaty of Rome, containing the obligation to achieve the result of a Directive in Article 189, was signed.[457]

Based on such dates of conclusion, if follows from the analysis set out in Annex 1 that the obligation to achieve the result of a Directive would be part of a 'later' treaty as compared to 413 Extra-EU Treaties (27.4 % of all Extra-EU Treaties) and 233 Intra-EU Treaties (68.1 % of all Intra-EU Treaties).[458]

Whereas it might seem that the conclusion of, or accession to, the Treaty of Rome should be decisive for the purposes of Article 30 VCLT 1969, it should be borne in mind that the VLCT 1969 focuses on treaties as instruments instead of obligations.[459] This focus on treaties as instruments entails that the date of conclusion of the treaty, i.e., the instrument, containing the obligation to achieve the result of a Directive is decisive and not whether such obligation existed prior to the conclusion of such treaty. Hence, it is not decisive for the purposes of determining the 'successive' treaty within the context of Article 30 VCLT 1969 that the obligation to achieve the result of a Directive was included in the Treaty of Rome as signed on 25 March 1957. Instead, it is decisive in which treaty, i.e., instrument, such obligation is laid down at present. The focus on treaties as instruments instead of obligations thus entails that the date of conclusion of the Treaty of Maastricht is decisive for the purposes of Article 31 VCLT 1969 because such treaty replaced Article 189 Treaty of Rome, laying down the obligation to achieve the result of a directive.[460] The circumstance that the obligation, within the context of directives, has not materially changed, would then seem of no relevance given the focus of the VCLT 1969 on treaties as instruments irrespective of their obligations.

457. This is easy for Extra-EU Treaties, as well as those Intra-EU Treaties that have been concluded at a time when (i) both contracting states had not yet acceded to the EU (in that case the tax treaty will, in any event, be 'earlier' as compared to (the accession to) the Treaty of Rome) and (ii) when both contracting states had acceded to the EU (in that case, the tax treaty will, in any event, be 'later' as compared to (the accession to) the Treaty of Rome). It may, however, be more difficult for treaties concluded at a time when one of the two contracting states was a Member State and the other not (yet). Under the 'convergence of state consent approach', when faced with a multilateral treaty that has different dates for the states concerned, such as may be the case with respect to the Treaty of Rome, the date upon which both parties' consent to be bound by such multilateral treaty can be established would be decisive (*see* J. Pauwelyn, 2003, p. 374). Such approach entails that, for example, the tax treaty between the Netherlands and Croatia, signed on 23 May 2000, is to be regarded as 'earlier' compared to the TFEU because one of the contracting states, i.e., Croatia, signed its accession treaty after the conclusion of such tax treaty (i.e., on 9 December 2011) and notwithstanding the circumstance that such treaty would be 'later' for the Netherlands as compared to its accession to the EU by means of the signing of the Treaty of Rome. *See*, in general, regarding the difficulties that may arise when states accede to a multilateral treaty, such as, for example, the EU Treaties, at different times: J. Pauwelyn, 2003, p. 371.

458. Annex 1, para. 3.2.

459. *See*, to this effect, S. Rosenne, 1985, pp. 3-4, J. Pauwelyn, 2003, p. 368, and J. Klabbers in: The Law of Treaties Beyond the Vienna Convention (Cannizzaro ed.), 2011, p. 196.

460. *See* (60) Treaty of Maastricht ('Article 189 shall be replaced by the following:'). It is acknowledged that the wording of Article 189 Treaty of Maastricht, to the extent it relates to directives, is identical to that of Article 189 Treaty of Rome. This is, however, not relevant for the purposes of Article 30 VCLT 1969 because this provision considers the date of conclusion of the treaty – as an instrument – decisive (and not the date of the treaty obligation). As such, 'reconclusion' of a treaty (provision) results in a change of the date of conclusion for the purposes of Article 30 VCLT 1969 even if the relevant obligation has not been amended at all.

Hence, the 'reconclusion' of Article 288 TFEU by replacing Article 189 Treaty of Rome entails that the date of the conclusion of, or accession to, the Treaty of Maastricht would be decisive for the purposes of Article 30 VCLT 1969.

For the purposes of Article 30 VCLT 1969, a conflict between the obligation to achieve the result of a Directive (laid down, at present, in Article 288 TFEU) and a tax treaty is to be regarded as a conflict between the Treaty of Maastricht and a tax treaty.[461] As such, reference should be made to the date of conclusion of the Treaty of Maastricht, or the conclusion of a later accession treaty, in determining whether Article 288 TFEU is 'successive' or 'later' as compared to the date of conclusion of a tax treaty.

Following this instrument-based approach, it follows from the analysis set out In Annex 1 that the obligation to achieve the result of a Directive would be part of a 'later' treaty as compared to 626 Extra-EU Treaties (41.5% of all Extra-EU Treaties) and 251 Intra-EU Treaties (73.4% of all Intra-EU Treaties).[462] As such, the instrument-based approach underlying the VCLT 1969 entails that the obligation to achieve the result of a Directive would be 'later' vis-à-vis an additional 213 Extra-EU Treaties and 18 Intra-EU Treaties (as compared to an obligation-based approach that would consider the conclusion of, or accession to, the Treaty of Rome as decisive).

### ii Article 288 TFEU and the MLI as 'Successive' Treaties

While it may seem easy to determine whether the conclusion of the treaty containing Article 288 TFEU is 'later' as compared to a bilateral tax treaty, this may be more difficult with respect to determining whether Article 288 TFEU would be successive to a multilateral treaty that is open to signature, such as the MLI.[463] This can be demonstrated by the following example provided by Pauwelyn:

> Take the example of the WTO treaty (1994) in conflict with the Cartagena Biosafety Protocol (1999). States A and B are original WTO members which adopted the Protocol in 1999. State C acceded to the WTO in 2000 after it had adopted the Protocol in 1999. State D acceded to the WTO in 2001 and subsequently adopted the Protocol.[464]

In this example, between states A and B, the Cartagena Biosafety Protocol (1999) would be the later treaty as compared to the WTO treaty (1994). Between states A and B, on the one hand, and state C on the other, the WTO treaty (to which state C acceded

461. It is acknowledged in this context that Article 189 Treaty of Maastricht has been renumbered into Article 249 by means of the Treaty of Amsterdam (97/C 340/01) and subsequently into Article 288 by means of the Treaty of Lisbon (2007/C 306/01). In addition, paras 1 and 4 have also been amended by the Treaty of Lisbon (2007/C 306/01). Such amendments are, however, not relevant for present purposes because the 'treaty' conflict between the Directives and tax treaties relates to para. 3 of Article 288 TFEU.
462. Annex 1, para. 3.3. The same approach can also be applied to Extra-EU Treaties. *See* in this respect See tab: 'Annex 1 | Directives', cell: 'D46' in the excel file that can be accessed via https://doi.org/10.17026/dans-zku-ckqy. Article 288 TFEU would be 'later' as compared to 626 Extra-EU Treaties (+213).
463. J. Pauwelyn, 2003, p. 375.
464. J. Pauwelyn, 2003, p. 375.

in 2000) would be later as compared to the Cartagena Biosafety Protocol (which state C adopted in 1999). Finally, between states A, B, and C, on the one hand, and state D, on the other, the Cartagena Biosafety Protocol (adopted by state D after accession to the WTO treaty in 2001) would again be the later treaty.[465] It follows that the original date of conclusion of the WTO treaty (in 1994) and the Cartagena Biosafety Protocol (in 2001) would not be decisive. Instead, the order of accession to both treaties would be decisive.[466]

Applied to the case of Article 288 TFEU and the MLI, such issues do not (yet) arise. This is due to the circumstance that all Member States had acceded to the EU before the conclusion of the MLI, while Article 288 TFEU has also not been amended since the conclusion of the MLI. As such, for all Member States, the MLI is 'later' as compared to Article 288 TFEU.[467] If, however, signatories to the MLI would subsequently accede to the EU in the future, the MLI would seem 'earlier' as compared to their accession to (Article 288 of) the TFEU. In such case, the MLI would be 'later' between the current 27 Member States and 'earlier' in the relations between such Member States and the future Member State(s).

The situation wherein the MLI would be 'later' for the current 27 Member States and 'earlier' for future Member States could arise as soon as one of the following so-called candidate countries would accede to the EU:[468] Albania, North Macedonia, Serbia, Turkey or Ukraine. Each of these candidate countries has already signed the MLI.[469] As such, if one of these candidate countries would accede to the EU and become a Member State, the MLI would be 'earlier' as compared to such countries' conclusion of an agreement binding it to EU law.

With respect to such situations wherein one multilateral treaty compared to another multilateral treaty is 'later' for some of the parties and 'earlier' for the other parties, it becomes impossible to determine which treaty is 'earlier' or 'later'. Instead, this must be determined on a bilateral basis. Depending on the nature of the multilateral treaty (provision) as either 'multilateral' or 'bilateral' this may be contrary to the object and purpose of such treaty (provision). This could especially be the case with respect to 'multilateral' multilateral treaties if the result of the *lex posterior* rule of Article 30 VCLT 1969 would be that between some of the parties a multilateral treaty would no longer be applicable, whereas it would continue to be applicable between

465. J. Pauwelyn, 2003, p. 375.
466. J. Pauwelyn, 2003, p. 375.
467. With respect to the number of bilateral tax treaties affected by the MLI on 14 June 2022, reference can be made to See tab: 'Annex 2 | Amendments', in the excel file that can be accessed via https://doi.org/10.17026/dans-zku-ckqy. On 14 June 2022, the MLI was '*in effect*' with respect to 743 tax treaties concluded by the Member States (representing 40.2% of the total number of tax treaties concluded by such Member States).
468. On 28 July 2022, the candidate countries were Albania, Moldova, Montenegro, North Macedonia, Serbia, Turkey and Ukraine (*see* https://european-union.europa.eu/principles-countries-history/joining-eu_en (date accessed: 28 July 2022).
469. Based on the list of signatories, as published by the OECD and with the status of 28 June 2022, Albania (28 May 2019), North Macedonia (29 January 2020), Serbia (7 June 2017), Turkey (7 June 2017) and Ukraine (23 July 2018) will have signed the MLI before they would have acceded to the EU (*see* https://www.oecd.org/ctp/treaties/beps-mli-signatories-and-parties.pdf (date accessed: 28 July 2022).

other parties (*see* the example of Pauwelyn above). It is with respect to 'multilateral' multilateral treaties that are both open to signature and accession that, in the event that Article 30 VCLT 1969 would result in a 'bilateralisation' of a 'multilateral' multilateral treaty, that an application of Article 30 VCLT 1969 should be rejected on the ground that it cannot be established which 'multilateral' multilateral treaty is successive.[470]

At the same time, this argument would not be so strong with respect to a 'bilateral' multilateral treaty and a 'multilateral' multilateral treaty (such as the TFEU).[471] This is because affecting the application of a 'bilateral' multilateral treaty (provision) would not affect the rights of, or obligations towards, third states. As such, to the extent that the MLI would be 'bilateralisable', which would seem to be the case for its provisions aimed at affecting covered tax treaties,[472] it should be possible to determine the dates of conclusion of both the MLI and the TFEU based on the date upon which two states would have expressed their consent to be bound by the MLI affecting their bilateral tax treaty. At present, such date is 'later' as compared to Article 288 TFEU for each of the Member States considering that the most recent accession treaty (Croatia) was signed in 2011,[473] whereas the MLI has been signed as of 7 June 2017.[474]

#### 6.4.2.1.3 *The Requirement of 'Relating to the Same Subject Matter'*

Having established that a Directive, by means of Article 288 TFEU, and a tax treaty can be regarded as two successive treaties, the final question for the purposes of the scope of Article 30 VCLT 1969 is whether such treaties can be regarded as relating to the same subject matter.

##### i The TFEU and the Tax Treaties as 'Relating to the Same Subject Matter'

With respect to answering the question of whether the TFEU and tax treaties concluded by the Member States relate to the same subject matter for the purposes of Article 30 VCLT 1969, the starting point is that the term 'same subject matter' is not defined in the

470. J. Pauwelyn, 2003, p. 378.
471. The TFEU can be regarded as a 'multilateral' multilateral treaty in light of, for example, the ruling in CJEU, 15 July 1964, Case 6/64 (*Costa v. ENEL*), p. 594 that the 'executive force of Community law cannot vary from one State to another in deference to subsequent domestic law, without jeopardizing the attainment of the objective of the Treaty set out in Article 5(2)' and that 'the law stemming from the Treaty ... could not, because of its special and original nature, be overridden by domestic legal provisions, however framed, without being deprived of its character as Community law and without the legal basis of the Community itself being called into question'.
472. *See*, to that effect, also P. Baker, Bulletin for International Taxation 2021/11 & 12, p. 602 who notes that the part of the MLI that modifies covered tax treaties reflects bilateralism triumphing over multilateralism. *See also* D.M. Broekhuijsen, FED 2018/65, para. 5, D.W. Blum, Bulletin for International Taxation 2018/3, paras 2.2 and 3.2, and W.C. Haslehner, Bulletin for International Taxation 2020/4 & 5, p. 222.
473. The 2011 Accession Treaty (Croatia) was done at 9 December 2011.
474. *See*, to this effect, https://www.oecd.org/ctp/treaties/beps-mli-signatories-and-parties.pdf (date accessed: 28 July 2022).

VCLT 1969[475] and that its meaning has been - and still seems to be - subject to debate among legal scholars.[476] The different views regarding the meaning of the reference to the 'same subject matter' within this context, which are discussed in more detail below, can be summarised as follows:

(a) The *subject-based view*: the subject of a treaty in its entirety is decisive. As such, an environmental treaty and a trade treaty, irrespective of their content or substantive overlap, cannot be regarded as relating to the same subject matter for the purposes of Article 30 VCLT 1969.[477]
(b) The *conflict-based view*: two treaties related to the same subject matter for the purposes of Article 30 VCLT 1969 if they give rise to conflicting obligations. Based on this view, an environmental treaty and a trade treaty must be regarded as relating to the same subject matter if their simultaneous application gives rise to conflicting obligations irrespective of the overlap in their general topics or the extent to which their substance may overlap.[478]
(c) The *substance-based view*: whether two treaties related to the same subject matter must be determined on the basis of the issues dealt with by such treaties on an overall basis, i.e., based on their topic or substance.[479]

### ii The Subject-Based View

Under the subject-based view, the sameness of subject matter of two treaties for the purposes of Article 30 VCLT 1969 would have to be determined based on their (informal) labels or characterisations.[480] The subject-based view thus merely takes into account the overall 'subject' of the two treaties. It is not concerned with the nature of each treaty,[481] or the extent to which two treaties might overlap in practice.[482] As such, a trade treaty and an environmental treaty would not relate to the same subject matter because they deal with different subjects.[483] Similarly, tax treaties and the TFEU would also not relate to the same subject matter for the purposes of Article 30 VCLT 1969 under this subject-based view because they deal with different subjects ('elimination of

475. *See* ICSID, Case No. ARB/15/50 (*Eskosol S.p.a. v. Italian Republic*), para. 140.
476. C.J. Borgen in: The Oxford Guide to Treaties (Hollis ed.), 2012, para. Conclusion.
477. *See* J. Finke in: Research Handbook on the Law of Treaties (Tams, Tzanakopoulos & Zimmermann eds), 2014, p. 428. ('[E]ven though the term "subject matter" is not defined, its general usage implies that the treaties in question must address the same substantive area such as environmental law, trade law, and the like.')
478. This view is adopted by a number of legal scholars. *See* E.W. Vierdag, British Yearbook of International Law 1989, p. 100, as well as J. Pauwelyn, 2003, p. 367, C.J. Borgen in: The Oxford Guide to Treaties (Hollis ed.), 2012, para. Conclusion, A. Orakhelashvili in: The Vienna Conventions on the Law of Treaties (Corten & Klein eds), 2011, para. 30, and O. Dörr & K. Schmalenbach, 2018, pp. 544-545.
479. *See, e.g.*, PCA Case No. 2010-17 (*EURAM*), paras 169-170.
480. *See* J. Finke in: Research Handbook on the Law of Treaties (Tams, Tzanakopoulos & Zimmermann eds), 2014, p. 428.
481. Fragmentation Report, A/CN.4/L.682, p. 130, para. 254.
482. *See* C.J. Borgen in: The Oxford Guide to Treaties (Hollis ed.), 2012, para. Conclusion.
483. Fragmentation Report, A/CN.4/L.682, p.17, para. 21, as well as C.J. Borgen, 2005, pp. 603-604.

double taxation with respect to taxes on income and on capital and the prevention of tax evasion and avoidance'[484] versus 'the functioning of the European Union'[485]).

While the subject-based view seems to give effect to the understanding that the term 'same subject matter' 'should not be held to cover cases where a general treaty impinged indirectly on the content of a particular provision of an earlier treaty',[486] it has been rejected by the ILC in its Fragmentation Report (2006).[487] The reason for rejecting this view is that the 'characterizations ("trade law", "environmental law") have no normative value per se'.[488] Such characterisations merely 'describe the instruments from the perspective of different interests or different policy objectives' and have 'less to do with the 'nature' of the instrument than the interest from which it is described'.[489] As such, following a subject-based view, whether two treaties are relate to the same subject matter depends on how one classifies the subjects of the two treaties (without there being rules on how to classify such treaties).[490] According to the ILC, whether two treaties relate to the same subject matter under the subject-based view would 'be in fact dependent on argumentative success in pigeon-holing legal instruments as having to do with "trade", instead of "environment", "refugee law" instead of "human rights law", "investment law" instead of "law of development".'[491] As such, the subject-based view seems to lead to a 'reductio ad absurdum' that makes it possible for states to – for arbitrary reasons – avoid the same subject matter test to be fulfilled. They could, for example, conclude a treaty with the subject 'the law of human movement' in order to (attempt to) avoid such treaty as having the same subject matter as treaties dealing with 'refugee law'.[492] The subject-based view has, therefore, been described by the ILC as too narrow[493] and as not reflecting a reasonable interpretation of the term 'same subject matter'.[494]

### iii The Conflict-Based View

Under the second view, i.e., the 'conflict-based view', two successive treaties relate to the same subject matter as soon as their provisions give rise to conflicting obligations.[495] Pursuant to this view, the 'criterion of 'same subject-matter' seems already

484. *See* title of the OECD Model (2017).
485. *See* title of the TFEU.
486. ILC, 85th meeting, A/CONF.39/C1/SR.85222, para. 41.
487. Fragmentation Report, A/CN.4/L.682, pp. 17-18, paras 21-23. This report has been described in ICSID, Case No. ARB/15/50 (*Eskosol S.p.a. v. Italian Republic*), para. 142 as an 'important document'.
488. Fragmentation Report, A/CN.4/L.682, p. 17, para. 21.
489. Fragmentation Report, A/CN.4/L.682, p. 17, para. 21.
490. Fragmentation Report, A/CN.4/L.682, p. 18, para. 22.
491. Fragmentation Report, A/CN.4/L.682, p. 18, para. 22.
492. Fragmentation Report, A/CN.4/L.682, p. 130, para. 254.
493. Fragmentation Report, A/CN.4/L.682, p. 18, para. 22 as interpreted in ICSID, Case No. ARB/15/50 (*Eskosol S.p.a. v. Italian Republic*), para. 142.
494. Fragmentation Report, A/CN.4/L.682, p. 129, para. 253.
495. This view is adopted by a number of legal scholars. *See* E.W. Vierdag, British Yearbook of International Law 1989, p. 100, as well as J. Pauwelyn, 2003, p. 367, C.J. Borgen in: The Oxford Guide to Treaties (Hollis ed.), 2012, para. Conclusion, and A. Orakhelashvili in: The Vienna

fulfilled if two different rules or sets of rules are invoked in the same subject matter, or if, in other words, as a result of interpretation, the relevant treaties seem to point to different directions in their application by a party.'[496] With respect to the question of when two treaties may point in two different directions within the meaning of the conflict-based view, a wide notion and a stricter notion may be distinguished.

In its Fragmentation Report (2006), the ILC adopts a wide notion according to which two treaties point into different directions as soon as 'two rules or principles suggest different ways of dealing with a problem',[497] entailing that this would already be the case where a treaty would 'frustrate the goals of another treaty without there being any strict incompatibility between their provisions'.[498] Following such a wide notion of the conflict-based view, treaties would relate to the same subject matter if one treaty (i) strictly prevents the fulfilment of obligations under the other treaty or (ii) would undermine the object and purpose of such other treaty in one way or another.[499]

Legal scholars do not, however, necessarily agree with such a wide notion. Vierdag, for example, submits that two treaties point in two different directions if 'an attempted simultaneous application of two rules to one set of facts or actions leads to incompatible results'.[500] In addition, Pauwelyn argues that the requirement 'of "same subject-matter" relates rather to whether there is a genuine conflict (i.e., a material overlap) as between two specific treaty provisions in the particular circumstances of each case'.[501] Finally, reference can be made to Dörr and Schmalenbach who adopt the view that two treaties are only 'incompatible', thereby relating to the same subject matter, 'if their obligations cannot be complied with simultaneously, ie if a State Party to both treaties cannot comply with one of them without breaching the other'.[502] The main difference between the wide notion, as adopted by the ILC, and these stricter views is thus whether two treaties would also relate to the same subject matter if one treaty would undermine object and purpose of another treaty without strictly preventing the fulfilment of obligations under another treaty.

---

Conventions on the Law of Treaties (Corten & Klein eds), 2011, para. 30, and O. Dörr & K. Schmalenbach, 2018, pp. 544-545.

496. Fragmentation Report, A/CN.4/L.682, p. 18, para. 23. The ILC also addresses the question of what 'point in different direction' means. In that respect, a strict notion is distinguished from a wide notion. Under the strict notion, 'conflict exists if it is possible for a party to two treaties to comply with one rule only by thereby failing to comply with another rule'. Under a wider notion, however, treaties would also point in different directions if a 'treaty may frustrate the goals of another treaty without there being any strict incompatibility between their provisions' (*see* Fragmentation Report, A/CN.4/L.682, p. 19, para. 24).

497. Fragmentation Report, A/CN.4/L.682, p. 19, para. 25.

498. Fragmentation Report, A/CN.4/L.682, p. 19, para. 24. The wide notion can be distinguished from a strict notion according to which a 'conflict exists if it is possible for a party to two treaties to comply with one rule only by thereby failing to comply with another rule' (p. 19, para. 24).

499. Fragmentation Report, A/CN.4/L.682, p. 130, para. 254.

500. E.W. Vierdag, British Yearbook of International Law 1989, p. 100. It is acknowledged, however, that there are also scholars that adopt the wide notion. *See*, to that effect, C.J. Borgen in: The Oxford Guide to Treaties (Hollis ed.), 2012, para. C ('Conflicts between treaties').

501. J. Pauwelyn, 2003, p. 367.

502. O. Dörr & K. Schmalenbach, 2018, pp. 544-545, para. 13.

Leaving aside the disagreement regarding the scope of the conflict-based view, i.e., whether a wide or stricter notion is adopted, the basis for adopting the conflict-based view seems to be the immediate context of Article 30(1) VCLT 1969. It has, for example, been submitted that a conflict-based view follows from paragraphs (2) through (5) of Article 30 VCLT 1969. These paragraphs do not refer to the successive treaties relating to the same subject matter, but merely refer to such treaties as being 'incompatible'.[503] As such, when the term 'same subject matter' in Article 30(1) VCLT 1969 is read in light of these paragraphs (its 'context' within the meaning of Article 31(2) VCLT 1969), the ordinary meaning of such a term may be interpreted as requiring the existence of an incompatibility - or conflict - between two provisions of two successive treaties.[504] Based on such a conflict-based view of the term 'same subject matter' in Article 30 VCLT 1969, the TFEU and tax treaties concluded by the Member States would seem to relate to the same subject matter if the obligation to achieve the result of Directives would be at odds with obligations arising under tax treaties. As such, adopting the conflict-based view would entail that the TFEU and tax treaties, in the event of a conflict between their obligations, must be deemed to relate to the same subject matter for the purposes of Article 30 VCLT 1969. Whether a conflict-based view is adopted, is thus highly relevant for the purposes of the effect that the Directives, by means of Article 288 TFEU, may have on the application of tax treaties concluded by the Member States.

The case for the conflict-based view is, however, not ironclad. First, it must be acknowledged that the argument underlying the conflict-based view, i.e., paragraphs (2) through (5), has been explicitly rejected by an ICSID tribunal in *Eskosol*.[505] In *Eskosol*, the tribunal ruled that a conflict-based interpretation based on paragraphs (2) through (5) of Article 30 VCLT 1969 'would effectively require rewriting the text, to ignore a threshold provision ("the rights and obligations of State Parties to successive treaties relating to the same subject matter") which is expressly stated to be the foundational requirement for any of the following provisions of Article 30 even to apply ("shall be determined in accordance with the following paragraphs ...")'.[506] In addition, the tribunal concluded that a conflict-based view would also be incompatible with the 'comparators' in Article 30(1) and 30(3) VCLT 1969. Article 30(1) VCLT 1969 refers to whether the 'treaties' relate to the same subject matter, whereas Article 30(3) VCLT 1969 is only concerned with whether 'particular provisions' of such treaties are

503. *See* O. Dörr & K. Schmalenbach, 2018, pp. 544-545, para. 13.

504. J. Pauwelyn, 2003, p. 365. It is noted, in this respect, that this conflict-based understanding as to the meaning of 'relating to the same subject matter' is, in principle, limited to Article 30 VCLT 1969. Treaties may - outside the scope of Article 30 VCLT 1969 - be perceived as relating to the same subject matter without conflicting with each other. For example, the European Convention on Human Rights and the Charter of Fundamental Rights of the European Rights provide similar rights and, for that reason, seem to relate to the same subject matter, i.e., human rights. However, in the absence of a conflict, these treaties would not be considered to relate to the same subject matter for the purposes of Article 30 VCLT 1969. This would also not seem problematic given that Article 30 VCLT 1969 provides rules that govern situations wherein two treaties would conflict; when there would be no conflict, there is no need to apply this provision VCLT 1969. *See* for another example, J. Pauwelyn, 2003, p. 182.

505. ICSID, Case No. ARB/15/50 (*Eskosol S.p.a. v. Italian Republic*).

506. ICSID, Case No. ARB/15/50 (*Eskosol S.p.a. v. Italian Republic*), para. 136.

incompatible.[507] Taking this into account, the ICSID tribunal held that a conflict-based view would essentially entail reasoning from 'a part to a whole (i.e., that treaties necessarily relate to the same subject matter because specific provisions in different treaties might have different effects)'.[508] While it may be possible to reason from a whole to a part, the tribunal noted that this is not equally possible to reason in reverse from a part to a whole. As such, it ruled that a conflict-based view is contrary to the plain text of (the comparators set out in) Article 30 VCLT 1969.[509] Based on the arguments set out in the judgment of the ICSID in *Eskosol*, the case for adopting a conflict-based view seems less strong than might be expected.

Such case becomes even weaker if one takes into account that the *travaux préparatoires* of the VCLT 1969 regarding the meaning of the term 'same subject matter' seem to imply that its meaning should be understood more narrowly than would follow from the conflict-based view.[510] In particular, reference can be made to the following position expressed by the delegation of the United Kingdom:

> If, for example, a convention on such a specific topic as third-party liability in the field of nuclear energy contained a provision relating to the taking of legal action in the courts of one State and the giving effect to judgments in courts of another State, it could not be regarded as relating to the same subject-matter as a later treaty on the entirely different topic of the general reciprocal recognition and enforcement of judgments. The phrase in question should be construed strictly and should not be held to cover cases where a general treaty impinged indirectly on the content of a particular provision of an earlier treaty; in such question, the question involved was one of interpretation or of the application of such maxims as *generalia specialibus non derogant*.[511]

This position has subsequently been confirmed by Expert Consultant Waldock who expressed the view that the term 'same subject matter' 'should not be held to cover cases where a general treaty impinges indirectly on the content of a particular provision of an earlier treaty'.[512] As such, it can be derived from the drafting history of Article 30 VCLT 1969 that not each and every conflict between two treaties was intended to result in such treaties relating to the 'same subject matter' for the purposes of Article 30 VCLT 1969.

Finally, the case for a conflict-based view becomes even more difficult to accept when it is borne in mind that the *lex specialis* rule is also widely accepted as a conflict rule in public international law.[513] As such, there should be room for applying the *lex specialis* conflict rule. However, adopting a conflict-based view of the 'same subject matter' would seem to result in the *lex specialis* conflict rule being stripped of its

507. ICSID, Case No. ARB/15/50 (*Eskosol S.p.a. v. Italian Republic*), para. 137.
508. ICSID, Case No. ARB/15/50 (*Eskosol S.p.a. v. Italian Republic*), para. 137.
509. ICSID, Case No. ARB/15/50 (*Eskosol S.p.a. v. Italian Republic*), para. 137.
510. P. Merkouris, 2010, p. 153.
511. ILC, 85th meeting, A/CONF.39/C1/SR.85222, para. 41.
512. ILC, Summary of the plenary meetings and of the meetings of the Committee of the Whole, 9 April-22 May 1969 253, para. 41.
513. *See* section 6.4.1.

meaning and rendered ineffective.[514] The inapplicability of this also widely accepted conflict rule can be illustrated by means of the following line of reasoning. The *lex specialis* conflict rule applies when two treaty *provisions* relate to the same subject-matter and conflict with each other (it is, after all, a conflict rule).[515] If, however, a conflict-based view would be adopted of the term 'same subject matter' in Article 30 VCLT 1969, the very existence of such a conflict would entail that the treaties relate to the same subject matter within the meaning of Article 30 VCLT 1969. As a consequence, the existence of a conflict between (successive) treaties would entail that Article 30 VCLT 1969 is applicable, which would seem to leave little (to no) room for applying the *lex specialis* rule to such a conflict (or would give rise to situations wherein the *lex specialis* and *lex posterior* rules may be simultaneously applicable, which would then require determining the relationship of both conflict-solution techniques in the event of such simultaneous application).[516] As such, the existence of the *lex specialis* conflict rule also provides an argument against adopting the conflict-based view with respect to the meaning of the term 'same subject matter' in Article 30 VCLT 1969.

#### iv The Substance-Based View

Based on the preceding paragraphs, the subject-based view may be described as 'too narrow',[517] while the conflict-based view may be regarded as 'too broad'.[518] As such, it is unsurprising that tribunals have looked for another meaning of the term 'same subject matter' for the purposes of Article 30 VCLT 1969 that would be 'neither too narrow nor too broad'.[519] In *EURAM* and *A.M.F. Aircraftleasing*, for example, the PCA concluded that the 'subject matter' of a treaty 'is inherent in the treaty itself and refers to the issues with which its provisions deal, i.e., its topic or its substance'.[520] Under this 'substance-based view', two treaties do not necessarily relate to the same subject matter if they are applicable to the same facts, conflict with each other, or have the same purpose or goal.[521] Instead, it would have to be assessed based on the substance of such treaties whether they relate to the same subject matter. This view was also

514. P. Merkouris, 2010, p. 153. The *lex specialis* conflict rule is 'widely accepted' in public international law and has an 'independent role to play' as a conflict rule (*see* ICSID, Case No. ARB/15/50 (*Eskosol S.p.a. v. Italian Republic*), para. 142).
515. ICSID, Case No. ARB/15/50 (*Eskosol S.p.a. v. Italian Republic*), para. 142.
516. ICSID, Case No. ARB/15/50 (*Eskosol S.p.a. v. Italian Republic*), para. 142.
517. Fragmentation Report, A/CN.4/L.682, p. 18, para. 22 as interpreted in ICSID, Case No. ARB/15/50 (*Eskosol S.p.a. v. Italian Republic*), para. 142.
518. *See* ICSID, Case No. ARB/15/50 (*Eskosol S.p.a. v. Italian Republic*), para. 142.
519. *See*, to this effect, ICSID, Case No. ARB/15/50 (*Eskosol S.p.a. v. Italian Republic*), para. 142. *See also* PCA Case No. 2010-17 (*EURAM*), para. 168 where the PCA notes that such term must be given a '*balanced interpretation in good faith*'.
520. PCA Case No. 2010-17 (*EURAM*), para. 172 and PCA, Case No. 2017-15 (*A.M.F. Aircraftleasing v. Czech Republic*), para. 357.
521. PCA Case No. 2010-17 (*EURAM*), paras 170-172. It is, for example, mentioned by the PCA that 'a treaty on environmental protection and a treaty on trade may both apply to the same factual situation but the subject with which they deal is quite different' (para. 171) and that 'two treaties can each have the goal of enhancing the well-being of children, one providing for an international mechanism of monitoring of child labour, another in deciding that children under

adopted by an ICSID tribunal in *Eskosol* considering that such tribunal held that it 'agrees with the EURAM tribunal that the subject matter of a treaty "is inherent in the treaty itself and refers to the issues with which its provisions deal, i.e., its topic of substance".'[522]

With respect to this substance-based view that has been formulated by the PCA and ICSID, it would seem that it deals with the main criticism in respect of the subject-based view and the conflict-based view. First, it deals with the criticism with respect to a subject-based view that the nature of successive treaties would be irrelevant. Second, the substance-based view recognises that mere incidental overlap between treaties would be insufficient for concluding that the two treaties as a whole relate to the same subject matter.[523] In addition, it would also seem to leave room for the application of the *lex specialis* conflict rule. Hence, the substance-based view seems to address the arguments against adopting both the subject-based and conflict-based views with respect to the meaning of the term 'same subject matter'. For that reason, the substance-based view seems appropriate for determining whether two treaties relate to the 'same subject matter' for the purposes of Article 30 VCLT 1969.

Support for adopting this 'substance-based view' can be implicitly derived from the Fragmentation Report (2006). In this report, within the context of cross-regime treaty conflicts, i.e., treaties that would neither be linked institutionally nor be envisaged as part of the same concerted effort,[524] the ILC notes that the 'straightforward priority of one treaty over another ... on a merely chronological basis' cannot be reasonably assumed in the event of such cross-regime treaties.[525] This is because such treaties may have been concluded 'with no conscious sense that they are part of the "same project".'[526] These arguments against adopting a conflict-based approach with respect to cross-regime treaty conflicts also seem valid within the context of conflicts between the TFEU and tax treaties given that they are not institutionally linked,[527] nor

fourteen may not be married against their will. Yet no reasonable person would consider that those two treaties, although pursuing the same goal, the same overall purpose, have the same subject matter' (para. 172).

522. ICSID, Case No. ARB/15/50 (*Eskosol S.p.a. v. Italian Republic*), para. 146.
523. Such a view is in line with PCA, no. 2008-13 (*Eureko*), para. 242.
524. *See*, regarding this definition, ICSID, Case No. ARB/15/50 (*Eskosol S.p.a. v. Italian Republic*), para. 144.
525. Fragmentation Report, A/CN.4/L.682, p. 138, para. 272.
526. Fragmentation Report, A/CN.4/L.682, p. 130, para. 255.
527. The absence of such an institutional link can be derived from the case law of the CJEU pursuant to which the Member States have retained their competence, in the absence of unifying or harmonising measures for the elimination of double taxation at the level of the EU, 'for determining the criteria for taxation and capital with a view to eliminating double taxation by means, *inter alia*, of international agreements. In that context, the Member States are free to determine, in the framework of bilateral conventions for the avoidance of double taxation, the connecting factors for the purpose of allocating powers of taxation' (Case C-602/17 (*Sauvage*), para. 22). Based on the Member States having retained their competences and freedom to conclude tax treaties, the tax treaties are not to be regarded as part of the same regime as the TFEU or the Directives (*See* for a similar line of reasoning PCA Case No. 2010-17 (*EURAM*), para. 183 where the tribunal notes that it would seem difficult to argue that the EU Treaties have the same subject matter as a bilateral investment treaty if the EU has no competence to deal with the matters dealt with in such bilateral treaty.).

are they part of the same concerted effort.[528] As such, the ILC also seems to recognise that 'a more nuanced approach', as compared to the subject-based and conflict-based views, would be needed within the context of such conflicts than merely applying the *lex posterior* rule of Article 30 VCLT 1969.[529] Such more nuanced approach seems to have been subsequently formulated by the PCA and ICSID tribunals by means of the substance-based view.

Application of the 'substance-based view' as formulated by the PCA and ICSID tribunals to conflicts between the Directives, by means of Article 288 TFEU, and tax treaties entails that it would have to be assessed whether the TFEU, based on its topic and substance, can be regarded as relating to the same subject matter as such tax treaties. In determining the topic or substance of the TFEU, reference can be made to the judgments of the PCA and ICSID tribunals. In *EURAM*, for example, the PCA ruled that the EU Treaties related to accession to 'an economic community'.[530] Similarly, in *A.M.F. Aircraftleasing*, the PCA held that the 'topic or subject of the EU treaties is to promote economic integration and to create and maintain a common market among the Member States'.[531] Moreover, the ICSID tribunal in *Eskosol* concluded that the topic or substance of the EU Treaties 'was the creation of a common market between EU Member States, governed by EU law'.[532] It would seem that the common denominator of these descriptions of the topic or substance of the EU Treaties is the creation of a common market between the EU Member States.

This topic should then be compared with that of tax treaties. In determining the topic of such treaties, there do not seem to be clear-cut guidelines for what factors are decisive. Nevertheless, it can be derived from the case law of the PCA and ICSID tribunals adopting a substance-based view that the following factors are relevant: (i) what do the treaties 'create',[533] (ii) what rights and obligations do the treaties give rise

528. As regards the question of whether the Member States envisage tax treaties as part of the same concerted effort as the EU Treaties, it would seem that there are no indications that this is the case. Whereas the conclusion of tax treaties may contribute to the functioning of the internal market, in the sense that such treaties seek to avoid double taxation, they are not concluded for the purposes of contributing to the functioning of the internal market; they are, ultimately, concluded as part of an 'overall policy of each state to encourage foreign investment or to assist the State's investors to participate in overseas trade and development' (*see* P. Baker, 1996, p. 5, para. 2-01). Whereas such purpose may contribute to a better functioning of the internal market, which functioning is among the purposes of the EU Treaties, it does not necessarily entail that the two treaties must be regarded as having the same subject matter for the purposes of Article 30 VCLT 1969. Tax treaties are – ultimately – different instruments that are concluded for a purpose that is not similar to the purpose of the EU Treaties (*see* by analogy ICSID, Case No. ARB/15/50 (*Eskosol S.p.a. v. Italian Republic*), para. 144, as well as PCA Case No. 2010-17 (*EURAM*), para. 184 where the tribunal noted that '[to] accede to an economic community is simply not the same as to set up a specific investment regime for investor-State arbitration').
529. Fragmentation Report, A/CN.4/L.682, p. 138, para. 272. *See also* ICSID, Case No. ARB/15/50 (*Eskosol S.p.a. v. Italian Republic*), para. 143.
530. PCA Case No. 2010-17 (*EURAM*), para. 184.
531. *See* PCA, Case No. 2017-15 (*A.M.F. Aircraftleasing v. Czech Republic*), para. 358.
532. ICSID, Case No. ARB/15/50 (*Eskosol S.p.a. v. Italian Republic*), para. 146.
533. *See* ICSID, Case No. ARB/15/50 (*Eskosol S.p.a. v. Italian Republic*), para. 146, as well as PCA Case No. 2010-17 (*EURAM*), para. 184.

to,[534] and (iii) what is the nature of the topics dealt with by the treaties ('coincident' or not).[535] Bearing this in mind, the following can be noted with respect to tax treaties. First, tax treaties create a bilateral agreement that is aimed at facilitating 'cross-border trade and investment by eliminating the tax impediments these cross-border flows'.[536] Such aim is achieved by eliminating double taxation by restricting the rights of the contracting states to tax cross-border income on a reciprocal basis.[537] As such, regarding the second factor, tax treaties give rise to reciprocal rights and obligations.[538] Such rights and obligations aimed at eliminating double taxation in practice are laid down in the distributive provisions of tax treaties and the provision that provides for the elimination of double taxation in the residence state by means of the credit or exemption method. These provisions together then create a bilateral 'system' wherein cross-border income should not be subject to double taxation. Such system then facilitates cross-border trade and investment. In addition to being aimed at eliminating double taxation, tax treaties are also aimed, nowadays, at preventing tax evasion and avoidance, as well as (double) non-taxation.[539] Such additional purpose is, especially after the 2017 Update of the OECD Model, reflected by the preamble of the OECD Model and Article 29 OECD Model regarding the 'Entitlement to benefits'.[540] This additional purpose does not, however, detract from the (nature of the) rights and obligations to which a tax treaty may give rise given that such a treaty can still not impose a duty to tax cross-border income; it can only impose limitations to the extent to which such income may be taxed by the contracting states.[541] Finally, regarding the nature of topic dealt with, it can be noted that tax treaties deal with the taxation of cross-border income from residents of either state. As such, the topic of substance of tax treaties may be described as eliminating double taxation of cross-border income of residents of the contracting states without creating opportunities for non-taxation or reduced taxation through tax avoidance or tax evasion.

534. *See* Arbitration Institute of the Stockholm Chamber of Commerce, No. 088/2004 (*Eastern Sugar*), paras 161-165.
535. ICSID, Case No. ARB/15/50 (*Eskosol S.p.a. v. Italian Republic*), para. 146.
536. B.J. Arnold, 2019, p. 144. *See also* J. Bossuyt, 2021, para. 8.1.2.6.3, no. 779 who refers to the main purpose of tax treaties as 'to facilitate and foster international trade and investment by alleviating and diminishing various barriers for taxpayers'. Reference can furthermore be made to the preamble of the OECD Model (2017) which indicates that it is the purpose of tax treaties to give effect to the desire to further developing the economic relationship between the two contracting states and to enhance their cooperation in tax matters.
537. B.J. Arnold, 2019, p. 144. *See also* W.C. Haslehner in: Klaus Vogel on Double Taxation Conventions (Reimer & Rust eds), 2021, p. 25, para. 29 who refers to avoidance of double taxation as the '*main purpose of tax treaties*', as well as F.A. Engelen, 2004, para. 10.3 who notes that it is the 'primary purpose of a tax treaty to avoid international juridical double taxation, in order to facilitate the international exchange of goods, services, capital, technology and persons'.
538. *See*, to this effect, B.J. Arnold, 2019, p. 137.
539. *See*, to this effect, B.J. Arnold, 2019, p. 145 and also W.C. Haslehner in: Klaus Vogel on Double Taxation Conventions (Reimer & Rust eds), 2021, p. 25, para. 29.
540. *See* W.C. Haslehner in: Klaus Vogel on Double Taxation Conventions (Reimer & Rust eds), 2021, p. 25, para. 29.
541. *See*, to this effect, Y. Brauner, Tax Treaty Monitor 2020/1, p. 29 who refers to 'the maxim that tax treaties do not impose taxation, but, rather, limit the powers of the treaty partners to enforce their domestic laws'.

Having established both topics, a comparison can be made under the substance-based view. The topic of the TFEU, as one of the two EU Treaties, is to create a common market between EU Member States, while the topic of tax treaties would be to, in short, eliminate double taxation in respect of bilateral cross-border income. These two topics are not the same: taxation of cross-border income cannot be regarded as the same as setting up an economic community or common market, notwithstanding that tax treaties may ultimately contribute to the creation of such common market.[542] This also seems to find support in the circumstance that the competence of determining the rules for the taxation of such activities remains with the Member States (while recognising that, in exercising such competence, the Member States must respect the laws of the EU).[543] Consequently, tax treaties and the TFEU are not regarded as relating to the same subject matter for the purposes of Article 30 VCLT 1969 under a 'substance-based view'.

v Conclusion as to the Meaning of 'Relating to the Same Subject Matter'

It has been the purpose of this section 6.4.2.1.3 to determine whether the TFEU and tax treaties can be regarded as 'relating to the same subject matter' within the meaning of Article 30 VCLT 1969. In that respect, it follows from the preceding paragraphs of this section that the answer to such question depends on the view adopted with respect to the meaning of the term 'same subject matter'. Under the 'subject-based' and 'substance-based' views, tax treaties do not relate to the same subject matter as the TFEU. They do, however, relate to the same subject matter under the 'conflict-based view'. It follows that the view one adopts essentially determines whether conflicts between Directives – by means of Article 288 TFEU – and tax treaties fall within the scope of Article 30 VCLT 1969.

In this respect, the present author adopts the 'substance-based view' pursuant to which two treaties relate to the same subject matter for the purposes of Article 30 VCLT 1969 if they relate to the same topic or have the same substance. The reasons for adopting this view are that it addresses the criticism that applies with respect to the 'subject-based view' and the 'conflict-based view'. In addition, this view has been adopted by the ICSID and the PCA when interpreting the term 'same subject matter' in Article 30 VCLT 1969 while searching for a meaning that was neither too narrow ('subject-based view') nor too broad ('conflict-based view'). The consequence of

542. *See*, in this respect, ICSID, Case No. ARB/15/50 (*Eskosol S.p.a. v. Italian Republic*), para. 147 where the tribunal noted that it was insufficient for concluding that two treaties related to the same subject matter that 'protections under both regimes could be afforded in certain circumstances to the same investors – at least in the context of direct rather than indirect investment'.

543. *See*, by analogy, PCA Case No. 2010-17 (*EURAM*), para. 183 where the PCA notes that '[i]t is also well-known that, until the Lisbon Treaty, foreign direct investment was not one of the competences of the EU. This would almost suffice to concluded that the two treaties, the Austria-Slovakia BIT and the ECT do not have the same subject matter. If the European Union had no jurisdiction to deal with direct investment, it would be difficult to argue that the EU Treaties have the same subject matter – direct investment – as the BITs, of which direct investment is one of the subject matters'.

adopting this view is, however, that the TFEU and tax treaties do not relate to the same subject matter and that Article 30 VCLT 1969 cannot be applied to conflicts between such treaties.

The same conclusion applies with respect to the MLI given that it is the purpose of the MLI to 'implement tax treaty related measures to prevent base erosion and profit shifting'.[544] This is achieved by the MLI providing rules that can 'replace' provisions of a tax treaty ('in the place of'), change the application of such provision ('applies to' or 'modifies'), or fill a gap in a tax treaty ('in the absence of'),[545] provided that such treaty is, at the very least, considered as a covered tax treaty within the meaning of Article 2(1)(a) MLI. Based on this understanding of the topic of the MLI, i.e., the modification of the application of tax treaty provisions to implement certain BEPS measures, it does not relate to the creation of a common market or anything similar.[546] As such, the MLI is considered as not relating to the same subject matter as the TFEU.

#### *6.4.2.1.4 Conclusion Regarding the Scope and Applicability of the Lex Posterior Rule of Article 30 VCLT 1969*

In order for conflicts between Directives and tax treaties to fall within the scope of the *lex posterior* rule of Article 30 VCLT 1969, three conditions must be met: there must be (i) two treaties, (ii) that are successive, while (iii) relating to the same subject matter. The first condition entails that Article 30 VCLT 1969 does not apply to conflicts between Directives, as decisions of an international organisation, and tax treaties. This is because decisions of an international organisation do not qualify as treaties within the meaning of Article 2(1)(a) VCLT 1969 and, hence, Article 30 VCLT 1969. However, the obligation to achieve the result of the Directives is part of a treaty, i.e., the TFEU. Therefore, viewed like a conflict between Article 288 TFEU and a tax treaty, a conflict between a Directive and a tax treaty would be the result of two treaties (implying that the first condition of Article 30 VCLT 1969 would be met). This does not, however, entail that Article 30 VCLT 1969 can be applied to such a treaty conflict.

The conditions of 'successive' and 'relating to the same subject matter' must also be met. With respect to whether the TFEU is 'successive' to a tax treaty, it has been concluded that this should be determined on the basis of when the Treaty of Maastricht, replacing Article 249 EC Treaty with (now) Article 288 TFEU, has become

544. *See also*, Explanatory Statement to the MLI, p. 3, para. 14 ('the purpose of the Convention is to swiftly implement the tax treaty-related BEPS measures'), as well as p. 8, para. 21 ('the overall purpose of the Convention to implement tax treaty-related measures produced as part of the Final BEPS Package in a swift, co-ordinated and consistent manner across the network of existing tax treaties without the need to bilaterally renegotiate each such treaty'.).

545. *See* Explanatory Statement to the MLI, p. 6, para. 15.

546. The MLI, by contrast, is (implicitly) regarded as relating to the same subject matter as tax treaties within the meaning of Article 30 VCLT 1969 by its Conference of the Parties. *See*, in this respect, Opinion of the Conference of the Parties of the MLI regarding Interpretation and Implementation Questions (3 May 2021), p. 4 where it is provided that 'to the extent that they are incompatible, a subsequent treaty (i.e. the MLI) prevails over a previously concluded treaty between the same Parties on the same subject matter (i.e. a Covered Tax Agreement). This rule is explicitly set out in Article 30(3) of the VCLT'.

binding on one Member State (for Extra-EU Treaties) or both Member States (for Intra-EU Treaties). This is due to the VCLT 1969 focusing on treaties as instruments. As such, the date of the treaty containing the current version of Article 288 TFEU is decisive, not whether such obligation already existed prior to the conclusion of such treaty. Based on the date of conclusion of the Treaty of Maastricht, Article 288 TFEU is 'successive' with respect to 251 Intra-EU Treaties (section 6.4.2.1.2).[547]

Whether the conflict rule of Article 30 VCLT 1969 is applicable with respect to those 251 earlier Intra-EU Treaties is dependent on the final condition of Article 30 VCLT 1969 being met: the TFEU and such Intra-EU Treaties must relate to the same subject matter. In that respect, it has been concluded that three different views can be distinguished regarding the meaning of the term 'same subject matter' in Article 30 VCLT 1969, i.e., a 'subject-based', a 'conflict-based', and a 'substance-based' view. It has moreover been concluded that it is highly relevant which view would be adhered to: under the 'subject-based' and 'substance-based' views, the TFEU and tax treaties do not relate to the same subject matter as tax treaties (thereby rendering Article 30 VCLT 1969 inapplicable); under the 'conflict-based' view, by contrast, the existence of a conflict would imply that two treaties related to the same subject matter. As such, under this view, the TFEU and tax treaties can be regarded as relating to the same subject matter (entailing that Article 30 VCLT 1969 would be applicable).

In light of the arguments against the 'subject-based' and 'conflict-based' views, as well as taking into account the interpretation accorded to the term 'same subject matter' by the PCA and an ICSID tribunal, the present author adopts the 'substance-based' view. Under such a view, the TFEU and tax treaties do not relate to the same subject matter because the TFEU relates to the creation of a common market or an economic community whereas tax treaties are concerned with taxation of cross-border income with an aim of eliminating double taxation. The creation of a common market is just different from providing a set of rules limited to avoiding double taxation with respect to cross-border income on a bilateral, reciprocal, basis. The former is much wider than the latter. Their topics would thus seem (very) different. The consequence of this conclusion would, however, be that the TFEU and tax treaties do not relate to the same subject matter for the purposes of Article 30 VCLT 1969. This, in turn, means that not all conditions for the application of Article 30 VCLT 1969 are met. The result of adopting a 'substance-based' view of the term 'same subject matter' is thus that conflicts between the Directives (via Article 288 TFEU) and tax treaties fall outside the scope of Article 30 VCLT 1969. As a consequence, the application of tax treaties cannot be affected by the Directives under Article 30 VCLT 1969.

547. It is noted that Article 288 TFEU would also be later as compared to 626 Extra-EU Treaties. This also implies that 91 Intra-EU Treaties and 881 Extra-EU Treaties are 'successive' to the Treaty of Maastricht (and, thus, Article 288 TFEU) (representing 52.6% of all tax treaties concluded by the Member States).

### 6.4.2.2 *An Analogous Application of the* Lex Posterior *Rule of Article 30 VCLT 1969*

#### *6.4.2.2.1 The Rationale for an Analogous Application of Article 30 VCLT 1969*

It follows from the preceding section 6.4.2.1 that conflicts between the Directives and tax treaties fall outside the scope of the codified *lex posterior* rule of Article 30 VCLT 1969 because the Directives are regarded as decisions of an international organisation and not as 'treaties' within the meaning of the VCLT 1969 (section 6.4.2.1.1). As such, a conflict between a Directive and a tax treaty does not qualify as a conflict between successive 'treaties'.[548] This, in turn, entails that a conflict between a Directive, as a decision of an international organisation, and a tax treaty cannot be resolved by means of the *lex posterior* conflict rule laid down in Article 30 VCLT 1969. As such, the starting point under public international law would be that conflicts between tax treaties and later Directives, as decisions of an international organisation, cannot be resolved by means of the *lex posterior* conflict rule of Article 30 VCLT 1969.

Notwithstanding the inapplicability of Article 30 VCLT 1969 to conflicts between treaties and later decisions of international organisations, it has been submitted by Pauwelyn that the broader principle to which Article 30 VCLT 1969 gives effect 'should apply ... in respect of a treaty norm in conflict with a later act of an international organisation.'[549] As such, according to Pauwelyn, conflicts between treaties and later acts of an international organisation should be resolved in accordance with the principle that 'a later expression of intention is to be presumed to prevail over an earlier one'.[550] This submission of Pauwelyn is highly relevant for present purposes because it would entail that a conflict between a tax treaty and a (later) Directive, as a decision - or act - of an international organisation, could be governed by the *lex posterior* rule notwithstanding the conclusion that Article 30 VCLT 1969 itself is not applicable to such a conflict.[551]

With respect to the submission of Pauwelyn that a later act of an international organisation should prevail over an earlier treaty on the basis of the broader principle to which Article 30 VCLT 1969 gives effect, the following must be acknowledged. The submission of Pauwelyn is based on the notion that 'all rules of international law - be they set out in a treaty or in custom - are, in principle of the same binding force. As a result, any later rule, that is, any later expression of state consent, normally overrules an earlier contradictory rule'.[552] Following such notion, conflicts between equally

548. Additionally, even if a conflict between a Directive and a tax treaty is viewed as a conflict between successive treaties via Article 288 TFEU, such conflict still falls outside the scope of Article 30 VCLT 1969 because the TFEU does not relate to the same subject matter as a tax treaty under a substance-based view (section 6.4.2.1.3).
549. J. Pauwelyn, 2003, p. 384.
550. J. Pauwelyn, 2003, p. 384.
551. This is also recognised by J. Pauwelyn, 2003, p. 384 given that he acknowledges that 'Article 30 applies only in respect of successive treaty norms. However, as we noted above, Article 30 is essentially but the logical consequence of a broader principle, namely that "a later expression of intention is to be presumed to prevail over an earlier one".'
552. J. Pauwelyn, 2003, pp. 96-97.

ranked sources of public international law, such as treaties and later decisions of international organisations, can be resolved by resorting to the principle that the latest expression of state intent should prevail.[553] Whereas the notion underlying the application of the *lex posterior* rule to conflicts between treaties and later decisions of international organisations may have merit, there does not seem to be any case law of the ICJ, ECtHR or arbitral tribunals anno 2022 confirming the application of the *lex posterior* principle, i.e., later expression of state consent prevails over earlier state consent, to such conflicts.[554] In the absence of such case law, this author adopts the view that it cannot be too readily assumed that the *lex posterior* rule, as reflecting a broader principle of public international law, can be applied to conflicts between treaties and later decisions of international organisations.[555] Whereas it might not be too readily assumed, the submission of Pauwelyn does indicate that it seems arguable that conflicts between treaties and later decisions of international organisations can be resolved by means of the *lex posterior* conflict rule as reflecting a broader principle of public international law.

Whereas it may seem arguable that the broader principle to which Article 30 VCLT 1969 gives effect should apply to conflicts between treaties and later decisions of an international organisation, the lack of support in the case law of the ICJ, ECtHR and arbitral tribunals for the application of such broader principle to such conflicts has lead this author to consider whether Article 30 VCLT 1969 can be applied by analogy to conflicts between treaties and later decisions of public international law. The key difference between these two approaches can be explained as follows. The submission of Pauwelyn assumes that there is a rule of public international law - the broader principle to which Article 30 VCLT 1969 gives effect - pursuant to which a conflict between a treaty and a later decision of an international organisation should be resolved in favour of such a decision. An analogous application of Article 30 VCLT 1969, by contrast, takes as a starting point the assumption that there is no such rule, which assumption would seem valid in light of the absence of case law of the ICJ, ECtHR and arbitral tribunals confirming the application of such a broader principle.[556] It thus presumes that public international law would only provide for the application of the *lex posterior* rule to successive treaties (the 'regulated' case) and not to conflicts between other sources of public international law or, for present purposes, in any event not to conflicts between treaties and later decisions of an international organisation (the 'unregulated' case). In determining whether the *lex posterior* rule of Article 30

553. *See* J. Pauwelyn, 2003, p. 384.
554. In support of this submission, *see* Annex 3.
555. In support of this view, this author refers to the circumstance that the application of the lex posterior conflict rule to conflicts between treaties and decisions of international organisations has, in any event, not been (explicitly) addressed or confirmed in the articles of C.J. Borgen (2005), A. Lindroos, Nordic Journal of International Law 2005/1, E. Vranes, The European Journal of International Law 2006/2, and W. Czaplinski & G.M. Danilenko, Netherlands Yearbook of International Law 2009/21. Additionally, it has also not been (explicitly) addressed in the sections regarding Article 30 VCLT 1969 in M.E. Villiger, 2009, A. Orakhelashvili in: The Vienna Convention on the Law of Treaties (Corten & Klein eds), 2011, A. Aust, 2013, R. Kolb, 2017, and O. Dörr & K. Schmalenbach, 2018.
556. *See* Annex 3.

VCLT 1969 (applicable to conflicts between treaties only) should also be applied by analogy to a conflict between a treaty and a later decision of an international organisation, it would be necessary to assess whether the adoption of such a later decision can be regarded as relevantly similar to the conclusion of a later treaty. In order to make such an assessment, it would be necessary to:

(a) draw a comparison between the 'regulated' case of successive treaties and the 'unregulated' case of a treaty and a successive decision of an international organisation (in this case a Directive);
(b) identify the similarities and differences between the 'regulated' and the 'unregulated' case; and
(c) ascertaining whether a 'rational judgment' can be made with respect to the similarities of the two cases being 'relevant for their legal evaluation' and with respect to their differences being regarded as 'irrelevant'.[557]

### *6.4.2.2.2 Comparison Between the Situation of Successive Treaties and the Situation of Treaties and Later Directives as Decisions of an International Organisation*

In comparing the 'regulated' case of successive treaties and the 'unregulated' case of a treaty and a successive Directive as a decision of an international organisation, the starting point is that, with respect to the 'regulated' case of successive treaties, the earlier treaty is followed by the conclusion of a later treaty. The conclusion of such later treaty then presupposes that states have (again) expressed their consent to be bound by such treaty in accordance with Article 11 VCLT 1969. Hence, the conclusion of a successive treaty can be regarded as reflecting a later expression of the intention of states.

With respect to the adoption of a later Directive, it seems arguable that the earlier treaty is followed by a (later) expression of the intention of a (Member) State(s) to be

557. In support of this process regarding an analogy in international law, *see* S. Vöneky in: Max Planck Encyclopedias of International Law 2008, para. 17. This 'process' of analogical reasoning in international law seems to be aligned with the more general process of analogical reasoning in law. For example, C.R. Sunstein, Harvard Law Review 1993/3, p. 745 considers the process of analogical reasoning to appear 'to work in four simple steps: (I) Some fact pattern A has a certain characteristic X, Y, and Z; (2) Fact pattern B differs from A in some respects but shares characteristic X, or characteristics X, Y, and Z; (3) The law treats A in a certain way; (4) Because B shares certain characteristics with A, the law should treat B the same way'. Essentially, Sunstein draws a comparison between two cases ((1) and (2)), reflecting the steps under a) and b), and then seeks to determine the relevance of their similarities and irrelevance of their differences based on the way the law would treat, in this case, later treaties ((3) and (4)), reflecting step c). Similar to Sunstein, W. Huhn, Villanova Law Review 2003/1, p. 312 describes analogical reasoning as a three-step process, which consist of 'similarity is seen between cases; next the rule inherent in the first case is announced; then the rule of law is made applicable to the second case'. This process, again, implies identifying the similarities and differences based on a comparison of two cases and establishing that they are relevantly similar based on the rule inherent in the first case, which inherent rule would seem to reflect the comparator for making a 'rational judgment'.

bound by, in this case, a decision of an institution of the European Union. This argument is based on the following line of reasoning. Directives within the area of direct taxation that are currently in force have been adopted on the basis of Article 115 TFEU. This provision entails that each Directive has been adopted after the Member States have unanimously voted in favour of the adoption of such Directive in the Council.[558] Hence, it seems arguable that each Directive reflects the consent of all Member States.[559] Second, such consent can be regarded as a consent to be bound by the Directive given that it follows from Article 288 TFEU that such Directives are binding upon the Member States.[560]

### i Similarities and Differences

Based on a comparison of the conclusion of a subsequent treaty and the adoption of a later Directive, as a decision of an international organisation, the following similarities and differences have been identified:

(a) *Similarity*: both the conclusion of a later (tax) treaty and the adoption of a later Directive require an expression of a consent to be bound by the relevant treaty or Directive.
(b) *Difference*: the consent to be bound by (tax) treaties is generally expressed by their signature, whereas the consent to be bound by a Directive is expressed by means of votes of the Member States within the Council.
(c) *Difference*: a treaty is binding (Article 26 VCLT 1969; section 6.2) whereas a Directive is (only) binding as to the result to be achieved (Article 288 TFEU).
(d) *Difference*: the consent to be bound is, in the event of a tax treaty, laid down in an agreement between states within the meaning of Article 2(1)(a) VCLT

558. For evidence of support of this position that each of the Directives currently in force has been adopted with the unanimous support of the Member States (and, hence, without abstentions), *see* Voting result regarding the Interest and Royalties Directive (2003/49/EC), Document 5926/3/03, Voting result regarding the Mutual Assistance Directive (2011/16/EU), Voting result regarding the Parent-Subsidiary Directive (2011/96/EC), no. 17931/11, Voting result regarding the amendment of the Parent-Subsidiary Directive (2014/86/EU), no. 17931/11, Voting result regarding the amendment of the Parent-Subsidiary Directive (2015/96/EU), no. 5636/15; Voting result regarding ATAD1 (2016/1164/EU), no. 5636/15, Voting result regarding ATAD2 (2017/952/EU), no. 9740/17, and Voting result regarding the Arbitration Directive ((EU) 2017/1852). With respect to the Merger Directive (2009), the present author has not been able to retrieve the voting result of the Council.
559. *See*, to this effect, L. de Broe in: Building Global International Tax Law: Essays in Honour of Guglielmo Maisto (Pistone ed.), 2022, para. 23.4.3 where he notes that 'in case of a conflict between an inter se treaty and a later directive, the pragmatic argument could be made that, since the Member States adopt these directives with unanimity, they simultaneously consent to amend their tax treaties and replace them with the provisions adopted under the directive'.
560. L. de Broe in: Building Global International Tax Law: Essays in Honour of Guglielmo Maisto (Pistone ed.), 2022, para. 23.4.3 even goes a step further in stating that it could be argued that such consent is to amend and replace tax treaties. In this author's view, the Directives currently in force do not provide explicit evidence of such an intention. As such, this author concludes that the adoption by unanimity of a Directive evidences only the consent of the Member States to be bound by a Directive and not necessarily – in the absence of explicit evidence – signals an intention to amend or replace their tax treaties.

1969 while the consent to be bound, in the event of a Directive, is laid down in a legal act of an institution of the European Union (i.e., a decision of an international organisation (*see* Chapter 2)).

### ii Relevance of Similarities and Differences

Bearing in mind the similarities and differences identified, the key question with respect to determining the case for an analogous application of Article 30 VCLT 1969 is whether the similarities and differences are relevant.[561] In determining this, it has been submitted by Vöneky that 'object and purpose identify the ground that indicates which similarities of the cases in question are relevant and which dissimilarities are irrelevant'.[562] As such, the object and purpose of Article 30 VCLT 1969 must be assessed before being able to make a 'rational judgment' regarding the relevance of the similarities and differences between later treaties and later decisions of international organisations for the purposes of an analogous application of Article 30 VCLT 1969.

In this respect, the starting point is that Article 30 VCLT 1969 can be regarded as 'no more than an application of the general principle that a later expression of intention is to be presumed to prevail over an earlier one'.[563] As such, Article 30 VCLT 1969 can be seen as 'nothing more than a logical consequence of states being their own law-makers, possessing the contractual freedom to 'change their minds': a later expression of consent prevails over an earlier one'.[564] Bearing this in mind, it would seem that it is the purpose of Article 30 VCLT 1969 to give effect to a presumption that states when entering into later commitments, share a common intention that their later intention prevails over their earlier intentions.[565] Based on this purpose of Article 30 VCLT 1969, it would seem that the similarity between the conclusion of a later treaty and the adoption of a later Directive is relevant given that both reflect an expression of intention of states, either expressed by signing a later treaty or voting in favour of a later Directive

Whereas the similarity may be relevant, an analogous application of the *lex posterior* rule would also require that the differences would be irrelevant in light of the purpose of Article 30 VCLT 1969. In that respect, it can be noted, first, that the means by which the consent is expressed seems irrelevant. This is due to Article 11 VCLT 1969 providing that the expression of consent to be bound by a treaty may be expressed by 'any other means if so agreed'. This reference to 'any other means if so agreed' seems to indicate that it is decisive that state consent has been expressed, not the way in which this has been done. As such, it would seem that negotiating states could agree

561. *See* M. Koszowski, 2019, p. 163 who regards determining the process of establishing the relevant similarities as 'crucial for any analogy'.
562. S. Vöneky in: Max Planck Encyclopedias of International Law 2008, para. 17.
563. YBILC 1966, Volume II, p. 217, para. 10. *See also*, ILC, 2006, A/CN.4/L.682, p. 119, para. 230 where it can be derived from that the ILC also considered the lex posterior maxim reflects 'a presumption of intent to derogate from the earlier agreement'.
564. J. Pauwelyn, 2003, p. 381.
565. *See* C.J. Borgen, 2012, para. D who notes that the lex posterior rule 'considers the parties' evolving intent and favours the most recent treaty by the same parties'.

that consent to be bound by a treaty would have to be given by means of a vote within the Council.[566] For that reason, the difference regarding the way in which consent to be bound by a treaty or a Directive does not seem relevant.[567] Second, the difference in terms of a treaty being binding and a Directive being only binding as to the result to be achieved also seems irrelevant in light of the purpose of Article 30 VCLT 1969. This is due to it being the purpose of Article 30 VCLT 1969 to give effect to the most recent expression of the intention of the parties. In the event of a later Directive, such consent relates to a certain outcome, such as the inclusion of (non-distributed) income of a controlled foreign company permanent establishment. Such outcome, in turn, reflects rather clearly the intention of the Member States to tax such income. Similarly, Article 23, in conjunction with Article 7 of an Intra-EU Treaty based on the OECD Model reflects an intention between two Member States that the resident Member State must exempt income attributable to a permanent establishment situated in the other Member State. Hence, both the Directive and the Intra-EU Treaty quite clearly reflect an expression of intent with respect to the taxation of profits attributable to a permanent establishment, notwithstanding the fact that the consent to be bound by ATAD1 only relates to the result to be achieved while the consent to be bound by the Intra-EU Treaty relates to the treaty as a whole. As such, this second difference seems irrelevant. Third, and finally, the difference regarding the form by means of which the consent to be bound is laid down can be regarded as irrelevant as well in light of the absence of a hierarchy among the sources of public international law.[568] The rationale for such absence seems to be the 'direct consequence of the assumption that all international norms, in one way or another, derive from state consent. Since, therefore, all norms essentially derive from the same source (state consent), it is presumed that they have the same binding value'.[569] What matters is thus that the relevant states have expressed their consent with respect to a rule of public international law. As such, the circumstance that a Directive is adopted in the form of a decision of an international organisation and a tax treaty in the form of a treaty would not be relevantly different within the context of ascertaining whether the *lex posterior* rule of Article 30 VCLT 1969 can be applied by analogy.[570]

566. *See, e.g.*, S. Szurek in: The Vienna Conventions on the Law of Treaties (Corten & Klein eds), 2011, para. 9 who notes that the expression of 'any other means if so agreed to' plays the role of an 'escape clause internal to the provision itself, meant to reserve all the innovations of the practice, belonging to the progressive development of law'. It would thus seem broad enough to also include an expression of consent to be bound by voting (unanimously) in favour of a treaty within the institutional framework of an international organisation.

567. *See* in this respect also H. Kelsen, 1952, p. 366 who notes that '[a] general norm adopted by a unanimous decision of an international organ composed of representative of all parties to the treaty establishing the organ is not different from a norm created by a treaty entered into by the states upon which the norm is binding'.

568. *See* regarding the absence of a hierarchy among the sources of public international law in general: M. Prost in: The Oxford Handbook of the Sources of International Law (Besson & d'Aspremont eds), 2018, para. I, as well as J. Pauwelyn, pp. 94-96.

569. J. Pauwelyn, 2003, p. 95.

570. In support of the irrelevance of the form in which state consent is expressed, *see* J. Pauwelyn, 2003, p. 384.

### iii Conclusion Regarding an Analogous Application of Article 30 VCLT 1969 to the Directives as Decisions of an International Organisation

Based on the previous sections, the adoption of a later Directive can be regarded as relevantly similar to the conclusion of a later treaty in light of the purpose of Article 30 VCLT 1969 (i.e., giving effect to the most recent expression of state consent). Based on this relevant similarity, it would thus seem arguable that Article 30 VCLT 1969 should be applied by analogy to conflicts between tax treaties and later Directives (as decisions of an international organisation).

With respect to this conclusion that it is arguable that Article 30 VCLT 1969 can be applied by analogy, the following observation needs to be made. As indicated above, there is no case law of the ICJ, ECtHR, or an arbitral tribunal confirming an analogous application of Article 30 VCLT 1969 to conflicts between treaties and later decisions of international organisations. As such, this author would not go as far as concluding that the *lex posterior* conflict rule *should* apply by analogy to conflicts between treaties and later decisions of international organisations. Instead, this author concludes that an analogous application of Article 30 VCLT 1969, based on the relevance of the similarities and differences identified, would only be 'arguable'.

#### *6.4.2.2.3 The Requirement of 'Successive' 'Treaties' under an Analogous Application of Article 30 VCLT 1969*

If the *lex posterior* rule of Article 30 VCLT 1969 would apply by analogy to successive decisions of international organisations and treaties, the relevant date would not be the conclusion of the Treaty of Maastricht (or the accession thereto). Instead, the date of adoption of a Directive would be decisive because such date reflects the Member States' expression of their intention to be bound by such Directive. In addition, if a Member State had not yet acceded to the EU at the time of such adoption, the date of conclusion of the accession treaty, by means of which they have expressed their intention to be bound by such Directive, should be considered decisive. The result of this approach, in terms of tax treaties concluded before each Directive, is as follows:[571]

| | *Pre-Directive Intra-EU Treaties*[572] | *Pre-Directive Extra-EU Treaties*[573] |
|---|---|---|
| Interest and Royalties Directive (2003/49/EC) | 270 (78.9%) | 889 (57.7%) |
| Merger Directive (2009/133/EC) | 305 (89.2) | 1097 (72.8%) |

571. It is acknowledged that the geographical scope of the Interest and Royalties Directive, Merger Directive, Mutual Assistance Directive, Parent-Subsidiary Directive and the Arbitration Directive is limited to situations between Member States only. For completeness' sake, however, it is also set out to what extent they have been adopted after the conclusion of an Extra-EU Treaty.
572. Annex 1, para. 3.4.2.
573. *See* Annex – Excel, para. 'Annex 1 | Directives', rows: 30 through 39.

| | *Pre-Directive Intra-EU Treaties*[572] | *Pre-Directive Extra-EU Treaties*[573] |
|---|---|---|
| Mutual Assistance Directive (2011/16/EU) and Parent-Subsidiary Directive (2011/96/EU) | 311 (90.9%) | 1216 (80.7%) |
| Parent-Subsidiary Directive (2014/86/EU) | 327 (95.6%) | 1340 (88.9%) |
| Parent-Subsidiary Directive (2015/121/EU) | 329 (96.2%) | 1369 (90.8%) |
| ATAD1 ((EU) 2016/1164) | 333 (97.4%) | 1416 (94%) |
| ATAD2 ((EU) 2017/952) and Arbitration Directive ((EU) 2017/1852) | 336 (98.2%) | 1443 (95.8%) |

As compared to the (regular) application of Article 30 VCLT 1969, an analogous application of such provision would result in an increase in the number of 'earlier' tax treaties. For example, under such a 'regular' application, the obligation to achieve the result of a Directive would be later as compared to 251 Intra-EU Treaties (73.4% of all such treaties) and 626 Extra-EU Treaties (41.5% of all such treaties). By contrast, under an analogous application of the *lex posterior* rule of Article 30 VCLT 1969, this number increases. Regarding Intra-EU Treaties, such an analogous application would entail that – with respect to ATAD2 – nearly all Intra-EU Treaties would be earlier as compared to a Directive (the number increases from 251 (73.4%) to 336 (98.2%). The same applies with respect to Extra-EU Treaties considering that the number of earlier treaties increases from 626 (41.5%) to 1,416 (94%).[574] As such, an analogous application of the *lex posterior* rule of Article 30 VCLT 1969 greatly increases the number of earlier tax treaties as compared to a 'regular' application of such provision.

With respect to the 'bilateral' provisions of the MLI, an analogous application of the *lex posterior* rule of Article 30 VCLT 1969 would seem to have the following implications. Twenty-six Member States signed the MLI on 7 June 2017. As such, the MLI would be 'earlier' as compared to the Arbitration Directive (adopted on 10 October 2017) and 'later' with respect to all other Directives (ATAD2, for example, was adopted on 29 May 2017). This is different, however, for Estonia because it signed the MLI on 29 June 2018, i.e., after adoption of the Arbitration Directive on 29 May 2017. As such, for Estonia, the Arbitration Directive would be 'earlier' as compared to the MLI.[575]

#### *6.4.2.2.4 The Requirement of 'Relating to the Same Subject Matter' under an Analogous Application of Article 30 VCLT 1969*

It follows from section 6.4.2.1.3 that this author adopts a 'substance-based view' of the term 'same subject matter' in Article 30 VCLT 1969. Based on such a view, under an

574. *See* tab: 'Annex 1 | Directives', in the excel file that can be accessed via https://doi.org/10.17026/dans-zku-ckqy.
575. *See* https://www.oecd.org/ctp/treaties/beps-mli-signatories-and-parties.pdf (date accessed: 28 July 2022).

analogous application of Article 30 VCLT 1969, the sameness of subject matter should be determined by comparing the topics of the Directives and the tax treaties (instead of comparing the topics of the TFEU and tax treaties under the 'regular' application of Article 30 VCLT 1969). With respect to comparing such topics, the starting point is that the topic of tax treaties can be described as eliminating double taxation of cross-border income of residents of the contracting states, by imposing limits to the right to tax, without creating opportunities for non-taxation or reduced taxation through tax avoidance or tax evasion. It should thus be assessed whether the topic of a Directive is similar to this. In order to make such an assessment, it will be determined below, with respect to each Directive (irrespective of whether it can give rise to obligations that are incompatible with those arising from a tax treaty), (i) what a Directive creates, (ii) what rights and obligations a Directive give rise to, and (iii) the nature of the topics dealt with by a Directive. In that respect, reference will be made to (a) the objective, (b) means to achieve such objective, (c) the geographical scope, and (d) personal scope of each of the Directives.

#### i The Topic or Substance of the Interest and Royalties Directive

Based on its heading, the Interest and Royalties Directive seeks to 'create a 'common system of taxation applicable to interest and royalty payments made between associated companies of different Member States'. This common system is then aimed at eliminating tax obstacles in respect of certain cross-border interest and royalty payments within the EU.[576] Such tax obstacles relate to the (risk of) double taxation with respect to interest and royalty payments between group companies resident in the EU.[577] The way in which this obstacle is eliminated is by requiring Member States to exempt these payments from taxation at source.[578] Based on these characteristics of the Interest and Royalties Directive, its topic would seem to be the elimination of source

576. *See* P. Farmer in: International and EC Tax Aspects of Groups of Companies (Maisto ed.), 2008, para. 4.2 ('designed to eliminate withholding tax obstacles in the area of cross-border interest and royalty payments within a group of companies ... Intra-EU'), and M. Helminen, 2021, para. 3.2.1 ('intragroup interest and royalty payments are taxed only once in a Member State'). *See also* M. Distaso & R. Russo, European Taxation 2004/4, pp. 152-153 who note that the 'main aim' of this Directive 'seems to be the direct application of the exemption from withholding tax on interest/royalties' and A. Cordewener in: European Tax Law (Wattel, Marres & Vermeulen eds), 2018, p. 401 ('the main aim is to eliminate remaining juridical double taxation and administrative and cash-flow disadvantages of cross-border intra-group interest and royalty payments as compared to similar purely domestic payments ... A collateral aim is to ensure that interest and royalty payments are taxed at least once in a Member State').

577. *See* Article 1(1) in conjunction with Articles 1(7) and 3 Interest and Royalty Directive.

578. P. Farmer in: International and EC Tax Aspects of Groups of Companies (Maisto ed.), 2008, para. 4.2 ('by abolishing withholding taxes on royalty and interest payments intra-EU'), Report from the Commission to the Council in accordance with Article 8 of Council Directive 2003/49/EC on a common system of taxation applicable to interest and royalty payments made between associated companies of different Member States, p. 3 ('the scheme consists of exempting interest and royalty payments from taxation at source ... while attempting to ensure that the beneficial owner of the payments is taxed in its MS of residence'), L. Adamczyk & A. Majdanska in: Introduction to European Tax Law on Direct Taxation (Lang, Pistone, Schuch & Staringer eds), 2014, p. 26, para. 46 ('it provides ... for no withholding tax on interest and

taxation of intra-group interest and royalty payments between companies that are resident in the EU Member States.

Such topic of the Interest and Royalties Directive seems to have aspects in common with the topic of tax treaties concluded between Member States. First, both the Directive and Intra-EU Treaties are aimed at eliminating double taxation of cross-border income of residents of the contracting states.[579] Second, the rights and obligations created to achieve such aim seem to be similar in the sense that both impose limitations on the extent to which Member States are permitted to tax cross-border income falling within their scope. Third, the interest and royalty payments falling within the scope of the exemption required by the Interest and Royalty Directive also fall within the scope of Articles 11 and 12 of Intra-EU Treaties resembling the OECD Model. For example, the Interest and Royalties Directive applies essentially, based on Article 1, to interest or royalty payments arising in a Member State and paid to an associated company of another Member State that is the beneficial owner of such payments. Similarly, Article 11 of an Intra-EU Treaty based on the OECD Model would apply to interest arising in a Member State and paid to a resident of another Member State, while Article 12 would apply to royalties arising in a Member State and beneficially owned by a resident of the other Member State. It thus seems likely that payments falling within the substantive scope of the Interest and Royalties Directives would also fall within the scope of Article 11 or 12 of an Intra-EU Treaty. As such, there seems to be substantive overlap in the sense that payments within the scope of the Interest and Royalties Directive would also fall within the scope of an Intra-EU Treaty. Based on these three aspects that the Interest and Royalties Directive would have in common with tax treaties, it would seem arguable that the topic of the Directive, i.e., eliminating double taxation of cross-border interest and royalty payments by imposing restrictions on the right to tax, resembles the topic of a tax treaty. Based on such resemblance of topic, the Interest and Royalties Directive may thus be regarded as relating to the same subject matter as an Intra-EU Treaty for the purposes of an analogous application of the lex posterior rule of Article 30 VCLT 1969.[580]

Whereas it may be regarded as arguable that the Interest and Royalties Directive relates to the same subject matter as Intra-EU Treaties, it is acknowledged that the topic of such Directive is more limited – or: more specific – than that of Intra-EU Treaties. First of all, the substantive scope of Intra-EU Treaties is wider. Such treaties relate to the elimination of double taxation in respect of cross-border income in general. As such, they provide for a set of rules wherein each type of cross-border income of

royalty payments between associated companies'), and A. Cordewener in: European Tax Law (Wattel, Marres & Vermeulen eds), 2018, p. 401 ('[t]he core rule is a prohibition of taxation in the source State').

579. *See*, in support of this position, L. de Broe in: Current Tax Treaty Issues (Maisto ed.), 2019, para. 16.2.1.

580. It does not relate to the same subject matter as Extra-EU Treaties in light of the geographical scope of the Interest and Royalties Directive. Such Directive is limited to interest and royalty payments between residents of the EU only (*see* Article 1 in conjunction with Article 3(a)(ii) Interest and Royalties Directive). For that reason, payments between a resident of the EU and a third state resident fall outside its scope and, hence, its subject matter.

residents of the two contracting states should fall within its substantive scope.[581] This is different from the Interest and Royalties Directive. This Directive only seeks to provide a set of rules for intra-group interest and royalty payments. As such, the substantive scope of the Interest and Royalties Directive is limited - or more specific - as compared to that of tax treaties. Second, with respect to the scope of Intra-EU Treaties regarding interest and royalty payments in particular, it can also be noted that such scope is more general than that of the Interest and Royalties Directive. Such Directive only applies to interest or royalty payments arising in a Member State and paid to an associated company of another Member State that is the beneficial owner of such payments. By contrast, Articles 11 and 12 of Intra-EU Treaties based on the OECD Model would also apply to such payments made to individuals as well as to non-associated companies. As such, the topic of the Interest and Royalties Directive may be perceived as more limited than that of tax treaties (and, hence, as different from the topic of such treaties).

### ii The Topic or Substance of the Merger Directive

The Merger Directive, based on its heading, seeks to 'create' a 'common system of taxation' applicable to certain corporate reorganisations between companies of different Member States. Such common system is aimed at removing tax obstacles, such as double taxation within the internal market,[582] that may arise in respect of cross-border restructuring operations within the EU.[583] This purpose is achieved by requiring Member States to apply a deferral (by rollover relief) of taxes that would have been due over (unrealised) capital gains as a consequence of a corporate reorganisation involving two companies that are tax resident in the EU.[584] Such Directive thus essentially imposes a limitation on the extent to which Member States may tax (unrealised) capital gains. The substance of the Merger Directive could thus be described as relating to the deferral of taxation of cross-border corporate reorganisations within the EU, by imposing a limitation on the right to tax capital gains, with a view to avoiding (double) taxation over unrealised capital gains.

581. *See*, to this effect, Article 21 OECD Model (2017) which provides a distributive rule with respect to items of income of a resident of a Contracting State, wherever arising, and 'not dealt with in the foregoing Articles of this Convention'.

582. Recital (14) of the Merger Directive (2009). Moreover, G.F. Boulogne, 2016, p. 286 notes that the 'Merger Directive has partly taken away the double taxation linked to cross-border restructuring'.

583. *See* G.F. Boulogne, 2016, p. 13 and pp. 17-18. *See also* M. Helminen, 2021, para. 3.3.1.2 ('abolish tax obstacles on cross-border company reorganizations in the European Union').

584. *See*, to this effect, G.F. Boulogne, 2016, p. 13 ('provides for deferral (by rollover relief) of tax claims that becomes due at the level of a company or a shareholder in the case of the cross-border mergers, (partial) divisions, transfers of assets and exchanges of shares taking place within the EU. Taxation of the capital gains is deferred until a later disposal of the asset (actual realization of profits)') and M. Helminen, 2021, para. 3.3.1.2 ('company reorganizations must not cause immediate direct tax consequences to the companies and their shareholders participating in a company reorganization. ... the taxation is deferred to the moment at which the assets will be transferred').

This topic of the Merger Directive seems to have common ground with that of Intra-EU Treaties. Both are aimed at avoiding double taxation. Such double taxation is avoided by imposing limitations on the extent to which capital gains may be taxed. The Merger Directive imposes a limitation to tax by requiring an exemption of taxation of unrealised capital gains in certain corporate reorganisations whereas Article 13 of Intra-EU Treaties based on the OECD Model provides rules aimed at limiting the extent to which the source or residence state may tax capital gains in general. As such, the obligations by both the Merger Directive and an Intra-EU Treaty can be regarded as being aimed at limiting the extent to which a capital gain may be taxed. Moreover, in terms of substantive overlap, it would seem that (deemed) capital gains arising from cross-border corporate reorganisations fall within the scope of Article 13 of Intra-EU Treaties based on the OECD Model.[585] Hence, there would be substantive overlap in the sense that the transactions covered by the Merger Directive would also fall within the scope of such provision. Based on these similarities between the Merger Directive and Intra-EU Treaties, it would seem arguable that the topic of the Directive, i.e., deferral of taxation of cross-border corporate reorganisations within the EU, by imposing a limitation on the right to tax capital gains, with a view to avoiding (double) taxation over unrealised capital gains, resembles the topic of Intra-EU Treaties. As such, it would thus seem arguable that the Merger Directive could be regarded as relating to the same subject matter for the purposes of an analogous application of the *lex posterior* rule of Article 30 VCLT 1969.[586]

At the same time, however, the same observations as were made with respect to the Interest and Royalties Directive seem applicable here. First, the personal scope of the Merger Directive is limited to companies (resident in the EU) only. As such, it does not apply to individuals. Second, the Merger Directive only relates to the taxation of cross-border reorganisations, whereas tax treaties relate to all forms of cross-border income.[587] Based on such differences, the topic of the Merger Directive does seem to be more limited – or more specific – than that of Intra-EU Treaties.

### iii The Topic or Substance of the Mutual Assistance Directive

The Mutual Assistance Directive provides rules regarding the exchange of information and other forms of administrative cooperation between the Member States.[588] As such, it is aimed at ensuring efficient administrative cooperation between Member States to overcome the negative effects of the increasing globalisation of the internal market.[589]

585. With respect to the overlap between the Merger Directive and Article 13 OECD Model, *see* G.F. Boulogne, 2016.
586. It does not relate to the same subject matter as Extra-EU Treaties in light of the geographical scope of the Interest and Royalties Directive. Such Directive is limited to interest and royalty payments between residents of the EU only (*see* Article 1 in conjunction with Article 3(a)(ii) Interest and Royalties Directive). For that reason, payments between a resident of the EU and a third state resident fall outside its scope and, hence, its subject matter.
587. *See*, to that effect, G.F. Boulogne, 2016 who refers to Article 13 OECD Model in this respect.
588. *See* Chapter II of the Mutual Assistance Directive (2011/16/EU).
589. Recital (29) Mutual Assistance Directive (2011/16/EU).

Such aim is then achieved by providing a set of rules aimed at providing a legal basis for Member States to exchange information on request, automatically, or spontaneously. Its topic can thus be described as providing for the exchange of information and other forms of administrative cooperation between Member States (with the aim of overcoming the negative effects of the increasing globalisation of the internal market).

Based on such a description of the topic of the Mutual Assistance Directive, its topic seems to be different from that of Intra-EU Treaties. As concluded in section 6.4.2.1.3, the topic or substance of tax treaties could be described as eliminating double taxation of cross-border income of residents of the contracting states, by imposing limitations on the right to tax such income, without creating opportunities for non-taxation or reduced taxation through tax avoidance or tax evasion. Such topic does not reflect the exchange of information and other forms of administrative cooperation, which is the topic of the Mutual Assistance Directive. This does not, however, entail that there would be no substantive overlap between the Mutual Assistance Directive and Intra-EU Treaties. Such overlap would, in fact, seem likely in light of Article 26 of Intra-EU Treaties following the OECD Model providing for the exchange of information on request, automatically, or spontaneously.[590] As such, information may be exchanged between Member States based on either an Intra-EU Treaty or the Mutual Assistance Directive. Moreover, in terms of the information that may be exchanged, there would also seem to be overlap. Under Article 26 of Intra-EU Treaties based on the OECD Model, the Member States 'shall exchange such information as is foreseeably relevant for carrying out the provisions of this Convention or to the administration or enforcement of the domestic laws concerning taxes of every kind and description imposed on behalf of the Contracting States, or of their political subdivisions or local authorities, insofar as the taxation thereunder is not contrary to the Convention'. By comparison, the Mutual Assistance Directive provides for the exchange of information regarding 'all taxes of any kind levied by, or on behalf of, a Member State or the Member State's territorial or administrative subdivisions, including the local authorities',[591] with the exception of 'value added tax and customs duties, or ... excise duties covered by other Union legislation on administrative cooperation between Member States'[592] or 'compulsory social security contributions payable to the Member State or a subdivision of the Member State or to social security institutions established under public law'.[593] It follows that both Article 26 of Intra-EU Treaties and the Mutual Assistance Directive relate to the exchange of information regarding all taxes of any kind levied by, or on behalf of, a Member State or the Member State's territorial or administrative subdivisions, including the local authorities. As such they would seem to have substantive overlap. Bearing in mind such substantive overlap, it would thus seem arguable that the Mutual Assistance Directive shares at least some aspects with Intra-EU Treaties. Whether this is sufficient for regarding it as relating to the same subject matter as such treaties is, in this author's view, unclear. This lack of clarity

590. *See* paras 9 and 9.1 of the OECD Commentaries (2017) to Article 26.
591. *See* Article 2(1) Mutual Assistance Directive (2011).
592. Article 2(2) Mutual Assistance Directive (2011).
593. Article 3(1) Mutual Assistance Directive (2011).

mainly arises from the circumstance that the exchange of information in tax treaties can be described as an 'ancillary objective',[594] whereas it is the main subject of the Mutual Assistance Directive.[595]

### iv The Topic or Substance of the Parent-Subsidiary Directive(s)

The Parent-Subsidiary Directive (2011/96/EU) seeks to 'create' a 'common system of taxation applicable in the case of parent companies and subsidiaries of different Member States' based on its heading. The purpose of such a common system would be to eliminate tax obstacles in respect of such profit distributions by requiring the Member States to exempt qualifying profit distributions from taxation at the source, as well as from taxation in the residence state.[596] Similar to the Interest and Royalties Directive, its scope is limited to intra-group cross-border payments, in this case in the form of profit distributions, between companies that are resident in EU Member States. Its topic can thus be described as eliminating double taxation of cross-border intra-group profit distributions, by imposing limitations on the right to tax such distributions, of companies that are resident in the EU.

Bearing in mind such topic, it would seem that it shares common ground with the topic of Intra-EU Treaties. Such common ground can, first of all, be based on both the Parent-Subsidiary Directive and Intra-EU Treaties being aimed at eliminating double taxation in respect of cross-border income of residents falling within their scope. Such aim is then achieved by means of imposing limitations on the extent to which profit distributions may be taxed either under Articles 4 and 5 Parent-Subsidiary Directive or by means of Articles 10 and 23 of Intra-EU Treaties based on the OECD Model. Moreover, it would seem that those profit distributions falling within the scope of such provisions of the Directive also fall within the scope of the limitations imposed by an Intra-EU Treaty based on the OECD Model. For example, Article 4 Parent-Subsidiary Directive requires the Member State of which the parent company is a resident to refrain from taxing profits received from a subsidiary resident in another Member State. By comparison, Article 23 of Intra-EU Treaties would require the parent company of a Member State to provide a credit for taxes paid in the source state on dividends paid by a resident of one Member State to a resident of another Member State. As such, it limits

594. *See* B.J. Arnold, 2019, p. 146. The ancillary nature of the exchange of information may also be derived from the circumstance that there is no reference to such exchange in the title of the OECD Model or preamble. This is different for the elimination of double taxation without creating opportunities for non-taxation or reduced taxation through tax evasion or avoidance.

595. This would, by means of comparison, seem different with respect to The Multilateral Convention on Mutual Administrative Assistance in Tax Matters.

596. P. Farmer in: International and EC Tax Aspects of Groups of Companies (Maisto ed.), 2008, para. 4.2 *See also* A. Cordewener in: European Tax Law (Wattel, Marres & Vermeulen eds), 2018, p. 399 and Joined Cases C-504/16 & C-613/16 (*Deister and Juhler*), para. 48 ('the Parent-Subsidiary Directive ... seeks ... to eliminate any disadvantage to cooperation between companies of different Member States as compared between companies of the same Member State and thereby to facilitate the grouping together of companies at EU level. That directive thus seeks to ensure neutrality from the tax point of view, of the distribution of profits by a company established in one Member State to its parent company established in another Member State'). *See also* M. Helminen, 2021, para. 3.1.1.

the extent to which the Member State of the parent company would be able to tax profit distributions as well (albeit by means of a different method, i.e., a credit method instead of an exemption method). Similarly, Article 5 Parent-Subsidiary Directive imposes a duty to exempt profit distributions from source taxation if such profits are paid by a subsidiary resident in one Member State to a parent company resident in another Member State, whereas Article 10 of Intra-EU Treaties, based on the OECD Model, would also limit the right of the source state to tax such distributions, i.e., dividends. Hence, the extent to which profit distributions falling within the scope of the Parent-Subsidiary Directive may be taxed is (also) governed by Intra-EU Treaties. Based on these areas of common ground, the topic of the Parent-Subsidiary Directive could be regarded as similar to that of Intra-EU Tax Treaties.

There are, however, also differences based on the substantive and personal scope of the Directive. With respect to the substantive scope, it can be noted that the Parent-Subsidiary Directive relates only to intra-group profit distributions whereas tax treaties deal with all cross-border profit distributions between residents of the contracting states, as well as to other types of cross-border income. As such, the substantive scope of the Parent-Subsidiary Directive is more limited - or more specific - than that of Intra-EU Treaties. In addition, regarding the personal scope, it follows that the application of the Parent-Subsidiary Directive is limited to profit distributions paid to companies only, while tax treaties apply to dividends paid to individuals and companies. As such, the personal scope is also more limited than that of Intra-EU Treaties. Based on such differences, the topic of the Parent-Subsidiary Directive, although sharing common ground with that of an Intra-EU Treaty, is more limited - or more specific - than that of Intra-EU Treaties.

It is furthermore acknowledged that this Directive has been amended in 2014 and 2015. With respect to such amendments, the following can be noted. Directive 2014/86/EU was aimed to amend the Parent-Subsidiary Directive (2011/96/EU) with a view to avoiding situations of double non-taxation.[597] In order to avoid such situations, Directive 2014/86/EU introduced a duty to impose a taxation on profit distributions at the level of the parent company if and to the extent that such distributions would be deductible by the subsidiary.[598] Such an obligation to tax is not laid down in Intra-EU Treaties. As such, the amendment by means of the Directive 2014/86/EU entails that the Parent-Subsidiary Directive can give rise to obligations that are different from that of tax treaties. Such an obligation to tax with a view to avoiding non-taxation would, however, seem to contribute towards achieving the aim of tax treaties to avoid creating opportunities for non-taxation. Hence, the topic of the Parent-Subsidiary Directive, following its amendment by Directive 2014/86/EU, can be described as eliminating double taxation of cross-border intra-group profit distributions, by imposing limitations on the right to tax such distributions, of companies that are resident in the EU 'without creating opportunities for non-taxation'. Based on such description, its topic would still be aligned with that of Intra-EU Treaties.

597. Recital (2) Parent-Subsidiary Directive (2014/86/EU).
598. *See* Recital (3) Parent-Subsidiary Directive (2014/86/EU), as well as Article 1(1) of such Directive amending Article 4(1)(a) Parent-Subsidiary Directive 2011/96/EU.

Additionally, the amendment resulting from Directive (EU) 2015/121 was founded upon it being considered necessary that the Parent-Subsidiary Directive (2011/96/EU) 'is not abused by taxpayers who fall within the scope of its application'.[599] In order to achieve such a result, Directive (EU) 2015/121 provided for the 'inclusion of a common minimum anti-abuse rule in Directive 2011/96/EU'.[600] As such following the amendment of the Parent-Subsidiary Directive (2011/96/EU) by this Directive, Member States are obliged to 'not grant the benefits of [the Parent-Subsidiary] Directive to an arrangement of a series of arrangements which have been put into place for the main purpose or one of the main purposes of obtaining a tax advantage that defeats the object or purpose of this Directive, are not genuine having regard to all relevant facts and circumstances'.[601] The amendment of the Parent-Subsidiary Directive by means of this Directive would thus seem to be aimed at avoiding tax avoidance by means of the Parent-Subsidiary Directive. In such a sense, it also contributes to the topic of Intra-EU Treaties to avoid creating opportunities for tax avoidance.

### v The Topic or Substance of ATAD1

With respect to ATAD1, it follows from its heading that it seeks to 'create' rules against 'tax avoidance practices that directly affect the functioning of the internal market'. As such, based on its preamble, it is the purpose of such Directive to improve the resilience of the internal market as a whole against cross-border tax avoidance practices,[602] while also avoiding the creation of other obstacles to the internal market, such as double taxation.[603] ATAD1 seeks to achieve this dual purpose by means of an interest deduction limitation provision, an exit taxation provision, a general anti-avoidance provision, a controlled foreign corporation regime and an anti-hybrid mismatch provision.[604] The effect of these provisions could be described as creating and extending the objective tax liability of corporate taxpayers in the EU by either requiring taxation of income or denying a deduction of payments.[605] It can furthermore be noted that, different from the Directives discussed in the previous sections, the geographical scope of ATAD1 is not limited to intra-EU cross-border activities only. Its provisions also apply to domestic situations,[606] as well as to situations involving taxpayers resident in third states.[607] Based on these characteristics, the topic of ATAD1 can be

599. Recital (2) Parent-Subsidiary Directive (EU) (2015/121).
600. Recital (5) Parent-Subsidiary Directive (EU) (2015/121).
601. Article 1 Parent-Subsidiary Directive (EU) (2015/121) replacing Article 1(2) Parent-Subsidiary Directive 2011/96/EU.
602. Recital (16) ATAD1.
603. Recital (5) ATAD1.
604. M. Helminen, 2021, para. 3.4.1. *See also* recital (16) ATAD1.
605. D.S. Smit in: European Tax Law (Wattel, Marres & Vermeulen eds), 2018, p. 492.
606. *See* recital (11) ATAD1 regarding the GAAR.
607. This applies to the exit taxation rules (*see* Article 5(1) ATAD1), the GAAR (*see* recital (11) ('to ensure that the GAARs apply in domestic situations, within the Union and vis-à-vis third countries in a uniform manner')) and the controlled foreign company rules (*see* recital (11) ('[i]t is desirable to address situations both in third countries and within the Union')).

described as the prevention of tax avoidance by means of measures extending corporate income tax liability of taxpayers within the EU.

Such topic would seem to share common ground with that of, at least, Intra-EU Treaties in the sense that both their topics relate to preventing the creation of opportunities for non-taxation or reduced taxation through tax avoidance or tax evasion. In that sense, ATAD1 could thus be seen as contributing towards the purpose of not creating opportunities for non-taxation or tax avoidance, especially if one takes into account that the commonly used abbreviation 'ATAD' means 'Anti Tax-Avoidance Directive'. There are, however, also differences between their topics. First, tax treaties either impose a limitation on the right to tax income or not if, for example, the principal purpose test of Article 29 OECD Model would provide that the treaty benefits shall not apply. ATAD1, by contrast, does not provide rules relating to the imposition of limitations to the right to tax income but rather requires the taxation of income by extending the corporate tax liability of taxpayers. In such a way, ATAD1 thus provides for different obligations than might arise under tax treaties. Another difference is that ATAD1 only applies to corporate taxpayers whereas tax treaties apply to individuals as well as companies, i.e., corporate taxpayers. Third, in terms of its substance, the topic of ATAD1 is more limited (or: more specific) to that of tax treaties. This can be illustrated as follows. ATAD1 contains, essentially, four anti-tax avoidance provisions with different degrees of overlap with matters dealt with by tax treaties.[608] The GAAR can apply to the same set of facts as tax treaties (including the PPT),[609] whereas the exit taxation rules may apply to situations where Article 13 OECD Model might be applicable.[610] Moreover, the controlled foreign company rules can apply to situations covered by Articles 7 and 23 OECD Model.[611] By contrast, the interest deduction limitation rule does not seem to have such overlap considering that it only affects the corporate tax base of a taxpayer in a Member State by limiting the deductibility of interest (and not the taxation of cross-border activities).[612] As such, three out of the four anti-tax avoidance provisions of ATAD1 can apply to situations covered by Intra-EU Treaties (as well as by Extra-EU, Treaties). Intra-EU Treaties apply, however, with respect to many more categories of cross-border income. As such, the substantive scope of ATAD1 is more limited – or more specific – than that of tax treaties.

It follows from the considerations above that reasons for regarding ATAD1 as relating to the same topic as tax treaties would have to be its substantive overlap with provisions of tax treaties and its purpose to prevent tax avoidance. It should, however, be acknowledged that such reasons for regarding the Directive as relating to the same subject matter as tax treaties would seem to make for a less strong case than would be

608. The fifth anti-tax avoidance rule, the hybrid mismatch rule, is discussed within the context of ATAD2.
609. *See* G. Maisto in: Thinker, Teacher, Traveler: Reimagining International Tax Essays in 1 Honor of H. David Rosenbloom (Kofler, Mason & Rust eds), 2021, para. 25.3.
610. *See*, in general regarding exit taxes, K. Moser, Bulletin for International Taxation 2019/10, pp. 526 et seq.
611. *See* F.A. Engelen, J. Vleggeert & T.M. Vergouwen, WFR 2019/257, p. 7314 and I. Panzeri, European Taxation 2021/4, p. 147.
612. *See* B.J. Arnold, Bulletin for International Taxation 2019/4, pp. 184-185.

the case with respect to the Interest and Royalties Directive, Merger Directive, and Parent-Subsidiary Directive. This is due to, first, those Directives relating to the (historically) main purpose of Intra-EU Treaties to eliminate double taxation whereas ATAD1 would relate to the (more recent) purpose of such treaties to avoid non-taxation. Additionally, those Directives provide for the imposition of an obligation to refrain from taxing cross-border income with a view to eliminating double taxation. In such a way, those three Directives thus provide obligations that are similar to those arising from Intra-EU Treaties. By contrast, ATAD1 is aimed at, essentially, imposing obligations to tax income instead of imposing limitations on the right to tax certain categories of cross-border income. As such, its obligations are not similar to those provided for by Intra-EU Treaties. Such considerations regarding the difference between ATAD1 and the Interest and Royalties Directive, Merger Directive, and Parent-Subsidiary Directive would thus seem to indicate that the sameness of the topic of ATAD1 and Intra-EU Treaties would be less likely than would be the case with respect to those three Directives. Nevertheless, it would still seem conceivable that it can be regarded as relating to the same subject matter as Intra-EU Treaties based on its (limited) substantive overlap and its purpose to avoid – or: prevent – tax avoidance.

#### vi The Topic or Substance of ATAD2

Whereas ATAD1 was aimed at introducing various measures aimed at improvising the resilience of the internal market against cross-border tax avoidance practices, including a provision regarding hybrid mismatches, it is the purpose of ATAD2 to improve such resilience against hybrid mismatches in particular.[613] Hence, its purpose is more limited in terms of types of cross-border avoidance practices that it seeks to address.

This is also reflected by its provisions. ATAD2 provides, first, for the replacement of the provision of ATAD1 regarding hybrid mismatches, i.e., Article 9 ATAD1, by a more extensive provision addressing hybrid mismatches. Whereas Article 9 ATAD1 provided for the denial of deductions with respect to hybrid mismatches resulting in a double deduction or deduction without inclusion within the EU before its amendment, Article 9 after amendment by ATAD2 relates to such mismatches also in the relations with third states, while also introducing an obligation to include income in the taxable base (Article 9(2)(b)). Additionally, ATAD2 extended the scope of the hybrid mismatches covered by ATAD1 to hybrid mismatches involving disregarded permanent establishments (Article 9(5)) and hybrid transfers (Article 9(6)). Also, ATAD2 resulted in the addition of provisions to ATAD1 regarding so-called reverse hybrid mismatches (Article 9a) and tax residency mismatches (Article 9b). Essentially, ATAD2 replaced a 'basic' hybrid mismatch provision in ATAD1 with a comprehensive set of hybrid mismatch provisions.

It thus seems that it is the topic of ATAD2 to extend the hybrid mismatch rules of ATAD1 both in terms of situations covered (from situations between Member States only to also in the relations with third states), in terms of obligations imposed (from

613. Recital (27) ATAD2.

denial of deduction only to also providing for the inclusion of income) and in terms of hybrid mismatches covered with a view to preventing tax avoidance. Bearing this in mind, the topic of ATAD2 can be phrased more generally as providing for rules that are aimed at tackling hybrid mismatches with a view to combatting tax avoidance. The aim of preventing tax avoidance seems to have common ground with the topic of tax treaties to the extent that such treaties seek to eliminate double taxation without creating opportunities for non-taxation and tax avoidance. The common ground with tax treaties would be even more strong if such treaty included a provision – Article 1(2) OECD Model – regarding transparent entities.[614] This provision, which was recommended in Chapter 14 of the BEPS Action 2 Final Report, sets out the way in which tax treaties are to be applied if income is derived by or through an entity that is transparent under the laws of one or both contracting states (thus also hybrid entities).[615] As such, this provision may be regarded as giving effect to the outcomes of the BEPS Action 2 Final Report. The objective of this provision would then seem similar to that of ATAD2 considering that the Commission proposal was aimed at providing 'for rules consistent with and no less effective than the rules recommended by the ... OECD BEPS report on Action 2'.[616] That this focus is consistent with the BEPS Action 2 Report is also reflected by the statement in the preamble that the Member States 'should use the applicable explanations and examples in the OECD BEPS report on Action 2 as a source of illustration or interpretation'.[617] It thus seems arguable that both Article 1(2) OECD Model and ATAD2 share a common objective in the sense of giving effect to the outcomes of the BEPS Action 2 Final Report with respect to hybrid mismatches.

In addition to both being aimed at giving effect to the outcomes of the BEPS Action 2 Report, it would seem conceivable that there is substantive overlap between ATAD2 and tax treaties with respect to income that is attributable to permanent establishments. This could, first of all, be the case where it concerns allocation mismatches. Such mismatches may arise, for example, if a deductible payment from an associated enterprise in a third state is made and such payment would be allocated by the head office state to a permanent establishment in another Member State under an Intra-EU Treaty, while the permanent establishment Member State would allocate that same payment to the head office under that same treaty (i.e., an allocation mismatch).[618] In such situation, there would be a deduction without inclusion outcome within the meaning of Article 9(2) ATAD2 that is the result of the application of the Intra-EU Treaty. The obligation under ATAD2, i.e., inclusion of the payment in the payee jurisdiction, would then touch upon the subject matter of tax treaties. Second,

614. *See* 2017 Update to the OECD Model, p. 2 ('[t]he addition of new paragraph 2 to Article 1 (the transparent entity provision) and of related Commentary changes. These changers appear in Chapter 14 of the Report on Action 2 (Neutralising the Effects of Hybrid Mismatch Arrangements)'). Article 1(2) OECD Model (2017) may also be part of tax treaties concluded before the 2017 Update to the OECD Model if Article 3 of the MLI, regarding transparent entities, would apply with respect to a covered tax treaty.
615. *See also* para. 26.3 of the Commentaries to the OECD Model (2017) to Article 1.
616. Recital (5) ATAD2.
617. Recital (28) ATAD2.
618. This would be a mismatch within the meaning of Article 1(9)(c) ATAD1 after amendment by ATAD2.

ATAD2 provides for the inclusion of income that is attributable to a so-called disregarded permanent establishment that is not taxed. In such a situation, Article 9(5) ATAD2 requires the Member State of the head office to include such income. As such, it essentially seeks to change the way in which the Intra-EU Treaty is applied and, hence, has substantive overlap with such Intra-EU Treaty. Moreover, if a deduction without inclusion outcome would be the result of a deductible payment that is allocated by a head office Member State to a disregarded permanent establishment situated in a third state under an Extra-EU Treaty,[619] Article 9(2)(b) ATAD2 would seem to also be aimed at affecting the application of such treaty.[620] As such, ATAD2 can also have substantive overlap with such treaties with respect to deduction without inclusion outcomes involving deductible payments that are attributable to a disregarded permanent establishment in a third state. Moreover, ATAD2 also provides rules concerning the taxation of deemed payments involving permanent establishments, which also seems to indicate that its provisions can overlap with Article 7 of tax treaties based on the OECD Model given that such provision relates to the allocation of income between a permanent establishment and a head office.[621] These examples demonstrate that ATAD2 can have substantive overlap with situations covered by Article 7 of tax treaties based on the OECD Model. Such substantive overlap is, however, limited to very specific situations, i.e., situations involving hybrid mismatches within the meaning of ATAD2. Tax treaties, by contrast, have a much wider scope in the sense that they provide for rules regarding the taxation of business profits in general by means of Article 7 OECD Model, while also providing rules with respect to the taxation of, essentially, all other categories of cross-border income. Hence, whereas there may be substantive overlap, such overlap only concerns a small area covered by tax treaties. Such scope is even more limited if it is borne in mind that ATAD2 only relates to corporate taxpayers, whereas tax treaties also apply to individuals.

Bearing these considerations in mind, the case for regarding ATAD2 as relating to the same topic as tax treaties would have to be based on the circumstance that they have (limited) substantive overlap and relate to the purpose of avoiding non-taxation and tax avoidance. As such, it can be considered 'conceivable' that it relates to the same topic as tax treaties concluded by the Member States. Nevertheless, there would also seem to be arguments for concluding that the topic of ATAD2 is different from that of tax treaties because its topic, based on its purpose and the scope of their substantive overlap, seems to relate only to a very limited part of the topic covered by tax treaties.

619. This would be a mismatch within the meaning of Article 1(9)(d) ATAD1 after amendment by ATAD2.

620. It is acknowledged that Article 9(5) ATAD2 provides for a carve-out with respect to non-taxation outcomes with respect to disregarded permanent establishments whose income must be exempt under Extra-EU Treaties. This would seem to entail, at first glance, that ATAD2 would not impose an obligation to tax such a deductible payment arising from a third state that is allocated to a permanent establishment in a third state under an Extra-EU Treaty. Such payment would, however, also fall within the scope of Article 9(2)(b) ATAD2. In accordance with recital (29) of the preamble to ATAD2, Article 9(2)(b) could be applicable here because the Article 9(5) does not result in adjustment of the mismatch outcome. Hence, Article 9(2) ATAD2 would still seem applicable.

621. *See* Article 1(9)(f) ATAD1 after amendment by ATAD2.

### vii The Topic or Substance of the Arbitration Directive

The final Directive to be discussed within the context of an analogous application of Article 30 VCLT 1969 is the Arbitration Directive. This Directive seeks to establish an effective and efficient procedure to resolve disputes in the context of the proper functioning of the internal market,[622] in particular disputes leading to double taxation.[623] In order to achieve such objective, the Arbitration Directive introduces a mechanism on which both individuals and companies would be able to rely[624] that is aimed at resolving disputes between Member States concerning the interpretation and application of bilateral tax treaties.[625]

In the preamble of the Arbitration Directive, it is recognised that tax treaties also contain mechanisms aimed at effective resolution of such disputes. Such mechanisms might, however, 'not achieve the effective resolution of such disputes in all cases in a timely manner'.[626] Therefore, the Arbitration Directive has been adopted to provide such an effective resolution of disputes relating to the interpretation and application of tax treaties. Taking into consideration that the Arbitration Directive is expressly aimed at dispute resolution in respect of tax treaties, this would seem to indicate that it relates to the (same) subject matter of tax treaties. Its provisions are, in any event, aimed at effective resolution of disputes regarding, in principle, each provision of a tax treaty, while also applying to all taxpayers that are subject to taxes on income and capital covered by bilateral tax treaties.[627] In addition, the Arbitration Directive expressly seeks to ensure effective dispute resolution leading to double taxation (and hence, to avoid such double taxation), which seems to relate to the purpose of tax treaties.[628] In terms of substantive overlap with provisions of tax treaties, it can furthermore be noted that this would be conceivable if an Intra-EU Treaty contained a provision similar to Article 25(5) OECD Model. Such a provision is aimed at providing for a dispute resolution mechanism, whereas such a mechanism is also provided for by the Arbitration Directive because the tax treaty-based dispute resolution mechanism, according to the preamble of the Arbitration Directive, does not always function effectively. As such, the Arbitration Directive effectively seeks to provide an alternative, more effective, dispute resolution mechanism than that provided for in Intra-EU Treaties containing a provision such as Article 25(5) OECD Model.

622. Recital (10) Arbitration Directive ((EU) 2017/1852).
623. Recital (2) Arbitration Directive ((EU) 2017/1852).
624. Article 1 Arbitration Directive ((EU) 2017/1852). *See also* recital (7) Arbitration Directive ((EU) 2017/1852).
625. Recital (2) in conjunction with recital (10) Arbitration Directive ((EU) 2017/1852), as well as Article 1 Arbitration Directive ((EU) 2017/1852).
626. Recital (3) Arbitration Directive ((EU) 2017/1852).
627. Recital (7) Arbitration Directive ((EU) 2017/1852).
628. Recital (2) Arbitration Directive ((EU) 2017/1852).

### viii Summary of the Sameness of the Subject Matter of the Directives and Tax Treaties

Based on the preceding paragraphs regarding each Directive, the Table 6.1 summarises the overlap between each Directive and tax treaties in terms of their (i) objectives, (ii) substantive scope, (iii) geographical scope, and (iv) personal scope.

*Table 6.1 Summary of Sameness of Subject Matter of the Directives and Tax Treaties*

| *Directive* | *Objective* | *Substantive Scope* | *Geographical Scope* | *Personal Scope* |
|---|---|---|---|---|
| Interest and Royalties Directive | Partial, only to the extent that it concerns the elimination of double taxation on interest and royalty payments. | Partial, only Articles 11 and 12 OECD Model. | Only for Intra-EU Treaties. | Partial, only for companies. |
| Merger Directive | Partial, only to the extent that it concerns the elimination of double taxation on capital gains resulting from corporate reorganisations. | Partial, only Article 13 OECD Model. | Only for Intra-EU Treaties. | Partial, only for companies. |
| Mutual Assistance Directive | No, the exchange of information is not the (main) purpose of tax treaties. | Partial, only Article 26 OECD Model. | Only for Intra-EU Treaties. | Yes, both individuals and companies. |
| Parent-Subsidiary Directive as amended by (2014/86/EU) and (2015/121/EU) | Partial, only to the extent that it concerns the elimination of double taxation on dividend payments without creating opportunities for tax avoidance. | Partial, only Articles 10 and 23 OECD Model. | Only for Intra-EU Treaties | Partial, only for companies. |
| ATAD1 | Partial, ATAD1 primarily focuses on tackling tax avoidance without creating double taxation (tax treaties is other way around). | Partial, in any event, Articles 7, 13, 23 and 29 OECD Model. | Intra-EU and Extra-EU Treaties | Partial, corporate taxpayers only. |

| *Directive* | *Objective* | *Substantive Scope* | *Geographical Scope* | *Personal Scope* |
|---|---|---|---|---|
| ATAD2 | Partial and limited, ATAD2 is only aimed at tackling tax avoidance arising from hybrid mismatches. | Partial, in any event, Articles 1(2), 7 and 23 OECD Model. | Intra-EU and Extra-EU Treaties | Partial, corporate taxpayers only. |
| Arbitration Directive | Partial, the Arbitration Directive is aimed at introducing an effective dispute resolution mechanism. However, such mechanism is in particular aimed at disputes leading to double taxation (and hence, seeks to eliminate such double taxation). | Full, in the sense that its measures can apply to the interpretation and application of each tax treaty provision. Also, overlap with Article 25 OECD Model. | Only for Intra-EU Treaties | Yes, individuals and companies. |

### ix Conclusion of the Sameness of the Subject Matter of the Directives and Tax Treaties

Based on the preceding paragraphs, it would seem that the topic of the Arbitration Directive would seem most likely to be regarded as relating to that of Intra-EU Treaties. This is due to this Directive being the only Directive that is directly linked to the interpretation and application of Intra-EU Treaties given that it seeks to provide an effective dispute resolution mechanism aimed at resolving in an effective way disputes regarding the interpretation and application of such treaties. Additionally, it could relate to the same topic, i.e., dispute resolution with respect to tax treaties, as Article 25(5) OECD Model while also having the same personal scope as Intra-EU Treaties in the sense that individuals as well as companies would fall within the scope of the Arbitration Directive.

Moreover, the topics of the Interest and Royalties Directive, the Merger Directive and the Parent-Subsidiary may also be likely to be regarded as relating to that of tax treaties. This is due to such Directives having the same general purpose of eliminating double taxation as Intra-EU Treaties. They also impose similar obligations as Intra-EU Treaties in the sense that their application limits the extent to which certain cross-border categories of income may be taxed. Moreover, with respect to the amendments to the Parent-Subsidiary Directive, it would seem that they also relate to the subject matter of Intra-EU Treaties because they are aimed, if read in conjunction with the

Directive that they amended, at avoiding elimination of double taxation without creating opportunities for non-taxation or tax avoidance. Hence, also those amendments seem to relate to the same subject matter notwithstanding that especially the 2014 amendment imposes a duty to tax, which duty is not imposed by tax treaties. The reason for regarding the topic of these three Directives as likely – and not: most likely – as relating to the same topic as that of Intra-EU Treaties is based on the differences in terms of substantive overlap and personal overlap as compared to the Arbitration Directive. Whereas the Arbitration Directive may be resorted to for the purposes of dispute resolution regarding the interpretation or application of any Intra-EU Treaty provision, the overlap between the Interest and Royalties Directive, the Merger Directive and the Parent-Subsidiary extend only to articles in Intra-EU Treaties based on Articles 10, 11, 12, 13 and 23 of the OECD Model. As such, the substantive overlap of each of these Directives would seem less than that of the Arbitration Directive. Moreover, the personal scope of these Directives is limited to companies only, whereas the provisions of Intra-EU Treaties also relate to individuals. It would thus seem that the topics of the Interest and Royalties Directive, the Merger Directive and the Parent-Subsidiary, although sharing common ground with Intra-EU Treaties, must also be regarded as more limited than that of Intra-EU Treaties.

Less likely, although still conceivable, would be that the topics of ATAD1 and ATAD2 relate to the same topic as that of Intra-EU Treaties. Reasons for regarding them as relating to the same topic would be that ATAD1 and ATAD2 can have substantive overlap with Intra-EU Treaties and that such Directive provide rules aimed at tackling tax avoidance without, in case of ATAD1, resulting in double taxation. As such, these Directives do not relate to the (historically main) purpose of tax treaties, i.e., the elimination of double taxation, but only to the (more recent) purpose of preventing non-taxation and tax avoidance. The sameness of the topics of ATAD1 and ATAD2 would thus have to be based on such latter purpose, as well as on the basis of their provisions being able to relate to the some of the situations that are also covered by Intra-EU Treaties. As such, the main difference between the topics of ATAD1 and ATAD2 with the topics of the Interest and Royalties Directive, the Merger Directive and the Parent-Subsidiary Directive would seem to be that the former do not relate to the elimination of double taxation whereas the latter are not – with the exception of the Parent-Subsidiary Directive – relating to the prevention of non-taxation or tax avoidance. As such, it is concluded that it seems less likely, yet still conceivable, that ATAD1 and ATAD2 can be regarded as relating to the same topic as an Intra-EU Treaty.

Least likely, yet still conceivable, would seem to be that the topic of the Mutual Assistance Directive would be the same as that of Intra-EU Treaties. The reason for regarding this least likely is that the objective of the Mutual Assistance Directive, i.e., the exchange of information and other forms of administrative cooperation between Member States, is not reflected in the topic of Intra-EU Treaties as eliminating double taxation of cross-border income of residents of the contracting states, by imposing limit to the right to tax, without creating opportunities for non-taxation or reduced taxation through tax avoidance or tax evasion. This difference can be explained by the circumstance that the exchange of information seems to reflect only an ancillary objective and not one of the main objectives of an Intra-EU Treaty. Such difference would then seem to make it less likely that it relates to the same subject as Intra-EU Treaties as compared to the other Directives that are linked to the objectives of Intra-EU Treaties to eliminate double taxation without creating opportunities for non-taxation or reduced taxation through tax avoidance or tax evasion. Apart from such difference, the Mutual Assistance Directive does seem to have substantial overlap with Intra-EU Treaties containing a provision similar to Article 26 OECD Model. Additionally, the personal scope of the Mutual Assistance Directive is - contrary as is the case with respect to the other Directives with the exception of the Arbitration Directive - similar to that of Intra-EU Treaties in the sense that it extends to both individuals and companies. Based on such similarities, it can thus nevertheless be considered conceivable that the Mutual Assistance Directive would have to be regarded as relating to the same topic as that of an Intra-EU Treaty.

Whereas it is considered conceivable that each of the Directives can be regarded as relating to the same topic as tax treaties, it should be acknowledged that as a general observation their topics, with the exception of the Arbitration Directive and the Mutual Assistance Directive, seem more limited than that of tax treaties in terms of cross-border income falling within their scope, i.e., only specific categories are covered by the Directives whereas in principle all categories of cross-border income are covered by Intra-EU Treaties, and in terms of the personal scope, i.e., corporate taxpayers or companies only as compared to companies as well as individuals. As such, the topic of such Directive seems to be, in any event, more limited - or: more specific - than that of tax treaties. This does not, however, have to entail that they cannot relate to the same subject matter in light of the common ground identified above, but this limited scope should be borne in mind when ascertaining whether these Directives would have to be regarded as relating to the same subject matter as an Intra-EU Treaty.

#### *6.4.2.2.5 Conclusion Regarding the Scope and Applicability of an Analogous Application of Article 30 VCLT 1969*

Whereas Article 30 VCLT 1969 cannot be applied to conflicts between the Directives and tax treaties, it has been concluded that it is arguable that the *lex posterior* rule of Article 30 VCLT 1969 can be applied by analogy to conflicts between the Directives, as decisions of an international organisation, and tax treaties. The basis for considering this arguable is that there are arguments for regarding the adoption of the Directives relevantly similar to the conclusion of tax treaties in light of the purpose of Article 30 VCLT 1969 and the lack of a hierarchy between treaties and decisions of international organisations under public international law.

If applied by analogy, conflicts between Directives and tax treaties would fall within the scope of the *lex posterior* rule of Article 30 VCLT 1969 if they are successive and relate to the same subject matter. With respect to the first condition, it has been concluded that it is possible to establish whether a Directive is 'successive' as compared to a tax treaty and vice versa (section 6.4.2.2.3).[629] As such, whether the *lex posterior* rule can be applied by analogy essentially depends on whether a Directive and a tax treaty can be regarded as relating to the same subject matter. In that respect, it has been concluded that it is conceivable that each of the Directives may be regarded as relating to the same subject matter as Intra-EU Treaties based on the understanding of the topic of such treaties as relating to the elimination of double taxation of cross-border income of residents of the contracting states, by imposing limits to the right to tax, without creating opportunities for non-taxation or reduced taxation through tax avoidance or tax evasion.

There are, however, differences in the extent to which this would seem conceivable. The strongest arguments seem to apply with respect to the Arbitration Directive because such Directive is aimed at introducing an effective dispute resolution mechanism regarding disputes with respect to the interpretation and application of provisions of Intra-EU Treaties. Hence, it is clearly linked to Intra-EU Treaties. Such a clear link is absent with respect to other Directives. Nevertheless, there are still good arguments regarding the Interest and Royalties Directive, the Merger Directive, the Parent-Subsidiary Directive as relating to the same topic as Intra-EU Treaties based on such Directives being aimed at eliminating double taxation with respect to cross-border income by imposing limitations on the right to tax such income while the Parent-Subsidiary Directive also provides rules aimed at preventing non-taxation and tax avoidance. There are, however, also differences with Intra-EU Treaties in the sense that the substantive and personal scope of such Directives are limited as compared to the substantive and personal scope of Intra-EU Treaties. Viewed from that perspective, the topic of these Directives can be regarded as more specific than that of Intra-EU Treaties (and, for this reason, as different from the topic of such tax treaties), while still having common ground with such treaties. Moreover, the arguments underlying the sameness of the subject matter of ATAD1 and ATAD2 and Intra-EU Treaties would be based on such Directives being aimed at preventing non-taxation and tax avoidance, while also having substantive overlap with such treaties in the sense that some of the provisions of these Directives imposing an extension of the corporate tax liability could apply to situations that would also be covered by Intra-EU Treaties. Based on such substantive overlap, as well as the similarities between their purposes, there would be common ground that would seem to make it arguable that ATAD1 and ATAD2 relate to the same topic – and subject matter – as Intra-EU Treaties for the purposes of an analogous application of Article 30 VCLT 1969. As was the case with the topics of the Interest and Royalties Directive, the Merger Directive, the Parent-Subsidiary Directive, however, the topics of ATAD1 and ATAD2 are in any event more limited than that of Intra-EU Treaties based on the differences in substantive overlap and personal scope. As such, the topics of ATAD1 and ATAD2 share aspects with the subject matter of Intra-EU

629. The main difference with a (regular) application of Article 30 VCLT 1969 in this respect would be that it is not the date of (accession to) Article 288 TFEU that is decisive, but rather (accession to or adoption of) the relevant Directive. This would, in turn, entail that the Directives would be successive as compared to at least 270 Intra-EU Treaties and 884 Extra-EU Treaties (representing 62.4% of all treaties) to, at best, 336 Intra-EU Treaties and 1,416 Extra-EU Treaties (representing 94% of all treaties).

Treaties, but their subject matters are more limited. Finally, the least strong connection in terms of similarity of subject matter would seem to exist between the Mutual Assistance Directive and Intra-EU Treaties. This is due to such Directive relating to an ancillary objective of such treaties and not (directly) to either the elimination of double taxation or to the prevention of non-taxation or tax avoidance or tax evasion. The absence of such a link with the main objectives of Intra-EU Treaties does not, however, entail that the similarity in substantive scope is very different from that of the other Directives in the sense that the subject matter of the other Directives, as compared to that of Intra-EU Treaties, also shares common ground with one (or more) provision(s) of an Intra-EU Treaty (in this case with provisions based on Article 26 OECD Model). Hence, there would be substantive overlap whereas the personal scope - different from the other Directives with the exception of the Arbitration Directive - is similar to that of Intra-EU Treaties. As such, the sameness of the subject matter of the Mutual Assistance Directive may be based on the substantive overlap with Article 26 OECD Model, if part of an Intra-EU Treaty. It does not, however, relate to the main purposes of Intra-EU Treaties, which seems to make the position that this Directive relates to the same topic as Intra-EU Treaties less strong as compared to the other Directives, yet still arguable or conceivable.

It follows from the above that it is considered arguable, and hence conceivable, that each of the Directives can be regarded as relating to the same subject matter as Intra-EU Treaties. If relating to the same subject matter, the consequence would be that conflicts between them could fall within the scope of, and be resolved by, an analogous application of the *lex posterior* rule of 30 VCLT 1969.

### 6.4.2.3 *The Consequences of the* Lex Posterior *Conflict Rule (Article 30(3) and (4) of the VCLT 1969)*

#### *6.4.2.3.1 General*

Based on the conclusions of section 6.4.2.1, a conflict between a Directive and a tax treaty cannot fall within the scope of Article 30 VCLT 1969. It has, however, also been concluded in section 6.4.2.2 that it is arguable that Article 30 VCLT 1969 may be applied by analogy to conflicts between such a Directive and a tax treaty. Taking into account this conclusion, the present section sets out the rule of Article 30 VCLT 1969 that would then be applicable to successive Directives, as decisions of an international organisation, and tax treaties relating to the same subject matter.

The starting point in this respect is that it follows from Article 30(1) VCLT 1969 that the rights and obligations of the states that are bound by such treaties and Directives would be determined in accordance with paragraphs 2 through 5 of Article 30 VCLT 1969. For present purposes, paragraphs 3 and 4 are most relevant because such paragraphs contain the *lex posterior* conflict rule. Therefore, these paragraphs are discussed in detail below. In discussing them, three different situations of conflicts between Directives and tax treaties will be addressed:

(a) a conflict between a later Directive and an earlier Intra-EU Treaty (section 6.4.2.3.2);
(b) a conflict between a later Intra-EU Treaty and an earlier Directive (section 6.4.2.3.3); and
(c) conflicts between Directives and Extra-EU Treaties (section 6.4.2.3.4).

The reason for drawing such distinction is that paragraph 3 of Article 30 VCLT 1969 applies only when all the parties to the earlier treaty are also parties to the later treaty (or, under an analogous application, the later Directive). This provision thus only applies to the situation wherein a Directive, to which (by analogy) the 27 Member States are parties, and an earlier Intra-EU Treaty, to which only two Member States have been parties. By contrast, paragraph 4 applies when the parties to the later treaty (or Directive) are not also the same parties as to the earlier treaty (or Directive). This would be the case if an Intra-EU Treaty, concluded between two Member States, is later as compared to a Directive, 'concluded' between 27 Member States, as well as with respect to Extra-EU Treaties. With respect to the MLI, it can be noted that, to the extent that the MLI would be bilateralisable and affecting an Intra-EU Treaty, the same consequences apply as with respect to earlier and later Intra-EU Treaties. To the extent that it is bilateralisable and affecting an Extra-EU Treaty, the consequences of Extra-EU Treaties apply, while such consequences also apply to the extent that the MLI would be regarded as multilateral.

As noted above, the present section focuses on paragraphs 3 and 4 of Article 30 VCLT 1969. The reason for not discussing paragraph 2 is that such paragraph merely provides that the *lex posterior* conflict rule is not applicable if one of the two conflicting sources of international law would provide that it is subject to the other by means of so-called subordination clauses.[630] Such subordination clauses may, for example, provide that the treaty 'is subject to', 'is not inconsistent with', 'is without prejudice to' or 'shall not affect' another treaty.[631] As such, subordination clauses essentially provide evidence of a common intention between the parties regarding how to resolve conflicts with certain other treaties or sources of international law. Examples of such clauses may be found in the TFEU with respect to pre-accession Extra-EU Treaties (Article 351),[632] as well as in a few tax treaties vis-à-vis their obligations under the EU

630. O. Dörr & K. Schmalenbach, 2018, p. 546, para. 16. This paragraph does not, by contrast, relate to treaties providing that they claim priority over another treaty (by means of so-called supremacy clauses). *See*, to that effect, M. Villiger, pp. 404-405, para. 12.
631. J.B. Mus, Netherlands International Law Review 1998/2, pp. 214-215. It is noted that Mus does not refer to 'shall not affect'.
632. *See* A. Orakhelashvili in: The Vienna Conventions on the Law of Treaties (Corten & Klein eds), 2011, para. 61 and O. Dörr & K. Schmalenbach, 2018, p. 546, para. 16.

Treaties.[633] If such a clause is included in a treaty, it follows from Article 30(2) VCLT 1969 that a conflict is to be resolved in accordance with such a clause and not by reference to the *lex posterior* rule of paragraphs 3 and 4 of Article 30 VCLT 1969.

Paragraph 5 is also not further discussed. This paragraph provides that application of Article 30(4) VCLT 1969 does not affect (i) the regime of modifications of a multilateral treaty by means of a treaty to which only some of the parties to such treaty are a party (Article 41 VCLT 1969), (ii) termination or suspension of a treaty under Article 60 VCLT 1969, and (iii) any question of state responsibility that arises from the conclusion or application of a treaty what would be incompatible with an earlier treaty. With respect to Article 41 VCLT 1969, it suffices to note that it only applies to the modification of multilateral treaties. As such, it cannot modify bilateral tax treaties. In addition, regarding the MLI, there would not be any indications that the Directives are intended to amend the MLI in any way.[634] In addition, Article 60 VCLT 1969 cannot, by its very nature, result in the Directives affecting the application of tax treaties because it can merely 'entitle' a party to terminate such a treaty or suspend its operation in whole or in part in case of a material breach of such a tax treaty.[635] Such a party may also resort to other measures outside the scope of Article 60 VCLT 1969, such as taking

633. A search in the IBFD Tax Treaty Database (performed on 24 January 2022) on the term 'European Union' revealed that 26 treaties contain – specific or general – subordination clauses granting priority to EU law. Such clauses may include wording indicating that it is agreed or that it is understood that (i) the laws of the EU shall prevail over the tax treaty (Protocol to the Netherlands-Germany Tax Treaty 2012), (ii) the tax treaty shall be applied in full compliance with international obligations arising from EU Membership (Article 29(3) Italy-Kosovo Treaty 2021), (iii) the tax treaty shall not affect legal acts of the EU (Protocols to the Luxembourg-Poland Tax Treaty 2012 and the Hungary-Luxembourg Tax Treaty 2015), or (iv) the tax treaty shall in no way prejudice obligations arising from membership of the EU (Protocols to the Hungary-Armenia Tax Treaty 2009, the Hungary-Taiwan Tax Treaty 2010, the Hungary-Hong Kong Tax Treaty 2010, the Hungary-Denmark Tax Treaty 2011, the Hungary-Georgia Tax Treaty 2011, the Hungary-Mexico Tax Treaty 2011, the Hungary-United Arab Emirates Tax Treaty 2013, the Hungary-Bahrain Tax Treaty 2014, the Hungary-Kyrgyzstan Tax Treaty 2020, and the Hungary-Andorra Tax Treaty 2021, as well as Article 29 Hungary-Kosovo Tax Treaty 2013 and Article 30 Hungary-Iraq Tax Treaty 2016). In addition, such subordination clauses may also take the form of a joint declaration (Joint Declaration to the Hungary-Liechtenstein Income and Capital Tax Treaty 2015), a unilateral understanding (Protocol to the Hungary-San Marino Income Tax Treaty 2009 and Article 27 of the Hungary-Qatar Income Tax Treaty 2012), or a unilateral declaration (Protocol to the Hungary-Saudi Arabia Income and Capital Tax Treaty 2014 and Protocol to the Hungary-Iran Income and Capital Tax Treaty 2015). What is of particular interest with respect to these general subordination clauses in the tax treaties concluded by the Member States is that they have mainly been included in tax treaties concluded with third states (81%) (general subordination clauses have been included in 4 treaties concluded between Member States whereas they have been included in 17 treaties concluded with third states).

634. Even if this would be the case, however, it should be established that either (i) the MLI provides for such a possibility of modification or (ii) that the modification is not prohibited by the MLI. Based on Article 33 MLI, it would seem that amendments are only permitted upon a proposal that it considered by a Conference of the Parties.

635. M.E. Villiger, 2009, pp. 741-742, para. 12 as well as B. Simma & C.J. Tams in: The Vienna Convention on the Law of Treaties (Corten & Klein eds), 2011, paras 1 and 12.

countermeasures,[636] asserting its right to performance of the treaty,[637] or to present an international claim for compensation.[638] As this provision cannot affect the application of tax treaties directly, it is not further discussed. Finally, the confirmation that Article 30(4) VCLT 1969 does not affect any question of state responsibility is relevant, but its effect is discussed separately in section 6.5.

#### *6.4.2.3.2 Intra-EU Treaties and Later Directives (Analogous Application of Article 30(3) VCLT 1969)*

In the event of a conflict between an earlier Intra-EU Treaty and a later Directive, all the parties to the earlier treaty would also be parties (by analogy) to the later Directive. In such a situation, an analogous application of Article 30(3) VCLT 1969 would provide that the earlier Intra-EU Treaty applies only to the extent that its provisions would be compatible with those of the later Directive (as the *lex posterior*).[639] As such, later Directives relating to the same subject matter as an earlier Intra-EU Treaty would effectively set aside such a treaty.[640] This then entails that the application – in the sense of: applicability – of earlier Intra-EU Treaties could be affected by the Directives under an analogous application of Article 30 VCLT 1969.

> The effect of an analogous application of the *lex posterior* rule of Article 30 VCLT 1969 to a conflict between a Directive an earlier Intra-EU Treaty can be illustrated as follows. The State Secretary of Finance of the Netherlands has indicated that Dutch national laws cannot override obligations under tax treaties concluded by the Netherlands, even if such national laws are aimed at implementing a Directive.[641] As such, the national legislation providing for the taxation of profits attributable to a disregarded permanent establishment,[642] as required by Article 9(5) ATAD2, would be set aside by Intra-EU Treaties concluded by the Netherlands if the taxation of such profits would be incompatible with such treaties.[643] Such an incompatibility would seem to arise if, for example, a Dutch corporate taxpayer would have a disregarded permanent establishment situated in Luxembourg to which income is allocated under the tax treaty with Luxembourg given that such income must be exempted by the Netherlands in accordance with Article 23 of such tax treaty. If, however, it would be accepted that the *lex posterior* conflict rule of Article 30 VCLT 1969 can be applied by analogy to conflicts between Directives, as decisions of an international organisation, and earlier Intra-EU Treaties and that ATAD2 relates to the same subject matter as the Intra-EU Treaty between the

636. M.E. Villiger, 2009, p. 748, para. 26, B. Simma & C.J. Tams in: The Vienna Convention on the Law of Treaties (Corten & Klein eds), 2011, para. 4 and O. Dörr & K. Schmalenbach in: 2011, p. 1044, para. 74.
637. M.E. Villiger, 2009, p. 738, para. 6.
638. M.E. Villiger, 2009, p. 748, para. 26 and O. Dörr & K. Schmalenbach in: 2011, p. 1035, para. 45.
639. Article 30(3) VCLT 1969, to the extent relevant, provides the following: 'the earlier treaty applies only to the extent that its provisions are compatible with those of the later treaty'.
640. It is acknowledged that Article 30(3) VCLT 1969 only affects the applicability of a provision in an earlier treaty; it does not invalidate or terminate such earlier treaty. *See* J. Pauwelyn, 2003, p. 363.
641. Dutch Parliamentary Proceedings II 2021-2022, 22 112, no. 3397, p. 10.
642. *See* Article 15e(9) Dutch Corporate Income Tax Act 1969.
643. Dutch Parliamentary Proceedings II 2018-2019, 35 241, no. 3 p. 17.

> Netherlands and Luxembourg, such an incompatibility would not arise in practice. This is because it would follow from such *lex posterior* conflict rule that the earlier Intra-EU Treaty between the Netherlands and Luxembourg, concluded in 1968, is applicable only to the extent compatible with (the provisions of) the later Directive, i.e., (Article 9(5) of) ATAD2. As the exemption of income attributable to the disregarded permanent establishment under such tax treaty would be incompatible with Article 9(5) ATAD2, such exemption would thus not be applicable. The inapplicability of the exemption in the tax treaty would then, in turn, entail that the Dutch national laws providing for the taxation of the profits attributable to the Luxembourg disregarded permanent establishment are not incompatible with such treaty and that such profits would be taxed by the Netherlands notwithstanding the fact that, pursuant to the provisions of the Intra-EU Treaty between the Netherlands and Luxembourg, the Netherlands would have been required to exempt those profits.[644]

It follows that (provisions of later) Directives can affect the application of (earlier) Intra-EU Treaties under an analogous application of Article 30 VCLT 1969. It must, however, be acknowledged that Article 30(3) VCLT 1969 refers to its *lex posterior* conflict rule being subject to the earlier Intra-EU Treaty not having been terminated or suspended in operation under Article 59 VCLT 1969. This makes sense considering that no conflict should arise if the earlier Intra-EU Treaty would have been terminated or suspended, i.e., no longer be in force or governing the relations between the Member States.[645] In that event, only the Directive would be applicable. As such, it should first be established whether the Directives would affect the application of earlier Intra-EU Treaties under (an analogous application of) Article 59 VCLT 1969.

According to (an analogous application of) Article 59 VCLT 1969, an earlier Intra-EU Treaty would be terminated or suspended if it relates to the same subject matter as the Directive and the adoption of a Directive implied the termination or suspension of the earlier Intra-EU Treaty.[646] With respect to the condition regarding the 'same subject matter', the prevailing view is that such sameness must be determined on the basis of the two successive treaties as a whole (or, under an analogous application, on the basis of a treaty and a Directive as a whole).[647] This thus requires a comparability to a certain degree of generality.[648] The reason for this general approach regarding the sameness of subject matter is that Article 59 VCLT 1969 can only result in the termination or suspension of the earlier Intra-EU Treaty as a whole.

644. Within this context reference can be made to L. de Broe in: Building Global International Tax Law: Essays in Honour of Guglielmo Maisto (Pistone ed.), 2022, para. 23.4.3 who indicates that a similar line of reasoning has been adopted by the Belgian legislator in justification of its amendment of Belgium's controlled foreign company legislation 'when it reversed its earlier position that it could not adopt CFC rules on low-taxed PEs established in treaty countries'.

645. *See*, to this effect, S.A. Sadat-Akhavi, 2003, p. 50. *See also* N. Matz-Lück in: The Max Planck Encyclopedia of Public International Law (Wolfrum ed.), 2010, para. 18 and O. Dörr & K. Schmalenbach in: 2012, para. 548, p. 22.

646. *See* the title of Article 59 VCLT 1969 ('implied by conclusion of a later treaty').

647. The view that Article 59 VCLT 1969 only covers termination of suspension of the earlier treaty in full, and not partially, has been expressed by S.A. Sadat-Akhavi, 2003, p. 49 and O. Dörr & K. Schmalenbach in: 2012, para. 1018, para. 26.

648. F. Dubuisson in: The Vienna Convention on the Law of Treaties (Corten & Klein eds), 2011, para. 25.

As such, a limited degree of overlap between such a treaty and a later treaty (or Directive) should not be able to justify the termination or suspension of such an Intra-EU Treaty in full.[649] Moreover, termination or suspension on the basis of Article 59 VCLT 1969 requires that the Directives would reflect an implicit intention of the Member States to terminate or suspend their earlier Intra-EU Treaties in full. The Directives adopted to this date do not, however, reflect such an intention. The Interest and Royalties Directive, Merger Directive, Parent-Subsidiary Directive, ATAD1 and ATAD2 apply only to corporate taxpayers and only partially overlap with provisions of tax treaties concluded by the Member States. Hence, they do not reflect by any means an implicit intention to terminate such tax treaties in full. In addition, the Mutual Assistance Directive only overlaps with Article 26 OECD Model and contributes to an ancillary objective of Intra-EU Treaties. Such a limited overlap would not reflect an implicit intention to terminate or suspend the operation of such treaties. Finally, the application of the Arbitration Directive is dependent on Intra-EU Treaties considering that it seeks to provide a dispute resolution mechanism with respect to the interpretation and application of such treaties. Hence, it requires their existence. Therefore, the Arbitration Directive cannot be said to reflect an implicit intention to terminate or suspend an earlier Intra-EU Treaty. It thus follows that earlier Intra-EU Treaties are not terminated or suspended (in full) by (an analogous application of) Article 59 VCLT 1969.

Given that earlier Intra-EU Treaties are not terminated or suspended under an analogous application of Article 59 VCLT 1969, the *lex posterior* rule of Article 30 VCLT 1969 can be applied by analogy to conflicts between Directives and earlier Intra-EU Treaties. If applicable, it follows from such rule that earlier Intra-EU Treaties only apply to the extent compatible with later Directives relating to the same subject matter. As such, under an analogous application of Article 30 VCLT 1969 the application – in terms of applicability – of earlier Intra-EU Treaties could be affected in the event of a conflict with such a later Directive.

#### *6.4.2.3.3 Directives and Later Intra-EU Treaties (Article 30(4) VCLT 1969)*

In the event of a conflict between a later Intra-EU Treaty and an earlier Directive, the (2) parties to the later bilateral treaty do not include all the (27) 'parties' to the earlier Directive. Hence, a conflict between such a treaty and Directive falls outside the scope of an analogous application of Article 30(3) VCLT 1969. Instead, Article 30(4) VCLT 1969 would have to be applied by analogy. This provision would have the following two consequences:

(a) between the Member States that are parties to the later Intra-EU Treaty the *lex posterior* rule of Article 30(3) VCLT 1969 applies. As such, in their bilateral relation, the later Intra-EU Treaty would take precedence over the earlier

649. *See*, to that effect, F. Dubuisson in: The Vienna Convention on the Law of Treaties (Corten & Klein eds), 2011, para. 26.

Directive (Article 30(4)(a) VCLT 1969). In such a way, it would seem that the application of the Directive would be affected by the conclusion of a later Intra-EU Treaty (instead of the Intra-EU Treaty's application being affected by a Directive);[650] and

(b) between the Member States to such later Intra-EU Treaty and the other Member States that are 'parties' to the Directive, the Directive would continue to govern their mutual rights and obligations (Article 30(4)(b) VCLT 1969). Hence, in those relations the later Intra-EU Treaty would not, in accordance with the principle of *pacta tertus*, affect the application of the Directives. Consequently, the two Member States to the later Intra-EU Treaty remain obliged to achieve the result of the earlier Directive vis-à-vis the other 25 Member States.

With respect to these two consequences, the following can be noted. The first consequence reflects the *lex posterior* rule in the sense that it provides that between the parties to the later Intra-EU Treaty, such treaty would take precedence over the earlier Directive. The second consequence, by contrast, confirms the application of the earlier treaty in the relations with the Member States that are not also parties to the later Intra-EU Treaty. As such, this second consequence reflects the *lex prior in tempore, potior in jure* rule pursuant to which an earlier norm prevails over a later norm.[651]

Within the context of conflicts between a later Intra-EU Treaty and an earlier Directive, the *lex prior* conflict rule entails that if Member State A and Member State B conclude a later Intra-EU Treaty, such Member States remain under a duty to achieve the result of a Directive in their bilateral relation vis-à-vis the other 25 Member States. As such, concluding a later Intra-EU Treaty and giving effect to such a treaty over a conflicting Directive with respect to cross-border income between Member State A and Member State B would entail a failure to achieve the result of such Directive. Such a failure would, in turn, mean that the rights of, or obligations towards, the other 25 Member States under the TFEU would be violated. That outcome is at odds with Article 30(4)(b) VCLT 1969 which provides that the TFEU and the Directives would continue

650. Whether the application of the Directives could be affected in such a respect assumes that Article 30(4)(a) VCLT 1969 could be applied as such. Based on Article 5 VCLT 1969, however, the application of the rules of the VCLT 1969 is 'without prejudice to any relevant rules of the [international] organization'. As such, if it would be established that the relevant rules of the EU as an international organisation do not allow later Intra-EU Treaties relating to the same subject matter as the Directives to take precedence under the *lex posterior* rule of Article 30(4)(a) VCLT 1969, this effect should not arise.

651. *See* J. Pauwelyn, 2003, p. 424, M.E. Villiger, 2009, pp. 399-400, para. 1, and C.J. Borgen in: The Oxford Guide to Treaties (Hollis ed.), 2012, para. 2. Pauwelyn refers to this principle within the context of 'the earlier AB norm prevail[s] over the later conflicting AC norm (lex prior principle or prior in tempore potior in jus)'). Moreover, Villiger writes that the principle of *lex prior in tempore, potior in jure* is among the principles serving to resolve conflicts between successive treaties. According to him, the *lex prior* principle is aimed 'in particular at conflicting treaties with diverging membership'. Finally, Borgen considers the lex priori principle 'most likely to be used when there is no commonality between the two treaties (eg AB:AC) or where there may be partial commonality overall (eg ABCD:ABEF) but no commonality among the specific counterparties to the conflict (eg comparing A's obligations to C or D to its obligations to E or F)'.

to govern the relations between Member States A and B and the other Member States. As such, giving effect to a later Intra-EU Treaty over a Directive would entail violation of the *pacta sunt servanda* principle because the obligations arising from the Directive (and Article 288 TFEU) would not be performed in full. Moreover, even the mere conclusion of such a later incompatible Intra-EU Treaty may be considered as a violation of such principle vis-à-vis the other Member States given that the CJEU has held that Member States must respect EU law when concluding treaties.[652] As such, the conclusion of a later Intra-EU Treaty that conflicts with an earlier Directive is contrary to the rights of, and obligations towards, the other Member States, which rights and obligations are not affected by the conclusion of a later Intra-EU Treaty under Article 30(4)(b) VCLT 1969. This illustrates the issue of Article 30(4) VCLT 1969 that it does not 'solve the principal dilemma of breach of the pacta sunt servanda rule if the fulfilment of two incompatible obligations is owed by a party'.[653] It merely confirms that between Member States A and B, the later Intra-EU Treaty would be governing their rights and obligations while simultaneously confirming that between such Member States A and B and the other 25 Member States, the earlier Directive (and TFEU) continue(s) to govern their mutual rights and obligations.

It thus follows that (an analogous application of) Article 30(4) VCLT 1969 does not resolve a conflict between a later Intra-EU Treaty and an earlier Directive. This provision merely confirms that the Member States concluding a later Intra-EU Treaty can apply such a treaty in their mutual relations while also remaining bound to achieve the result of a Directive vis-à-vis the other 25 Member States. Hence, it only provides that the Intra-EU Treaty and the Directive would be valid and equally applicable. As such, it cannot be concluded that the application of later Intra-EU Treaties is affected by earlier Directives under the conflict rules of Article 30(4) VCLT 1969 (or that the application of the Directives is affected by the later Intra-EU Treaties).[654]

---

652. *See*, to this effect, Case C-467/98 (*Open Skies (Denmark)*), para. 112. Such a duty to not conclude incompatible treaties follows from the duty of Union loyalty pursuant to which Member States 'shall take any appropriate measure ... to ensure fulfilment of the obligations arising out of the Treaties or resulting from the acts of the institutions of the Union', while also being obliged to 'refrain from any measure which jeopardizes the attainment of the Union's objectives'. Moreover, it would seem that the conclusion of a later Intra-EU Treaty 'contracting out' of the Directives would be contrary to the 'fundamental premise that each Member State shares with all the other Member States, and recognizes that they share with it, a set of common values on which the EU is founded', which premise 'implies and justifies the existence of mutual trust between the Member States that those values will be recognized, and therefore that the law of the EU that implements them will be respected' (*see*, to this effect, Case C-284/16 (*Achmea*), para. 34).
653. N. Matz-Lück in: The Max Planck Encyclopedia of Public International Law (Wolfrum ed.), 2010, para. 25.
654. It is acknowledged, as noted by L. de Broe in: Building Global International Tax Law: Essays in Honour of Guglielmo Maisto (Pistone ed.), 2022, para. 23.4.3, that Member States 'should, because of their duty of sincere cooperation, refrain from concluding treaties that collide with primary and secondary EU law'. As such, if it is assumed that the Member States adhere to this duty, there should, in principle, be no later Intra-EU Treaties that conflict with earlier Directives. To the extent that there would be such a conflict, De Broe notes that later Intra-EU Treaties 'would have to be disregarded on the grounds of the primacy doctrine and of Article 4(3) of the TEU'. With respect to such consequences based on the EU law perspective, reference is made to Chapter 7 of this thesis.

#### 6.4.2.3.4 *Extra-EU Treaties and Directives (Article 30(4) VCLT 1969)*

The situation of Extra-EU Treaties differs from Intra-EU Treaties because the parties to an earlier Extra-EU Treaty would not also be (by analogy) parties to the later Directive. This is due to third states not having voted in favour of a Directive, nor have they otherwise expressed their consent to be bound by such Directives. As such, it follows from an analogous application of Article 30(4)(b) VCLT 1969 that the mutual rights and obligations of the parties to an Extra-EU Treaty are not affected by the adoption of a later (or, for that matter, an earlier) Directive. Such outcome in terms of effect of the Directives on the application of Extra-EU Treaties is in line with the *pacta tertiis* principle pursuant to which the rights and obligations of third states should not be affected by a source of international law to which they have not consented. Consequently, the application of Extra-EU Treaties cannot be affected by the Directives under an analogous application of Article 30 VCLT 1969.

Whereas the application of Extra-EU Treaties is not affected, it should be borne in mind that the Directive governs the mutual rights and obligations between the Member States that are not parties to the Extra-EU Treaty. This is because such an Extra-EU Treaty is a *res inter alios acta* for those Member States which should, in accordance with the *pacta tertiis* principle, not affect the mutual rights and obligations of the Member States under the Directives. As such, Member States do remain obliged to achieve the result of the Directives irrespective of whether this would be compatible with an (earlier or later) Extra-EU Treaty.

> Bearing in mind the comments made earlier regarding the superiority of tax treaties concluded by the Netherlands vis-à-vis national legislation aimed to give effect to Directives (section 6.4.2.3.2), an analogous application of Article 30 VCLT 1969 to a conflict between a (later) Directive and an (earlier) Extra-EU Treaty concluded by the Netherlands would thus not be resolved. As such, national laws of the Netherlands aimed at giving effect to the obligation of ATAD1 to tax income of a controlled foreign company permanent establishment situated in a third state would continue to be set aside if a tax treaty with such a third state provides for an exemption of such income.

### 6.4.2.4 *Conclusion Regarding the* **Lex Posterior** *Rule*

It has been the purpose of this section 6.4.2 to determine to what extent the Directives may affect the application of tax treaties concluded by the Member States under the *lex posterior* rule of Article 30 VCLT 1969. Based on the previous sections, a distinction may be drawn between a 'regular' application of Article 30 VCLT 1969 and an 'analogous' application of such provision for the purposes of determining the effect of the Directives on the application of tax treaties.

With respect to a 'regular' application of Article 30 VCLT 1969, it has been concluded that this provision is not applicable to conflicts between Directives, as decisions of an international organisation, and tax treaties because the Directives do not qualify as 'treaties' within the meaning of Article 2(1)(a) VCLT 1969. If, however, a conflict between Directives and tax treaties would be regarded as a conflict between the obligation to achieve the result of a Directive laid down in Article 288 TFEU and a tax treaty, there would be (a conflict between) two treaties within the meaning of such provision of the VCLT 1969. This would, however, not result in the application of the *lex posterior* conflict rule to earlier Intra-EU Treaties. This is due to Article 30 VCLT 1969 requiring two treaties that relate to the same subject matter. With respect to such sameness of subject matter, this author concludes that the topic of the TFEU, i.e., the creation of a common market, is different from that of tax treaties, i.e., eliminating double taxation of cross-border income of residents of the contracting states without creating opportunities for non-taxation or reduced taxation through tax avoidance or tax evasion. As such, even if a conflict between a Directive and a tax treaty would be regarded as a treaty conflict between Article 288 TFEU and a tax treaty, the *lex posterior* rule would not be applicable because such treaties do not relate to the same subject matter. The consequence of this conclusion is that the application of tax treaties cannot be affected by the (treaty obligation to achieve the result of the) Directives under Article 30 VCLT 1969.

This is different under an analogous application of the *lex posterior* rule of Article 30 VCLT 1969. Under an analogous application of such provision, the *lex posterior* rule of Article 30 VCLT 1969 would be applicable to conflicts between a Directive, a decision of an international organisation, and a tax treaty. Such an analogous application is considered arguable – or: conceivable – based on argument that the adoption of a Directive can be regarded as relevantly similar to the conclusion of a subsequent treaty in light of the purpose of Article 30 VCLT 1969 and the absence of a hierarchy between a treaty and a decision of an international organisation under public international law. If applied by analogy, the *lex posterior* rule would apply to conflicts between Directives and tax treaties if they would relate to the same subject matter. With respect to such sameness of subject matter, it has been concluded that this is conceivable with respect to each of the Directives, although the degree of sameness of subject matter (and thereby the conceivability of them relating to the same subject matter as a tax treaty) may differ from one Directive to another.

If relating to the same subject matter, earlier Intra-EU Treaties would not be applicable under an analogous application of the *lex posterior* rule of Article 30 VCLT 1969 to the extent that such treaties would be incompatible with (the result of (the provisions of)) the Directives. As such, the applicability of 270 (pre-Interest and Royalty Directive) to 336 (pre-ATAD2) Intra-EU Treaties may be affected by the Directives in the event of a conflict. Whereas the application of such earlier Intra-EU Treaties may be affected under an analogous application of the *lex posterior* rule of Article 30 VCLT 1969, this is not the case with respect to later Intra-EU Treaties, i.e., post-Directive Intra-EU Treaties, and Extra-EU Treaties. This is because the parties to later Intra-EU Treaties do not include all 'parties' to the earlier Directive while third states are also not 'parties' to the Directives, irrespective of whether such a Directive is earlier of later as compared to an Extra-EU Treaty.

### 6.4.3 The *Lex Specialis* Conflict Rule

#### *6.4.3.1 General*

In section 6.4.2, it has been concluded that it is arguable that the Directives can, by means of an analogous application of the *lex posterior* rule of Article 30 VCLT 1969, affect the application of Intra-EU Treaties that are earlier as compared to the Directives. Such an analogous application of Article 30 VCLT 1969 would not, however, be able to resolve all conflicts between Intra-EU Treaties and the Directives given that it is effectively only capable of resolving such conflicts if the Intra-EU Treaty is earlier as compared to a Directive. Hence, it would not affect the application of an Intra-EU Treaty that would be later as compared to a Directive nor would it be able to affect the application of such a treaty if the Directive would have to be regarded as not relating to the (same) subject matter as the Intra-EU Treaty.[655]

It is with respect to those situations wherein an analogous application of the *lex posterior* rule of Article 30 VCLT 1969 would not be applicable that, in any event, the other '*widely recognised*' conflict rule of public international law pursuant to which a more specific rule should take precedence over a more general rule (*lex specialis derogate legi generali*), may be relevant and resorted to.[656] It should, however, be stressed that the application of the *lex specialis* conflict rule is not dependent on the inapplicability of the *lex posterior* conflict rule. Both rules may be resorted to at the same time. As such, the *lex specialis* conflict rule would potentially be relevant with respect to each conflict between a treaty and a Directive, irrespective of the application of the (analogous application of the) *lex posterior* rule (regarding their interaction, *see* section 6.4.5). Given the relevance of the *lex specialis* conflict rule, its application is discussed below. First, the legal basis of the *lex specialis* conflict rule is set out (section 6.4.2). This is followed by an assessment of whether conflicts between Directives and tax treaties fall within the scope of this conflict rule (section 6.4.3). Subsequently, the conflict rule itself is addressed (section 6.4.4). Finally, this section 6.4 ends with a conclusion (section 6.4.5).

655. It should be acknowledged in this respect that, especially within the context of Intra-EU Treaties, Member States are precluded from concluding tax treaties that would be incompatible with, at that time, Directives. Such a duty would follow from the duty of Union loyalty pursuant to which Member States shall 'refrain from any measure which could jeopardise the attainment of the Union's objectives'. Entering into an Intra-EU Treaty that would be incompatible with the result to be achieved by a Directive would then be contrary to such duty. *See*, by analogy, also Case C-55/00 (*Gottardo*), para. 32 where the CJEU held that Member States 'may not disregard Community rules but must exercise their powers in a manner consistent with Community law'. As such, the situation of a conflict between a Directive and a later Intra-EU Treaty should – if the duty of Union loyalty is complied with – be non-existent. This also seems to be acknowledged by L. de Broe in: Building Global International Tax Law: Essays in Honour of Guglielmo Maisto (Pistone ed.), 2022, para. 23.4.3 who notes that 'Member States should, because of their duty of sincere cooperation, refrain from concluding treaties that collide with primary and secondary EU law'.

656. *See* Fragmentation Report, A/CN.4/L.682, pp. 34-35, para. 56.

#### *6.4.3.2 The Legal Basis of the* Lex Specialis *Conflict Rule*

Whereas the *lex posterior* conflict rule has been codified in the VCLT 1969, this is not the case for the *lex specialis* conflict rule.[657] The absence of such a codification does not, however, seem to detract from its status as a widely accepted conflict resolution rule under public international law.[658] In resolving conflicts, the *lex specialis* stipulates that a more specific norm prevails over a more general norm. The rationale for resolving conflicts in such a way is that the *lex specialis* conflict rule presumes that 'the special norm reflects most closely, precisely and/or strongly the consent or expression of will of the states in question'.[659] Such presumed intention differs from that underlying the lex posterior conflict rule, which is that the latest state consent should prevail because it reflects the most recent will of the parties.[660] Both conflict rules discussed in this chapter thus seek to give priority to presumed intentions of the parties to a treaty, i.e., either the more specific or later legislative intent must prevail in the event of a conflict between sources of public international law. Underlying both conflict rules is thus the notion that conflicts should be resolved in accordance with the intention of the parties to both treaties. There can, however, be situations wherein there would be no clear evidence of an intention between the parties regarding the resolution of a conflict. In those situations, reference can then be made to the conflict rules such as the *lex posterior* and *lex specialis*. This is due to such conflict rules being aimed at resolving conflicts with a view to giving effect to *presumed* intentions of the parties.[661] As such, the legal basis for the *lex specialis* conflict rule is that it seeks to resolve conflicts in accordance with the intentions of the parties. This is then achieved by presuming that such parties intended to give priority to a norm that is more special as compared to another more general norm in the event of a conflict.

#### *6.4.3.3 The Scope of the* Lex Specialis *Conflict Rule*

With respect to determining whether Directives may affect the application of tax treaties under the *lex specialis* conflict rule, it needs to be assessed whether conflicts

---

657. The absence of a codification of the *lex specialis* may be understood in light of the focus of the VCLT 1969 on treaties as 'instruments and not as obligations' (*see* J. Klabbers, 2017, p. 80, as well as J. Klabbers in: The Law of Treaties Beyond the Vienna Convention (Cannizzaro ed.), 2011, p. 201).
658. In support of such wide recognition, *see* Fragmentation Report, A/CN.4/L.682, p. 34, para. 56, as well as by I. Sinclair, 1984, p. 96, E. Vranes, European Journal of International Law 2006/2, p. 396, P. Merkouris, 2010, p. 131, J. Finke in: Research Handbook on the Law of Treaties (Tams, Tzanakopoulos & Zimmermann eds), 2014, p. 422, P. Niemelä, 2017, p. 27, and D.M. Broekhuijsen, 2018, p. 174. An example wherein a tribunal recognised the *lex specialis* conflict rule is ICSID, Case No. ARB/15/50 (*Eskosol S.p.a. v. Italian Republic*), para. 142.
659. J. Pauwelyn, 2003, p. 387. This also seems to be recognised in the Fragmentation Report, A/CN.4/L.682, p. 37, para. 60 ('lex specialis may also seem useful as it may provide better access to what the parties may have willed').
660. *See* J. Pauwelyn, 2003, p. 388.
661. Such presumption can, of course, be rebutted. *See*, to that effect, J. Pauwelyn, 2003, p. 388. This is also reflected by Article 30(2) VCLT 1969 regarding 'subordination clauses'. An example of a case wherein a presumed legislative intention was rebutted concerns ECtHR, Application No. 10593/09 (*Nada v. Switzerland*), para. 172 regarding the presumption against conflict with earlier international law.

between such Directives and tax treaties fall within the scope of such conflict rule (as has also been determined with respect to the *lex posterior* conflict rule above). In order to determine this, it will first be assessed whether the *lex specialis* conflict rule can be applied to conflicts between treaties and decisions of international organisations (its 'formal' scope; section 6.4.4.3.1). Subsequently, it will be assessed under what circumstances a conflict between sources of public international law would fall within the (material) scope of the *lex specialis* conflict rule (its 'material' scope; section 6.4.4.3.2).

### *6.4.3.3.1 The 'Formal' Scope of the Lex Specialis Conflict Rule*

With respect to the 'formal' scope of the *lex specialis* conflict rule, the starting point is that the *lex specialis* conflict rule can be applied to conflicts between the same sources of public international law.[662] Within the context of tax law, an often cited example of the application of the *lex specialis* rule is that Article 31 VCLT 1969 (as *lex generalis*) applies only if a tax treaty (term) cannot be interpreted on the basis of Article 3(2) OECD Model (as *lex specialis*).[663] The case law of the ICJ, however, also indicates that the *lex specialis* conflict rule can resolve conflicts between different sources of public international law given that this court has applied *lex specialis* conflict rule to a conflict between a treaty within the meaning of Article 38(1)(a) ICJ Statute and customary international law within the meaning of Article 38(1)(b) ICJ Statute.[664] Bearing this

662. With respect to a conflict between two different treaties to which the *lex specialis* rule was applied, *see* PCIJ, 1924, Collection of Judgments (*The Mavrommatis Palestine Concessions*), p. 31 where the Court concluded that 'in cases of doubt, the Protocol, being a special and more recent agreement, should prevail'.
    With respect to conflicts between two sources of customary international law, *see* ICJ, 12 April 1960 (*Case concerning Right of Passage over Indian Territory (Portugal v. India)*), Merits, Judgment, p. 44 where the Court found a 'practice clearly established between two States which was accepted by the Parties as governing the relations between them' and ruled that 'the Court must attribute decisive effect to that practice for the purpose of determining the specific rights and obligations. Such a particular practice must prevail over any general rules.' In support of regarding this case as evidencing the application of the lex specialis rule to two customary rules of international law, *see* J. Pauwelyn, 2003, pp. 394-395 and W. Czaplinski & G.M. Danilenko, Netherlands Yearbook of International Law 2009, p. 20 and P. Merkouris, 2010, p. 167.
663. *See*, to that effect, F.A. Engelen, 2004, para. 10.10.2, R.A. Bosman, 2015, para. 3.3.1, A.P. Dourado, G. Kofler, E. Reimer, A. Rust, R. Ismer & J. Ruß in: Klaus Vogel on Double Taxation Conventions (Reimer & Rust eds), 2022, p. 235, para. 129, and J. Bossuyt, 2021, para. 8.2.2.1. This matter has also been addressed in sections 3.1 and 3.5.
664. *See* ICJ, 27 June 1986 (*Nicaragua v. United States of America*), Judgment, p. 137, para. 274 where it was held that '[i]n general, treaty rules being lex specialis, it would not be appropriate for a State should bring a claim based on customary law rule if it has by treaty already provided means for settlements of such a claim'. Reference can also be made to ICJ, 20 February 1969 (*North Sea Continental Shelf Cases (Federal Republic of Germany/Denmark; Federal Republic of Germany/Netherlands)*), Judgment, p. 42, para. 72 where the Court held that 'rules of [general] international law can, by agreement, be derogated from in particular cases or as between particular parties', as well as to ICJ, 24 February 1982 (*Case concerning the Continental Shelf (Tunisia/Libyan Arab Jamahiriya)*), Judgment, p. 38, para. 24 where the ICJ stated that 'it would no doubt have been possible for the Parties to identify in the Special Agreement certain specific developments in the law of the sea [...], and to have declared that in their bilateral

application of the *lex specialis* rule in mind, it would seem that there is support for applying the *lex specialis* conflict rule to conflicts between two different sources of public international law of equal rank.[665] Given then that decisions of international organisations are of equal rank as treaties, similar to treaties and customary international law being of the same rank, there would seem to be no reason to exclude conflicts between Intra-EU Treaties[666] and the Directives as decisions of an international organisation from the scope of the *lex specialis* conflict rule.[667] There is, however, no case law of the ICJ that confirms an application of the *lex specialis* conflict rule to conflicts between treaties and later decisions of an International organisation. As such, the application of the *lex specialis* conflict rule to such conflicts is considered as merely arguable on the basis of the ICJ having applied this conflict rule to a conflict between two different sources of public international law of equal rank (i.e., customary international law and a treaty).

#### *6.4.3.3.2 The 'Material' Scope of the Lex Specialis Conflict Rule*

Based on the conclusion that conflicts between Intra-EU Treaties and Directives can fall within the 'formal' scope of the *lex specialis* conflict rule, it should subsequently be determined whether such conflicts can also fall within the 'material' scope of such conflict rule. In that respect, the first condition would seem to be that two sources of public international law must relate to the same subject – or substantive – matter and

relations in the particular case such rules should be binding as lex specialis'. The application of the *lex specialis* conflict rule to treaties and customary international law has also been recognised by the Iran-US Claims Tribunal given that it held that 'as a lex specialis in the relations between the two countries, the Treaty supersedes the lex generalis, namely customary international law' (IUSCT, Case No. 56 (*(Amoco International Finance Corporation v. Islamic Republic of Iran)*, Partial Award (Award No. 310-56-3), para. 112).

The application of the *lex specialis* conflict rule to conflicts between treaties and custom has also been recognised by various legal scholars, as well as the ILC. Reference can, for example, be made to J. Pauwelyn, 2003, pp. 391-394 and Fragmentation Report, A/CN.4/L.682, p. 39, para. 66 where the ILC notes that 'there is no reason to limit the operation of lex specialis to relationships between treaties', while also stating that the lex specialis conflict rule 'is often held to regulate the relationship between treaty (as lex specialis) and custom (as "general law")'.

665. *See* P. Merkouris, 2010, pp. 166-167 who notes that the *lex specialis* rule does not require the two rules dealing with the same subject to be laid down in the same source of public international law. As such, he concludes that the *lex specialis* rule can be applied to conflicts between two different sources of international law or between two non-treaty sources. Merkouris refers, within this context, to R. Jennings & A. Watts, 1992, p. 1280 who point out that the lex specialis principle is not restricted to treaty law and that it functions as a 'discretionary aid' which is 'expressive of common sense and normal grammatical usage' (p. 167, footnote 767). Reference is also made to this point may by Jennings & Watts in Fragmentation Report, A/CN.4/L.682, p. 39, para. 66.

666. Bearing in mind the *pacta tertiis* principle (section 6.3), the Directives should not be able to affect the application of Extra-EU Treaties. Hence, the *lex specialis* conflict rule may only be applicable with respect to Intra-EU Treaties.

667. There is, at least to the extent that this author is aware, no case law of the ICJ, ECtHR, or tribunals rejecting the application of the *lex specialis* conflict rule to such conflicts.

conflict with each other.[668] With respect to the requirement of sameness of subject matter, the starting point would seem to be that the content of this term is different from the term same subject matter within the context of the *lex posterior* rule (*see* section 6.4.2.1.3). Instead of determining whether a treaty as a whole relates to the same topic or substance, the *lex specialis* conflict rule would seem to require sameness of subject matter at the level of the conflicting provisions. Support for such a view regarding the sameness of subject matter within the context of the *lex specialis* rule can be derived from the Commentaries to Article 55 of the Draft articles on responsibility of States for Wrongful Acts where it is mentioned that the *lex specialis* rule applies if two provisions deal with the same subject matter and would be inconsistent.[669] As such, in determining whether a conflict between an Intra-EU Treaty and Directive falls within the scope of the *lex specialis* conflict rule, it would have to be assessed whether they relate to the same subject - or substantive - matter on a per provision, or case-by-case, basis.

Based on this nature of the sameness of subject matter test (and adopting a substance-based view of the term 'same subject matter'; *see* section 6.4.2.1.3), it would seem that the mere partial substantive overlap of Directives and Intra-EU Treaties is not an argument against concluding that they relate to the same subject matter for the purposes of the *lex specialis* conflict rule.[670] This can be illustrated as follows. In section 6.4.2.2.4, it was concluded that it was conceivable that the topics of ATAD1 and ATAD2 would relate to the same topic as that of Intra-EU Treaties. The reasons for regarding it merely 'conceivable' are that ATAD1 and ATAD2 only have partial substantive and personal overlap with Intra-EU Treaties, while also not relating to the (historically main) purpose of avoiding double taxation, but only to preventing

668. Regarding the condition of the same subject - or substantive - matter, *see* G. Fitzmaurice, British Yearbook of International Law 1957, p. 237 (*lex specialis* 'can only apply where both the specific and general provisions concerned with the same substantive matter'), paras 4-5 of the Commentaries to Article 55 of the Draft articles on Responsibility of States for Internationally Wrongful Acts with commentaries ('For the lex specialis principle to apply it is not enough that the same subject matter is dealt with by two provisions; there must be some actual inconsistency between them, or else a discernible intention that one provision is to exclude the other.'), J. Pauwelyn, 2003, p. 389 ('Although necessarily dealing with the "same subject-matter" - if not, there would be no conflict.'), A. Lindroos, Nordic Journal of International Law 2005/1, p. 45 ('it may be argued that application of the lex specialis maxim presupposes that the rules in question deal with the same subject matter and are in conflict'), and the ILC in Fragmentation Report, A/CN.4/L.682, pp. 62-63, para. 116 ('Because only those that are in some respect similar can be compared - and indeed can enter into conflict - it must be assumed, together with Fitzmaurice, that lex specialis "can only apply where both the specific and general provisions concerned deal with the same substantive matter".'). The condition of a conflict is adopted by paras 4-5 of the Commentaries to Article 55 of the Draft articles on Responsibility of States for Internationally Wrongful Acts with commentaries and A. Lindroos, Nordic Journal of International Law 2005/1, p. 45.

669. *See* para. 4 of the Commentaries to Article 55 of the Draft articles on Responsibility of States for Internationally Wrongful Acts with commentaries. According to A. Lindroos, Nordic Journal of International Law 2005/1, p. 45, this paragraph entails that 'it may be argued that application of the lex specialis maxim presupposes that the rules in question deal with the same subject matter and are in conflict'.

670. *See* section 6.4.2.2.4 regarding this assessment in the context of an analogous application of the *lex posterior* conflict rule.

non-taxation and tax avoidance. As such, there seem to be reasons for concluding that these two Directives would not relate to the same substance or topic as Intra-EU Treaties as a whole. For the purposes of the sameness of subject matter test of the *lex specialis* conflict rule, however, it should not be assessed whether ATAD1 and ATAD2 relate to the same subject matter as an Intra-EU Treaty, but merely whether a provision of ATAD1 or ATAD2 relates to the same topic or substance as a provision of an Intra-EU Treaty. The difference in substantive scope between ATAD1 and ATAD2 would, in that event, seem irrelevant. What is decisive, is whether on a provision level it can be concluded that the Directive and the Intra-EU Treaty relate to the same topic or substance. Taking this nature of the sameness of subject matter test for the purposes of the *lex specialis* conflict rule into account, it would seem that Article 9(5) of ATAD2 and Article 23 (in conjunction with Article 7) of an Intra-EU Treaty based on the OECD Model can be regarded as relating to the same subject matter in the event of a conflict, although only to the extent that it concerns corporate taxpayers. This sameness of subject matter can be construed as follows. First, the subject matter of the relevant provisions of the Intra-EU Treaty can be regarded as providing rules with respect to the taxation of business profits attributable to a permanent establishment at the level of the head office.[671] Similarly, the subject of Article 9(5) ATAD2 can be described as also providing rules regarding the taxation of such profits at the level of the head office. Hence, such provision could be regarded as relating to the same topic or substance as Article 23 (in conjunction with Article 7) of an Intra-EU Treaty based on the OECD Model.[672] This example indicates that partial substantive overlap between an Intra-EU Treaty and a Directive may be sufficient – or may even indicate – that such a treaty and a Directive relate to the same subject matter for the purposes of the *lex specialis* conflict rule (whereas partial overlap may be seen as an argument against sameness of subject matter within the context of the *lex posterior* conflict rule; section 6.4.2.2.4). As such, it seems that the partial overlap between each of the Directives with provisions of Intra-EU Treaties indicates that they can relate to the same subject matter for the purposes of the *lex specialis* conflict rule when their application would give rise to a conflict with an Intra-EU Treaty. Hence, such conflicts would thus seem capable of falling within the 'material' scope of the *lex specialis* conflict rule.

671. This can be illustrated as follows: Article 23 of an Intra-EU Treaty based on the OECD Model (2017), in conjunction with Article 7, would provide that the Member State of the head office shall exempt profits attributable to a permanent establishment in another Member State if such profits may be taxed in that other Member State. At the same time, Article 7(2) ATAD1 provides that (certain categories of) profits attributable to a controlled foreign company permanent establishment situated in a Member State shall be included in the tax base of the Member State head office. The provisions of the Intra-EU Treaty and ATAD1 would thus both relate to the same topic of taxation of profits attributable to a permanent establishment at the level of the head office situated in a Member State.

672. Article 9(5) ATAD2 provides that the Member State of the head office 'shall require the taxpayer to include the income that would otherwise be attributed to the disregarded permanent establishment' whereas Article 23 (in conjunction with Article 7) of such Intra-EU Treaty would provide for the exemption of that same income.

### 6.4.3.4 *Determining the* Lex Specialis *and* Lex Generalis

Once a conflict between a Directive, such as ATAD1 or ATAD2, and an Intra-EU Treaty falls within the scope of the *lex specialis* conflict rule, this conflict rule provides that the *lex specialis* prevails over the *lex generalis*.[673] As such, in order for a Directive to affect the application of an Intra-EU Treaty under the *lex specialis* conflict rule, it would need to be determined that the Directive (provision) would be the *lex specialis* vis-à-vis the Intra-EU Treaty (provision).[674] In making such determination, the starting point is that this requires a 'relational assessment'[675] in the sense that it must be assessed whether the rule of a Directive is special in regard to the rule of the Intra-EU Treaty.[676] This is due to a rule never being 'general' or 'special' in abstract terms, but only in relation to another rule.[677] In determining the special nature of the rules of a Directive vis-à-vis the rules of an Intra-EU Treaty, reference can be made to both the subject matter of those rules as well as to the membership to both rules.[678]

With respect to comparing the subject matter of two conflicting rules, it may be established that one provision 'addresses the particular subject matter ... more directly or precisely', i.e., 'the material scope of one norm can be more precise or limited than another'.[679] The application of the subject matter test within the context of the *lex specialis* conflict rule is illustrated by Pauwelyn as follows:

> the material scope of one norm can be more precise or limited than another. On that basis, a WTO rule dealing with countermeasures for breach of WTO obligations is lex specialis as opposed to general international law dealing with countermeasures generally, for any breach of international law. Equally an obligation to do something in events A to Z is less specific than an obligation not to do this something in the specific events A and B. or a WTO obligation not to restrict trade, irrespective of the product involved, must be seen as less specific than an obligation (or permission) to restrict trade in the specific products A and B.[680]

Bearing in mind this illustration, it would seem that the partial overlap of Directives with provisions of tax treaties indicates that, in the event of a conflict, a Directive

673. *See* J. Pauwelyn, 2003, p. 385. The relevant criterion for resolving a conflict is thus specialty instead of time (as is the case under the *lex posterior* rule) (*see* J. Pauwelyn, 2003, p. 388). *See also* J. Finke in: Research Handbook on the Law of Treaties (Tams, Tzanakopoulos & Zimmermann eds), 2014, pp. 423-424 ('the principle of lex specialis provides that in case of conflict, the more specific provision should prevail over the more general one').
674. It is acknowledged, within this context, that in the event that the Intra-EU Treaty would be the *lex specialis* vis-à-vis a Directive this would not entail that the Intra-EU Treaty prevails over the Directive as the *lex generalis*. This is due to the 'parties' to the Directive, i.e., the 27 Member States, not also being parties to the relevant (bilateral) Intra-EU Treaty. In that case, the principle of *pacta tertiis* (section 6.3) precludes the Intra-EU Treaty from affecting the Directive because this would affect the rights of, and obligations towards, Member States that have not consented to (and are hence not bound by) such Intra-EU Treaty.
675. Fragmentation Report, A/CN.4/L.682, p. 62, para. 116.
676. By analogy, *see* Fragmentation Report, A/CN.4/L.682, p. 61, para. 112.
677. Fragmentation Report, A/CN.4/L.682, p. 61, para. 112.
678. *See*, to this effect, J. Pauwelyn, 2003, pp. 388-389, as well as Fragmentation Report, A/CN.4/L.682, p. 35, para. 60 and p. 61, para. 112.
679. J. Pauwelyn, 2003, p. 389.
680. J. Pauwelyn, 2003, p. 389.

(provision) would be likely to qualify as the *lex specialis* vis-à-vis the provision of a tax treaty. This can be illustrated as follows with respect to provisions of the Directives imposing a duty to tax income, i.e., the Parent-Subsidiary Directive, ATAD1 and ATAD2, and Intra-EU Treaties imposing a duty to refrain from taxing that same income. In general terms, these Directives only apply to corporate taxpayers. Hence, the personal scope of the provisions of such Directives is likely to be more limited than those of a provision of an Intra-EU Treaty (*see* section 6.4.2.2.4). Additionally, the substantive scope of these Directives is also likely to be more limited than those of the provisions of Intra-EU Treaties relating to the same subject matter. This can be illustrated as follows.

With respect to conflicts between the duty to tax dividends under Article 4(1)(a) of the Parent-Subsidiary Directive (the anti-hybrid rule) and Article 10 in conjunction with Article 23 of an Intra-EU Treaty requiring an exemption of dividends at the level of the parent company (in derogation from the credit method provided for in the OECD Model),[681] the starting point would seem to be that they both relate to the topic of cross-border dividend payments. A comparison of both provision reveals, however, that the scope of the anti-hybrid rule of the Parent-Subsidiary Directive is more limited than that of Article 10 of an Intra-EU Treaty. This is due to the anti-hybrid rule only being applicable to (i) dividends paid by a company in which the parent company holds an interest of, essentially, at least 10% and (ii) only to the extent that such dividends are deductible at the level of the company paying the dividends. Article 10 in conjunction with Article 23 of the Intra-EU Treaty, by contrast, applies to all cross-border dividends irrespective of the shareholding held and irrespective of the deductibility of such dividends (although an exemption in such a treaty would generally require a certain minimum shareholding to be held by the shareholder receiving the dividend). As such, the anti-hybrid rule of the Parent-Subsidiary Directive seems to address the particular subject matter of cross-border dividends in a more precise way (in terms of Pauwelyn's illustration, Article 10 in conjunction with Article 23 of an Intra-EU Treaty applies to events A to Z whereas the anti-hybrid rule of the Parent-Subsidiary Directive only applies in specific events A and B). Consequently, the anti-hybrid rule would seem to be the *lex specialis* with respect to Article 23 in conjunction with Article 10 of the Intra-EU Treaty.

681. Examples of Intra-EU Treaties providing for an exemption of inter-company dividends in the residence state would be the tax treaties concluded by Germany with the Czech Republic (1980), Portugal (1980), Slovak Republic (1980), Italy (1989), Sweden (1992), Denmark (1995), Estonia (1996), Latvia (1997) and Lithuania (1997). Such Intra-EU Treaties provide that Germany exempts dividends paid to a German resident company owning at least a certain percentage of the voting shares or capital of the company paying the dividends that is resident in the other contracting state irrespective of the deductibility of such dividends. There are, however, also more recent Intra-EU Treaties concluded by Germany that explicitly provide that no exemption is provided if the dividends have been deductible (*see*, to that effect, the tax treaties concluded with Austria (2000), Romania (2001), Poland (2003), Croatia (2006), Slovenia (2006), Bulgaria (2010), Malta (2010), Hungary (2011), Ireland (2011), Spain (2011), Luxembourg (2012), the Netherlands (2012), Finland (2016)). Generally, such more recent German Intra-EU Treaties provide that the exemption only applies to dividends 'which were not deducted when determining the profits of the company distributing the dividends'.

The same line of reasoning can be applied with respect to a conflict between the controlled foreign company provision(s) of ATAD1 with respect to permanent establishments and an Intra-EU Treaty's provision laying down an exemption of profits attributable to such permanent establishments. The provisions of ATAD1 regarding the taxation of profits attributable to a (controlled foreign company) permanent establishment and Article 23 in conjunction with Article 7 of an Intra-EU Treaty based on the OECD Model would both relate to the topic of taxation of profits attributable to a permanent establishment. While relating to the same topic, a comparison of Article 7 ATAD1 with Article 23 in conjunction with Article 7 of an Intra-EU Treaty based on the OECD Model indicates that ATAD1 only applies to (i) permanent establishments of corporate taxpayers, (ii) qualifying as controlled foreign companies within the meaning of Article 7(1) ATAD1, and (iii) only to non-distributed income of such controlled foreign companies as set out in Article 7(2) ATAD1. Article 23 of the Intra-EU Treaty provides, by contrast, for an exemption of income attributable to a permanent establishment that may be taxed in the state where such permanent establishment is situated. Such obligation would then apply irrespective of whether it concerns the permanent establishment of a corporate or individual taxpayer, irrespective of whether it qualifies as a controlled foreign company, and irrespective of the type of income. Hence, the Intra-EU Treaty would apply to situations A to Z when it concerns the taxation of profits attributable to a permanent establishment whereas ATAD1 only applies to situations A and B (in terms of Pauwelyn's illustration). As such, Article 7 ATAD1 would seem to be the *lex specialis* vis-à-vis the *lex generalis* of Article 23 in conjunction with Article 7 of an Intra-EU Treaty. The same applies with respect to Article 9(5) ATAD2 given that this provision only applies to profits attributable to disregarded permanent establishments of corporate taxpayers. As such, it applies only to one particular situation whereas the relevant provisions of the Intra-EU Treaties apply to all situations wherein income is attributable to a permanent establishment in another Member State. Hence, Article 9(5) ATAD2 would also seem to qualify as a *lex specialis* vis-à-vis Article 23 in conjunction with Article 7 of an Intra-EU Treaty.

With respect to each of the situations set out above, the Directive can be regarded as the *lex specialis* based on the circumstance that its provision applies to the subject matter dealt by an Intra-EU Treaty in a more specific – or limited – way. In terms of the illustration of Pauwelyn, the Directive provision applies to situations A and B whereas the Intra-EU Treaty's provision applies to situations A to Z. To the extent that other provisions of Directives than set out above would also only apply to situations A and B, it would thus seem that they are also to be regarded as having a more 'special' subject matter than the provision of an Intra-EU Treaty with which they would conflict.

In addition to determining the special nature of a Directive provision based on a comparison of its subject matter with the subject matter of a(n incompatible) tax treaty provision, the special nature of a Directive vis-à-vis an Intra-EU Treaty may also be determined on the basis of membership, i.e., by means of the number of actors whose behaviour is regulated.[682] In general terms, application of this criterion would seem to

682. *See* Fragmentation Report, A/CN.4/L.682, p. 61, para. 112, as well as p. 35, para. 60. *See also* J. Pauwelyn, 2003, p. 390.

imply that Directives would be the *lex generalis* vis-à-vis Intra-EU Treaties given that there are 27 actors whose behaviour is regulated by a Directive whereas there are only 2 in case of an Intra-EU Treaty. This would, in turn, seem to imply that resort to the subject matter and membership for establishing the *lex generalis* point to different directions: the subject matter seems to indicate that the provisions of the Directives are more special as compared to the provisions of Intra-EU Treaties whereas membership would point towards the Intra-EU Treaties as more special.

This contradictory outcome does not, however, entail that it cannot be concluded that a Directive's provision would, based on their subject matter, be the *lex specialis* vis-à-vis a provision of an Intra-EU Treaty. With respect to membership, it has been argued that membership may merely provide an indication that a treaty may go further 'either in terms of detail or in terms of the objectives pursued' because there are fewer parties.[683] As such, the reference to membership within the context of determining the *lex specialis* can be regarded as an assumption as to the subject matter of a source of public international law. Upon review of the subject matter of the provisions of a source, it may still become apparent that the source of public international law that regulates the behaviour of states A, B and C would do so in a more special - or specific - way than the source of public International law seeking to govern the behaviour of states A and B only. This can be illustrated as follows. The subject matter of the TEU and TFEU, being concluded (by accession) between 27 Member States, seems more general (i.e., creating a common market between EU Member States) than the subject matter of tax treaties with only two parties (i.e., taxation of cross-border activities). At the same time, however, it would seem arguable that the subject matter of the Directives, adopted by 27 Member States, is more specific than that of such tax treaties (in terms of substantive and personal scope). As such, membership merely provides an indication that the nature of the subject matter of a provision would be more specific. Whether this indication would, in practice, justify the source of public international law with fewer parties as more specific depends on the subject matter of such source as compared to the other source. Hence, the comparison of the subject matter of the two conflicting sources of public international law, in this case an Intra-EU Treaty's provision and a Directive's provision, would, ultimately, seem to be decisive for the purposes of the *lex specialis* conflict rule.

#### *6.4.3.5 Application of the* Lex Specialis *Conflict Rule*

If it would be determined that (i) a provision of a Directive relates to the same subject matter as a provision of an Intra-EU Treaty, (ii) that such provisions conflict with each other, and (iii) that the Directive provision is the *lex specialis* as compared to the provision of the Intra-EU Treaty (as *lex generalis*), the *lex specialis derogate legi generali* conflict rule provides that the Directive provision would prevail over the relevant

683. J. Pauwelyn, 2003, p. 390.

(incompatible) Intra-EU Treaty provision.[684] In light of the conclusion that the subject matter of Directive provisions imposing duties to tax is likely to be more specific than that of Intra-EU Treaties (in terms of personal scope and situations covered), the *lex specialis* conflict rule would seem likely to be able to attribute priority to provisions of a Directive in case such provisions would conflict with provisions of an Intra-EU Treaty. As such, Directives would seem capable of affecting the application of Intra-EU Treaties under the *lex specialis* conflict rule:

> Applied to the example provided in section 6.4.2.3.2 above regarding a conflict between the exemption in the tax treaty between the Netherlands and Luxembourg and the disregarded permanent establishment rule of ATAD2, the following can be noted if the *lex specialis* conflict rule would be resorted to (instead of, or in addition to, the *lex posterior* conflict rule (regarding their relation, *see* section 6.4.4)). It follows from section 6.4.3.3.3 that the subject matter of Article 9(5) ATAD2 seems to be more specific than that of Article 7 of the Intra-EU Treaty between the Netherlands and Luxembourg in conjunction with Article 23 of that Intra-EU Treaty. As such, it would seem arguable that Article 9(5) ATAD2 can be regarded as a '*lex specialis*' as compared to such provisions of the Intra-EU Treaty. In that case, the *lex specialis* rule would provide that the more specific legislative intention, i.e., taxation of profits attributable to a disregarded permanent establishment, must prevail over the more general legislative intention, i.e., profits attributable to any permanent establishment, including a disregarded one, must be exempt. In such a way, the *lex specialis* conflict rule could thus result in ATAD2 affecting the application of an Intra-EU Treaty under public international law.

#### *6.4.3.6 Conclusion Regarding the* Lex Specialis *Conflict Rule*

This section 6.4.3 has been aimed at answering the question of whether the application of tax treaties concluded by the Member States may be affected by the Directives under the *lex specialis* conflict rule. In that respect, it has been concluded that, based on the application of the *lex specialis* conflict rule to conflicts between different sources of public international law, i.e., treaties and customary international law, it is arguable that it can be applied to conflicts between treaties and decisions of an international organisation because such sources of public international law are also of equal rank. As such, it is considered arguable that the *lex specialis* conflict rule can be resorted to for the purposes of resolving conflicts between Intra-EU Treaties and Directives (as decisions of an international organisation that are of equal rank as such Intra-EU Treaties).

With respect to the resolution of such conflicts, it has furthermore been concluded that provisions of Directives can relate to the same subject matter as that of

684. *See* J. Pauwelyn, 2003, p. 385. The relevant criterion for resolving a conflict is thus specialty instead of time (as is the case under the *lex posterior* rule) (*see* J. Pauwelyn, 2003, p. 388). *See also* J. Finke in: Research Handbook on the Law of Treaties (Tams, Tzanakopoulos & Zimmermann eds), 2014, pp. 423-424 ('the principle of lex specialis provides that in case of conflict, the more specific provision should prevail over the more general one'.). J. Finke in: Research Handbook on the Law of Treaties (Tams, Tzanakopoulos & Zimmermann eds), 2014, pp. 423-424.

provisions of Intra-EU Treaties and that the Directive provisions are likely to provide rules with respect to such subject matter in a more specific way (as compared to provisions of Intra-EU Treaties) because their personal and substantive scope - in terms of situations covered - is generally more limited than that of provisions of Intra-EU Treaties. Hence, it would seem arguable that a provision of a Directive could be regarded as the *lex specialis* vis-à-vis provisions of Intra-EU Treaties with which such a Directive provision conflicts. In case a Directive provision qualifies as the *lex specialis*, application of the *lex specialis* conflict rule would entail that the application of the incompatible Intra-EU Treaty provision is affected in the sense that it would not be applicable to the extent incompatible with the more specific Directive provision. Such non-application as a result of the *lex specialis* conflict rule would then be based on the presumption that the Directive, being more specific than the Intra-EU Treaty, reflects most closely, precisely and/or strongly the consent or expression of will of the Member States with respect to a particular situation.

### 6.4.4 The Interaction Between the *Lex Posterior* and *Lex Specialis* Conflict Rules

As noted in section 6.4.1, the *lex posterior* conflict rule may be regarded as the conflict rule of first resort under public international law. Nevertheless, the *lex posterior* conflict rule is not necessarily more important than the *lex specialis* conflict rule.[685] Both conflict rules may be applied to conflicts between sources of public international law. If both would result in the same result, this would create a strong presumed common intention as to how to resolve a conflict between two such sources.[686] It may, however, be conceivable that the *lex posterior* and *lex specialis* conflict rules would give rise to contradictory outcomes. The question that would arise with respect to such a situation of contradictory outcomes is whether there exists a rule pursuant to which an earlier more specific source of public international law would take precedence over a later more general source of public international law.

Diverging opinions have been expressed regarding the answer to such question.[687] Pauwelyn, for example, expresses the view that the *lex specialis* principle

685. *See*, implicitly, N. Matz-Lück in: The Max Planck Encyclopedia of Public International Law (Wolfrum ed.), 2010, para. 24 who notes that if 'both agreements lack conflict clauses or if the conflict clauses contradict one another, either Articles 30(3) and (4) VCLT as specific codifications of the lex posterior maxim can function as derogation norm or the application of a general lex posterior or lex specialis rule must be taken into consideration'. He does not, as such, *see* a formal hierarchy between the *lex posterior* rule and *lex specialis* rule.

686. *See*, for example, wherein the court relied on both such conflicts rules to give effect to one (later) treaty over another (earlier) treaty, PCIJ, 1924, Collection of Judgments (*The Mavrommatis Palestine Concessions*), p. 31 where the PCIJ ruled that 'in cases of doubt, the protocol, being a special and more recent agreement, should prevail'. Reference may furthermore be made to PCIJ 1932, Advisory Opinion No. 23 (*Danzig*), and PCIJ, 1927, Advisory Opinion (*Jurisdiction of European Commission of Danube*), wherein the PCIJ gave priority to later bilateral agreements that were also more specific (*see*, regarding such an interpretation, J. Pauwelyn, 2003, pp. 395-396).

687. N. Kontou, 1994, p. 24 noted, for example, that '[s]ome authors take the view that the lex posterior always repeals the lex prior, even if the prior rule is more specific. Others suggest that

cannot 'overrule the lex posterior principle in Article 30'.[688] By contrast, Czaplinski and Danilenko submit that 'judicial practice tends to favour the lex specialis derogat legi generali principle in particular'.[689] Moreover, Vranes took the position that there can be no absolute or even abstract hierarchy between the *lex specialis* and *lex posterior* conflict rules.[690] In his view, it should be established for each individual case which of the two conflict rules is to be awarded priority.[691] Such an approach would seem aligned with the idea that both conflict rules seek to resolve conflicts by resorting to presumed common intentions, which may both be rebutted. As such, a case-by-case approach would provide room for determining which of the two presumed common intentions may most closely reflect the intentions of the parties. This position also seems to be defended by Kolb who notes that 'none has automatic priority. The issue is one of object and purpose and of intention of the parties'.[692] Bearing in mind that the *lex posterior* and *lex specialis* conflict rules are both based on presumptions regarding the common intentions between the parties,[693] the approach of Vranes and Kolb seems most aligned with the notion that a conflict should be resolved in accordance with the common intentions of the parties.[694] As a consequence, it cannot be determined in the abstract whether the *lex posterior* or *lex specialis* conflict rule should prevail in the event that they would point in different directions with respect to the resolution of a conflict between a Directive and an Intra-EU Treaty.

### 6.4.5 The Residual Role of the *Lex Posterior* and *Lex Specialis* Conflict Rules

In the previous section, it was concluded that the choice between the *lex posterior* and *lex specialis* conflict rule, to the extent that it may arise, should be dependent on the common intentions between the Member States that are parties to an Intra-EU Treaty. In this section, the interaction of the *lex posterior* and *lex specialis* conflict rules with conflict clauses in tax treaties are addressed.

The starting point in determining this interaction is that the *lex posterior* and *lex specialis* conflict rules are aimed at resolving conflicts based on presumed intentions of

the lex specialis rule limits the scope of the application of the lex posterior: a later law, general in character, does not repeal an earlier law that is special in character (lex posterior generalis non derogat legi priori specialis)'. Moreover, J. Finke in: Research Handbook on the Law of Treaties (Tams, Tzanakopoulos & Zimmermann eds), 2014, p. 423 considers the relation between the *lex specialis* and *lex posterior* conflict rules 'obscure'.

688. *See* J. Pauwelyn, 2003, p. 409.
689. W. Czaplinski & G.M. Danilenko, Netherlands Yearbook of International Law 2009, p. 21.
690. E. Vranes, Zeitschrift für ausländisches öffentliches Recht und Völkerrecht 2005/2, p. 402.
691. E. Vranes, Zeitschrift für ausländisches öffentliches Recht und Völkerrecht 2005/2, p. 402.
692. R. Kolb, 2016, pp. 189-190.
693. This is also recognised by R. Michaels & J. Pauwelyn, p. 6 who note that 'both lex specialis and lex posterior are presumptions as to the intent of the lawmaker or legislator on the issue in question'.
694. Such notion is, for example, reflected by Article 30(2) VCLT 1969 providing that the *lex posterior* conflict rule is not applicable in the event of a subordination clause attributing priority to another, perhaps earlier, treaty.

the parties,[695] i.e., either the presumed latest legislative intent or the most specific legislative intent should prevail. The circumstance that both conflict rules seek to resolve conflicts in accordance with presumed intentions entails that they are subject to rebuttal of such presumed intentions. For example, if a tax treaty would contain a conflict clause stipulating that its provisions are without prejudice to obligations arising from EU membership (a subordination clause),[696] such clause would provide evidence of a clear intention of the parties with respect to a tax treaty regarding the resolution of conflicts between obligations under a tax treaty and obligation arising from EU membership. In that case, a conflict should be resolved in accordance with the relevant conflict clause irrespective of the outcome of a resolution of a conflict under the *lex posterior* and/or *lex specialis* conflict rule. To the extent that such latter conflict rules would provide for presumed different intentions regarding the resolution of a conflict between a Directive and a tax treaty, such presumed intentions would be rebutted by means of the clear conflict clause. As such, the *lex posterior* and *lex specialis* conflict rules can be regarded as residual in the sense that they are subject to rebuttal by means of, for example, conflict clauses in the tax treaties themselves.

The residual nature of the *lex posterior* and *lex specialis* conflict rules also entails that it seems arguable that the presumed intentions to which they seek to give effect may be rebutted by the Directives, as decisions of an international organisation. If such Directives would provide evidence of an intention among the Member States regarding the effect that a Directive should have on the application of an Intra-EU Treaty, it would seem conceivable that such evidence could rebut the presumed intentions justifying application of the *lex posterior* and *lex specialis* conflict rules. Examples of provisions of (proposals for) Directives that would seem to provide evidence of a clear common

695. *See* sections 6.4.2 (*lex posterior*) and 6.4.4.2 (*lex specialis*).

696. A search in the IBFD Tax Treaty Database (performed on 24 January 2022) on the term 'European Union' revealed that 26 treaties contain – specific or general – subordination clauses granting priority to EU law. Such clauses may include wording indicating that it is agreed or that it is understood that (i) the laws of the EU shall prevail over the tax treaty (Protocol to the Netherlands-Germany Tax Treaty 2012), (ii) the tax treaty shall be applied in full compliance with international obligations arising from Membership (Article 29(3) Italy-Kosovo Treaty 2021), (iii) the tax treaty shall not affect legal acts of the EU (Protocols to the Luxembourg-Poland Tax Treaty 2012 and the Hungary-Luxembourg Tax Treaty 2015), or (iv) the tax treaty shall in no way prejudice obligations arising from membership of the EU (Protocols to the Hungary-Armenia Tax Treaty 2009, the Hungary-Taiwan Tax Treaty 2010, the Hungary-Hong Kong Tax Treaty 2010, the Hungary-Denmark Tax Treaty 2011, the Hungary-Georgia Tax Treaty 2011, the Hungary-Mexico Tax Treaty 2011, the Hungary-United Arab Emirates Tax Treaty 2013, the Hungary-Bahrain Tax Treaty 2014, the Hungary-Kyrgyzstan Tax Treaty 2020, and the Hungary-Andorra Tax Treaty 2021, as well as Article 29 Hungary-Kosovo Tax Treaty 2013 and Article 30 Hungary-Iraq Tax Treaty 2016). In addition, such subordination clauses may also take the form of a joint declaration (Joint Declaration to the Hungary-Liechtenstein Income and Capital Tax Treaty 2015), a unilateral understanding (Protocol to the Hungary-San Marino Income Tax Treaty 2009 and Article 27 of the Hungary-Qatar Income Tax Treaty 2012), or a unilateral declaration (Protocol to the Hungary-Saudi Arabia Income and Capital Tax Treaty 2014 and Protocol to the Hungary-Iran Income and Capital Tax Treaty 2015). What is of particular interest with respect to these general subordination clauses in the tax treaties concluded by the Member States is they have mainly been included in tax treaties concluded with third states (81%) (general subordination clauses have been included in 4 treaties concluded between Member States whereas they have been included in 17 treaties concluded with third states).

intention between the Member States regarding the intended effect of a Directive on an Intra-EU Treaty are Article 8 of the CCCTB proposal (2011),[697] Article 16(5) Arbitration Directive,[698] and Article 11 of the ATAD3 Proposal (2021).[699] Each of these provisions expressly refers to Intra-EU Treaties and, hence, evidences a rather clear intention of the intended effect of a Directive on the application of an Intra-EU Treaty. To the extent that application of the *lex posterior* and/or *lex specialis* conflict rules would confirm such intention, the presumed intentions could be regarded as reinforcing the intentions as reflected by the Directive. To the extent that, by contrast, they would indicate a different intention in terms of which source of international law would have to prevail, e.g., the application of a tax treaty should not be affected by a Directive, the Directive provision would seem to rebut the presumed intention underlying the *lex posterior* or *lex specialis* conflict rule. In case of such rebuttal, it would not seem justified to resort to such conflict rule(s). In that event, effect should thus be given to the intentions as follow from a Directive for the purposes of resolving a conflict between a Directive and an Intra-EU Treaty. This, again, highlights the residual role of the *lex posterior* and *lex specialis* conflict rules.

## 6.5 CONCLUSIONS REGARDING THE EFFECT OF THE DIRECTIVES ON THE APPLICATION OF TAX TREATIES UNDER THE RULES OF PUBLIC INTERNATIONAL LAW

It has been the purpose of this chapter to determine the effect of the Directives on the application of tax treaties under the rules of public international law. In that respect, the *pacta sunt servanda* and (section 6.2) the *pacta tertiis* principles have been discussed (section 6.3), as well as the *lex posterior* and *lex specialis* conflict rules (section 6.4). Based on such sections, the starting point in answering the effect of the Directives on the application of tax treaties under public international is that a distinction must be drawn between Intra-EU Treaties and Extra-EU Treaties.

Under the rules of public international law, the Directives cannot affect the application – in terms of applicability – of Extra-EU Treaties.[700] The application of Intra-EU Treaties may, by contrast, be affected by a Directive if such application would conflict with a Directive (in the absence of a conflict, the Directives also would not

697. Article 8 CCCTB Proposal (COM(2011) 121/4) provides that 'The provisions of this Directive shall apply notwithstanding any provision to the contrary in any agreement concluded between Member States.'

698. Article 16(5) Arbitration Directive ((EU) 2017/1852) provides that submission of a complaint on the basis of such Directive 'shall put an end to any other ongoing proceedings under the mutual agreement procedure or dispute resolution procedure under an agreement or convention that is being interpreted or applied in relation to the relevant question in dispute'.

699. Article 11 ATAD3 Proposal (COM(2021) 565 final) provides that tax treaties would have to be 'disregarded'.

700. The only exception would be if a third state would have agreed that the Extra-EU Treaty is subject to commitments under EU law. Such agreement could, for example, follow from the inclusion of subordination clause as included in some of the Hungarian Extra-EU Treaties. In the absence of such a clause granting priority to commitments under EU law, however, the *pacta tertiis* principle precludes the Directives from affecting Extra-EU Treaties.

affect the application of Intra-EU Treaties). With respect to those Intra-EU Treaties that are incompatible with (the result of) the Directives, it follows from this chapter that their application may be affected by the Directives under the *lex posterior* conflict rule as well as the *lex specialis* conflict rule. As such, the effect of the Directives on the application of tax treaties under public international law is limited, in any event, to Intra-EU Treaties and only to the extent that such treaties would be incompatible with such Directives. The conclusions regarding the effect that the Directives may have on the application of Intra-EU Treaties under such conflict rules of public international law are discussed in sections 6.5.1 through 6.5.3 below. With respect to such effect of the Directives it should, however, be acknowledged that both the *lex posterior* and *lex specialis* conflict rules seek to resolve conflicts on the basis of presumed intentions of the parties. As such, the application of these conflict rules would be subject to clear evidence of the parties regarding a different resolution of a conflict (i.e., presumed party intent underlying the *lex posterior* and *lex specialis* conflict rules may be rebutted by, for example, a conflict clause in the tax treaty or by provisions of a Directive evidencing a common intention between the Member States).[701]

### 6.5.1 Conclusion Regarding the Effect of the *Lex Posterior* Rule of Article 30 VCLT 1969

The application of Intra-EU Treaties is not affected by the Directives under the *lex posterior* rule of Article 30 VCLT 1969 because the Directives do not qualify as 'treaties' within the meaning of Article 30 VCLT 1969. As such, conflicts between Directives and tax treaties fall outside the scope of this conflict rule. This does not change if the conflict between a Directive would be perceived as a conflict between Article 288 TFEU, i.e., the treaty provision laying down the obligation to achieve the result of a Directive, and an Intra-EU Treaty because the TFEU does not relate to the same subject matter as tax treaties under a substance-based view of the term 'same subject matter' in Article 30 VCLT 1969. The creation of a common market, the subject matter of the TFEU (in conjunction with the TEU) is just not the same as the topic of tax treaties, i.e., eliminating double taxation of cross-border income of residents of the contracting states, by imposing limitations on the right to tax such income, without creating opportunities for non-taxation or reduced taxation through tax avoidance or tax evasion.

### 6.5.2 Conclusion Regarding the Effect of an Analogous Application of the *Lex Posterior* Rule of Article 30 VCLT 1969

Whereas it has been concluded that the application of Intra-EU Treaties cannot be affected by a 'regular' application of Article 30 VCLT 1969; it has also been concluded

701. An example of clear intention between the parties regarding the effect that Directives should have on Intra-EU Treaties may be found in some of the recent Hungarian treaties providing that their application is without prejudice to obligations arising from EU membership.

that an application of the *lex posterior* rule of Article 30 VCLT 1969 by analogy to conflicts between Directives, as decisions of an international organisation, and tax treaties can be regarded as 'arguable'. The argument for such an analogous application of the *lex posterior* conflict rule is that the conclusion of a later treaty can be regarded as relevantly similar to the adoption of a later Directive in light of (i) the absence of a hierarchy between decisions of international organisations and treaties under public international law, and (ii) the purpose of the rule of Article 30 VCLT 1969 to give effect to the latest legislative intention of the parties to a treaty, which intention may also be reflected by sources of international law other than a treaty such as a decision of an international organisation.

If the *lex posterior* rule of Article 30 VCLT 1969 can be applied by analogy to conflicts between earlier Intra-EU Treaties and later Directives, the Directives themselves may affect the application of Intra-EU Treaties provided that such Directives would be found to relate to the same topic or substance as such treaties. In this author's view, this would seem arguable with respect to all Directives in the sense that there are arguments for concluding that each Directive has a topic or substance that is, at least partially, similar to that of an Intra-EU Treaty. If relating to the same subject matter, a conflict between a later Directive and an earlier Intra-EU Treaty falls within the scope of the *lex posterior* conflict rule of Article 30 VCLT 1969 (applied by analogy). If falling within such scope and in the event of a conflict between such an earlier (incompatible) Intra-EU Treaty and a later Directive, the later Directive would then take priority. In terms of the number of Intra-EU Treaties whose application, in terms of applicability, may then be affected by the Directives, this would amount to 270 (pre-Interest and Royalties Directive) to 336 (pre-ATAD2) Intra-EU Treaties (out of 342 Intra-EU Treaties in total).[702] The application of those Intra-EU Treaties that have been concluded after the adoption of a Directive can, however, not be affected by the Directives under an analogous application of the *lex posterior* rule of Article 30 VCLT 1969.[703]

### 6.5.3 Conclusion Regarding the Effect of the *Lex Specialis* Rule

Whereas an analogous application of the *lex posterior* rule of Article 30 VCLT 1969 may affect the application of up to 336 (of the 342) Intra-EU Treaties, the Directives would be able to affect the application of all (342) Intra-EU Treaties under the *lex specialis* conflict rule. This is due to it being decisive for the purposes of the *lex specialis* conflict rule whether the subject of a provision of a Directive can be regarded as more specific

702. These numbers only demonstrate the number of Intra-EU Treaties whose application may be affected *if* they would conflict with a Directive. It does not intend to indicate anything regarding the question as to whether, for example, the Interest and Royalties Directives can conflict with such treaties.

703. In theory, however, no conflicts should arise between such later Intra-EU Treaties and the Directives given that Member States are, based on the duty of Union loyalty, precluded from concluding treaties that are incompatible with their obligations under such Directives. *See*, to this effect, L. de Broe in: Building Global International Tax Law: Essays in Honour of Guglielmo Maisto (Pistone ed.), 2022, para. 23.4.3.

as compared to a provision of a tax treaty and not whether a Directive has been adopted after the conclusion of an Intra-EU Treaty.

Whether a Directive could affect the application of an Intra-EU Treaty under the *lex specialis* conflict rule would thus be dependent on it being established that (provisions of) such a Directive reflect(s) a more specific intention with respect to a given situation than the intention that would follow from (the provisions of) an Intra-EU Treaty. Whether this is the case needs to be determined on a case-by-case basis, but it is considered arguable that, in any event, the Directives imposing an obligation to tax, i.e., the Parent-Subsidiary Directive, ATAD1 and ATAD2, given their partial (or limited) overlap in terms of substantive and personal scope with provisions of Intra-EU Treaties, can be regarded as the *lex specialis* with respect to the relevant (incompatible) provisions of the relevant Intra-EU Treaty. If a Directive (provision) would be regarded as the *lex specialis*, the *lex specialis* conflict rule provides that the *lex generalis* (the provision(s) of the Intra-EU Treaty) would have to be left inapplicable to the extent that such *lex generalis* is incompatible with the more specific provision(s) of such a Directive. In such a way, the Directives could thus affect the application of each of the Intra-EU Treaties by means of the *lex specialis* conflict rule (making it more relevant, in terms of treaties affected, than the effect on Intra-EU Treaties under an analogous application of the *lex posterior* rule of Article 30 VCLT 1969).

## 6.6 OBSERVATIONS REGARDING TREATIES WHOSE APPLICATION IS NOT AFFECTED BY THE DIRECTIVES

It follows from the conclusions regarding the effect of the *lex posterior* and *lex specialis* conflict rules set out in section 6.6 that the Directives may be able to affect the application of Intra-EU Treaties. They cannot, however, affect the application of Extra-EU Treaties. Hence, in the event of a conflict between the Directives and such treaties, the conflict is not resolved under the rules of public international law. This, in turn, entails that the Member States are bound by both the obligation to achieve the result of a Directive (vis-à-vis the other Member States and the European Union) and the obligations arising from such Extra-EU Treaties (vis-à-vis third states). With respect to such a situation, it follows from the *pacta sunt servanda* principle that both such obligations must be performed in good faith. This is, however, not possible in the event of a conflict. In the event of a conflict, a Member State would have to choose which treaty obligation to perform and which treaty obligation to breach.[704] This decision

704. *See* Fragmentation Report, A/CN.4/L.682, p. 62, para. 115. If and to the extent that a conflict between a Directive and an Intra-EU Treaty would not be resolved, the same choice may arise with respect to Intra-EU Treaties. This could, for example, be the case where a conflict would arise between a later Intra-EU Treaty (as compared to a Directive) and the Directive would not be considered as a *lex specialis* under the *lex specialis* conflict rule. In such an event, it would seem that the duty of Union loyalty would seem to require Member States to choose to give effect to the Directive instead of their Intra-EU Treaty, especially if one would take into account that the same duty would apply with respect to the other Member State. It also follows from such duty that Member States must refrain from any measures jeopardising the attainment of the goals of the EU, including the Directives. As such, if the decision would be made to apply

would then inevitably lead to state responsibility, considering that such (international) responsibility arises as soon as a state refuses to fulfil, or fails to fulfil, a treaty obligation.[705]

The legal consequences of such international responsibility can be found in Part Two of the Draft articles on Responsibility of States for Internationally Wrongful Acts.[706] Such legal consequences entail the obligation of the state responsible for the internationally wrongful act to (i) cease that act,[707] (ii) offer appropriate assurances and guarantees of non-repetition,[708] and (iii) make full reparation for the injury.[709] With respect to these legal consequences, it follows from Article 29 of the Draft articles on Responsibility of States for Internationally Wrongful Acts that they do not affect the continued duty of the state responsible for the internationally wrongful act to perform the obligation breached. It thus follows that, after a choice between two treaty obligations is made, the legal consequences mentioned are triggered, while the treaty obligation that was decided not to give effect to must still be performed.

With respect to the legal consequences that arise by operation of law once a state commits an internationally wrongful act, it should be mentioned that, in practice, the state whose obligations have been violated must inform the other state that it has

---

the Directive, the international responsibility of the Member State making such decision should not be invoked by the other Member State if that would be contrary to the Directive itself. *See*, to this effect, also D.S. Smit in: European Tax Law (Wattel, Marres & Vermeulen eds), 2018, p. 490 who notes that '[c]learly, Member States cannot object against their fellow Member States limiting bilateral tax treaty rights to honour their EU Directive obligations'.

705. *See* ICJ, 1950, Advisory Opinion (*Interpretation of Peace Treaties with Bulgaria, Hungary and Romania*), p. 228 ('it is clear that refusal to fulfil a treaty obligation involves international responsibility'). This principle, i.e., that a breach of international law by a state entails its international responsibility, has been codified in Article 1 of the Draft articles on Responsibility of States for Internationally Wrongful Acts, with commentaries, which provides that '[e]very internationally wrongful act of a State entails the international responsibility of that State'. Based on Article 2 of these draft articles, there is an internationally wrongful act of a State when conduct consisting of an action or omission constitutes a breach of an international obligation, which must be understood as referring to cover both treaty and non-treaty obligations (para. 7 of the Commentaries to Article 2 of the Draft articles on Responsibility of States for Internationally Wrongful Acts with commentaries). Such a breach arises if 'conduct attributed to a State as a subject of international law amounts to a failure by that State to comply with an international obligation incumbent upon it' (para. 1 of the Commentaries to Article 11 of the Draft articles on Responsibility of States for Internationally Wrongful Acts with commentaries. *See also* Article 12, as well as para. 3 of the Commentaries thereto, of the Draft articles on Responsibility of States for Internationally Wrongful Acts with commentaries). The essence of an internationally wrongful act may thus be regarded as 'the non-conformity of the State's actual conduct with the conduct it ought to have adopted in order to comply with a particular international obligation' (*see* para. 3 of the Commentaries to Article 11 of the Draft articles on Responsibility of States for Internationally Wrongful Acts with commentaries).
706. *See* Article 28 of the Draft articles on Responsibility of States for Internationally Wrongful Acts with commentaries.
707. Article 30(a) of the Draft articles on Responsibility of States for Internationally Wrongful Acts with commentaries.
708. Article 30(b) of the Draft articles on Responsibility of States for Internationally Wrongful Acts with commentaries.
709. Article 31 of the Draft articles on Responsibility of States for Internationally Wrongful Acts with commentaries.

committed the internationally wrongful act when seeking cessation or reparation.[710] As such, if a Member State gives priority to a Directive over obligations arising under an Extra-EU Treaty, the third state must give notice to such Member State if it intends to invoke the international responsibility of such Member State and, as such, intends to rely on the legal consequences of such international responsibility as set out in Part Two of the Draft articles on Responsibility of States for Internationally Wrongful Acts.

In sum, choosing between two mutually exclusive treaty obligations shall give rise to international responsibility for the Member State making such choice. Whether, as a matter of practice, such international responsibility would have legal consequences for such state depends on whether the state(s) to the other - violated - treaty invoke such responsibility.

710. Draft articles on Responsibility of States for Internationally Wrongful Acts with commentaries, p. 119, para. 2.

## CHAPTER 7

# The Effect of the Directives on the Application of Tax Treaties under EU Law

## 7.1 INTRODUCTION

Whereas the previous chapter has focused on the effect that the Directives may have on the application – in terms of the applicability – of tax treaties under public international law, this chapter is aimed at determining such effect under the laws of the EU. In determining the effect of the Directives on the application of tax treaties from the perspective of the laws of the EU, the focus will be on the primacy of EU law pursuant to which authorities of Member States are required to set aside (inter)national laws in the event of a conflict between such laws and rules of EU law.[711] In order to determine the extent to which the Directives may have such an effect on the application of tax treaties under the laws of the EU, the applicability – or scope – of the primacy of the Directives to conflicts between Directives and tax treaties is addressed first (section 7.2), followed by an assessment of the extent to which such primacy is enforceable before Member State courts (section 7.3). This chapter ends with an answer to the question to what extent Member State courts may be obliged to set aside tax treaties that conflict with the Directives (and thereby affect their application) under the laws of the EU (section 7.4).

711. *See, e.g.*, R. Schütze, 2021, para. 119 and M. Bobek in: European Union Law (Barnard & Peers eds), 2017, p. 162. For completeness' sake, it is noted that such primacy only affects the applicability of conflicting national laws (or tax treaties) and not their validity (*see*, to this effect, V. Trstenjak, Beijing Law Review 2013/2, p. 72, M. Klamert, 2014, p. 102, and M. Claes in: The Oxford Handbook of European Union Law (Chalmers ed.), 2015, p. 182).

## 7.2 THE SCOPE OF THE PRIMACY OF THE DIRECTIVES TO CONFLICTS WITH TAX TREATIES

### 7.2.1 General

This section aims to determine the extent to which the primacy of EU law applies to conflicts between the Directives and tax treaties. For these purposes, a conflict would exist if a Member State does not achieve the result of a Directive due to the applicability of a tax treaty within its legal order. This would, for example, be the case where, within a Member State legal order, tax treaties are superior to domestic law aimed at implementing a Directive. In such case, a Member State would not be able to achieve the result of a Directive by means of its national legislation because such legislation would have to be left inapplicable to the extent incompatible with the application of tax treaties concluded by the Member State. It is with respect to such a conflict that this section seeks to determine the extent to which the primacy of the Directives would apply and be able to result in the setting aside of the relevant (incompatible) tax treaty.

In determining the extent to which the primacy is applicable with respect to tax treaties, a distinction can be drawn between the primacy of the Directives vis-à-vis Intra-EU Treaties and Extra-EU Treaties. Regarding Intra-EU Treaties, it is settled case law of the CJEU that EU law, including secondary EU law such as the Directives,[712] takes precedence over all international agreements concluded between the Member States.[713] As a consequence, all 343 Intra-EU Treaties fall within the scope of the

712. *See* Case 278/82 (*Rewe and Hauptzollämter*), para. 29 ('[t]he Court has held, in its judgment of 26 February 1962 (Case 10/61, Commission v Government of the Italian Republic, [1962] ECR 1), that "the EEC Treaty ... takes precedence over agreements concluded between Member States before its entry into force". It is clear that the same effect must be attributed to secondary Community law: Directive 69/169/EEC could therefore, in any event, validly set aside the provisions of the New York Convention with regard to travel by sea between Member States.').

713. *See* Case 10/61 (*Commission v. Italy*), p. 10, Case 235/87 (*Matteucci*), paras 21-22, Case C-469/00 (*Ravil*), para. 37, and Case C-478/07 (*Budějovický Budvar*), para. 98. It is not relevant, in this respect, whether the incompatible international agreement between Member States has been concluded before or after accession. This follows from Case C-469/00 (*Ravil*), para. 37 where the CJEU held that the provisions of a treaty concluded by Italy and France on 28 April 1964, i.e., after both states had become Member States by means of the conclusion of the Treaty of Rome, 'cannot apply in the relations between those States if they are found to be contrary to the rules of the Treaty'. In addition, the primacy of EU law with respect to earlier international agreements between Member States follows from Case 10/61 (*Commission v. Italy*) which concerned a treaty signed on 23 May 1956 (before the accession of Italy), Case 235/87 (*Matteucci*) regarding a treaty signed on 24 September 1956 (before the accession of Belgium and Germany), and Case C-478/07 (*Budějovický Budvar*), para. 98 relating to an agreement concluded on 7 June 1979 between Austria and the Czech Republic (i.e., before the accession of both Austria and the Czech Republic). It is with respect to such earlier international agreements that Advocate General Wathelet has noted that the primacy of EU law position is consistent with Article 30(3) VCLT 1969, according to which 'when all the parties to the earlier treaty are parties also to the later treaty but the earlier treaty is not terminated or suspended in operation under Article 59, the earlier treaty applies only to the extent that its provisions are compatible with those of the later treaty' (*see* Opinion of Advocate General Wathelet in Case C-284/16 (*Achmea*), para. 47, footnote 51).

The 'absolute' primacy of EU law regarding treaties signed between Member States, i.e., primacy over all such treaties irrespective of their date of conclusion, has also been widely

primacy of the Directives.[714] While the primacy of the Directives thus applies to all Intra-EU Treaties, this is different for Extra-EU Treaties due to Article 351 TFEU. Article 351 TFEU provides that those Extra-EU Treaties 'concluded before 1 January 1958 or, for acceding States, before the date of their accession ... shall not be affected by the provisions of the Treaties'. Article 351 TFEU thus limits the applicability of, or can be regarded as an exception to,[715] the primacy of the Directives with respect to tax treaties. For that reason, its scope is relevant for the purposes of determining the extent to which the primacy of the Directives is applicable to conflicts with tax treaties.

### 7.2.2 The Scope of the Exception to the Primacy of the Directives (Article 351 TFEU)

As noted in the previous section, Article 351 TFEU essentially limits the applicability of the primacy of the Directives with respect to the Extra-EU Treaties that fall within the scope of such provision. With respect to such scope, a distinction will be drawn in this section between its temporal scope, i.e., which Extra-EU Treaties may be covered by the protection of Article 351 TFEU (section 7.2.2.1), and its substantive scope, i.e., what kind of rights and obligations are protected by Article 351 TFEU (section 7.2.2.2).[716] Within the context of determining the scope of Article 351 TFEU, it will furthermore be assessed whether the protection offered by the first paragraph of Article 351 TFEU is dependent on compliance of the relevant Member State with its duty to 'take all appropriate steps to eliminate incompatibilities' under the second paragraph of Article 351 TFEU (subsection 7.2.2.3). This section ends with a conclusion regarding the scope of Article 351 TFEU (7.2.2.4).

---

recognised by legal scholars. *See* A. Rosas, Fordham International Law Journal 2011/5, p. 1320, A. Dimopoulos, Common Market Law Review 2011/1, pp. 69-70, M. Klamert, 2014, p. 281, K. von Papp, Legal Issues of Economic Integration 2015/4, p. 6, M. Kellerbauer and M. Klamert in: The EU Treaties and the Charter of Fundamental Rights: A Commentary (Kellerbauer, Klamert & Tomkin eds), 2021, pp. 2070-2071, and L. de Broe in: Building Global International Tax Law: Essays in Honour of Guglielmo Maisto (Pistone ed.), 2022, para. 23.4.3.

714. *See*, to this effect, Opinion of Advocate General Wathelet in Case C-284/16 (*Achmea*), para. 47 who concludes that 'the provisions of such a convention between Member States are applicable in so far as they are compatible with the EU and FEU Treaties'. This effect is, in turn, based on the judgment of the CJEU in Case C-469/00 (*Ravil*), para. 37 where it held that 'the provisions of a convention between two Member States cannot apply in the relations between those States if they are found to be contrary to the rules of the Treaty'. In light of Case 278/82 (*Rewe and Hauptzollämter*), para. 29, this judgment should also apply to the Directives.

715. *See*, to this effect, K. von Papp, Legal Issues of Economic Integration 2015/4, p. 3, as well as W.C. Haslehner in: A Guide to the Anti-Tax Avoidance Directive (Haslehner, Pantazatou, Kofler & Rust eds), 2020, p. 61, para. 2.67 who refers to Article 351 TFEU as an 'exception to the general principle of effectiveness and primacy of EU law'.

716. *See*, in support of addressing both the temporal and substantive scope for the purposes of determining the 'protection' granted by Article 351 TFEU, Joined Cases C-364/95 & C-365/95 (*T-Port*), para. 61 ('for a Community provision to be deprived of effect as a result of an international agreement, two conditions must be fulfilled: the agreement must have been concluded before the entry into force of the Treaty and the third country concerned must derive from it rights which it can require the Member State concerned to respect').

#### *7.2.2.1 The Temporal Scope of Article 351 TFEU*

##### *7.2.2.1.1 General*

With respect to the temporal scope of Article 351 TFEU, the starting point is that, based on its wording, only those Extra-EU Treaties concluded by a Member State before, essentially, its accession to the EU shall not be affected by – or 'be protected from' – the primacy of EU law, which EU law includes the Directives.[717] The rationale for protecting such pre-accession Extra-EU Treaties seems to be the 'pacta sunt servanda principle of international law',[718] as well as the *pacta tertiis nec nocent nec prosunt* principle,[719] pursuant to which the accession of a Member State should have no effect on its commitments vis-à-vis third states.[720] This rationale can be derived from consistent references in the case law of the CJEU that it is the purpose of Article 351 TFEU to 'make clear, in accordance with the principles of international law, as set out in, *inter alia*, Article 30(4)(b) [VCLT] 1969, that the application of [the EU Treaties] does not affect the duty of the Member State concerned to respect the rights of non-member countries under a prior agreement and to perform its obligations thereunder.'[721] From this case law, it thus follows that Article 351 TFEU essentially aims to ensure that Member States would not become obliged, upon accession to the EU, to act in breach of international agreements entered into with third states before their accession,[722] which could give rise to state responsibility (*see* section 6.6).

At the same time, however, the wording of Article 351 TFEU also seems to indicate that it is not concerned with avoiding such state responsibility with respect to those Extra-EU Treaties that have been concluded by a Member State after its accession to the EU.[723] It has, however, been submitted by legal scholars, as well as Advocate

717. *See*, to this effect, Case C-435/22 PPU (*Generalstaatsanwaltschaft München*), paras 116-117 where the CJEU noted that Article 351 TFEU did not apply to an extradition treaty concluded by Germany with the United States on 20 June 1978 (i.e., after Germany's accession to the EU on 1 January 1958). Based on Case 812/79 (*Burgoa*), para. 7 it would seem that the CJEU would regard a treaty as 'concluded' for the purposes of Article 351 TFEU if it has been signed *and* ratified. This approach as to when a treaty is considered 'concluded' seems different from the interpretation accorded to the term 'concluded' in the VCLT 1969 (*see* section 6.4.2.1.1). *See*, regarding this approach of the CJEU, M. Kellerbauer & M. Klamert in: The EU Treaties and the Charter of Fundamental Rights: A Commentary (Kellerbauer, Klamert & Tomkin eds), 2021, p. 2066, footnote 5.
718. *See* Opinion of Advocate General Kokott in: Case C-366/10 (*Air Transport Association of America*), para. 56.
719. *See* Opinion of Advocate General Kokott in: Case C-366/10 (*Air Transport Association of America*), para. 57.
720. *See* sections 6.2 and 6.3.
721. *See, inter alia*, Case 812/79 (*Burgoa*), para. 8, Case C-158/91 (*Levy*), para. 12, Case C-324/93 (*Evans Medical Care*), para. 27, Case C-124/95 (*Centro-Com*), para. 56, Case C-84/98 (*Commission v. Portugal*), para. 53, Case C-216/01 (*Budějovický Budvar*), para. 145, Case C-249/06 (*Commission v. Sweden*), para. 34, and Case C-277/10 (*Luksan*), para. 61.
722. *See* to this effect Opinion of Advocate General Kokott in: Case C-366/10 (*Air Transport Association of America*), para. 56.
723. *See*, to this effect, Case C-476/98 (*Open Skies (Germany)*), para. 69 where the CJEU ruled that Article 351 TFEU 'applies to rights and obligations flowing from agreements concluded by Member States before the Treaty entered into force, it cannot apply to amendments which

General Kokott, that the protection offered by Article 351 TFEU may also apply with respect to those Extra-EU Treaties that have been concluded *after* accession but *before* adoption of a Directive (or a transfer of competences to the EU).[724] Such an application of Article 351 TFEU (by analogy) would seem to be based on the premise that the adoption of a Directive would be (relevantly) similar to accession to the EU. If applied by analogy, the number of treaties that would fall within the temporal scope of the protection provided by Article 351 TFEU increases substantially.[725] This can be illustrated as follows. There are 443 pre-accession Extra-EU Treaties whereas there would be, based on the year of adoption of the most recent Directive in 2017, up to 1,416 pre-ATAD2 Extra-EU Treaties.[726] Given this effect of an analogous application on the number of Extra-EU Treaties that would fall within the temporal scope of Article 351 TFEU, the question of whether the protection offered by Article 351 TFEU is to be applied by analogy to pre-Directive Extra-EU Treaties is relevant and discussed below in section 7.2.2.1.2.

Another question that needs to be addressed within the context of determining the temporal scope of Article 351 TFEU is to what extent amendments to treaties falling within the scope of Article 351 TFEU based on their original date of conclusion (hereinafter: 'Article 351 TFEU Treaties') could result in such date of conclusion 'shifting' to the date of amendment. This question is especially relevant for those Article 351 TFEU Treaties that have been amended after accession of the Member State to the EU (or, in case of an analogous application, after the date of adoption of a Directive) and is addressed in section 7.2.2.1.3.

---

Member States make to such agreements by entering into new commitments after the entry into force of the Treaty'. This would seem to be especially the case where the conclusion of such a post-accession Extra-EU Treaty would be incompatible with EU law at the time of its conclusion (*see, e.g.*, Case C-476/98 (*Open Skies (Germany)*), paras 135-137 where the CJEU ruled that Member States were precluded from entering into international commitments containing rules 'capable of affecting rules adopted by the [EU] or of altering their scope'. By nevertheless entering into such commitments, it found that Germany had failed to fulfil its obligations under EU law).

724. An analogous application of Article 351 TFEU has been advocated for by K.M. Meessen, Common Market Law Review 1974/4, p. 491, R.R. Churchill & N.G. Foster, The International and Comparative Law Quarterly 1987/3, pp. 504 et seq., and J.P. Terhechte, European Yearbook for International Economic Law 2010, p. 6. *See also* Opinion of Advocate General Kokott in: Case C-188/07 (*Commune de Mesquer*), para. 95 who considers an analogous application of Article 351 TFEU as 'conceivable'. There are, however, also legal scholars who reject an analogous application of Article 351 TFEU. *See*, to that effect, P. Manzini, European Journal of International Law 2001/4, p. 786 and C. Eckes in: 2011, p. 365.

725. *See* to this effect J.P. Terhechte, European Yearbook for International Economic Law 2010, p. 6 and R. Schütze in: Foreign Affairs and the EU Constitution: Selected Essays 2014, p. 168. Schütze, on p. 165, does highlight that, while referring to R.R. Churchill & N.G. Foster, The International and Comparative Law Quarterly 1987/3, p. 519 and Joined Cases C-176/97 & C-177/97 (*Commission v. Belgium and Luxembourg*), the CJEU seems to have implicitly rejected an analogous application in Case 181/80 (*Arbelaiz-Emazabel*). In these cases, the CJEU did not, however, explicitly reject an analogous application of Article 351 TFEU.

726. *See* Annex 1, para. 3.4.3.

### *7.2.2.1.2 The Temporal Scope and Post-accession, Pre-Directive Extra-EU Treaties (Analogous Application of Article 351 TFEU)*

As noted in the previous section, it has been submitted by Advocate General Kokott and legal scholars that the protection of Article 351 TFEU should also apply by analogy to post-accession, pre-Directive Extra-EU Treaties (hereinafter: 'PD Extra-EU Treaties').[727] The argument underlying such an analogous application would be that accession to the EU would have to be regarded as being relevantly similar to the EU exercising a new competence of adopting a legal act, such as a Directive, after a Member State has concluded a treaty with a third state. In support of the view that Article 351 TFEU should be applicable by analogy, the following line of reasoning could be adopted. It seems arguable that there are similarities between a Member State's accession to the EU and the EU exercising a certain competence or adopting a legal act after accession to the EU after the conclusion of an Extra-EU Treaty.[728] If similar, an

727. It is acknowledged that an analogous application would be based on the assumption that the conditions of Article 351 TFEU itself are not met with respect to PD Extra-EU Treaties (*see* J. Hage, Argumentation 2005/4, p. 403 who notes that an analogous application of a rule requires that the conditions of such rule are not satisfied ('otherwise it would be normal application')). Such assumption seems valid in light of the clear wording of Article 351 TFEU and the CJEU considering itself unable to depart from a meaning of a provision of EU law that is 'absolutely plain' (*see*, to this effect Case C-181/20 (*Vysocina Wind*), para. 39. This position is based on the settled case law in which the CJEU held that 'an interpretation cannot have the result of depriving the clear and precise wording of that provision of all effectiveness' (*see* Case C-220/03 (*ECB v. Germany*), para. 31, Case C-199/05 (*European Community v. Belgium*), para. 42, Joined Cases C-147/11 & C-148/11 (*Czop and Punakova*), para. 32, Joined Cases C-671/11 to C-676/11 (*FranceAgriMer*), para. 26, and, also, Case C-181/20 (*Vysocina Wind*), para. 39). Reference can also be made to K. Lenaerts & J.A. Gutiérrez-Fons, EUI Working Papers 2013/9, p. 7 who note that 'the ECJ will never ignore the clear and precise wording of an EU law provision').

In the event of Article 351 TFEU, the wording regarding its temporal scope seems to be 'absolutely plain' (*see* Opinion of Advocate General Capotorti in: Case 181/80 (*Arbelaiz-Emazabel*), para. 19 ('in the case of conventions on matters over which the Community did not start to exercise its powers for some time after the entry into force of the Treaty, the institutions' obligations not to obstruct observance of the commitments entered into by one or more Member States should extend also to the commitments entered into before such powers were exercised. But that view manifestly conflicts with the wording of the first paragraph of Article 234'), P. Manzini, European Journal of International Law 2001/4, p. 786 ('it is not consistent with the literal interpretation of paragraph 1, which, as seen above, unequivocally refers to the date of entry into force of the EC Treaty for each member state; this date cannot be confused with the moment of the effective exercise of functions by the Community'), J.P. Terhechte, European Yearbook for International Economic Law 2010, p. 6 ('the provision's wording makes a direct application of Article 351 TFEU impossible when Member States later on transfer powers to the Union'), A. Rosas, Fordham International Law Journal 2011/5, p. 1322 ('Article 351 does not cover agreements concluded by Member States after they have become EU members, even if the Union had not, at the time of the conclusion of the agreement, adopted common rules. ... The provision now refers explicitly to agreements concluded either "before 1 January 1958" or, for acceding states, "before the date of their accession" and thus does not seem to leave room for any margin of interpretation in this regard.'), and R. Schütze in: Foreign Affairs and the EU Constitution: Selected Essays 2014, p. 164 ('for the wording of the provision precluded its direct application to subsequent international agreements of the Member States')).

728. *See* J.P. Terhechte, European Yearbook for International Economic Law 2010, p. 6 ('leaving room for an analogy of Art. 351 TFEU, due to comparable situations in both cases'.).

analogous application of Article 351 TFEU could then be 'based on the idea that the conferral of a new competence upon the EU by way of primary law reform creates a situation that, from the viewpoint of Member States international engagements, is comparable to the very creation of the Union'.[729] Adoption of a Directive and accession to the EU would, following this line of reasoning, be relevantly similar if the purpose of Article 351 TFEU is understood as giving effect to a general principle pursuant to which Member States cannot be forced to violate their international law obligations provided that such obligations were not incompatible with those under the laws of the EU at the time of the entry into of such international law obligations.[730] In other words, Article 351 TFEU would seek to ensure that Member States are prevented from being forced to 'breach public international law obligations they entered into in good faith with a third country'.[731] Support for such a conclusion regarding the purpose of Article 351(1) TFEU could be derived from references in the case law of the CJEU to Article 351 TFEU being aimed at making it 'clear, in accordance with the principles of international law, as set out in, *inter alia*, Article 30(4)(b) [VCLT] 1969, that the application of [the EU Treaties] does not affect the duty of the Member State concerned to respect the rights of non-member countries under a prior agreement and to perform its obligations thereunder'.[732] Based on such an understanding of the purpose of Article 351 TFEU, the similarity between accession to the EU and the EU exercising a new competence or adopting a legal act could be regarded as relevant. If relevant, such similarity would provide an argument for an analogous application of Article 351 TFEU (regarding an application of rules by analogy, *see* section 6.4.2.2.2).

Whereas an analogous application of Article 351 TFEU could thus be considered arguable on the basis of accession to the EU and adoption of a Directive being relevantly similar, it must be acknowledged that the CJEU has recently (22 October 2022) rejected such an application of Article 351 TFEU in *Generalstaatsanwaltschaft München* (Case C-435/22 PPU). In *Generalstaatsanwaltschaft München*, a German court (*Oberlandesgericht München*) requested a preliminary ruling on, *inter alia*, whether Article 351 TFEU could be applied by analogy to a post-accession Extra-EU Treaty concluded before an amendment of the EU Treaties introducing the *ne bis in idem principle*. More specifically, the case concerned the question of whether a post-accession extradition treaty concluded between Germany and the United States in 1978 could be affected by the *ne bis in idem principle* as subsequently incorporated into

729. L. Pantaleo, European Foreign Affairs Review, 2014/2, pp. 308-309.
730. P. Ariginelli in: The External Tax Strategy of the EU in a Post-BEPS Environment (Jiménez ed.), 2019, para. 8.3.1.
731. W.C. Haslehner in: A Guide to the Anti-Tax Avoidance Directive (Haslehner, Pantazatou, Kofler & Rust eds), pp. 61-62.
732. *See, inter alia*, Case 812/79 (*Burgoa*), para. 8, Case C-158/91 (*Levy*), para. 12, Case C-324/93 (*Evans Medical Care*), para. 27, Case C-124/95 (*Centro-Com*), para. 56, Case C-84/98 (*Commission v. Portugal*), para. 53, Case C-216/01 (*Budějovický Budvar*), para. 145, Case C-249/06 (*Commission v. Sweden*), para. 34, and Case C-277/10 (*Luksan*), para. 61. Reference can furthermore be made to CJEU, Opinion 2/15 (*EU-Singapore Free Trade Agreement*), para. 254 and Case C-282/19 (*MIUR and Ufficio Scolastico Regionale per la Campania*), para. 55 wherein the CJEU ruled that Article 351 TFEU is 'intended to permit the Member States to respect the rights which third States derive, in accordance with international law, from those earlier agreements'.

EU law as a result of the amendment of the EU Treaties by means of the Treaty of Amsterdam in 2000 and the conclusion of the Charter of Fundamental Rights of the European Union.[733] In response to this question, the CJEU ruled that Article 351(1) TFEU must be interpreted as applying 'only to agreements concluded before 1 January 1958 or, in the case of acceding States, before the date of their accession'.[734] In support of this conclusion, the CJEU referred to the following three arguments. First, the CJEU referred to the circumstance that Article 351(1) TFEU allows for an exception to (the primacy of) the application of EU law and that exceptions are to be interpreted strictly.[735] Within the context of an analogous application of Article 351 TFEU, the CJEU highlights that a 'strict interpretation is particularly necessary as regards [Article 351(1) TFEU], since that provision allows derogation not from a specific principle but from the application of any provisions of the Treaties'.[736] Second, the Court made a reference to a 'strict interpretation ... also [being] necessary in light of the obligation of the Member States under [Article 351(2) TFEU] to take all appropriate steps to eliminate existing incompatibilities between an agreement and the Treaties'.[737] Third, and finally, the CJEU also referred to the circumstance that the wording of Article 351 TFEU has been the subject of negotiations in connection with the Treaty of Amsterdam in light of the circumstance that the phrase 'before the entry into force of this Treaty' was replaced by the phrase 'before 1 January 1958 or, for acceding States, before the date of their accession'.[738] According to the Court, the Member States were aware, when concluding the Treaty of Amsterdam, that 'the competences of the European Union may evolve significantly over time, including in fields which were the subject of agreements concluded with third countries'. Nevertheless, the Member States 'did not provide for the possibility of taking into account, for the purposes of [Article 351 (1) TFEU, the date on which the European Union became competent in a given area'.[739] It thus seems as if the CJEU considers the conclusion of the Treaty of Amsterdam to reflect a confirmation of a common intention between the Member States that Article 351 TFEU should only apply to pre-accession treaties with third states. As such, the CJEU seems to presume (a contrario) that the Member States had a common intention at the time of conclusion of the Treaty of Amsterdam that the EU Treaties should be able to affect post-accession treaties that would become incompatible with EU law in the future. Based on such a presumed intention, as well as the case law that exceptions should be interpreted strictly, it is unsurprising that the CJEU concluded that Article 351 TFEU cannot be applied by analogy to post-accession treaties with third states. For the purposes of this book, this entails that Article 351 TFEU can only protect the 413 pre-accession Extra-EU Treaties (and not up to 1,416 pre-Directive Extra-EU Treaties).

733. *See* C-435/22 PPU (*Generalstaatsanwaltschaft München*), para. 115.
734. C-435/22 PPU (*Generalstaatsanwaltschaft München*), para. 126.
735. *See* C-435/22 PPU (*Generalstaatsanwaltschaft München*), paras 119-120.
736. C-435/22 PPU (*Generalstaatsanwaltschaft München*), para. 121.
737. C-435/22 PPU (*Generalstaatsanwaltschaft München*), para. 122.
738. Case C-435/22 PPU (*Generalstaatsanwaltschaft München*), paras 123-124.
739. Case C-435/22 PPU (*Generalstaatsanwaltschaft München*), para. 125.

*7.2.2.1.3 The Temporal Scope and Amendments*

The starting point with respect to the temporal scope of Article 351 TFEU is the date on which an Extra-EU Treaty has been concluded. It must be established with respect to such date whether the Member State concerned had acceded to the EU. If on that date the Member State had not yet acceded to the EU, the relevant Extra-EU Treaty would fall within the temporal scope of Article 351 TFEU. Based on the analysis of the EU tax treaty network in Annex 1, there would be 413 Extra-EU Treaties that qualify as pre-accession Extra-EU Treaties.[740] Of these 413 pre-accession Extra-EU Treaties, 54 have been bilaterally amended after the accession of the relevant Member State to the EU, while 139 have been amended by means of the MLI.[741] The question that is addressed in the present section is under what circumstances those post-accession amendments to pre-accession Extra-EU Treaties would be able to result in such treaties as a whole falling outside the temporal scope of Article 351 TFEU. In answering this question, a distinction can be drawn, based on the so-called *Open Skies* case law of the CJEU,[742] between amendments by means of a replacement of the 351 TFEU Treaty,[743] or by means of amendments to a 351 TFEU Treaty without such a replacement.[744]

With respect to amendments that result in a replacement of a 351 TFEU Treaty by a new Extra-EU Treaty, the CJEU adopts a formal approach. Under this formal approach, the date of the new treaty becomes decisive for the purposes of determining whether the relevant Extra-EU Treaty falls within the temporal scope of Article 351 TFEU. If the date of the conclusion of the new treaty lies after the date of accession, Article 351 TFEU is no longer applicable because the rights and obligations arise, 'not from an agreement before, but from an agreement after the accession' of the Member

740. *See* Annex 1, para. 3.2. For the purposes of calculating the number of pre-accession Extra-EU Treaties, accession is deemed to have taken place in the year in which an Accession Treaty has been concluded while a tax treaty is considered as concluded before such accession if it has been concluded in any year before such an Accession Treaty has been concluded. The CJEU seems, however, to adopt a different approach by focusing on whether an Extra-EU Treaty has been concluded and entered into force before accession to the EU (*see*, to that effect, Case 812/79 (*Burgoa*), para. 7).
741. *See* Annex 2, para. 3.
742. The *Open Skies* case law concerns infringement proceedings against several Member States for entering into so-called *open skies* type bilateral agreements with the United States (i.e., agreements that facilitate, in particular, 'free access to all routes, the granting of unlimited route and traffic rights, the fixing of prices in accordance with a system of "mutual disapproval" and the possibility of sharing code'). Such agreements were concluded after the Commission obtained a limited mandate to negotiate with the United States to replace bilateral agreements previously concluded with certain European states that were, at that time, not Member States of the EU. According to the Commission, by concluding those agreements, the Member States infringed the external competence of the EU (except for the case against the United Kingdom) and infringed the right of establishment (*see* Press Release No 89/02 (Judgments in Cases C-466/98, C-467/98, C-468/98, C-469/98, C-471/98, C-475/98 & C-476/98), para. 1).
743. Case C-466/98 (*Commission v. United Kingdom*).
744. Case C-467/98 (*Commission v. Denmark*), Case C-468/98 (*Commission v. Sweden*), Case C-469/98 (*Commission v. Finland*), Case C-471/98 (*Commission v. Belgium*), Case C-472/98 (*Commission v. Luxembourg*), Case C-475/98 (*Commission v. Austria*), and Case C-487/98 (*Commission v. Germany*).

State.[745] The circumstance that some provisions may contain obligations that are substantially similar or would not have been amended by the post-accession Extra-EU Treaty is of no relevance in this respect.[746]

While amendments may take the form of a replacement of a 351 TFEU Treaty in full, they may also take the form of an amendment of only part of such a treaty by means of, for example, a protocol or an exchange of diplomatic notes. Such partial amendments can, based on the *Open Skies* case law, also result in the date of amendment becoming decisive for the purposes of establishing whether an Extra-EU Treaty falls within the scope of Article 351 TFEU. The relevant criterion in that respect is whether it can be established that a partial amendment to such treaty has been the result of a renegotiation of the relevant treaty in its entirety.[747]

The reason for applying this criterion seems to be that Member States are under a duty to refrain from maintaining in force those provisions that would be incompatible with EU law.[748] As such, when renegotiating a treaty in its entirety, Member States are precluded from (implicitly) confirming the (continued) application of provisions that are incompatible with the laws of the EU.[749] At the same time, however, if there is no evidence of negotiations regarding an amendment of a treaty in its entirety, it follows that the date of conclusion of the 351 TFEU Treaty does not shift to the date of amendment of a 351 TFEU Treaty. With respect to those pre-accession Extra-EU Treaties that have been amended after accession of the Member State without (evidence of) a renegotiation regarding the treaty in full, a distinction should thus be drawn between, on the one hand, those provisions that have not been amended (falling within the temporal scope of Article 351 TFEU) and those provisions that have been amended (falling outside the scope of Article 351 TFEU).[750]

With respect to those pre-accession Extra-EU Treaties that have been – bilaterally or multilaterally by means of the MLI – amended, it should thus be examined whether the relevant amendment has been the result of a renegotiation in full. With respect to each of the 54 post-accession bilateral amendments of pre-accession Extra-EU Treaties,

745. Case C-466/98 (*Commission v. United Kingdom*), paras 26-27.

746. *See*, to this effect, the argument put forward by the United Kingdom in Case C-466/98 (*Commission v. United Kingdom*), para. 17, which was rejected by the CJEU.

747. *See* Case C-467/98 (*Open Skies (Denmark)*), para. 39 where the CJEU held that 'while some provisions of the agreement were not formally modified by the amendments made in 1995 or were subject only to marginal changes in drafting, the commitment arising from those provisions were none the less confirmed during the renegotiation. In such a case, the Member States are prevented not only from contracting new international commitments but also from maintaining such commitments in force if they infringe [EU] law'.

748. Case C-467/98 (*Open Skies (Denmark)*), para. 39.

749. Case C-467/98 (*Open Skies (Denmark)*), para. 39.

750. *See*, to this effect, Case C-476/98 (*Open Skies (Germany)*), para. 69 ('although article 234 of the Treaty ... applies to rights and obligations flowing from agreements concluded by Member States before the treat entered into force, it cannot apply to amendments which Member States make to such agreements by entering into new commitments after the entry into force of the Treaty'). M. Kellerbauer & M. Klamert in: The EU Treaties and the Charter of Fundamental Rights: A Commentary (Kellerbauer, Klamert & Tomkin eds), 2021, p. 2068, para. 8 come to a similar conclusion given that they note that an amended pre-accession Extra-EU Treaty would 'not fall under Article 351(1) TFEU if the Agreement in its entirety was renegotiated and the commitment arising from it were confirmed during the renegotiation'.

it should thus be assessed whether the scope of the negotiations leading to such amendments related to the treaty as a whole or were limited to certain provisions only. The same applies regarding amendments by means of the MLI, which amendments would seem less likely to result in the date of conclusion of a 351 TFEU Treaty shifting to the date of amendment by means of the MLI because it has been the purpose of the MLI to avoid bilateral renegotiations to (partially) implement the contents of the BEPS Action Plan.[751] In the absence of bilateral renegotiations, it would thus seem unlikely that modifications of covered tax treaties by means of the MLI would reflect the result of a renegotiation of such agreements in full.

#### *7.2.2.1.4 Conclusions Regarding the Temporal Scope of Article 351 TFEU*

It follows from the preceding sections that Article 351 TFEU only applies to pre-accession Extra EU-Treaties (representing 27.4% of all Extra-EU Treaties, or 22.3% of all treaties concluded by the Member States) and that an analogous application of Article 351 TFEU should be rejected in light of the judgment of the CJEU in *Generalstaatsanwaltschaft München* (Case C-435/22 PPU). With respect to the 413 pre-accession Extra-EU Treaties falling within the scope of Article 351 TFEU, it needs, however, to be borne in mind that they could fall outside the temporal scope of Article 351 TFEU if they would be amended by a Member State after its accession to the EU following a renegotiation of such treaty in full. Whether an amended pre-accession Extra-EU Treaty would continue to fall within the temporal scope of Article 351 TFEU is thus dependent on the nature of the negotiations that resulted in its post-accession amendment. If no (re)negotiation in full has taken place, a distinction should be drawn for the purposes of Article 351 TFEU between those provisions that have not been amended (falling within the temporal scope of Article 351 TFEU) and those that have been amended (falling outside the temporal scope of Article 351 TFEU).

### *7.2.2.2 The Substantive Scope of Article 351 TFEU*

#### *7.2.2.2.1 The 'Protected' Rights and Obligations*

Article 351 TFEU provides that the 'rights and obligations' arising from pre-accession Extra-EU Treaties shall not be affected by the EU Treaties. While this might seem to indicate a broad substantive scope of Article 351 TFEU, it follows from the case law of the CJEU that this is not the case. According to the CJEU, the term 'rights' refers to the 'rights of third states', whereas the term 'obligations' must be understood as being limited to the 'obligations of the Member States'.[752] With respect to those rights of, and

751. *See* BEPS Action 15 (Final Report), p. 16, para. 8 where it is noted that one of the advantages of a multilateral instrument would be that it allows for 'all existing bilateral tax treaties to be modified in a synchronized way with respect to BEPS issues, without a need to individually address each treaty within the 3000+ treaty network'.

752. CJEU, 27 February 1962, Case 10/61 (*Commission v. Italy*), p. 10 where the CJEU held that the 'application's interpretation is well founded' whereas such interpretation of the applicant

obligations towards, third states, it is settled case law of the CJEU that they are only to be protected if their observance is required. As such, if the observance of rights and obligations under a treaty falling within the scope of Article 351 TFEU would be 'discretionary' in the sense that Member States would not be required to give effect to (part of) a provision of a pre-accession Extra-EU Treaty, but would be allowed to give effect to such (a part of) a provision. In other words, Article 351 TFEU does not apply to 'discretionary' provisions in Extra-EU Treaties.[753]

The rationale underlying this substantive scope of the rights and obligations that shall not be affected by the EU Treaties is that, according to the CJEU, the Member States have 'by assuming a new obligation which is incompatible with the rights held under a prior treaty a state ipso facto gives up the exercise of these rights to the extent necessary for the performance of its new obligations'.[754] Accession to the EU by a Member State must thus be understood as entailing that such Member State is presumed, in accordance with the principle of international law as set out in, *inter alia*, Article 30(4)(b) VCLT 1969, to have given up any rights under pre-existing Extra-EU Treaties.[755] While such presumption can be regarded as following from the CJEU's interpretation of Article 351 TFEU, it would seem that basing such presumption on the principles of international law would not seem entirely justified. This is because Article 30(4)(b) VCLT 1969 merely confirms that between the Member States that are parties to the EU Treaties (following accession), the EU Treaties govern their mutual rights and obligations while also confirming that between the Member State and the third state that are parties to an Extra-EU Treaty, their mutual rights and obligations are governed by such Extra-EU Treaty. The consequence is that the third state concerned would continue to be under an obligation, in accordance with the principle of *pacta sunt servanda*, to give effect to the rights of, and obligations towards, Member States under a pre-accession Extra-EU Treaty. Hence, it does not follow from Article 30(4)(b) VCLT 1969 that the Member States can be presumed to have given up their rights under

entailed that 'the terms "rights and obligations" in article 234 [now: Article 351] refer, as regards the "rights", to the rights of third countries and, as regards the "obligations", to the obligations of Member States'.

753. Case C-324/93 (*Evans Medical Care*), para. 32 ('when an international agreement allows, but does not require, a Member State to adopt a measure which appears to be contrary to Community law, the Member States must refrain from adopting such a measure'). This position has subsequently been confirmed in Case C-124/95 (*Centro-Com*), para. 60, Case C-277/10 (*Luksan*), para. 62, and Case C-466/12 (*Svensson and Others*), para. 39 (regarding a directive). This position of the CJEU is also recognised by J. Klabbers, 2008, p. 149, J.P. Terhechte, European Yearbook for International Economic Law 2010, p. 6, R. Geiger in: European Union Treaties (Geiger, Khan & Kotzur eds), 2015, p. 1048, para. 5, and M. Kellerbauer & M. Klamert in: The EU Treaties and the Charter of Fundamental Rights: A Commentary (Kellerbauer, Klamert & Tomkin eds), 2021, p. 2067, para. 6.

754. CJEU, 27 February 1962, Case 10/61 (*Commission v. Italy*), p. 10.

755. In CJEU, 27 February 1962, Case 10/61 (*Commission v. Italy*), p. 10 the CJEU seems to confirm the applicant's position that such presumption is valid 'by virtue of the principles of international law'. In that respect it can be noted that the CJEU has subsequently referred to Article 351 TFEU as being aimed at making 'clear, in accordance with the principles of international law, as set out in, *inter alia*, Article 30(4)(b) [VCLT] 1969, that the application of [the EU Treaties] does not affect the duty of the Member State concerned to respect the rights of non-member countries under a prior agreement and to perform its obligations thereunder'.

pre-accession Extra-EU Treaty.[756] It would rather seem that Article 351 TFEU is aimed at allowing Member States to respect the principle of *pacta tertiis*, as laid down in Article 34 VCLT 1969, vis-à-vis third states with respect to their pre-accession Extra-EU Treaties (while excluding the application of such principle with respect to their post-accession Extra-EU Treaties).

Notwithstanding these comments regarding the basis upon which Member States must be presumed to have given up their rights under pre-accession Extra-EU Treaties, the fact is that it follows from Article 351 TFEU, as interpreted by the CJEU, that Member States are precluded from relying on such rights. This in turn entails that such rights under pre-accession Extra-EU Treaties fall outside the substantive scope of Article 351 TFEU and, as such, fall within the scope of the primacy of EU law. National courts would thus be required to, in principle, set aside any rights of Member States under pre-accession Extra-EU Treaties if such rights are contrary to the result to be achieved under the Directives. Whether this is the case would seem to be up to such national courts to determine.[757]

#### *7.2.2.2.2 The 'Protected' Rights and Obligations in Tax Treaties*

It follows from the preceding section that the protection of Article 351 TFEU applies only to rights of, and obligations towards, third states under pre-accession Extra-EU Treaties. The present section seeks to determine whether tax treaties can be regarded as containing such rights and obligations. In that respect, legal scholars seem to agree that Article 351 TFEU can be applicable to pre-accession concluded between Member States with third states, i.e., Article 351 TFEU Treaties,[758] which implies that such tax treaties should contain rights and obligations falling within the substantive scope of Article 351 TFEU.

---

756. *See*, to this effect, K. von Papp, Legal Issues of Economic Integration 2015/4, p. 15.

757. *See*, to this effect, Case C-124/95 (*Centro-Com*), para. 58 ('in proceedings for a preliminary ruling, it is not for this Court but for the national court to determine which obligations are imposed by an earlier international agreement on the Member State concerned and to ascertain their ambit so as to be able to determine the extent they thwart application of the provisions of [EU] law'), as well as Case C-324/93 (*Evans Medical Care*), para. 28 and Case C-158/91 (*Levy*), para. 21.

Within the context of an infringement proceeding, this would seem to be different considering that the existence of such rights and obligations may be decisive for the purposes of determining whether a Member State has failed to fulfil its EU law obligations. As such, the CJEU does seem to consider itself competent to determine whether rights of, and obligations towards, third states are laid down in Article 351 TFEU Treaties within the context of an infringement proceeding. Support for such view can be derived from Case C-84/98 (*Commission v. Portugal*), paras 54-55 where the CJEU essentially determined, by means of an interpretation of the relevant pre-accession Extra-EU Treaty, whether Portugal would have violated the rights and obligations of Yugoslavia if it had denounced such treaty. Reference can also be made to Case C-203/03 (*Commission v. Austria*), paras 62-64 where the CJEU concluded that, based on an interpretation of the relevant pre-accession Extra-EU Treaty, Austria could not have denounced such treaty and that it had, for that reason, not acted contrary to Article 351 TFEU.

758. *See*, *e.g.*, A.C.G.A.C. de Graaf, 2004, pp. 259-260, C.H.J.I. Panayi, EC Tax Review 2007/3, pp. 121-122, and M. Helminen, 2021, para. 1.5.3.2.

This seems to be unsurprising given that the provisions of tax treaties quite clearly stipulate what rights and obligations are entered into, especially within the context of the distributive provisions. With respect to such rights and obligations, reference can be made to the following (translated) example of de Graaf (2004):

> Assume Member State X and third state Z have agreed in a tax treaty prior to 1 January 1958 that the source state may tax interest paid on savings up to a maximum of 10%. Subsequently, the EU adopts a regulation or directive relating to 'interest on savings'. According to this rule of EU law Member States would be required to levy a withholding tax of at least 20% over interest paid to entities resident in third states of which the shares are held by a resident of other Member States.[759]

With respect to this example, De Graaf notes that the limitation of source taxation on interest payments laid down in the pre-accession Extra-EU Treaty shall not be affected by the regulation or directive in question under Article 351 TFEU. This makes sense given that Member State X has entered into an obligation vis-à-vis third state Z pursuant to which it shall only tax interest payments up to 10%. Such an obligation towards Member States Z would be affected by the regulation or directive if Member State X would give effect to its obligation under such regulation or directive and tax such payments at a rate of at least 20%. Similarly, Member States may enter into an obligation to exempt profits of a permanent establishment situated in a third state (*see* Article 23 OECD Model (2017)). If they would refuse to exempt such profits due to obligations under, for example, ATAD1 or ATAD2, the obligations vis-à-vis third states would also seem to be affected because investments in such third state would become less attractive than initially agreed to with the Member State under the relevant pre-accession Extra-EU Treaty. It thus follows that Extra-EU Tax Treaties are likely to include provisions that give rise to rights of, and obligations towards, third states. As such, limitations imposed by, for example, the distributive provisions can be regarded as falling within the substantive scope of Article 351 TFEU as reflecting rights of, or obligations towards, third states.

#### *7.2.2.2.3 Reliance on the 'Protected' Rights and Obligations in Tax Treaties*

Given that tax treaties are likely to contain rights of and obligations towards, third states that fall within the scope of Article 351 TFEU, the question that subsequently arises is whether taxpayers can rely on such protected rights and obligations before a Member State court in order to escape the primacy of Directives and, as such, to avoid the setting aside of the relevant (the provision(s) of) the pre-accession Extra-EU Treaty.

759. A.C.G.A.C. de Graaf, 2004, pp. 259-260. The example has been translated by the present author. In Dutch the example reads as follows: 'Stel lidstaat X en derde staat Z zijn in een vóór 1 januari 1958 gesloten belastingverdrag onderling overeengekomen dat de bronstaat maximaal 10% belasting over rente uitgekeerd op spaartegoeden mag heffen. Vervolgens stelt de Gemeenschap een verordening dan wel richtlijn op "rente op spaartegoeden" vast. Volgens deze gemeenschapsregeling moeten de lidstaten een bronbelasting van ten minste 20% heffen over rente betaald aan een in een derde staat gevestigde vennootschap waarvan alle aandelen worden gehouden door een inwoner van de andere lidstaten.'

In that respect, the starting point would be that Article 351 TFEU does not, in and of itself, directly confer rights on taxpayers.[760] Nevertheless, taxpayers can indirectly rely on this provision by arguing that the primacy of Directives is not allowed to affect the rights of, and obligations towards, third states entered into under a pre-accession Extra-EU Treaty. If respecting such rights and obligations would then be beneficial for the taxpayer in a dispute before a national court, the consequence would be that such a taxpayer can de facto rely on Article 351 TFEU.[761] Applied to the example of De Graaf in the previous section, a taxpayer could indirectly rely on Article 351 TFEU by arguing that any withholding taxes imposed on interest payments in excess of the 10% would be contrary to the rights of, or obligations towards, third state Z. In such a situation, a Member State court should then conclude that, based on Article 351 TFEU, the primacy of the regulation or directive would not be applicable with respect to the pre-accession treaty with third state Z in order to avoid the rights of, and obligations towards, third state Z would be affected by the regulation or directive. In the absence of such primacy, such regulation or directive would then not be able to set aside the 10% withholding tax limit laid down in such tax treaty as a matter of EU law. As such, taxpayers would seem to be able to rely on Article 351 TFEU by referring to rights of, or obligations towards, third states vis-à-vis third states being violated if a pre-accession Extra-EU Treaty would be set aside due to the primacy of a Directive.

#### *7.2.2.3 Conclusions Regarding the Scope of Article 351 TFEU*

Based on the preceding sections, it is concluded that the temporal scope of Article 351 TFEU is limited to Extra-EU Treaties that have been concluded prior to the accession of a Member State to the EU while not having been amended, post-accession, following a renegotiation of such a treaty in full. In addition, it has been concluded that an application of Article 351 TFEU by analogy to post-accession, pre-Directive Extra-EU Treaties should be rejected in light of the judgment of the CJEU in *Generalstaatsanwaltschaft München* (Case C-435/22 PPU). As such, only (413) pre-accession Extra-EU Treaties (out of 1,507 Extra-EU Treaties in total) fall within the temporal scope of Article 351 TFEU.

With respect to the substantive scope of Article 351 TFEU, it is concluded that only rights of, and obligations towards, third states arising under Article 351 TFEU Treaties are protected. In general, it has furthermore been concluded that pre-accession Extra-EU Treaties generally contain rights of, and obligations towards, third states that fall within such substantive scope by means of, in any event, those provisions that limit the right to tax of the contracting states. In addition, it has been concluded that taxpayers can, effectively, rely on those rights of, and obligations towards, third states falling within the substantive scope of Article 351 TFEU in order to avoid such a pre-accession Extra-EU Treaty from being set aside by means of the primacy of (an incompatibility with) a Directive. Whereas there thus seem to be rights of, and

760. Case 812/79 (*Burgoa*), para. 10.
761. *See* K. von Papp, Legal Issues of Economic Integration 2015/4, p. 8.

obligations towards, third states that are not to be affected by the primacy of the Directives, it should be borne in mind that the rights of, and obligations towards, Member States under Article 351 TFEU Treaties, as well as any rights and obligations under non-Article 351 TFEU Treaties, must be regarded as falling outside the scope of such protection against the primacy of the Directives.

### 7.2.3 The Protection of Article 351 TFEU and the Duty to Eliminate Incompatibilities

#### *7.2.3.1 The Duty to Eliminate Incompatibilities*

While it may be clear that Article 351 TFEU, based on its first paragraph, is aimed at protecting rights of, and obligations towards, third states under pre-accession Extra-EU Treaties in the event that such rights and obligations would be incompatible with, for present purposes, a Directive, it follows from the second paragraph of Article 351 TFEU that such protection should only apply on a temporary basis.[762] This paragraph provides that the Member States are obliged to take all appropriate steps to eliminate any incompatibility between a 351 TFEU Treaty and, for present purposes, a Directive.

Such appropriate steps include, in any event, (attempting to) interpret(ing) a 351 TFEU Treaty in a way that is consistent with the result of the (incompatible) Directive,[763] commencing negotiations with a goal of eliminating the incompatibility,[764] and termination of the 351 TFEU Treaty.[765] In principle, or as a starting point, Member States are free to determine the steps they consider appropriate to eliminate an incompatibility arising between a 351 TFEU Treaty and a Directive.[766] However, the duty to take all appropriate steps is one of result: it is a duty to eliminate the incompatibility, not merely attempt to eliminate an incompatibility.[767]

Although the duty is to achieve a result, the CJEU has consistently held that Member States are not required under Article 351, second paragraph, TFEU to violate the rights of and obligations towards, the third states under the incompatible pre-accession Extra-EU Treaty.[768] This entails, *inter alia*, that an obligation to denounce

762. *See* Opinion of Advocate General Ruiz-Jarabo Colomer in: Case C-284/05 (*Commission v. Finland*), para. 194.
763. *See*, to that effect, Chapter 4.
764. *See* M. Kellerbauer & M. Klamert in: The EU Treaties and the Charter of Fundamental Rights: A Commentary (Kellerbauer, Klamert & Tomkin eds), 2021, p. 2069, para. 13.
765. M. Kellerbauer & M. Klamert in: The EU Treaties and the Charter of Fundamental Rights: A Commentary (Kellerbauer, Klamert & Tomkin eds), 2021, p. 2069, para. 13. Regarding denunciation as an appropriate step, *see* Case C-62/98 (*Commission v. Portugal*), para. 49, Case C-216/01 (*Budějovický Budvar*), para. 170, Case C-203/03 (*Commission v. Austria*), para. 54, and Case C-264/09 (*Commission v. Slovak Republic*), para. 44.
766. Case C-264/09 (*Commission v. Slovak Republic*), para. 44.
767. *See* Opinion of Advocate General Maduro in: Joined Cases C-205/06 (*Commission v. Austria*) & C-249/06 (*Commission v. Sweden*), para. 68.
768. *See* Case C-62/98 (*Commission v. Portugal*), para. 45 ('the Portuguese Republic must in all cases respect the rights which the Republic of Angola derives from the contested agreement').

such a treaty only arises if this is permitted under the terms of the treaty,[769] and that the agreed term for denunciation must be respected.[770]

The interesting question for present purposes is, however, as of which moment a duty to denounce a 351 TFEU Treaty may arise. In that respect, it has been submitted that a duty to denounce should only arise after a 'reasonable period of time' has been afforded to the Member State concerned to eliminate an incompatibility between a pre-accession Extra-EU Treaty and a source of EU law by other means.[771] It is, however, unclear whether the CJEU agrees with this submission. It has, in any event, not provided guidelines for establishing when a duty to negotiate turns into a duty to terminate. This may, however, be explained by the circumstance that in each of the cases wherein it ruled on a duty to terminate, a substantial amount of time had already passed between the receipt by the Member State of a first notification of a (potential) incompatibility from the European Commission and a judgment of the CJEU. In the cases *Commission v. Portugal* (Case C-62/98), *Commission v. Austria* (Case C-203/03) and *Commission v. Slovakia* (Case C-264/09), for example, five to seven years had expired between the first letter of the European Commission to the Member State concerned and the date of the judgment of the CJEU.[772] As such, at the time the case had to be assessed by the CJEU, Member States would seem likely to have had some time to commence negotiations with a goal of eliminating an incompatibility. As such,

769. *See* Case C-264/09 (*Commission v. Slovak Republic*), para. 46 ('the contract at issue in the present case does not contain any clause providing for a possibility of denunciation').

770. *See* Case C-203/03 (*Commission v. Austria*), paras 62-64. In this case, an incompatibility had arisen between a directive and a pre-accession Extra-EU Treaty concluded by Austria as of its accession in 1995. Austria was, however, only informed of such (a potential for an) incompatibility by the European Commission on 29 September 1998 (para. 55) whereas it could not denounce the relevant pre-accession Extra-EU Treaty until 30 May 2007 (para. 55). The Court found that, given that it was not sufficiently clearly established on 30 May 1997 (the first opportunity to denounce the Extra-EU Treaty after accession) that it was incompatible with EU law (which seems based on the fact that Austria was notified of such incompatibility after 30 May 1997), Austria had not violated its obligation under Article 351(2) TFEU by not denouncing the pre-accession Extra-EU Treaty on 30 May 1997. Moreover, considering that at the time of the judgment of the CJEU on 1 February 2005 the next opportunity to denounce such treaty had not yet taken place, it is unsurprising that the Court ruled that Austria had not failed to take all appropriate steps under Article 351(2) TFEU by not denouncing its pre-accession Extra-EU Treaty. *See also* Case C-62/98 (*Commission v. Portugal*), para. 46 wherein the Court rules that 'the contested agreement contains a clause (Article XV) which expressly enables the contracting parties to denounce it, so that denunciation by the Portuguese Republic would not encroach upon the rights which the Republic of Angola derives from that agreement'.

771. *See* Opinion of Advocate General Mischo in: Joined Cases C-62/98 & C-84/98 (*Commission v. Portugal*), para. 69, C.N.K. Franklin, European Foreign Affairs Review 2005/10, p. 100, and Opinion of Advocate General Kokott in: Case C-74/16 (*Congregacioìn de Escuelas Pìas Provincia Betania*), para. 100.

772. With respect to Case C-62/98 (*Commission v. Portugal*), it follows from the judgment of the CJEU that the first letter indicating that such treaties would have to be adjusted was sent on 3 December 1992 (paras 10 and 11), whereas the judgment issued on 4 July 2000 (more than seven years); in *Commission v. Austria* (Case C-203/03), the first letter was sent on 29 September 1998 (para. 55) and the judgment was issued on 1 February 2005 (more than six years); in *Commission v. Slovakia* (Case C-264/09), the Commission sent a letter of formal notice on 10 April 2006 (*see* the Opinion of Advocate General Jääskinen in: Case C-264/09 (*Commission v. Slovakia*), para. 27) while the judgment of the CJEU was delivered on 15 September 2011 (more than five years).

Member States would seem to have had, in practice, a period of time for such negotiations with a view to eliminating the relevant incompatibility.

#### *7.2.3.2 The Effect of Compliance with the Duty to Eliminate Incompatibilities*

Taking into account the duty to eliminate incompatibilities between a pre-accession Extra-EU Treaty and a Directive, as well as the conclusion of the CJEU that a Member State can fail to comply with such duty,[773] the question may arise whether the protection granted by the first paragraph of Article 351 TFEU would be dependent on compliance with such duty. The answer to such question must be that this is not the case in light of the judgments of the CJEU in *Budějovický Budvar* (Case C-216/01) and *Ferrari* (Joined Cases C-720/18 & C-721/18).

In both judgments, the CJEU made it explicitly clear that the first paragraph of Article 351 TFEU permits a Member State to continue to apply a pre-accession Extra-EU Treaty to the extent that it concerns rights of, and obligations towards, third states, 'pending the success of one of the methods referred to in [the second paragraph of Article 351 TFEU]',[774] or 'until such time as one of the steps referred to in the second paragraph of Article 351 TFEU makes it possible to eliminate any incompatibilities between the TFEU and that convention'.[775] As such, the protection granted by the first paragraph of Article 351 TFEU to treaties falling within its scope is not affected by a Member State's compliance with the duty to eliminate incompatibilities on the basis of its second paragraph.

This conclusion would also seem consistent with the judgment of the CJEU in *Commission v. Portugal* (Case C-62/98) where it ruled that the rights that the third state concerned derived from the incompatible pre-accession Extra-EU Treaty had to be respected by Portugal 'in all cases'.[776] If the protection of Article 351, first paragraph, TFEU would be dependent on a Member State's with its obligations under Article 351, second paragraph, TFEU, this would entail that the rights of third states would be respected as long as such Member State has taken all appropriate steps. Such an interpretation would be at odds with the judgment of the CJEU that these rights are to be respected 'in all cases'.[777] It can thus be concluded that it follows from case law of the CJEU that the duty to eliminate incompatibilities has no effect on the protection granted by Article 351, first paragraph, TFEU to pre-accession Extra-EU Treaties.[778]

---

773. *See*, to that effect, Case C-62/98 (*Commission v. Portugal*).
774. Case C-216/01 (*Budějovický Budvar*), para. 173.
775. Joined Cases C-720/18 & C-721/18 (*Ferrari*), para. 72.
776. *See* Case C-62/98 (*Commission v. Portugal*), para. 45.
777. Further support for concluding that compliance with the duty under the second paragraph of Article 351 TFEU would have no effect on the protection granted by its first paragraph can be derived from the Opinion of Advocate General Tesauro in: Case C-158/91 (*Levy*) wherein he rejects such a link because this 'scarcely conforms to the letter and, still less, to the spirit of Article [351 TFEU] or, more generally, to the principles of international law. On consideration, this would lead to penalisation not only and not so much of the Member State concerned, but precisely of those non-member countries whose rights Article [351] is intended to protect'.
778. It is noted that the finding of the CJEU, in the context of an infringement proceeding, that a Member State would have violated its obligations under Article 351(2) TFEU would not affect

#### *7.2.3.3 Conclusion Regarding the Scope of the Primacy of the Directives*

Based on sections 7.2.1 and 7.2.2, the following conclusions apply with respect to the applicability of the primacy of Directives regarding tax treaties:

(a) All Intra-EU Treaties are subject to the primacy of the Directives.

(b) Extra-EU Treaties are subject to the primacy of the Directives unless Article 351 TFEU applies. As such:

   (i) the primacy of the Directives does not apply to Extra-EU Treaties that (i) have been concluded before the accession of the relevant Member State (temporal scope) and (ii) only to the extent that such treaties contain rights of or obligations towards, third states (which is likely to be the case with respect to, in particular, distributive provisions of tax treaties) (substantive scope).

   By contrast, the primacy of the Directives does apply with respect to (i) post-accession Extra-EU Treaties, as well as (ii) pre-accession Extra-EU Treaties to the extent it concerns the rights of or obligations towards, the Member States.

   With respect to the temporal scope of Article 351 TFEU, it has furthermore been concluded that post-accession, pre-Directive Extra-EU Treaties do not fall within the scope of Article 351 TFEU because the CJEU has rejected an analogous application of such provision in *Generalstaatsanwaltschaft München* (Case C-435/22 PPU).

   (ii) the primacy of the Directives applies with respect to those pre-accession Extra-EU Treaties that have been amended after accession of the relevant Member State to the EU if such amendment would be the result of a renegotiation in full (irrespective of the scope of the actual amendments). If amended without full renegotiation, only the amended provisions would be subject to the primacy of the Directives; the unamended provisions continue to fall within the scope of Article 351 TFEU.

---

the applicability of the pre-accession Extra-EU Treaty concerned. The purpose of infringement proceedings is to make EU Member States 'comply with and fulfil their obligations under the [EU] Treaties' (*see* C.E. Koops, 2014, p. 99). As such, an infringement proceeding on the basis of a failure to comply with Article 351(2) TFEU seeks to, ultimately, force an EU Member State to take all appropriate steps, including denunciation, if required, to eliminate an incompatibility between a pre-accession Extra-EU Treaty and a source of EU law. This also follows from Article 260 TFEU which provides that '[i]f the [CJEU] finds that a Member State has failed to fulfil an obligation of the treaties', e.g., failure to have taken all appropriate steps under Article 351(2) TFEU, 'the State shall be required to take the necessary means to comply with the judgment of the Court', e.g., ensure that the appropriate steps are taken by, for example, denouncing the relevant pre-accession Extra-EU Treaty. The judgment of the Court will, however, only oblige the EU Member State to take action; it will not stipulate, for example, that the pre-accession Extra-EU Treaty can no longer be applied. This would be contrary to the objective of an infringement proceeding and would also result in a violation of the rights of the third state concerned, whose rights must at all times be respected (*see*, to that effect, Case C-62/98 (*Commission v. Portugal*), para. 45).

The rationale for such a negotiation-based approach towards amendments is that the Member States would have been under a duty to amend incompatible provisions of a pre-accession Extra-EU Treaty during such negotiations. By refraining from that, they must be presumed to have confirmed the application of such incompatible provisions, which confirmation is contrary to their duty under the second paragraph of Article 351 TFEU to eliminate incompatibilities when amending a pre-accession Extra-EU Treaty.

## 7.3 THE ENFORCEABILITY OF THE PRIMACY OF THE DIRECTIVES

### 7.3.1 General

Based on the findings of the previous section, it can be determined whether a Directive enjoys primacy with respect to a tax treaty concluded by a Member State. If a Directive would enjoy primacy this does not, however, entail that such a Directive will also affect the application of such a tax treaty under the laws of the EU, by setting it aside, in the event of a conflict. This would only be the case if such primacy of a Directive would be enforceable. As such, the enforceability of the primacy of the Directives is relevant for determining the extent to which the Directives may affect the application of tax treaties under the laws of the EU. Taking this into account, the present section aims to answer to what extent the primacy of the Directives is enforceable with respect to tax treaties.

The answer to this question depends on whether a Directive provision would have direct effect (section 7.3.2). This follows from, *inter alia*, *Poplawski* (Case C-573/17) where the CJEU explicitly held that 'a provision of EU law which does not have direct effect may not be relied on ... in a dispute coming under EU law in order to disapply a provision of national law that conflicts with it'.[779] However, the mere finding that a provision of a Directive would have direct effect does not, in and of itself, entail that the primacy of such provision is enforceable before a national court. The enforceability of the primacy of a directly effective (provision of a) Directive is therefore discussed separately in sections 7.3.3 and 7.3.4. If a Directive would either not have direct effect or its direct effect would not be enforceable, the Directive (provision) would be 'nominally supreme but in practice left outside the gates of the national legal order'[780] and not be enforceable. If not enforceable, such primacy cannot result in a Directive affecting the application of a tax treaty (by setting aside such a treaty) in the event of conflict under the laws of the EU.[781]

779. Case C-573/17 (*Poplawski*), para. 62.
780. *See* M. Bobek in: European Union Law (Barnard & Peers eds), 2017, p. 163.
781. It is acknowledged, in this respect, that the non-enforceability of the primacy of a provision of a Directive under the laws of the EU does not entail that a court of a Member State is prohibited from setting aside – or disapplying – a provision of a tax treaty on the basis the laws of such Member State with a view to ensuring the relevant Member State achieves the result of a Directive. *See*, to this effect, Case C-261/20 (*Thelen Technopark Berlin*), paras 33 and 48.

### 7.3.2 The Requirement of Direct Effect

As noted in the previous section, the obligation to set aside tax treaty provisions that are incompatible with a provision of a Directive only arises if such a provision has direct effect.[782] Based on case law of the CJEU, this would be the case if such a provision would be (i) clear,[783] (ii) unconditional, and (iii) 'not contingent on any discretionary implementing measures'.[784] These conditions essentially limit the primacy of the Directives to those provisions that, by their very nature, can be applied by a Member State court without any further action on the side of the Member State being required.[785] It thus follows that it would have to be established, in the event of a conflict between a (provision of a) Directive and a tax treaty that is subject to the primacy of such a Directive (provision), whether the relevant Directive (provision) is 'sufficiently operational in itself to be applied by a court'.[786] If this were the case, Member State courts would, in principle, be required to set aside – and hence affect the applicability of – an incompatible (provision of a) tax treaty that is subject to the primacy of a Directive (subject to the limitations set out in the next two sections below). If, however, a provision of a Directive would not have direct effect, national courts would be under no such duty (entailing that the applicability of tax treaties cannot be affected by such non-directly effective, yet 'nominally supreme', Directives).[787]

782. M. Bobek in: European Union Law (Barnard & Peers eds), 2017, p. 163. *See*, in general, S. Prechal, 2009, pp. 231-234.

783. According to T.C. Hartley, 2010, p. 210, a provision would not be sufficiently precise if it 'merely lays down a general objective or policy to be pursued, without specifying the appropriate means to attain it'. In cases, 'it can hardly be regarded as a legal rule suitable for application by a court of law. In such cases, further legislation is necessary before it can become operative'.

784. *See* Case 44/84 (*Hurd*), para. 47. *See also* Case 8/81 (*Becker*), para. 25 and Case C-282/10 (*Dominguez*), para. 33. Reference may also be made to T.C. Hartley, 2010, p. 210 and K. Lenaerts & P. van Nuffel, 2011, p. 810, para. 21-056. This would, for example, entail, within the context of directives, that the deadline for implementation must have passed (*see* Case 148/78 (*Ratti*), para. 46; reference may also be made to S. Switzer, 2009, pp. 65-65. For an example of a provision, within the area of indirect taxation, of a provision that required further implementation and, for that reason, was denied direct effect is Article 13A(1)(n) of Directive 77/388/EEC, which refers to 'certain cultural services' (*see*, to that effect, Case C-592/15 (*British Film Institute v. HMRC*), paras 22-24).

785. *See* T.C. Hartley, 2010, p. 210.

786. B. de Witte in: The Evolution of EU Law (Craig & De Búrca eds), 2011, p. 331.

787. It is acknowledged within the context of the enforceability of the primacy of Directives that the question as to whether a Member State may be held liable to pay compensation for non-transposition of a Directive that was intended to confer rights upon individuals may arise (*see*, in this respect, Joined Cases C-6/90 & C-9/90 (*Francovich*)). The conditions for such state liability are that (i) the result to be achieved under a directive entails the grant of rights to individuals, (ii) while the content of those rights is identifiable on the basis of the provisions of such a directive, and (iii) a causal link exists between the failure of the Member State's obligation to implement a directive and the loss and damage suffered (*see*, to this effect, Joined Cases C-178/94, C-179/94, C-188/94, C-189/94 & C-190/94 (*Dillenkofer*), para. 29). Whereas the liability arising from the so-called Francovich doctrine may (theoretically) arise in connection with a Member State's failure to transpose a Directive due to the applicability of a(n incompatible) tax treaty, it is noted that the finding of such liability cannot affect the applicability of such tax treaty. It can merely result in a Member State being required to pay

### 7.3.3 The Enforceability of (Detrimental) Directly Effective Provisions of a Directive

If an incompatibility arises between a directly effective provision of a Directive and a tax treaty with respect to which such Directive enjoys primacy, Member State courts would, in principle, be required to set aside such incompatible tax treaty. This obligation to set aside a tax treaty is, however, subject to the prohibition of reverse vertical direct effect pursuant to which the setting aside of a tax treaty by relying on the primacy of a Directive is prohibited if this would result in the imposition of an obligation on a taxpayer, such as a higher tax burden.[788]

The rationale for this limitation is that the need to rely on a directly effective provision of a Directive should only arise because of a Member State's failure to implement such Directive. Such a failure may arise as a consequence of the laws of a Member State providing that tax treaties set aside any rules of national laws, including those aimed at implementing a Directive,[789] or because a Member State would not have amended its national laws in a way that would be adequate to achieve the result of a Directive, irrespective of whether a tax treaty could set aside such national laws. According to the CJEU, a failure on the side of the Member State to adequately implement a Directive is not allowed to be relied upon to the detriment of the citizens of a Member State.[790]

It thus follows that Member State courts cannot set aside tax treaty provisions that would be incompatible with directly effective provisions of a Directive if that would be detrimental to a taxpayer. The consequence of this limitation to the enforceability of the primacy of the Directives is that the application of tax treaties may only be affected by the primacy of a Directive, under the laws of the EU, to the extent that this would, essentially, be beneficial for a taxpayer.

compensation. Taking this result of the so-called Francovich doctrine into account, in the sense that it cannot affect the applicability – or application – of tax treaties, it is not further discussed in this thesis.

788. S. Prechal, 2009, p. 55. *See also* Case 8/81 (*Becker*), para. 24, Case 80/86 (*Kolpinghuis*), para. 8, Joined Cases C-6/90 & C-9/90 (*Francovich*), para. 11, Case C-321/05 (*Kofoed*), para. 42, and Joined Cases C-115/16, C-118/16, C-119/16 & C-299/16 (*N Luxembourg 1*), para. 114.

789. This would, for example, be the case in the Netherlands considering that the Dutch State Secretary of Finance has confirmed that Article 94 Dutch Constitution entails that national laws, even those aimed at implementing Directives, must be set aside to the extent incompatible with tax treaties concluded by the Netherlands (*see* Parliamentary Proceedings II 2020-2021, 25 087, no. 260, p. 28).

790. Case 152/84 (*Marshall*), para. 47 ('a Member State which has not adopted the implementing measures required by the directive within the prescribed period may not plead, as against individuals, its own failure to perform the obligations which the directive entails'.). *See also* S. Prechal, 2009, p. 219, R. Schütze, 2021, para. 90, and A. Dashwood, M. Dougan, B. Rodger, E. Spaventa & D. Wyatt, 2011, p. 260. It can thus be concluded that the direct effect of the Directives resembles a 'one way street' in the sense that only individuals (or entities) may rely on such direct effect vis-à-vis a Member State (*see* G.W. Kofler in: Principles of Law: Function, Status and Impact in EU Tax Law (Brokelind, ed.), 2014, para. 12.2.3).

This is especially relevant for those Directives that are aimed at increasing the tax burden of taxpayers, such as ATAD1 and ATAD2.[791] Reliance on directly effective provisions of such (tax burden increasing) Directives is, in light of their purpose, likely to be detrimental to a taxpayer entailing that, based on the prohibition of reverse vertical direct effect, the primacy of such provisions is not enforceable if relied upon by a (tax authority of a) Member State.[792] As such, although being potentially supreme vis-à-vis tax treaties concluded by the Member States, such primacy would not be enforceable in practice before Member State courts.[793]

### 7.3.4 The Enforceability of (Beneficial) Directly Effective Provisions of a Directive

Based on the previous section, the primacy of (for a taxpayer) detrimental directly effective provisions of a Directive cannot be relied upon by a (tax authority of a) Member State to set aside tax treaties concluded by such Member State. Directives may, however, also provide for directly effective provisions that are beneficial for a taxpayer. With respect to such beneficial provisions, the prohibition of reverse vertical direct effect does not apply. As such, taxpayers would be able to rely on the primacy of such (beneficial) provisions of a Directive with a view to setting aside incompatible provisions of tax treaties. An example of a (beneficial) directly effective Directive

791. *See*, in this respect, also the Pillar 2 proposal (COM(2021) 823 final) and the ATAD3 Proposal (COM(2021) 565 final).

792. *See*, regarding the applicability of the prohibition of reverse direct effect with respect to directives aimed at tackling tax avoidance, Case C-251/16 (*Cussens*), para. 49 where the Court held that 'in the event that the referring court were to find that the leases preceding the sales of the properties at issue in the main proceedings constituted an abusive practice, any liability of those sales would have to be based on the relevant provisions of national legislation providing for such liability. [The Sixth Directive 77/388/EEC] cannot of itself impose obligations on an individual and cannot therefore be relied on as such against a person before a national court'. With respect to the objective of Directive 77/388/EEC, it can be noted that the CJEU has held that this directive recognises and encourages the objective of preventing tax avoidance (*see* Joined Cases C-131/13, C-163/13 & C-164/13 (*Schoenimport 'Italmoda' Mariano Previti*), para. 42). As such, it follows that the CJEU in *Cussens* upheld the prohibition of reverse vertical direct effect with respect to a directive that has been aimed at, *inter alia*, combating tax avoidance.

793. *See* for a similar conclusion F.A. Engelen, J. Vleggeert & T.M. Vergouwen, WFR 2019/257, p. 1558. It is noted, in this respect, that the prohibition of reverse vertical direct effect also seems applicable where a taxpayer would be found guilty of abusive or fraudulent conduct (*see*, to that effect, Case C-251/16 (*Cussens*), para. 49 and Joined Cases C-115/16, C-118/16, C-119/16 & C-299/16 (*N Luxembourg 1*), paras 114-120). The rationale for upholding the prohibition of reverse vertical direct effect in abusive or fraudulent situations is that the Member State itself can also be said to be 'guilty of abusive conduct' because such a Member State would, first, 'not have transposed a directive addressed to it (even though it could) and, second it would by relying on a possibility of preventing abuse that was contained in a directive which it had not transposed' (*see* Opinion of Advocate General Kokott in: Case C-117/17 (*Y Denmark Aps*), para. 99). At the same time, however, it should be noted that the duty of consistent interpretation can, by contrast, result in an interpretation of a provision of (inter)national law that would, in fact, be detrimental for an individual (*see* Joined Cases C-116/16 & C-117/16 (*T Danmark*), para. 87 and Case C-321/05 (*Kofoed*), para. 45, as well as section 4.5).

provision would be Article 5(1) of the Parent-Subsidiary Directive, which provides that intra-group cross-border profit distributions shall be exempt from withholding taxes. Given its direct effect, the primacy of the exemption from withholding taxes vis-à-vis tax treaties would be enforceable.[794] Given the enforceability of such primacy, the exemption from withholding taxes under the Parent-Subsidiary Directive could not be made subject to an Intra-EU Treaty.

Whereas the primacy of a beneficial directly effective provision of a Directive would be enforceable vis-à-vis a tax treaty, it should be acknowledged that the CJEU has held 'that EU law cannot be relied on for abusive or fraudulent ends' (hereinafter: the 'general EU anti-abuse principle').[795] As such, the primacy of a directly effective Directive provision such as Article 5(1) of the Parent-Subsidiary Directive would not be enforceable by a taxpayer if relied upon for abusive or fraudulent ends.[796] The general EU anti-abuse principle would, however, go further than merely precluding reliance on Article 5(1) of the Parent-Subsidiary Directive. The principle requires Member State authorities and courts to *refuse* the exemption from withholding tax on profits distributed in the event of abuse or fraud. The relevance of the obligation to refuse such an exemption can be illustrated as follows.

It has been concluded that the need to rely on the primacy of directly effective provisions of a Directive would only arise if a Member State does not achieve the result of a Directive (section 7.2.1). As such, if a Member State achieves such result by, for example, exempting profit distributions in accordance with Article 5(1) of the Parent-Subsidiary Directive under its domestic law, there would, in principle, be no need to rely on the direct effect of such Directive provision. Instead of relying on such a provision, a taxpayer would only rely on the domestic law provision whose application results in the exemption of the relevant profit distribution. If a taxpayer would rely on

794. *See*, to this effect, Case C-294/99 (*Athinaiki Zinthopiia*), para. 32 where the CJEU held that 'the rights conferred on economic operators by Article 5(1) of the [Parent-Subsidiary] Directive are unconditional and a Member State cannot make their observance subject to an agreement concluded with another Member State'.

795. Joined Cases C-115/16, C-118/16, C-119/16 & C-299/16 (*N Luxembourg 1*), para. 118 and Joined Cases C-116/16 & C-117/16 (*T Danmark*), para. 70. It is noted that an abusive or fraudulent situation would arise if granting EU law benefits would be inconsistent with the objective of the rules containing such benefits 'although the conditions for benefitting from that advantage are fulfilled only formally' (Joined Cases C-115/16, C-118/16, C-119/16 & C-299/16 (*N Luxembourg 1*), para. 102. Support for applying this general EU anti-abuse principle to Directives can be derived from Joined Cases C-115/16, C-118/16, C-119/16 & C-299/16 (*N Luxembourg 1*), para. 101 where the CJEU states that 'the principle that abusive practices are prohibited nonetheless constitutes a general principle of EU law which applies irrespective of whether the rights and advantages that are abused have their basis in the Treaties, in a regulation or in a directive').

There would be an abusive or fraudulent situation if, for example, it were established that transactions have taken place outside the context of 'normal commercial transactions', while being 'purely formal' and 'designed solely to obtain' the benefit of a Directive (*see*, to this effect, Joined Cases C-115/16, C-118/16, C-119/16 & C-299/16 *(N Luxembourg 1*), para. 99).

796. *See*, to this effect, Joined Cases C-116/16 & C-117/16 (*T Danmark*), para. 95 where the CJEU held that 'where there is a fraudulent or abusive practice, the national authorities and courts are to refuse a taxpayer the exemption from withholding tax on profits distributed by a subsidiary to its parent company, provided for in Article 5 of Directive 90/435, even if there are no domestic or agreement-based provisions providing for such a refusal'.

such domestic law provision for abusive or fraudulent ends, it would seem arguable that such taxpayer is relying on domestic law and not EU law for such ends. If such argument would be upheld, the taxpayer would be able to de facto rely on the benefits of Article 5(1) of the Parent-Subsidiary Directive for abusive or fraudulent ends.

This argument should, however, be rejected. The circumstance that the general EU anti-abuse principle requires national authorities and courts to *refuse* the benefits of a Directive in the event of abuse or fraud indicates that such a taxpayer cannot be allowed to rely on the benefits of the Parent-Subsidiary Directive. The obligation to *refuse* such benefits thus entails that such authorities and courts must ensure that the benefits are not provided to a taxpayer in fact. Applied to the example of Article 5(1) of the Parent-Subsidiary Directive, the general EU anti-abuse principle would require national authorities and courts to refuse a taxpayer the exemption from withholding taxes on profit distributions falling within the scope of such provision. Such refusal should be distinguished from the imposition of an obligation as discussed in section 7.3.3. This is due to the refusal of benefits of a Directive having to be regarded as the result of the application of 'the general principle of EU law that EU law cannot be relied on for abusive or fraudulent ends',[797] whereas the prohibition of reverse vertical effect seeks to ensure that directives are precluded 'from being able by themselves to create obligations for individuals and therefore from being capable of being relied upon per se by the Member State as against individuals'.[798] The difference thus seems to be that in the event of an abusive or fraudulent situation, it is not the Directive itself that results in the imposition of an obligation on a taxpayer, but the general EU anti-abuse principle.

Based on the above, it follows that national authorities and courts of a Member State can be under an obligation to deny, for example, an exemption of withholding taxes on profit distributions if granting such an exemption would result in a taxpayer claiming the benefits of Article 5(1) of the Parent-Subsidiary Directive for abusive or fraudulent ends. Given this obligation to deny an exemption, it would seem arguable that benefits of a treaty that would be similar to benefits of Article 5(1) of the Parent-Subsidiary Directive would also have to be denied.[799] The arguments for

797. Joined Cases C-116/16 & C-117/16 (*T Danmark*), para. 90. Directive 'although the conditions for benefitting from that advantage are fulfilled only formally'. This would, for example, be the case if it were established that transactions have taken place outside the context of 'normal commercial transactions', while being 'purely formal' and 'designed solely to obtain' the benefit of a Directive (*see*, to this effect, Joined Cases C-115/16, C-118/16, C-119/16 & C-299/16 (*N Luxembourg 1*), para. 99).

798. Joined Cases C-116/16 & C-117/16 (*T Danmark*), para. 86.

799. *See* O.C.R. Marres & I.M. de Groot, European Taxation 2021/8, para. 5.1 where they note that 'one may argue that tax treaty benefits must also be denied in abusive cases'. *See also* L.C. van Hulten & J.J.A.M. Korving, WFR 2019/129, para. 4.2 who write that it is arguable that application of reduced withholding tax rates in tax treaty situations can be contrary to the duty of Union loyalty in the event of a fraudulent or abusive situation, as well as O.C.R. Marres & I.M. de Groot, European Taxation 2021/8, para. 5.2 who note that 'granting equivalent benefits to abusers would result in the obligation under EU law to combat abuse being frustrated and would be contrary to the principle of sincere cooperation of EU law'. For a different view, *see* S.C.W. Douma, BNB 2020/9, para. 5 who writes that the so-called *Danish Cases* do not provide for a ground or the setting aside of tax treaties.

denying tax treaty benefits in the event of a fraudulent or abusive situation within the meaning of the general EU anti-abuse principle would be as follows. First, granting treaty benefits that are similar to the benefits of Directive in the event of such fraud or abuse 'would undermine the effectiveness of the general [EU anti-abuse] principle and hinder its coherent application'.[800] Second, granting such treaty benefits could be regarded as being incompatible with the principle of Union loyalty because Member States would then be allowed to 'circumvent the obligation to deny [EU] treaty benefits in abusive situations by way of a [tax treaty]'.[801] Bearing in mind these arguments, as well as the fact that the CJEU requires the refusal of the benefits of a Directive, this author agrees that it is arguable that tax treaties can provide for benefits that are also provided for by Directives. This would, for example, seem to be the case if an Intra-EU Treaty provides for an exemption of withholding taxes with respect to dividends that fall within the scope of Article 5(1) of the Parent-Subsidiary Directive.[802] Such an exemption would effectively provide for the same benefit as Article 5(1) of the Parent-Subsidiary Directive, i.e., an exemption from withholding taxes on cross-border intra-group dividends. Given that Intra-EU Treaty provides for the same benefit, it would seem that such benefit would also have to be refused by a Member State authority or court if such authority or court is required to refuse the benefit of Article 5(1) of the Parent-Subsidiary Directive under the general EU anti-abuse principle. Any other conclusion would effectively allow Member States to grant benefits of such Directive provision for abusive or fraudulent ends and, thereby, undermine the effectiveness and coherent application of the general EU anti-abuse principle.

Bearing in mind the previous paragraphs, it follows that the primacy of beneficial directly effective provisions of a Directive provision vis-à-vis a tax treaty is enforceable unless such provisions would be relied upon for abusive or fraudulent ends. Additionally, if it would be established that a benefit of a Directive would be granted for abusive or fraudulent ends, the non-enforceability of the directly effective Directive provision is accompanied by a duty for the Member State authorities and courts to ensure refusal of the benefits of such Directive provision. This refusal of a benefit of a Directive provision could then require such authorities and courts to set aside tax treaties concluded by the Member States providing for benefits that are similar to those benefits of the Directive that must be refused. As such, in abusive or fraudulent situations within the meaning of the general EU anti-abuse principle, the application of tax treaties can be affected to the extent that such tax treaties provide for benefits that must

800. *See* S. Baerentzen, A. Lejour & M. van 't Riet, World Tax Journal 2020/5, p. 271, as well as O.C.R. Marres & I.M. de Groot, European Taxation 2021/8, para. 5.2 who note it would result in 'the obligation under EU law to combat abuse being frustrated'.

801. *See* S. Baerentzen, A. Lejour & M. van 't Riet, World Tax Journal 2020/5, p. 271. *See also* I.M. de Groot, NLF 2019/0597 who considers it strongly arguable (*goed verdedigbaar*) that national authorities and courts would be required to set aside an exemption of withholding taxes in a tax treaty in abusive or fraudulent situations within the meaning of the general EU anti-abuse principle. *See also* O.C.R. Marres & I.M. de Groot, European Taxation 2021/8, para. 5.2 who write that granting similar treaty benefits in the event of fraud or abuse 'would be contrary to the principle of sincere cooperation of EU law'.

802. *See, e.g.*, Article 10(2) of the Intra-EU Treaty between the Netherlands and Sweden.

be refused pursuant to such principle. Such refusal would then be the result of the application of the general EU anti-abuse principle (and not the Directive itself).

### 7.3.5 Conclusion

It has been the purpose of this section 7.3 to determine the enforceability of the primacy of the Directives with respect to tax treaties. Based on sections 7.3.1 through 7.3.4, it is concluded that:

(a) The primacy of provisions of Directives with respect to tax treaties can only be enforceable if such provisions are directly effective, i.e., they are clear, unconditional, and not contingent on any discretionary implementing measures.

(b) If directly effective, the primacy of provisions of a Directive with respect to tax treaties is enforceable except for those situations wherein:

   (i) Member States, including their tax authorities, would rely on directly effective provisions of Directives with a view to setting aside a tax treaty in order to increase the tax burden of a taxpayer (i.e., impose an obligation on the taxpayer to pay (additional) taxes) (the prohibition of reverse vertical direct effect).

   (ii) Taxpayers would rely on rights laid down in directly effective provisions of Directives for fraudulent or abusive ends (due to the general EU anti-abuse principle).

   With respect to fraudulent or abusive situations within the meaning of (ii), it has furthermore been concluded that Member State courts are obliged to deny the benefits of a Directive to taxpayers. This obligation to deny benefits entails that, to the extent that a tax treaty would provide for the benefits of a Directive that must be denied in accordance with the general EU anti-abuse principle, Member State courts would be obliged to set aside such tax treaties pursuant to such anti-abuse principle.

## 7.4 CONCLUSIONS REGARDING THE EFFECT OF THE DIRECTIVES ON THE APPLICATION OF TAX TREATIES UNDER THE LAWS OF THE EU

It has been the purpose of this chapter to determine the extent to which the Directives may affect the application of tax treaties under the laws of the EU. More specifically, this chapter has been aimed at answering the question of to what extent the primacy of the Directives would require Member State courts to set aside tax treaties concluded by the Member States. Based on sections 7.2 and 7.3, the answer to this question is as follows.

The primacy of the Directives applies with respect to those (rights and obligations of) tax treaties concluded by the Member States falling outside the scope of Article 351 TFEU. As such, the Directives have primacy with respect to all 342 Intra-EU Treaties, all 1,094 post-accession Extra-EU Treaties, and those pre-accession Extra-EU Treaties that would have been amended after accession to the EU following a renegotiation in full. In addition, with respect to those pre-accession Extra-EU Treaties that have not been amended following such renegotiations, it depends on the nature of the rights and obligations provided by the remaining 416 post-accession Extra-EU Treaties whether the Directives would also enjoy primacy with respect to such treaties. Only rights of, or obligations towards, third states fall outside the scope of such primacy.

If a Directive enjoys primacy with respect to a tax treaty, such primacy would only be enforceable before a Member State court if the relevant provision that would be incompatible with a tax treaty has direct effect[803] while setting aside the tax treaty, by relying on the primacy of such directly effective (Directive) provision, would not result in the imposition of an obligation on a taxpayer.[804] It follows that, in practice, the primacy of directly effective provisions of Directives vis-à-vis tax treaties would only be enforceable to the extent that the setting aside of such tax treaties would be beneficial for a taxpayer. It should, however, be acknowledged that such enforceability of beneficial directly effective Directive provisions is subject to the following caveat. If the benefits of such provisions are relied upon for fraudulent or abusive ends, the general EU anti-abuse principle precludes reliance on the primacy of beneficial directly effective provisions of a Directive (with a view to the setting aside of a tax treaty). As such, the primacy of beneficial directly effective Directive provisions would not be enforceable vis-à-vis Intra-EU Treaties if relied upon for fraudulent or abusive ends.

In addition to the effect that the Directives themselves may have on the application of tax treaties, it has been concluded that EU law can require the setting aside of a tax treaty if such a treaty would provide for benefits similar to those of a Directive in fraudulent or abusive situations. This would, for example, be the case where a tax treaty provides for an exemption of withholding taxes on intra-group cross-border dividends falling within the scope of Article 5(1) of the Parent-Subsidiary Directive. In the event of a fraudulent or abusive situation, the general EU anti-abuse principle requires a Member State authority or court to refuse the benefit of Article 5(1) of the Parent-Subsidiary Directive. As such, the exemption from withholding taxes would have to be refused. In the event that a tax treaty would provide for such an exemption that must be refused, a Member State authority or court would seem to be required to refuse, i.e., set aside, such an exemption under the relevant tax treaty in order to ensure that the benefits of the Directive are not granted (in fact) in fraudulent or abusive situations. As such, the application of a tax treaty can be affected by the general EU anti-abuse principle in the event that a tax treaty would provide for benefits

803. The requirement of direct effect entails that the relevant provision is clear, unconditional, and not contingent on any discretionary implementation measures.
804. In short and in different terms: the setting aside of a tax treaty by a directly effective Directive provision must be beneficial for a taxpayer.

that are similar or identical to those of a Directive, while the general EU anti-abuse principle requires refusal of such Directive benefits.

## 7.5 OBSERVATIONS REGARDING TREATIES WHOSE APPLICATION IS NOT AFFECTED BY THE DIRECTIVES UNDER THE LAWS OF THE EU

Based on the conclusions of the previous sections, there are tax treaties that cannot be set aside, i.e., whose application cannot be affected by the Directives in the event of a conflict. This may be due to (i) Article 351 TFEU being applicable, (ii) the relevant Directive provision not having direct effect, or (iii) the setting aside of the treaty by relying on a directly effective provision of a Directive resulting in the imposition of an obligation on a taxpayer. With respect to each of these situations, it should, however, be noted that the Member States remain under a duty to achieve the result of a Directive under Article 288 TFEU. As such, the conclusion that the application of a tax treaty would not be affected by a Directive in the event of an incompatibility implies that a Member State would have failed to achieve such result. This, in turn, entails that such Member State would have failed to fulfil its obligations under Article 288 TFEU.

The finding of such a failure has no direct consequences for the application of tax treaties concluded by the Member States. However, Member States do remain under an obligation, under Article 288 TFEU, to achieve the result of the Directives. In order to ensure that a Member State would still achieve such result, the Commission (and Member States) could bring the failure of such Member State to achieve the result of a Directive before the CJEU under Article 258 (or, for the Member States, 259) TFEU by means of a so-called infringement proceeding. Such an infringement proceeding would then be aimed to 'make Member States comply with and fulfil their obligations under the Treaties'.[805]

For present purposes, it is especially relevant to note that infringement proceedings can only result in a finding that the Member State has failed to fulfil its obligations under the EU Treaties, more specifically Article 288 TFEU. Such a finding does not, however, have direct consequences for the Member State. It merely declares that the Member State has failed to fulfil its obligations under the EU Treaties without attaching direct consequences to that finding. The Member State is, however, required 'to take the necessary measures to comply with the judgment of the Court' (Article 260 TFEU). Non-compliance with such judgment, which judgment would be aimed at requiring the Member State to comply with its obligations under the EU Treaties, can again be brought before the CJEU. If the CJEU would then conclude that the Member State concerned has not complied with its judgment, it may impose a lump sum or penalty on the Member State concerned (Article 260(2) TFEU). This is, however, the only consequence that may arise from an infringement proceeding. As such, the direct effect

805. C.E. Koops, 2014, p. 145.

of infringement proceedings is limited in the sense that they cannot have consequences for the application, or applicability, of non-affected tax treaties.[806]

806. This must not be understood, however, as meaning that infringement proceedings in general cannot have an indirect effect on the application of non-affected, incompatible, tax treaties. If the Member States would, based on the commencement of an infringement proceeding, renegotiate such tax treaties so as to make them compatible with their obligation under Article 288 TFEU, their application is – by means of such amendment – nevertheless affected. This effect is, however, rather indirect in the sense that it requires the Member State to actively change the content of such tax treaties. This does not occur by law, as would be the case with the affected tax treaties. Their application is directly affected by the Directives due to their (enforceable) primacy.

CHAPTER 8

# The Effect of Directives on the Application of Tax Treaties: Bringing the Public International Law and EU Law Perspective Together

It has been the purpose of Part III of this thesis to answer the question to what extent the Directives may affect the application, in terms of applicability, of tax treaties concluded by the Member States (after such treaties would have been interpreted), under the public international law perspective (Chapter 6) and the perspective of the laws of the EU (Chapter 7). It is the purpose of this chapter to combine the findings of both perspectives with a goal of determining the extent to which the Directives can affect, or are 'allowed' to affect, the application of tax treaties (under public international law) is aligned with the extent to which such Directives must affect, or are 'required' to affect, the application of such treaties (under the laws of the EU).

The starting point in this respect is that the Directives cannot affect (public international law), and are not required to affect (EU law), the application of tax treaties in the absence of a conflict between a Directive and a tax treaty. As such, a conflict is required in order for the Directives to be able to affect the application of tax treaties. With respect to the public international law perspective, such a conflict would arise if the obligations under a Directive would be incompatible with those under a tax treaty. From the perspective of the laws of the EU, a conflict exists if a Member State fails to achieve the result of a Directive due to, for present purposes, a tax treaty concluded by such Member State (*see*, with respect to this Member State perspective, section 1.4.3). It is with respect to these types of conflicts that it will be assessed below what effect the Directives may have on the application – in terms of applicability – of Intra-EU Treaties (section 8.1) and on Extra-EU Treaties (section 8.2).

## 8.1 THE EFFECT OF THE DIRECTIVES ON THE APPLICATION OF INTRA-EU TREATIES

In Chapter 6, it has been concluded that it is arguable that conflicts between Directives, as decisions of an international organisation, and Intra-EU Treaties may be resolved by means of an analogous application of the *lex posterior* conflict rule of Article 30 VCLT 1969 and/or the *lex specialis* conflict rule. Under an analogous application of the *lex posterior* rule, an earlier Intra-EU Treaty would be inapplicable to the extent that its provisions are incompatible with the obligations of a Member State under a later Directive (provided that the Intra-EU Treaty and Directive are found to relate to the same topic or substance). Under the *lex specialis* conflict rule, the relevant criterion for awarding precedence to a provision of a Directive with respect to a provision of an Intra-EU Treaty in the event of a conflict is specialty. If a Directive provision would be found to be more special as compared to an incompatible provision of an Intra-EU Treaty, which seems arguable with respect to, at least, the Parent-Subsidiary Directive, ATAD1 and ATAD2, the Intra-EU Treaty – as *lex generalis* – would be inapplicable to the extent the application of a provision of an Intra-EU Treaty is incompatible with a provision of a Directive – as *lex specialis*.

Whereas the application of Intra-EU Treaties may thus be affected by later Directives relating to the same subject matter – under an analogous application of the *lex posterior* rule – and/or Directives whose provisions are more special than those of an Intra-EU Treaty – under the *lex specialis* conflict rule – the following is acknowledged. First, both the *lex posterior* rule and *lex specialis* rule seek to resolve conflicts based on a presumption regarding the intentions of the parties with respect to, in this case, a conflict between an Intra-EU Treaty and a Directive. As such, the effect of Directives on the application of Intra-EU Treaties under the *lex posterior* and *lex specialis* rules is subject to evidence of a contrary common intention between the Member States as regards the way in which a conflict should be resolved. Second, it must be acknowledged that there is no case law from the ICJ, ECtHR, or arbitral tribunals (as published on italaw.com), that confirms an application of the *lex posterior* conflict rule to conflicts between (earlier) treaties and (later) decisions of international organisations. Additionally, there also does not seem to be case law of such courts and tribunals confirming (or rejecting) an application of the *lex specialis* rule to conflicts between treaties and decisions of international organisations. There is, however, case law of the ICJ that confirms the application of the *lex specialis* conflict rule to conflicts between different sources of public international law of equal rank. Such case law would thus seem to provide support for concluding that conflicts between treaties and decisions of international organisations, as different sources of public international law of equal rank, can be resolved by means of the *lex specialis* conflict rule. Whereas there may be support for such an application of the *lex specialis* conflict rule, this author is hesitant to conclude that the *lex specialis* conflict rule should – or must – be applicable to conflicts between Directives, as decisions of an international organisation, and tax treaties. Such hesitance is based on the absence of case law explicitly confirming such an application of the *lex specialis* conflict rule. Taking into account the comments above, this author adopts the view that it cannot be concluded that the Directives are capable, or should be capable, of affecting the application of Intra-EU Treaties under (an analogous application of) the *lex posterior* rule or *lex specialis* conflict rule. Instead, this author concludes that such an effect can only be considered 'arguable' in the sense that, notwithstanding explicit support in case law, there would be (sound) arguments for adopting the view that the application of Intra-EU Treaties can be affected by the Directives under either an analogous application of the *lex posterior* conflict rule of Article 30 VCLT 1969 or the *lex specialis* conflict rule.

If applicable to a conflict between an (earlier or more general) Intra-EU Treaty and a (later or more specific) Directive, the consequence of the *lex posterior* and *lex specialis* conflict rules would be that the (earlier or more general) Intra-EU Treaty is inapplicable to the extent such application would be incompatible with the (later or more specific) (result of a) Directive. This entails that the application of Intra-EU Treaties would be affected in such a way that they are not applicable - under public international law - to the extent that their application would be incompatible with the obligations under a (later or more specific) Directive. The inapplicability of the Intra-EU Treaty under public international law then implies that the obligations thereunder do not have to be performed. This, in turn, entails that - under public international law - a Member State would only need to perform the obligations arising from the Directive; the obligations relating to the Intra-EU Treaty would - as a result of the application of the *lex posterior* and/or *lex specialis* conflict rule(s) - no longer be applicable and, hence, would not need to be performed to the extent that such treaty conflicts with the Directive. As a consequence, the *lex posterior* and/or *lex specialis* conflict rule would entail that the Member State would be allowed under public international law to not give effect to the provisions of the Intra-EU Treaty in order to ensure that effect is given to the provisions of a Directive.

Assume Company A, resident in Member State Y, has a permanent establishment situated in Member State Z. Assume further that such permanent establishment must be treated as a controlled foreign company within the meaning of Article 7(1) ATAD1. In such a situation, Article 7(2) ATAD1 obliges Member State Y to include in the tax base (qualifying) income of the permanent establishment. Assume further that the Intra-EU Treaty between Member States Y and Z stipulates that profits attributable to a permanent establishment must be exempt. In this situation, Member State Y faces two - mutually exclusive - obligations: (i) tax the income of the permanent establishment situated in Member State Z (and achieve the result required by Article 7(2) ATAD1) and (ii) exempt the income of such permanent establishment (and achieve the result required by the Intra-EU Treaty with Member State Y).

With respect to such a situation of mutually exclusive - or conflicting - obligations, reference could be made to the conflict rules of public international law to determine whether the tax treaty obligation to exempt the profits attributable to the permanent establishment under the Intra-EU Treaty would be inapplicable in light of obligations arising from ATAD1. Under an analogous application of the *lex posterior* conflict rule, the Intra-EU Treaty between Member States Y and Z would, if such treaty has been concluded before the adoption of ATAD1 and based on the assumption that ATAD1 and such Intra-EU Treaty would relate to the same topic of substance, be applicable *'only to the extent that its provisions are compatible with those of the later treaty'*. Applied to the present example, an analogous application of the *lex posterior* conflict rule would entail that the

> Intra-EU Treaty obligation to exempt profits attributable to the permanent establishment situated in Member State Y would be rendered inapplicable because such exemption would be incompatible with obligations of a later decision of an international organisation (Article 7(2) ATAD1). Similarly, if it is assumed that the way in which Article 7(2) ATAD1 deals with the taxation of profits attributable to permanent establishments is (sufficiently) more specific than the way in which Articles 7 and 23 of an Intra-EU Treaty deal with the taxation of such profits, the *lex specialis* conflict rule would also provide for the inapplicability of the obligation to exempt the profits of the (controlled foreign company) permanent establishment under public international law. In this example, taking into account the assumptions made, the *lex posterior* and *lex specialis* conflict rules would thus both provide for the inapplicability of the Intra-EU Treaty to the extent that it is incompatible with the obligation to tax profits of a controlled foreign company permanent establishment laid down in Article 7(2) ATAD1. As a result, the Intra-EU Treaty would not require, and thereby de facto allow, Member State Y to tax the profits of the controlled foreign company permanent establishment notwithstanding the exemption provided for such profits in the Intra-EU Treaty with Member State Z.

If a Directive would affect the application of Intra-EU Treaties under public international law as a result of the *lex posterior* and/or *lex specialis* conflict rule(s), this could be relevant for the extent to which a Directive would (also) (be required to) affect the application of such treaties under the laws of the EU. This can be explained as follows. Under the laws of the EU, a Directive would only be able to affect the application of tax treaties concluded by the Member States - by means of the primacy of such Directive - in the event that a Member State fails to achieve the result of a Directive. Whether a Member State fails to achieve such a result depends, ultimately, on the national laws of such Member State and the status of tax treaties under such national laws. As indicated in section 1.4.3, tax treaties seem to be superior to national laws in most of the Member States. If superior, it would seem relevant whether the application of an Intra-EU Treaty is affected by a Directive under the rules of public international law if it is assumed that the superiority of treaties with respect to national laws only applies if such treaties are applicable under public international law. Such relevance can be illustrated as follows with respect to the example of the Netherlands as set out in section 6.4.2.3.2. In the Netherlands, being one of the Member States in which tax treaties are superior to national legislation (*see* section 1.4.3), national legislation aimed at implementing a Directive must be set aside if such legislation would be incompatible with (the obligations of the Netherlands under) an Intra-EU Treaty. Therefore, (superior) Intra-EU Treaties can result in the setting aside of national laws (aimed at implementing a Directive). Such setting aside then jeopardises, in principle, the extent to which the Netherlands may be able to achieve the result of a Directive if such result is incompatible with Intra-EU Treaties concluded by the Netherlands. If, however, the application of an Intra-EU Treaty would be affected by (the result of) a Directive under public international law in such a way that the Intra-EU Treaty is rendered inapplicable to the extent required for the purposes of achieving the result of a Directive, this would seem to entail that the national legislation aimed at achieving this result of a Directive would no longer be incompatible with the provisions of the Intra-EU Treaty because such provisions would - as a matter of public international law - be inapplicable to the extent they conflict with the result of the Directive that such national legislation seeks to implement. In the absence of an incompatibility between the national legislation aimed at implementing a Directive and an Intra-EU Treaty, it would then seem that such legislation is not set aside by such treaty and that, as a consequence, the result of the Directive is achieved notwithstanding the superiority of the (inapplicable) provisions of an Intra-EU Treaty. In the case of the Netherlands, the effect that a Directive may have on the application of Intra-EU Treaties under public international law might thus be relevant for the extent to which it is able to achieve the result of Directives notwithstanding the status of such treaties within the legal order of the Netherlands as superior with respect to national legislation (aimed at implementing a Directive). With respect to those Member States wherein tax treaties are not superior to national legislation, the effect of the Directives on the application of tax treaties under public international law would seem less relevant due to the circumstance that such Member States being able to achieve the result of such Directives irrespective of the (in)applicability of their Intra-EU Treaties under public international law. This does not mean, however, that the effect of the Directives under public international law on Intra-EU Treaties would be irrelevant for such Member States. This is due to the circumstance that the inapplicability of such treaties would entail that the Member States cannot incur international responsibility for not giving effect to their obligations under such treaties with a view to achieving the result of a Directive.

With respect to those Member States wherein tax treaties are superior to national legislation, the inapplicability of an Intra-EU Treaty under public international law due to its incompatibility with a Directive would seem highly relevant. This is because the inapplicability of such an Intra-EU Treaty would entail that national legislation of such Member States aimed at implementing such a Directive would no longer be incompatible with the Intra-EU Treaty (because such Intra-EU Treaty would, under public international law, be inapplicable to the extent incompatible with (the national legislation aimed at giving effect to such) a Directive). The setting aside of an Intra-EU Treaty by a Directive under public international law thus entails that such Member States would be able to achieve the result of a Directive and, hence, to comply with their obligations under Article 288 TFEU. Achievement of such a result and compliance with such obligations, in turn, would entail that there is no conflict for the purposes of the conflict rule of EU law because such conflict rule requires the non-achievement of, or failure to achieve, the result of a Directive.

It follows that the extent to which a Directive is able to affect the applicability of an Intra-EU Treaty under public international law would affect the extent to which such a Directive would (also) be able to affect applicability under the laws of the EU. Bearing this in mind, this author adopts the view that the effect of the Directives on Intra-EU Treaties under public international law should be addressed first.

As noted above, this author considers it only 'arguable' that the application of an Intra-EU Treaty can be affected by a Directive under an analogous application of the *lex posterior* or the *lex specialis* conflict rule. It can, therefore, not be excluded that the application of such a treaty would not be affected by these conflict rules of public international law. This would, for example, be conceivable if (i) the adoption of a Directive would have to be considered as relevantly different from the conclusion of a treaty (resulting in a rejection of an analogous application of the *lex posterior* conflict rule), (ii) a Directive would be found not to relate to the same subject matter as an Intra-EU Treaty (within the context of an analogous application of the *lex posterior* conflict rule), or (iii) the subject matter of a provision of a Directive would be found not sufficiently more precise than that of an Intra-EU Treaty (for the purposes of the *lex specialis* conflict rule).

If a conflict between obligations arising from a Directive and an Intra-EU Treaty is not resolved under the rules of public international law, the consequence would be that the application of an Intra-EU Treaty is not affected by a Directive and that, as a consequence, both the Directive, as a decision of an international organisation, and the Intra-EU Treaty remain applicable under public international law. As such, the obligations relating to both the Directive and the Intra-EU Treaty must both be performed in good faith. The applicability of the Intra-EU Treaty, although conflicting with the Directive, may then entail that a Member State would not be able to achieve the result of a Directive, especially if such an Intra-EU Treaty would be superior – within the legal order of a Member State – to the national legislation that is adopted for the purposes of implementing such Directive. If the applicability of an Intra-EU Treaty within the Member State's legal order entails that the result of a Directive is not achieved, this would mean that a Member State would have failed to fulfil its obligations under Article 288 TFEU. Such failure to achieve the result of a Directive by a Member State would then give rise to a conflict to which the conflict rule of the laws of the EU, i.e., the primacy of a Directive, applies. In determining whether such a conflict arises, it is thus required to determine the effect of (national laws implementing) a Directive on an Intra-EU Treaty under both the public international law and the Member State perspective first. This is necessary because it could follow from either perspective that the result of a Directive is achieved by a Member State. Only after it would become apparent that the application of a tax treaty is not affected in such a way that the result of a Directive is achieved under the public international law perspective and Member State perspective, would the primacy of EU law conflict rule become relevant.

With respect to the effect of the primacy EU law conflict rule on the application of Intra-EU Treaties it has been concluded in Chapter 7 that, as a starting point, each Directive enjoys primacy over, and would be able to set aside, each incompatible provision of an Intra-EU Treaty. This primacy must not, however, be understood as entailing that a Member State court must, at all times, set aside Intra-EU Treaties in the event that they preclude a Member State from achieving the result of a Directive (and fulfilling its obligations under Article 288 TFEU). The primacy of a Directive is only enforceable if (i) the relevant Directive provision has direct effect, i.e., the provision is clear, unconditional, and not contingent on any discretionary implementing measures, and (ii) the setting aside of, in this event, an Intra-EU Treaty does not result in the imposition of an obligation on the taxpayer concerned (due to the prohibition of reverse vertical direct effect). If one of these two conditions would not be met, the primacy of a Directive would not be enforceable. If not enforceable, Member State courts would not be required, as a matter of EU law, to set aside an Intra-EU Treaty whose application is incompatible with (the result of) a Directive.[807] As such, under the laws of the EU, a Member State court would de facto be 'allowed' to apply such (incompatible) Intra-EU Treaty in the event that the primacy of a Directive provision would not be enforceable.

> The conclusion that a Directive's primacy is not enforceable if this would result in the imposition of an obligation on a taxpayer would seem highly relevant with respect to provisions of Directives that impose a duty to tax income, such as provisions of ATAD1 and ATAD2. This is due to such provisions being aimed at increasing the tax burden of taxpayers (and, as such, at imposing an obligation of taxpayers). As such, it already seems to follow from the purpose of the provisions of ATAD1 and ATAD2 that their primacy with respect to Intra-EU Treaties would be unenforceable. The would seem to hold true with respect to the income inclusion rule of the on 31 October 2022 pending Pillar 2 Proposal (section 1.2).[808] Additionally, the obligation laid down in the on 31 October 2022 pending ATAD3 Proposal to 'disregard' Intra-EU Treaties would also seem to be aimed at imposing obligations on taxpayers given that the 'to be disregarded' tax treaties would generally have resulted in a lower tax burden for taxpayers. As such, it would seem that the Article 11 of the ATAD3 Proposal, containing the obligation to disregard Intra-EU Treaties, is aimed at resulting in a *de facto* higher tax burden for taxpayers (and, hence, the imposition of an obligation on such taxpayers).[809] It follows that the primacy of Article 11 of the ATAD3 Proposal would also seem unenforceable.

> If a Directive's primacy – or superiority – vis-à-vis an Intra-EU Treaty is unenforceable due to the prohibition of reverse vertical direct effect, this would entail that the Intra-EU Treaty cannot be set aside by a national court on the basis of the primacy of such a Directive. This, in turn, entails that a conflict between a provision of a Directive imposing a duty to tax income and a provision of an Intra-EU Treaty imposing a duty to refrain from taxing that same income is de facto resolved in favour of the Intra-EU Treaty under the laws of the EU. It is de facto resolved in favour of the Intra-EU Treaty because the laws of the EU do not require a Member State court to set aside such a treaty. As such, the application of the provisions of the Intra-EU Treaty would not be (required to be) affected by (the

807. It is acknowledged, in this respect, that the non-enforceability of the primacy of a provision of a Directive under the laws of the EU, due to such a provision not having direct effect or due to the prohibition of reverse vertical direct effect, does not entail that a court of a Member State is prohibited from setting aside – or disapplying – an incompatible provision of an Intra-EU Treaty on the basis the laws of such Member State. *See*, to this effect, Case C-261/20 (*Thelen Technopark Berlin*), paras 33 and 48. The question as to whether a Member State court is able to set aside tax treaties under the laws of the Member States seems, however, to precede the question as to whether a Directive's primacy can result in the setting aside of a treaty (*see* this section 8.1 where it is stated that it is required 'to determine the effect of (national laws implementing) a Directive on an Intra-EU Treaty under both the public international law and the Member State perspective first. This is necessary because it could follow from either perspective that the result of a Directive is achieved by a Member State. Only after it would become apparent that the application of a tax treaty is not affected in such a way that the result of a Directive is achieved under the public international law perspective and Member State perspective, would the primacy of EU law conflict rule become relevant').
808. *See* Chapter 2 of Pillar 2 proposal (COM(2021) 823 final). *See* regarding the incompatibility of the income inclusion rule with tax treaties: M.F. de Wilde, NLF-O 2022/4, V. Chand, A. Turina & K. Romanovska, World Tax Journal 2022/2, and L. de Broe in: Building Global International Tax Law: Essays in Honour of Guglielmo Maisto (Pistone ed.), 2022, para. 23.2.2.
809. *See* Article 11 ATAD3 Proposal (COM(2021) 565 final).

> unenforceable primacy of) a Directive and taxpayers would, as a matter of EU law be able to rely on such provisions to their benefit. Whereas the application of provisions of an Intra-EU Treaty is not to be affected in practice by the primacy of the Directives if such primacy is unenforceable, this does not entail that a Member State would no longer be required to achieve the result of a Directive. In fact, the finding that an incompatible provision of an Intra-EU Treaty would not be set aside by (the primacy of) a Directive and, as such, remains applicable entails that the relevant Member State fails to achieve the result of such Directive. The failure to achieve such result would then provide a ground for the European Commission and/or Member States to commence an infringement proceeding on the basis of Article 258 (European Commission) or Article 259 (Member States) TFEU. The outcome of such an infringement proceeding cannot, however, be that the Intra-EU Treaty would no longer be applicable. This is due to an infringement proceeding only being capable of resulting in the imposition of financial penalties; it cannot, by contrast, result in a change in the national laws or tax treaties of a Member State. Such laws of treaties would have to be amended by the Member State itself.

If it were established that a Directive has direct effect and that the setting aside of a tax treaty would not result in the imposition of an obligation on a taxpayer, such as a higher tax burden, the primacy of such Directive would be enforceable with respect to an incompatible Intra-EU Treaty. This indicates that, in practice, only beneficial (from a taxpayer's perspective) directly effective Directive provisions would be able to set aside incompatible provisions of Intra-EU Treaties. As such, taxpayers can enforce the setting aside of Intra-EU Treaties that would - in a Member State legal order - limit the extent to which benefits of directly effective Directive provisions can be relied upon, by invoking the primacy of such Directive provisions.[810]

Whereas taxpayers would be able to rely on the benefits of directly effective Directive provisions to set aside incompatible provisions of Intra-EU Treaties, it must be acknowledged that such setting aside would be precluded if the benefits of the Directive are relied upon for abusive or fraudulent ends. If relied upon for abusive or fraudulent ends, the general EU anti-abuse principle provides that such benefits must be denied. As such, the primacy of beneficial directly effective Directive provisions would not be enforceable with respect to Intra-EU Treaties if relied upon for fraudulent or abusive ends.

In addition to rendering the primacy of beneficial directly effective Directive provisions unenforceable, the general EU anti-abuse principle also entails a duty to refuse granting the benefits of such provisions to a taxpayer in fraudulent or abusive situations. Such requirement to refuse Directive benefits would then entail a duty to set aside a tax treaty if such a treaty provides for benefits that are similar to the benefits of the Directive that must be refused in accordance with the general EU anti-abuse principle. As such, the general EU anti-abuse principle has two relevant consequences within the context of the effect that Directives may have on the application of tax

810. *See*, to this effect, Case C-294/99 (*Athinaiki Zinthopiia*), para. 32 where the CJEU held that 'the rights conferred on economic operators by Article 5(1) of the [Parent-Subsidiary] Directive are unconditional and a Member State cannot make their observance subject to an agreement concluded with another Member State'.

treaties. First, it can render the primacy of beneficial directly effective Directive provisions unenforceable. Second, the general EU anti-abuse principle can require the application of a tax treaty to be affected in an abusive or fraudulent situation if such treaty provides benefits that are similar to those of a Directive.

In the event that the general EU anti-abuse principle requires the refusal of a benefit that is (de facto) provided by a provision of an Intra-EU Treaty, such general principle would give rise to obligations that are incompatible with the obligation under such Intra-EU Treaty such benefit (that is similar to that of a Directive). In the event of such an incompatibility (or conflict), the approach adopted in this thesis entails that it should be established first whether the application of the Intra-EU Treaty would be affected by the general EU anti-abuse principle under the rules of public international law before resorting to the setting aside of such treaty on the basis of the rules of the EU. With respect to the effect of the general EU anti-abuse principle on the application of Intra-EU Treaties, the starting point would be that the general EU anti-abuse principle belongs to primary EU law.[811] As part of primary EU law, the general EU anti-abuse principle would, ultimately, seem to be based on the EU Treaties and, as such, part of the sources of public international law.[812] This entails that a conflict between the general EU anti-abuse principle and a tax treaty could be regarded as a conflict between two treaties under public international law, i.e., the EU Treaties and the Intra-EU Treaty. With respect to the resolution of such conflict, it follows from section 6.4.2.1.3 that the Intra-EU Treaties would not, based on a substance-based view, relate to the same subject matter as the EU Treaties for the purposes of Article 30 VCLT 1969. As such, a conflict between the general EU anti-abuse principle and an Intra-EU Treaty falls outside the scope of the *lex posterior* conflict rule of this provision of the VCLT 1969. This conclusion entails that the application of an Intra-EU Treaty cannot be affected by the general EU anti-abuse principle by means of the *lex posterior* conflict rule. The same conclusion would also seem applicable with respect to the effect of the general EU anti-abuse principle under the *lex specialis* conflict rule because the subject matter of the TEU and TFEU seems more general than the subject matter of tax treaties (section 6.4.4.4). The same would seem to apply with respect to the general EU anti-abuse principle as compared to the provision of a tax treaty providing for a benefit that would have to be refused pursuant to such principle. The general EU anti-abuse principle provides that each rule of EU law cannot be relied on for abusive or fraudulent ends. It has, as such, a general scope and is not limited to, for example, those laws of

811. *See*, A. Arnull in: Prohibition of Abuse of Law: A New General Principle of EU Law? (R. de la Feria & S. Vogenauer eds), 2011, p. 12. *See also* K. Lenaerts & J.A. Gutierrez-Fons, Common Market Law Review 2010/6, p. 1641, R. Szudoczky, 2013, p. 17 and L. de Broe, World Tax Journal 2022/8, p. 442, who state that general principles of EU law have the status of primary EU law or rank equal to primary EU law.

812. It is acknowledged that there are scholars that distinguish general principles of EU law as a category of primary EU law distinct from the EU Treaties (*see* R. Szudoczky, 2013, p. 55). Nevertheless, this author concludes that the general EU anti-abuse principle would seem to be based, ultimately, on the EU Treaties. This conclusion is based on the fact that Member States are only required to comply with such principle as a result of their conclusion of the EU Treaties or their accession thereto. As such, the obligation to comply with such principle arises, ultimately, from the EU Treaties.

the EU within the context of (direct) taxation; it applies to all EU law, including those laws that relate to taxation.[813] By contrast, a provision of a tax treaty providing for a benefit that must be refused pursuant to the general EU anti-abuse principle would have a more limited scope. Such a provision would provide a benefit with respect to a certain type of income in a bilateral situation. As such, it seems likely that a tax treaty provision would have a more specific subject matter than the general EU anti-abuse principle. As a consequence, such tax treaty provision would have to be regarded as the *lex specialis* as compared to the general EU anti-abuse principle. It then follows that the application of a tax treaty, being the *lex specialis*, would not be affected by the general EU anti-abuse principle under the *lex specialis* conflict rule. The conclusion would be that the application of Intra-EU Treaties would not be affected by the general EU anti-abuse principle under the conflict rules of public international law. In the absence of an effect under the laws of public international law, it can still be determined whether the general EU anti-abuse principle has an effect on the application of tax treaties under the Member State perspective or the EU law perspective. If not affected under the Member State perspective, application of the EU law perspective would entail that Member State courts are required to refuse the benefits of a Directive being granted (irrespective of whether this would be detrimental for a taxpayer) and, as such, ensure that such benefits are granted to a taxpayer by means of an Intra-EU Treaty. In ensuring that the benefits of a Directive are not provided by means of an Intra-EU Treaty in a fraudulent or abusive situation, a Member State court would seem required to set aside such an Intra-EU Treaty pursuant to the general EU anti-abuse principle to the extent that application of such treaty would entail that a Directive benefit is granted in such a fraudulent or abusive situation.

## 8.2 THE EFFECT OF THE DIRECTIVES ON THE APPLICATION OF EXTRA-EU TREATIES

The effect that the Directives may have on the application of Extra-EU Treaties under the rules of public international law and the laws of the EU differs from their effect with respect to Intra-EU Treaties. First, under public international law, the Directives – as *res inter alios* between the Member States – cannot have any effect on the application of Extra-EU Treaties. This is because the *pacta tertiis* principle provides that such Directives cannot create either obligations or rights for third states without their consent (Article 34 VCLT 1969) nor can they affect the mutual rights and obligations of Extra-EU Treaties in the event of a conflict (Article 30(4)(b) VCLT 1969). As such, the rights and obligations under Extra-EU Treaties remain binding and must be performed in good faith in the event of a conflict with obligations arising from a Directive (Article 26 VCLT 1969).

Second, under the laws of the EU, a distinction must be drawn between those rights and obligations of Extra-EU Treaties that fall within the scope of Article 351 TFEU

813. *See* as to this effect, L. de Broe, World Tax Journal 2022/8, p. 442 who concludes that no distinction can be drawn between the general EU anti-abuse principle as applied in the various areas of law or in various types of cases.

and those that do not. To the extent rights and obligations under Extra-EU Treaties fall outside the scope of Article 351 TFEU, the effect of the Directives on the application of Extra-EU Treaties would be identical to that of Directives on the application of Intra-EU Treaties as set out in section 8.1. If, however, rights and obligations fall within the scope of Article 351 TFEU, they shall not be affected by the Directives. As such, it is highly relevant whether a treaty falls within the scope of Article 351 TFEU. If an Extra-EU Treaty falls within the scope of such provision, the Directives are precluded, under the laws of the EU, from having any effect on the application of a tax treaty.

This does not, however, entail that Member States are relieved from their duty to achieve the result of a Directive as soon as a tax treaty falls within the scope of Article 351 TFEU. Based on the second paragraph of Article 351 TFEU such Member States would remain under an obligation to take all appropriate steps to eliminate the incompatibility between such a treaty and the result to be achieved pursuant to a Directive. Such duty to take appropriate steps, which includes renegotiation as well as termination, does not, however, entail that the application of pre-accession Extra-EU Treaty can be affected by the Directives if a Member State fails to take the appropriate steps. As such, Article 351 TFEU ensures that the application of pre-accession Extra-EU Treaties cannot be affected by the Directives pending the successful elimination of an incompatibility.

The starting point with respect to the scope of Article 351 TFEU is that it applies to pre-accession Extra-EU Treaties only (the temporal scope). With respect to this temporal scope of Article 351 TFEU, it has been submitted by legal scholars that its rule, i.e., pre-existing rights and obligations arising from Extra-EU Treaties shall not be affected by later EU law, may also be applied by analogy to post-accession, pre-Directive Extra-EU Treaties. An analogous application of Article 351 TFEU would entail that the application of all pre-Directive Extra-EU Treaties, to the extent it concerns the rights of, and obligations towards, third states, shall not be affected by the Directives. In terms of treaties whose application shall not be affected, an analogous application would have great consequences. This can be illustrated as follows: there are only 413 pre-accession Extra-EU Treaties (27.4% of all Extra-EU Treaties) while there are 1,416 pre-ATAD2 Extra-EU Treaties (94% of all Extra-EU Treaties). As such, an analogous application of Article 351 TFEU greatly affects the number of Extra-EU Treaties that may fall within the scope of the primacy of the Directives. While potentially greatly affecting the number of Extra-EU Treaties that may be affected by the primacy of the Directives, it has been concluded in Chapter 7 that an analogous application of Article 351 TFEU must be rejected in light of the CJEU's ruling in *Generalstaatsanwaltschaft München* (Case C-435/22 PPU). As such, Article 351 TFEU is not applicable with respect to each of the 1,094 post-accession Extra-EU Treaties.

If an Extra-EU Treaty falls within the scope of Article 351 TFEU, it would have to be subsequently determined the rights and obligations that may be affected by means of (the primacy of) the Directives fall within the scope of the 'protection' granted by Article 351 TFEU (the substantive scope). The starting point with respect to such protection is that Article 351 TFEU only protects the rights of, and obligations towards, third states under pre-accession Extra-EU Treaties. This entails, for example, that Member States are obliged to adhere to limitations to their right to tax income as agreed to under pre-accession Extra-EU Treaties. As such, the obligation to tax certain categories of non-distributed income of a controlled foreign company permanent establishment laid down in Article 7(2) ATAD1 would not be able to affect the obligation vis-à-vis third states under a pre-accession Extra-EU Treaty requiring an exemption of that income under the laws of the EU. This would not be possible because taxing such income attributable to the controlled foreign company permanent establishment would amount to ATAD1 affecting the rights of, or obligations towards, the third state under such pre-accession Extra-EU Treaty. In such a way, the effect under the laws of the EU on the application of an Extra-EU Treaty, i.e., none, would be similar to the effect that a Directive would have under public international law, i.e., none.

If a tax treaty falls outside the (temporal or substantive) scope of Article 351 TFEU, the conclusions regarding the effect of the Directive on the application of an Extra-EU Treaty under the laws of the EU are identical to the conclusions with respect to the effect that such Directive may have on the application of an Intra-EU Treaty (section 8.1). With respect to post-accession Extra-EU Treaties, the effect of a Directive under public international law (none) may thus differ from that under the laws of the EU (setting aside of the Extra-EU Treaty provided that the primacy of a Directive provision would be enforceable). In addition to the difference between the public international law and EU law perspective in terms of the effect of Directives on the application of those Extra-EU Treaties falling outside the temporal scope of Article 351 TFEU, there is also another difference. It follows from case law of the CJEU that the Directives shall only not affect the rights of, and obligations towards, third states under pre-accession Extra-EU Treaties. Hence, the rights of, and obligations towards, Member States fall outside the 'protection' offered by Article 351 TFEU. Such rights of, and obligations towards, Member States may thus be affected by the Directives notwithstanding the conclusion that this would not be allowed under public international law. As such, also with respect to such rights of, and obligations towards, Member States, the same conclusions apply as set out in section 8.1.

## 8.3 THE EFFECT OF THE DIRECTIVES ON THE APPLICATION OF THE MLI

The effect of the Directives on the MLI under the rules of public international law depends, first and foremost, on whether it can be bilateralised. If bilateralisable and affecting an Intra-EU Treaty, the conclusions as set out in section 8.1 apply. If bilateralisable and affecting an Extra-EU Treaty, or if multilateral, the conclusions of section 8.2 apply with it being understood that the MLI does not fall within the temporal scope of Article 351 TFEU because the MLI has been concluded by each of the Member States after it had acceded to the EU.

# Part IV Conclusions and Recommendations

# Chapter 9
# Conclusion

It has been the purpose of this thesis to provide an answer to the following research question (*see* section 1.3):

> *To what extent do the Directives affect the interpretation and application of tax treaties concluded by the Member States?*

With respect to the answer to the research question set out in this chapter, the following preliminary observations apply:

(a) The research question is addressed from the perspectives of public international law and the laws of the EU. The question to what extent the interpretation and application of tax treaties concluded by the Member States may also be affected under the national laws of each of the 27 Member States is, therefore, out of its scope.

(b) The starting point for the purposes of the public international law perspective is that the Directives have a dual nature: they are both a source of public international law – as decisions of the European Union as an international organisation – and a source of the law that is in force in each of the Member States (*see* Chapter 2).

The relevance of this starting point, in particular the classification of the Directives as a source of public international law, will be illustrated in the sections below by indicating what the consequences would have been if the Directives are only regarded as part of the laws of the Member States (and not as a source of public international law).

Bearing these observations in mind, this chapter sets out the answer to the research question. In setting out such an answer, a similar structure is adhered to as applied throughout this thesis. This means that the conclusions regarding the effect of the Directives on the interpretation of tax treaties (section 9.1) are discussed before the effect that such Directives may have on the application – in terms of applicability – of tax treaties is set out (section 9.2). The rationale for such order of discussion is that the application of a tax treaty must be preceded by its – conscious or subconscious – interpretation.

## 9.1 THE EFFECT OF THE DIRECTIVES ON THE INTERPRETATION OF TAX TREATIES

With respect to the effect that the Directives have on the interpretation of tax treaties, it follows from Chapter 4, reflecting the EU law perspective, that the duty of consistent interpretation requires a Member State court to interpret a tax treaty 'so far as possible' in light of the wording and the purpose of a Directive with a view to ensuring that the result of such Directive is achieved. Whereas this might seem, at first glance, to indicate a far-reaching duty to interpret tax treaties in a way that is compatible with the result of the Directives, it has been consistently held by the CJEU that duty of interpretation applies only 'so far as possible'. This reference to 'so far as possible' entails, *inter alia*, that a Member State court is only required to interpret a tax treaty in a way that is consistent with the result of a Directive to the extent that this would be allowed for when applying the national methods of interpretation. In the event of the interpretation of a tax treaty, such national interpretative methods would be identical for each Member State court: Articles 31-33 VCLT 1969 and Article 3(2) OECD Model, if included in a tax treaty (or Article 2(2) in case of the MLI). As such, the obligation of a Member State court to interpret a tax treaty in light of the wording and purpose of Directive with a view to ensuring that such treaty is interpreted in a way that is consistent with such a Directive only applies to the extent that Articles 31-33 VCLT 1969 and Article 3(2) OECD Model (or Article 2(2) in case of the MLI) would allow for such a Directive consistent interpretation of a tax treaty.

Based on the conclusion that the duty of consistent interpretation, applied to the interpretation of tax treaties, would de facto require a Member State to comply with Articles 31-33 VCLT 1969 and Article 3(2) OECD Model (or Article 2(2) in case of the MLI), it follows that the 'required' effect of the Directives on the interpretation of tax treaties (under the duty of consistent interpretation and the EU law perspective) seems linked to the 'allowed' effect (under public international law) in the sense that the 'required' effect (under the laws of the EU) essentially follows the 'allowed' effect (under public international law). This link, then, entails that it would not be relevant to draw a distinction between the effect of the Directives on the interpretation of tax treaties under the perspective of public international law and the laws of the EU.

Whereas it would not be relevant to draw a distinction between the 'allowed' (under public international law) and 'required' (under EU law) effect of the Directives on the interpretation of tax treaties, it is relevant for the purposes of this section 9.1 to draw a distinction between the tax treaties whose interpretation may be affected by the Directives (section 9.1.1) and the way in which Directives may affect the interpretation of those treaties whose interpretation may be affected by them (section 9.1.2). Such a distinction reflects the idea that it should first be established whether a Directive may be taken into account as a means of interpretation under Articles 31-33 VCLT 1969,

Article 3(2) OECD Model or Article 2(2) MLI before determining the effect that such a Directive may have on the interpretation of a tax treaty.

### 9.1.1 The Treaties Whose Interpretation May Be Affected by the Directives

The interpretation of bilateral tax treaties is, in principle, governed by Article 3(2) OECD Model (as *lex specialis*) or by the general rule of interpretation of the VCLT 1969 as laid down in Article 31 VCLT 1969 (as *lex generalis*). Depending on the applicable interpretative provision, the number of tax treaties whose interpretation may be affected by the Directives. This can be illustrated as follows.

Under Article 3(2) OECD Model, the starting point is that undefined treaty terms have the meaning of such terms under the laws of the state applying the tax treaty. The reference to the 'laws of that state' has been interpreted in this thesis as meaning the laws in force within the state applying the treaty (and not as merely those laws enacted by a domestic legislator). Such interpretation entails that, based on the status of the Directives in the Member State legal order as part of the laws in force, the Directives, irrespective of their transposition into domestic law by a Member State legislator, can be resorted to for the purposes of giving meaning to undefined treaty terms. As part of the laws of a Member State applying a tax treaty (irrespective of transposition), the Directives can affect the interpretation of both Intra-EU Treaties and Extra-EU Treaties when determining the meaning of undefined terms in such treaties, provided that it is a Member State that would be applying the relevant tax treaty.

In addition to being part of the laws of the Member State applying a tax treaty, the Directives - or the obligation to achieve their result - may also be regarded as part of the 'context' within the meaning of Article 3(2) OECD Model with respect to Intra-EU Treaties and affect the interpretation of such treaties in the capacity as part of the context. While being aware of the lack of consensus among legal scholars concerning the meaning of the term 'context' in Article 3(2) OECD Model, the OECD Commentaries (2017) provide support for regarding the Directives as part of such context. This is due to such Commentaries providing that the context within the meaning of Article 3(2) OECD Model is determined by, in particular, the common intentions of the contracting states at the time of conclusion of the tax treaty, as well by the laws of the other contracting state. Based on the reference to such common intentions, the presumption against conflict with earlier obligations under public international law seems to provide support for regarding - at the time of conclusion: existing - Directives, as decisions of an international organisation, or the obligation to achieve their result under Article 288 TFEU, as part of the context. Pursuant to such a presumption, Member States would be presumed to have had an intention not to derogate from such earlier obligations in connection with the, at the time of conclusion, already existing Directives. It has also been submitted that a presumed common intention, at the time of conclusion, against conflict with pre-existing Directives can be based on the duty of Union loyalty pursuant to which Member States, when concluding a tax treaty, must act in accordance with their obligations under EU law. In addition to referring to the context being determined in particular by the common intentions at the time of conclusion of a tax treaty, the

OECD Commentaries (2017) also refer to the laws of the other contracting state. This reference thus seems to also provide support for regarding Directives as part of the context given that such Directives are part of the laws in force in the Member States.

Whereas the OECD Commentaries (2017) may provide support for regarding the Directives as part of the context within the meaning of Article 3(2) OECD Mode, it should be acknowledged that the effect of the Directives as 'context' is more limited in terms of number - or type - of treaties whose interpretation may be affected (as compared to the Directives as 'laws of that state'). This is because the Directives would only be part of the context within the meaning of Article 3(2) OECD Model, as interpreted in accordance with the OECD Commentaries (2017), to the extent that it relates to Intra-EU Treaties. Hence, the 'contextual' effect of the Directives would not extend to the interpretation of the 1,507 Extra-EU Treaties. The reasons for not extending such effect are that, first, the Directives cannot reflect any (presumed) common intention between a Member State and a third state and, second, that the Directives are not part of the laws of the third state as the 'other contracting state'.

Under Article 31 VCLT 1969, the effect of the Directives on the interpretation of tax treaties concluded by the Member States is also limited to Intra-EU Treaties only. This is because the general rule of interpretation of Article 31 VCLT 1969 seeks to give effect to the common intentions of the parties. This purpose is also reflected by the means that must be taken into account under such rule of interpretation: only means that may reflect the common intentions of the parties. As a consequence, the Directives can only affect the interpretation of the 342 Intra-EU Treaties under Article 31 VCLT 1969.

It follows that the (maximum) number of bilateral tax treaties whose interpretation can be affected by the Directives, per interpretative provision and capacity, can be summarised as follows:

| *Provision* | *Capacity* | *Treaties Affected* | | |
|---|---|---|---|---|
| | | *Intra-EU Treaties* | *Extra-EU Treaties* | *% All Treaties* |
| Article 3(2) OECD Model | 'laws of that State' | 342 | 1507 | 100 |
| | 'context' | 342 | 0 | 18.5 |
| Article 31 VCLT 1969 | 'rules of international law' | 342 | 0 | 18.5 |

**What if the Directives would not qualify as a source of international law?**

*If the Directives would not qualify as a source of international law, this would have two consequences for the effect that they could have on the interpretation of bilateral tax treaties. First, under Article 3(2) OECD Model, the Directives would only qualify as context in their capacity as laws of the other contracting states. They would not reflect common intentions at the time of conclusion of an Intra-EU Treaty in their capacity as 'relevant rules of international law applicable in the relations between the parties'. Second, the Directives cannot be taken into account under Article 31 VCLT 1969. This is because no reference is made to the laws of the contracting states in the general rule of interpretation. As a consequence, the Directives would have no effect on the interpretation of Intra-EU Treaties when resorting to Article 31 VCLT 1969 (in addition to already not having any effect on the interpretation of Extra-EU Treaties if qualifying as a source of international law).*

Finally, with respect to the effect that the Directives may have on the interpretation of the MLI, the following is concluded. The starting point when interpreting the MLI would be Article 2(2) MLI as a *lex specialis* vis-à-vis the rules on the interpretation of treaties of the VCLT 1969. Under Article 2(2) MLI, undefined MLI terms shall have the meaning they have under a covered tax treaty (CTA). If such an undefined MLI term would not be defined in the CTA, reference can be made to the interpretative provision of Article 3(2) OECD Model that is generally part of such a CTA. If reference is made to that interpretative provision, it follows from the conclusions set out above that a Directive would be able to affect the interpretation of undefined terms in a CTA. If a Directive would affect the interpretation of an undefined term in a CTA, such effect could extend to the interpretation of undefined MLI terms via the reference in Article 2(2) MLI to the meaning that such an undefined term has under a CTA. Additionally, if a Directive would affect the interpretation of the undefined MLI term that is part of an Intra-EU Treaty by means of Article 31 VCLT 1969, such effect may also extend to the interpretation of such undefined MLI term if this term in the MLI is interpreted in accordance with Article 2(2) MLI. It should, however, be acknowledged here that a meaning of an undefined MLI term on the basis of a CTA is subject to the context of the MLI requiring otherwise. As such, any effect that a Directive may have on the interpretation of undefined MLI terms via the reference to the meaning that such terms have under a CTA is subject to the context of the MLI requiring otherwise. The Directives may be considered as part of such MLI context if two conditions are met: (i) the provision of the MLI that is being interpreted can be regarded as being of a 'bilateral' nature, and (ii) such a provision would affect an Intra-EU Treaty. If both conditions are met, it is considered conceivable that the Directives can be regarded as part of the context of the MLI with respect to the interpretation of the relevant undefined MLI term. If either condition it not met, i.e., because the 'bilateral' provision relates to an Extra-EU Treaty or because it concerns a 'multilateral' provision of the MLI, the Directives cannot be part of the MLI context due to such Directives not being able to reflect any common intention between the parties to (tax treaty being affected by) the MLI. The distinction between MLI provisions qualifying as 'bilateral' and affecting an Intra-EU Treaty and those that do not is also relevant for the purposes of the effect that the Directives may have under Article 31 VCLT 1969 on the interpretation of the MLI. Under Article 31 VCLT 1969, the Directives may only have an effect on the interpretation of 'bilateral' MLI provisions affecting an Intra-EU Treaty. In all other cases, the Directives would not be applicable in the relations between the parties and, hence, would not qualify as any of the means of interpretation of the general rule of interpretation of Article 31 VCLT 1969.

**What if the Directives would not qualify as a source of international law?**

*Similar to the consequences with respect to the interpretation of bilateral tax treaties, Directives would not be able to qualify as 'context' of 'bilateral' provisions of the MLI affecting an Intra-EU Treaty as a relevant rule of public international law applicable in the relations between the parties. As such, the 'contextual' effect of the Directives under Article 2(2) MLI would be limited to that of domestic legislation in general. Additionally, when interpreting a provision of the MLI in accordance with the general rule of interpretation of the VCLT 1969, the Directives cannot be taken into account as a means of interpretation under Article 31 VCLT 1969. This, in turn, would entail that the Directives cannot have an effect on the outcome of the interpretation of 'bilateral' provisions of the MLI affecting an Intra-EU Treaty under the general rule of interpretation of the VCLT 1969 (in addition to already not having any effect on the interpretation of 'multilateral' MLI provisions and 'bilateral' MLI provisions affecting Extra-EU Treaties if the Directives would have qualify as a source of international law).*

### 9.1.2 The Way in Which the Interpretation of Tax Treaties May Be Affected by the Directives

#### *9.1.2.1 The Directives as … 'Laws of That State' (Article 3(2) OECD Model)*

As 'laws of that State' within the meaning of Article 3(2) OECD Model, Directives may give meaning to, and hence affect the interpretation of, undefined treaty terms, irrespective of whether such a Directive meaning would have been transposed into domestic law. An example of an undefined tax treaty term that may be interpreted by reference to the meaning such term has under a Directive could be the (in the OECD Model) undefined 'beneficial owner' term that is used in, *inter alia*, Articles 11 and 12 of the OECD Model. With respect to interpreting such undefined term in a tax treaty, the starting point would be Article 3(2) OECD Model and its reference to the meaning of the term 'beneficial owner' under the 'law of the state' applying the tax treaty. Such law of the state applying the tax treaty would include if it is a Member State that applies the relevant tax treaty, the definition of the term 'beneficial owner' laid down in Article 1(4) Interest and Royalties Directive, as interpreted by the CJEU in the *Danish Cases*. As part of the laws of the (Member) State applying a tax treaty, the undefined 'beneficial owner' term in a tax treaty could then be given the meaning such term has under the Interest and Royalties Directive (as interpreted by the CJEU).

Whereas the 'beneficial owner' definition of the Interest and Royalties Directive may thus affect the interpretation of the undefined 'beneficial owner' term in tax treaties concluded by the Member States as part of the laws of the Member States, it must be recalled that any meaning on the basis of the laws of the state applying a tax treaty is subject to the context requiring otherwise under Article 3(2) OECD Model. Such context may require otherwise, even with respect to Intra-EU Treaties whose context may include the obligation to achieve the result of a Directive (*see* section 9.1.2.2 below). As such, the circumstance that an undefined tax treaty term would be given the meaning such term has in a Directive, as part of the law of the Member State applying such a tax treaty, does not entail that such a Directive-based meaning must be adopted. One should still determine whether the 'context requires otherwise'.

### 9.1.2.2 *The Directives as … 'Context' (Article 3(2) OECD Model)*

As context within the meaning of Article 3(2) OECD Model, the obligation to achieve the result of the Directives may affect the interpretation of Intra-EU Treaties (section 9.1.1). Such effect could take the form of such obligation providing strong arguments for:

(a) confirming a meaning of an undefined treaty term under the laws of the Member State applying the Intra-EU Treaty that is compliant with the result to be achieved under such Directives (i.e., not requiring otherwise); or
(b) rejecting a meaning of an undefined treaty term under the laws of the Member State applying the Intra-EU Treaty that would be incompatible with the result to be achieved under such Directives (i.e., requiring otherwise).

The (potential) 'contextual' effect that a Directive may have on the interpretation of an Intra-EU Treaty can be illustrated by means of the following example based on the *Schneider Electric* judgment of the French Supreme Court (*Conseil d'État*). In *Schneider Electric*, the French Supreme Court ruled that the term 'profits' in Article 7(1) of the French-Swiss tax treaty had to be interpreted by reference to the meaning such term had under French law. Under such laws, the profits did not include the profits of a Swiss resident-controlled foreign company subsidiary. As such, the profits of the Swiss-controlled foreign company could not be taxed under Article 7(1) of the tax treaty unless the context would have provided otherwise (which it did not). If this interpretation, based on the laws of France as the state applying the treaty, is applied to Article 7(1) of an Intra-EU Treaty anno 2022, the consequence would be that France is still precluded from taxing profits attributable to a controlled foreign entity (and hence cannot achieve the result required by ATAD1). It should, however, be recalled that in *Schneider Electric* the French Supreme Court found that the context did not require otherwise. If, however, the context of an Intra-EU Treaty would include (the obligation to achieve the result of) ATAD1, the result to be achieved by ATAD1 could provide a strong argument for rejecting a meaning on the basis of the laws of France pursuant to which profits of a controlled foreign company would have to be exempt by France because adopting such a meaning would be incompatible with the result to be achieved under the controlled foreign entity rules of ATAD1.

With respect to such a 'contextual' effect of the Directives on the interpretation of Intra-EU Treaties, it should, however, be borne in mind that Article 3(2) OECD Model refers to '*the context requires otherwise*' (singular). As such, it would seem that it needs to be determined whether the context as a whole requires otherwise, which context could comprise of more elements than (the result to be achieved under) the Directives. If the context comprises of more than the Directives, it would seem that it must be assessed on the basis of all contextual elements whether the context as a whole requires a meaning to be adopted or rejected. Such an assessment would then have to be made in good faith without *a priori* attributing decisive weight to the sound arguments derived from the (obligation to achieve the result of the) Directives. The effect that the Directives, as context, may have on the interpretation of Intra-EU

Treaties can thus not be determined in the abstract, but requires an assessment on a case-by-case basis.

#### *9.1.2.3 The Directives as … 'Relevant Rules of International Law Applicable in the Relations Between the Parties' (Article 31 VCLT 1969)*

With respect to the effect of the Directive on the interpretation of Intra-EU Treaties under the general rule of interpretation of Article 31 VCLT 1969, the starting point is that such interpretative rule is aimed at giving effect to the (objectified) common intention of the contracting states with respect to such a treaty. As such, the effect of the Directives would, essentially, be dependent on the extent to which it may be established that they contain indications reflecting such a common intention. Such indications may be derived from both the Directives themselves as well as from the result that is to be achieved by them.

With respect to the Directives themselves, indications regarding a common intention with respect to Intra-EU Treaties may be derived from explicit language in (the preamble or (a) provision(s) of) a Directive addressing its relationship with the tax treaties concluded by the Member States or from similarities between terminology used in a Directive and an Intra-EU Treaty. An example of explicit language in a Directive would, for example, be recital (11) of ATAD2 which provides that adjustments under such Directive 'should in principle not affect the allocation of taxing rights between jurisdictions laid down under a double taxation treaty'. Moreover, Article 8 of the proposal for a CCCTB and Article 11 of the ATAD3 proposal also provide clear indications of the intended effect of such Directive(s) (proposals) vis-à-vis Intra-EU Treaties. In addition to such indications of a common intention with respect to the intended effect of a Directive on Intra-EU Treaties, a common intention as to the ordinary meaning of a term in an Intra-EU Treaty may also be derived from terminology in Directives that is similar to that used in a tax treaty. As such, the definition of the term 'beneficial owner' in the Interest and Royalties Directive, as interpreted by the CJEU, could be deemed to reflect the ordinary meaning of the undefined 'beneficial owner' term in an Intra-EU Treaty if interpreted under Article 31 VCTL 1969.

Additionally, the Directives may be taken into account as reflecting a common intention between the contracting states by means of the result that must be achieved by them. This can, first of all, be the case with respect to Intra-EU Treaties concluded after the adoption of a Directive. Based on the presumption against conflict, which is part of the principle of good faith that must be taken into account when interpreting a tax treaty under Article 31 VCLT 1969, it may be presumed that the Member States did not intend to conclude an Intra-EU Treaty that is incompatible with the result to be achieved under a pre-existing Directive. A presumed common intention to not derogate from pre-existing Directives could also be based on the duty of Union loyalty that provides that Member States, when concluding a tax treaty, must act in accordance with their (pre-existing) obligations under the laws of the EU. At the same time, it would seem arguable that it follows from the duty of Union loyalty that Member States can be presumed to have a general intention to not act contrary to pre-existing as well as future obligations under the laws of the EU. From that point of view, the duty of Union loyalty would provide support for presuming that the Member States also do not intend their Intra-EU Treaties to be incompatible with later Directives. With respect to such presumed common intentions, it should, however, be noted that the presumption against conflict with pre-existing obligations is widely accepted in public international law whereas a general presumption against conflict with, especially future, EU law has not yet been recognised in case law. As such, the general presumption against conflict with EU law would only seem 'conceivable' at present.

Whereas the Directives may provide indications of a common intention between Member States regarding the way in which their Intra-EU Treaties should be applied, it must be acknowledged that the effect of such indications should not be overstated. This is because the indications of a common intention based on the Directives must be weighed against the other means of interpretation referred to in Article 31 VCLT 1969 - ordinary meaning, object and purpose, and other (internal and external) context - in good faith. As such, the effect of the Directives on the interpretation under Article 31 VCLT 1969 depends on, on the one hand, the extent to which the Directives (can be presumed to) reflect common intentions of the Member States with respect to their Intra-EU Treaties and, on the other, the evidence of common intentions between the Member States that would appear from the other elements of interpretation referred to in Article 31 VCLT 1969.

### 9.1.3 The Role of Directives when Interpreting the MLI

With respect to determining the role of the Directives when interpreting provisions of the MLI, a distinction can be drawn between such an interpretation based on Article 2(2) MLI (as *lex specialis*) and Article 31 VCLT 1969 (as *lex generalis*). Under Article 2(2) MLI, Directives can affect the interpretation of an undefined MLI term by means of the reference to the meaning such term has under a covered tax treaty (CTA). As such, if the interpretation of a term in a CTA is affected by a Directive, either by means of Article 3(2) OECD Model or Article 31 VCLT 1969, this would also affect the interpretation of that same term in the MLI under Article 2(2) MLI. Such effect under Article 2(2) MLI via a CTA is, however, subject to the context of the MLI requiring otherwise. With respect to such context, it is conceivable that the Directives would be part of it to the extent that it relates to the interpretation of a provision of the MLI that is 'bilateral' and affects an Intra-EU Treaty. In all other situations, the Directives would not be part of such context. If part of the context of the MLI, the Directives could then require a CTA-based meaning to be either adopted or rejected. Whether this would be the case depends, however, on an assessment of whether the context as a whole, including the Directives, requires otherwise. As such, if the Directives would be part of the context within the meaning of Article 2(2) MLI, this does not entail that it would - at all times - require a Directive-compliant meaning to be given to undefined MLI terms. Instead, the required interpretation by a Directive must be weighed against other elements of the context indicating that a certain interpretation should, or should not, be adopted. Additionally, under Article 31 VCLT 1969, the role of the Directives depends on the provision in question being 'bilateral' and affecting an Intra-EU Treaty. If so, the effect of the Directives under Article 31 VCLT 1969 would be similar to the effect they can have on Intra-EU Treaties. If not, they cannot affect the interpretation of the MLI because the MLI would then have to be regarded as an Extra-EU Treaty. As an Extra-EU Treaty, the Directive would not be applicable in the relations between the parties within the meaning of Article 31(3)(c) VCLT 1969. In that case, the Directives can thus not be taken into account under Article 31 VCLT 1969.

## 9.2 THE EFFECT OF THE DIRECTIVES ON THE APPLICATION OF TAX TREATIES

With respect to answering the question to what extent the Directives may be able to affect the application – in terms of applicability – of tax treaties, a distinction must be drawn between such effect under public international law (section 9.2.2) and under the laws of the EU (section 9.2.3). Such a distinction is necessary because the effect that the Directives may have under the laws of the EU is not 'linked' to the effect that such Directives may have under public international law (as would seem to be the case with respect to the effect of such Directives on the interpretation of tax treaties (section 9.1)). As such, the effect of the Directives on the application of tax treaties under public international law, i.e., the 'allowed' effect, can differ from the effect that such Directives would be required to have under the laws of the EU, i.e., the 'required' effect. Bearing this in mind, the conclusions with respect to the effect of the Directives on the application of tax treaties are set out for each individual perspective first, after first discussing the order in which such perspectives should be resorted to (section 9.2.1). Section 9.2 ends with a comparison of the outcomes under both perspectives (section 9.2.4).

### 9.2.1 The Required 'Conflict' under Public International Law and the Laws of the EU

In setting out the conclusions below regarding the effect of the Directives on the application – in terms of applicability – of tax treaties under both perspectives, the following preliminary observation must be made. Under both perspectives, the Directives would only affect the application of tax treaties if it would be established that such tax treaties conflict with a Directive.

In determining whether such a conflict exists, a distinction must be drawn between a conflict for public international law purposes and a conflict for EU law purposes. This can be illustrated as follows. Under public international law, a conflict would arise if a Directive and a tax treaty give rise to incompatible obligations, such as a duty to tax income (e.g., ATAD1 or ATAD2) and a duty to not tax income (e.g., elimination of double taxation by means of an exemption). By comparison, for the purposes of the laws of the EU, a Directive could only conflict with a tax treaty concluded by a Member State if such Member State fails to achieve the result of such Directive. Such a failure to achieve the result of a Directive requires an assessment of the way in which a Directive has been implemented in the national legal order of a Member State and whether the result of such a Directive is achieved by that Member State. In assessing whether a Member State has achieved such result, the effect of the Directive under public international law on the application of a tax treaty may be relevant. For example, if tax treaties would be superior to national legislation aimed at achieving the result of a Directive, a Member State would, in principle, not be able to achieve the result of such Directive if such a result requires the setting aside of (superior) tax treaties. If, however, the application of such (superior) tax treaties would be affected under the rules of public international in such a way that they are not applicable to the extent such application would be incompatible with a Directive, the legislation aimed at achieving the result of such a Directive would no longer be incompatible with the relevant (superior) tax treaty. In that case, the Member State concerned would be able to achieve the result of a Directive without overriding its tax treaties (because such tax treaties, as a matter of public international law, are inapplicable to the extent they would frustrate achieving the result of the Directive). This effect of the Directives under public international law on the ability of a Member State to achieve the result of a Directive can be illustrated as follows (in addition to the example provided in section 8.2).

> Assume Member State X has transposed Articles 7 and 8 of ATAD1 in its domestic legislation while also having concluded a tax treaty with Member State Y that provides for an exemption of profits attributable to permanent establishments. Assume further that tax treaties, to the extent applicable under public international law, are superior to domestic legislation.
>
> Company A, resident in Member State X has a permanent establishment in Member State Y that qualifies as a controlled foreign company within the meaning of ATAD1. Based on the domestic legislation of Member State X, the non-distributed income of such permanent establishment must be taxed at the level of Company A in Member State X. At the same time, however, Member State X would be obliged to exempt the profits of such permanent establishment under its tax treaty with Member State Y. Based on the superiority of the tax treaty, Member State X exempts the income of the permanent establishment in Member State Y. In that event the result of ATAD1 is not achieved by Member State X. In case of such a failure to achieve the result of ATAD1, the primacy of EU law conflict rule may be resorted to.
>
> If, however, it would be established that as a matter of public international law the tax treaty between Member States X and Y is not applicable to the extent incompatible with ATAD1, there would be no conflict for the purposes of the laws of the EU. This can be illustrated as follows. If the tax treaty with Member State Y is inapplicable to the extent that ATAD1 requires the taxation of non-distributed income attributable to a permanent establishment, the tax treaty cannot be incompatible with national legislation aimed at giving effect to this requirement of ATAD1 because such treaty is inapplicable as a matter of public international law. In such a way, the effect of the Directives under public international law would affect the extent to which a conflict for the purposes of the laws of the EU would arise (and, hence, affects the extent to which the application of a tax treaty may be required to be affected under the primacy of EU law rule).

This example illustrates that the effect that a Directive may have under the rules of public international law on a tax treaty is relevant for the extent to which a Member

State may be able to achieve the result of a Directive notwithstanding the superiority of such treaties over domestic legislation (aimed at implementing a Directive). For that reason, this author adopts the view that it should be assessed first whether a conflict exists under public international law, followed by its resolution. In the event that the application of a tax treaty would not be affected by a Directive in such a way that it allows for the result of the Directive to be achieved, it should then be determined whether the Member State concerned has been able to override such a tax treaty (as a matter of the national laws of such Member State). If the tax treaty's application is overridden by such a Member State, the result of the Directive is achieved. It may, however, be conceivable that Member States would not be able to override tax treaties as a matter of their national (constitutional) law (section 1.4.3). In the event that a tax treaty is not, or cannot be, overridden, the Member State concerned would not be able to achieve the result of a Directive to the extent that such result be incompatible with such tax treaty. It is only in that event, i.e., a Member State cannot achieve the result of a Directive because the national legislation aimed at achieving such result is set aside by a tax treaty under its national (constitutional) law, that a conflict between a tax treaty and a Directive would seem to exist for the purposes of the laws of the EU. As such, it follows that the extent to which a Directive would require the setting aside of a tax treaty is dependent on an assessment of the effect of such a Directive on the application of a tax treaty under public international law and whether the Member State concerned is able to achieve the result of a Directive notwithstanding tax treaties concluded by such Member State (within which context the effect of the Directives on the application of a tax treaty under public international law may be relevant).

### 9.2.2 The Effect of the Directives on the Application of Tax Treaties under Public International Law

With respect to the effect that the Directives may have on the application of tax treaties under public international, the starting point is that a distinction must be drawn between Extra-EU Treaties and Intra-EU Treaties. With respect to Extra-EU Treaties, it follows from the *pacta tertiis* principle that their application shall not be affected by the Directives because third states have not consented to be bound by such Directives, as decisions of an international organisation. The situation of Intra-EU Treaties is different from that of such Extra-EU Treaties because the Member States are bound by, and have expressed their consent (by voting within the Council) to be bound by, the Directives under Article 288 TFEU. As such, the application of Intra-EU Treaties may be affected by the Directives under public international law by the *lex posterior* conflict rule (Article 30 VCLT 1969 (section 9.2.2.1) or an analogous application of Article 30 VCLT 1969 (section 9.2.2.2)) and/or by the 'widely recognised' *lex specialis* conflict rule (section 9.2.2.3).

#### *9.2.2.1 The Effect of the Directives on the Application of Intra-EU Treaties under Article 30 VCLT 1969*

With respect to the effect that the Directives may have under the codified *lex posterior* rule of Article 30 VCLT 1969, it has been concluded in Chapter 6 that such conflict rule cannot result in the Directives affecting the application of Intra-EU Treaties. This is due to the scope of Article 30 VCLT 1969 being limited to successive 'treaties', which treaties must also 'relate to the same subject matter'.

Based on the application of Article 30 VCLT 1969 being limited to successive 'treaties', it does not apply to a conflict between a treaty (an Intra-EU Treaty) and a decision of an international organisation (a Directive) (*see* Chapter 2). Therefore, a conflict between an Intra-EU Treaty and a Directive falls outside the scope of Article 30 VCLT 1969. Whereas a conflict between a Directive, as a decision of an international organisation, and an Intra-EU Treaty falls outside its scope, it is acknowledged that the obligation to achieve the result of a Directive is laid down in Article 288 TFEU, i.e., in a treaty. As such, a conflict between the result to be achieved pursuant to (the provisions of) a Directive and an Intra-EU Treaty can be regarded as qualifying as a conflict between successive treaties within the meaning of Article 30 VCLT 1969 if it is regarded as a conflict between Article 288 TFEU (and not the Directive itself) and an Intra-EU Treaty. If, however, a conflict between a Directive and an Intra-EU Treaty would be regarded as a conflict between the TFEU and an Intra-EU Treaty as successive treaties, it must still be determined whether such treaties relate to the same subject matter. With respect to such sameness of subject matter, it has been concluded that - based on a comparison of the topic and substance of both the TFEU and Intra-EU Treaties in general - they do not relate to the same subject matter. The topic of the TFEU, i.e., the creation of a common market, is not the same as that of Intra-EU Treaties, i.e., eliminating double taxation of cross-border income of residents of the contracting states, by imposing limitations on the right to tax such income, without creating opportunities for non-taxation or reduced taxation through tax avoidance or tax evasion. Given this difference in subject matter, conflicts between (the obligation to achieve the result of a Directive under) Article 288 TFEU and an Intra-EU Treaty would fall outside the scope of Article 30 VCLT 1969. Taking this into account, it follows that the application of Intra-EU Treaties cannot be affected under Article 30 VCLT 1969 by the Directives themselves, as decisions of an international organisation, or by the obligation to achieve their result as laid down in Article 288 TFEU.

#### *9.2.2.2 The Effect of the Directives on the Application of Intra-EU Treaties under an Analogous Application of Article 30 VCLT 1969*

Notwithstanding the conclusion of Chapter 6 that the application of Intra-EU Treaties cannot be affected by the Directives by means of Article 30 VCLT 1969 (section 9.2.2.1), it has also been concluded in Chapter 6 that this author considers it 'arguable' that the application of Intra-EU Treaties can be affected by the Directives under an analogous application of the *lex posterior* rule of Article 30 VCLT 1969. The reason for considering such an analogous application 'arguable' is that the adoption of a Directive can be regarded as relevantly similar to the conclusion of a tax treaty. Such similarity would be based on both the adoption of a Directive and the conclusion of an Intra-EU Treaty requiring - and thus reflecting - the consent to be bound of the Member States. Such similarity could then be considered relevant in light of the purpose of Article 30

VCLT 1969 that it must be presumed that parties intend their latest expression of (legislative) intent to prevail over their earlier (legislative) intent, whereas the difference in form by means of which such intent is expressed would seem irrelevant based on the Intra-EU Treaty and Directive, as a decision of an international organisation, being of equal rank under public international law. Based on these considerations, the adoption of a later Directive and the conclusion of a later Intra-EU Treaty can thus be regarded as relevantly similar, thereby providing support for an analogous application of Article 30 VCLT 1969. Although providing such support, this author does acknowledge that the ICJ, ECtHR, and arbitral tribunals have not (yet) applied Article 30 VCLT 1969 by analogy to conflicts between treaties and later decisions of international organisations (*see* Annex 3). In the absence of such case law, this author concludes that an analogous application of Article 30 VCLT 1969 should only be regarded as 'arguable'.

If applicable by analogy, the *lex posterior* rule of Article 30 VCLT 1969 would be applicable to conflicts between successive Intra-EU Treaties and Directives, as decisions of an international organisation, provided that they relate to the same subject matter. With respect to such sameness of subject matter, it is concluded that this is conceivable with respect to each of the Directives in the sense that there are similarities that would support the conclusion that such Directives relate to the same subject matter as that of an Intra-EU Treaty while there are also differences in topic or substance that might indicate a different subject matter. The extent to which it is conceivable differs, however. The Arbitration Directive, for example, seems to have most common ground with Intra-EU Treaties given that it provides for a mechanism aimed at resolving disputes relating to the interpretation and application of such treaties. This is different for the other Directives given that they do not have such an explicit link with Intra-EU Treaties. This does not, however, entail that they have no aspects in common with Intra-EU Treaties. The Interest and Royalties Directive, Merger Directive and Parent-Subsidiary Directive would, for example, seem to relate to the same purpose as tax treaties, i.e., elimination of double taxation, while providing rules aimed at imposing limitations on the extent to which certain categories of cross-border income may be taxed while the extent to which such income may be taxed may simultaneously be governed by an Intra-EU Treaty. Hence, there would seem to be, at least partial, overlap in the topic or substance of such Directives and that of an Intra-EU Treaty. Similarly, ATAD1 and ATAD2 are aimed at avoiding non-taxation and tax avoidance, which is also an objective of Intra-EU Treaties. These two Directives also provide for rules that apply to situations that are also covered by Intra-EU Treaties. ATAD1 and ATAD2, however, may also be regarded as having a different subject matter because they contain obligations that differ in nature from those arising under Intra-EU Treaties. Such obligations are different from those of Intra-EU Treaties in the sense that they are aimed at extending the corporate tax liability whereas such treaties would only provide for rules limiting the extent to which taxes may be levied. As such, ATAD1 and ATAD2 seem to have common ground with Intra-EU Treaties but, based on the nature of the obligations arising from these two Directives being different from those arising from Intra-EU Treaties, seemingly less common ground than would be the case with respect to the Interest and Royalties Directive, Merger Directive and

Parent-Subsidiary Directive that contain obligations that are similar to those arising under Intra-EU Treaties. Finally, the Mutual Assistance Directive also has common ground with Intra-EU Treaties if such treaties contain a provision similar to Article 26 OECD Model. While there may be similarities between Directives and Intra-EU Treaties, it should be acknowledged that there are also differences in terms of subject matter. For example, Intra-EU Treaties provide for a comprehensive set of rules aimed at eliminating double taxation with respect to, in principle, all categories of cross-border income derived by individuals as well as companies. Hence, the substantive and/or personal topic of such treaties seems wider than those of the Directives (with, it would seem, the exception of the Arbitration Directive). Notwithstanding such wider scope, the aspects that each of the Directives seems to have in common with Intra-EU Treaties would support the conclusion that it is conceivable that they relate to the same subject matter as Intra-EU Treaties.

If it would be concluded that an Intra-EU Treaty relates to the same subject matter as a later Directive, an analogous application of the *lex posterior* rule would entail that such an (earlier) Intra-EU Treaty would not be applicable to the extent incompatible with the later Directive. As such, the application of 270 (pre-Interest and Royalty Directive) to 336 (pre-ATAD2 and pre-Arbitration Directive) Intra-EU Treaties may be affected by the Directives if the *lex posterior* conflict rule of Article 30 VCLT 1969 can be applied by analogy to conflicts between the Directives and Intra-EU Treaties. Whereas the application of pre-Directive Intra-EU Treaties may be affected by the Directives under an analogous application of the *lex posterior* rule, it should also be acknowledged that the application of post-Directive Intra-EU Treaties would not be affected by such Directives. As such, to the extent that a conflict would arise between an earlier Directive and a later Intra-EU Treaty, which conflict should not arise given that a Member State is - as a matter of EU law - precluded from concluding tax treaties that are incompatible with (existing) obligations under EU law, the application of such a later treaty would not be affected by an analogous application of the *lex posterior* conflict rule.

### *9.2.2.3 The Effect of the Directives on the Application of Intra-EU Treaties under the* Lex Specialis *Rule*

In addition to the effect that the Directives may have on the application of Intra-EU Treaties under an analogous application of the *lex posterior* conflict rule of Article 30 VCLT 1969, the application of such treaties may also be affected under public international law by the 'widely recognised' *lex specialis* conflict rule. The starting point with respect to the application of the this conflict rule is that it has been confirmed by the ICJ that it can be applied with respect to conflicts between different sources of public international law that are of equal rank, i.e., customary international law and treaties. Taking this application of the *lex specialis* rule into account, it seems arguable that conflicts between other equally ranked sources of public international law, such as treaties and decisions of international organisations, also fall within its scope.

If falling within its scope, the *lex specialis* conflict rule could result in the Directives affecting the application of Intra-EU Treaties in the event of a conflict between their provisions. In order to affect the application of an Intra-EU Treaty, it should be established, first, that the provision of a Directive conflicting with a provision of an Intra-EU Treaty relates to the same topic or substance. This condition would seem likely to be met in the event of a conflict between a Directive providing for the taxation of income and an Intra-EU Treaty requiring the non-taxation of that same income. For example, the controlled foreign company rules of ATAD1 would seem to relate to the taxation of profits attributable to a permanent establishment, whereas Article 7 in conjunction with Article 23 of an Intra-EU Treaty based on the OECD Model would also seem to relate to such topic. If it is established that the conflicting provisions of a Directive and Intra-EU Treaty relate to the same topic or substance, it should be determined which provision reflects more closely, precisely and/or strongly the consent of the Member States with respect to a given situation. Given that, generally, the Directives have a more limited substantive and personal scope as compared to Intra-EU Treaties, it would seem likely that provisions of Directives can be regarded as more closely, precisely or strongly reflecting the intentions of the Member States (as compared to such intentions based on an Intra-EU Treaty) with respect to the subject matter covered by both such a Directive and an Intra-EU Treaty. If regarded as more closely, precisely or strongly reflecting such intentions, the Directive can be regarded as the *lex specialis* vis-à-vis the Intra-EU Treaty as the *lex generalis*. Under the *lex specialis* conflict rule, the consequence would then be that the Intra-EU Treaty (as *lex generalis*) would be inapplicable to the extent incompatible with a Directive (as *lex specialis*).

#### *9.2.2.4 Summary of the Effect of the Directives on the Application of Tax Treaties under Public International Law*

With respect to the effect of the Directives on the application of tax treaties under public international law, a distinction must be made between Intra-EU Treaties and Extra-EU Treaties. With respect to the effect of Directives on the application – in terms of applicability – of Intra-EU Treaties, it follows from the conclusions set out in sections 9.2.2.1 through 9.2.2.3 that it is considered arguable that the application of Intra-EU Treaties can be affected by the Directives under public international law by means of either an analogous application of the *lex posterior* conflict rule of Article 30 VCLT 1969 or under the *lex specialis* conflict rule. Such an effect is, however, only considered 'arguable' because this author has not found any case law of the ICJ, ECtHR or an arbitral tribunal wherein the *lex posterior* or *lex specialis* conflict rule has been applied to conflicts between a treaty and a decision of an international organisation. If it is assumed that such conflict rules can be applied to such conflicts, it should be acknowledged – in terms of their importance – that they seek to resolve conflicts based on presumed intentions between the parties (in case of an Intra-EU Treaty: the Member States). As such, it would seem that their application is subject to indications of a different intention between the Member States with respect to resolving conflicts between Intra-EU Treaties and Directive, which intentions may be laid down in, for example, conflict clauses in the treaty and/or Directive itself.

**What if the Directives would not qualify as a source of international law?**

*If the Directives would not qualify as a source of international law, they cannot fall within the scope of an analogous application of Article 30 VCLT 1969 or the lex specialis conflict rule. As such, the consequence would be that the application of none of the Intra-EU Treaties would be affected under the rules of public international law. This would then entail that the application of both Intra-EU and Extra-EU Treaties would not be 'allowed' to be affected by the Directives under public international law.*

### 9.2.3 The Effect of the Directives on the Application of Tax Treaties under the Laws of the EU

As indicated in section 9.2.1, the effect of the Directives on the application of tax treaties under the laws of the EU is dependent upon a Member State not being able to achieve the result of a Directive, which may be due to such Member State incorrectly transposing the relevant Directive into national law or due to national laws not being able to set aside (superior) tax treaties. In the event that a Member State fails to achieve the result of a Directive, a conflict arises in respect of which the primacy of EU law conflict rule applies. Such primacy of EU law conflict rule then provides for the following resolution of a conflict between a Directive and, for present purposes, a tax treaty: all tax treaties concluded by a Member State must be set aside with a view to ensuring that the obligations under EU law are complied with.

With respect to the primacy of EU law conflict rule, two exceptions apply. First, (rights and obligations of) tax treaties falling within the scope of Article 351 TFEU shall not be affected by the primacy of EU law. As such, they fall outside the scope of the primacy of EU law conflict rule (section 9.2.3.1). Second, with respect to those treaties falling within the scope of the primacy of EU law, such primacy must be enforceable. If not enforceable, the application of a tax treaty that is incompatible with the result of a Directive cannot be affected by the primacy of EU law conflict rule and, therefore, cannot be set aside by means of such primacy (section 9.2.3.2).

#### *9.2.3.1 The Scope of the Primacy of EU Law*

As mentioned in the previous section, the scope of the primacy of EU law is limited by Article 351 TFEU. Pursuant to Article 351 TFEU, rights and obligations arising from pre-accession Extra-EU treaties 'shall not be affected by the provisions of the EU Treaties', including thus the Directives. The scope of Article 351 TFEU thus de facto determines the extent to which the application of tax treaties may be affected by the Directives by the primacy of EU law. Whether a treaty right or obligation falls within such can be established as follows.

First, it must be established whether the tax treaty concerns an Intra-EU or Extra-EU Treaty. This is necessary because Article 351 TFEU only applies to Extra-EU

Treaties. Hence, treaty obligations laid down in the 342 Intra-EU Treaties fall within the scope of the primacy of the Directives. Second, it would have to be determined whether an Extra-EU Treaty falls within the temporal scope of Article 351 TFEU. In that respect, it has been concluded that Article 351 TFEU is limited to those Extra-EU Treaties that have been concluded before accession of the Member State concerned to the EU and does not apply (by analogy) to post-accession, pre-Directive Extra-EU Treaties.

Third, and finally, if an Extra-EU Treaty falls within the scope of (an analogous application) of Article 351 TFEU, it must be established whether the primacy of the Directive would result in the rights of, and obligations towards, third states being affected. In this context, it can be noted the setting aside of provisions of tax treaties imposing limitations on the right to tax income would generally affect such rights of, and obligations towards, third states.

#### *9.2.3.2 The Scope of the Enforceability of the Primacy of EU Law*

With respect to those rights and obligations under tax treaties that fall outside the scope of Article 351 TFEU, the primacy of the Directives applies. This entails that such rights and obligations must be set aside if that would ensure that the result of a Directive (provision) is achieved, provided that the primacy of such a Directive (provision) is enforceable in a Member State. With respect to such enforceability, two cumulative conditions apply. First, the relevant Directive provision that is relied upon with a view to setting aside a tax treaty in accordance with the primacy of EU law conflict rule must have direct effect. As such, the Directive provision must be clear, unconditional, and not contingent on any discretionary implementing measures. Second, if directly effective, the result of the setting aside of a tax treaty does not result in the imposition of an obligation on the taxpayer concerned (due to the prohibition of reverse vertical direct effect). As such, the primacy of the Directives is, essentially, only enforceable to the extent that the setting aside of a tax treaty would be beneficial for a taxpayer. This second condition regarding the enforceability of the primacy of Directives seems of particular relevance with respect to those (recent) Directives that seek to increase the tax burden of taxpayers, such as ATAD1 and ATAD2. In the event of a conflict between a Directive's obligation to tax income and a tax treaty's obligation to not tax that same income, the primacy of such a Directive cannot be enforced and, as such, be relied upon. As a result of such non-enforceability, the primacy of provisions of Directives imposing a duty to tax is thus not capable of affecting the application of incompatible tax treaty provisions; such primacy can thus be described as a 'toothless tiger'.

#### *9.2.3.3 Summary of the Effect of the Directives on the Application of Tax Treaties under the Laws of the EU*

In summary, in the event that a Member State is not able to achieve the result of a (provision of a) Directive due to a tax treaty, the laws of the EU provide for a simple conflict rule: all laws of the EU, including a Directive, have primacy over all national law, including, from the perspective of the EU, tax treaties, of the Member States.

Whereas this conflict rule provides a clear starting point regarding the effect of the Directives on the application of tax treaties, it is not applicable to those (rights and obligations of) tax treaties falling within the scope of Article 351 TFEU ('Article 351 TFEU Treaties'). As such, in determining the effect of the Directives on the application of tax treaties, a distinction must be drawn, as a first step, between Article 351 TFEU Treaties and non-Article 351 TFEU Treaties. Only the application of non-Article 351 TFEU Treaties can be affected by the Directives under the laws of the EU.

With respect to those non-Article 351 TFEU Treaties to which the primacy of EU law conflict rule applies, it must be assessed whether the primacy of a Directive is enforceable. This requires an assessment of (i) the nature of the Directive provision and (ii) the effect of the setting aside of the non-351 TFEU Treaty for a taxpayer. With respect to the requirement under (i), it follows from case law of the CJEU that the primacy of Directive provisions is only enforceable if they are directly effecting i.e., such provisions must be clear, unconditional, and not contingent on any discretionary implementation measures. If a Directive's provision would be directly effective, this does not, however, in and of itself entail that its primacy is enforceable. This is due to the settled case law of the CJEU that the setting aside of national law, including treaties concluded by the Member States, on the basis of the primacy of a Directive's provision is not allowed to result in the imposition of an obligation on a taxpayer. As such, it must be determined, with respect to directly effective provisions of a Directive, whether the setting aside of a non-351 TFEU Treaty would result in the imposition of an obligation on the taxpayer (requirement (ii)). If the setting aside does not result in the imposition of an obligation on a taxpayer, the primacy of a Directive is enforceable; if it does result in imposing such an obligation the primacy if not enforceable due to the prohibition of reverse vertical direct effect.

The non-enforceability of the primacy of Directive provisions imposing an obligation on taxpayers entails that Directives such as ATAD1 and ATAD2 cannot, under the primacy of EU law conflict rule, affect the application of tax treaties concluded by the Member States. As such, although ATAD1 and ATAD2 would be supreme vis-à-vis incompatible tax treaties, such superior status cannot result in the non-applicability of such tax treaties. In other words: such Directives would not – under the primacy of EU law conflict rule – be able to affect the application of tax treaties concluded by the Member States.

This finding is of particular relevance in light of the conclusion in section 1.4.3 that tax treaties are superior to national legislation in the majority of the Member States. If such superiority extends to national legislation aimed at implementing a Directive, such as ATAD1 and ATAD2, the majority of the Member States would not be able to achieve the result of (provisions of) Directives that are aimed at increasing the tax liability of taxpayers to the extent that such result requires the inapplicability of a (from a Member State perspective: superior) tax treaty (after having determined the applicability of such tax treaty from the public international law perspective). The non-achievement of the result of the Directive would then, in principle, give rise to a conflict to which the primacy of the Directive would be applicable. Such primacy would, however, not be enforceable due to the setting aside of a tax treaty resulting in a higher tax burden for the taxpayer. This non-enforceability then entails that the result of a Directive is not achieved until, essentially, the tax treaty is amended (or the superiority of the tax treaty under national law is amended so as to not apply with respect to national legislation aimed at implementing a Directive). Until such amendment, however, the majority of the Member States would not seem able to achieve the result of (a provisions of) a Directive that is aimed at increasing the tax burden of taxpayers such as ATAD1 and ATAD2, by means of national legislation because the application of the (from a Member State: superior) tax treaties cannot be affected by the Directive under the laws of the EU (notwithstanding the superiority of such Directive under the perspective of the EU). The same considerations apply with respect to the on 31 October 2022 pending ATAD3 Proposal, to the extent requiring the disregarding of Intra-EU Treaties, and Pillar 2 Proposal, to the extent requiring the taxation of income. The majority of the Member States would not seem able to achieve their result due to the superiority of their tax treaties vis-à-vis national legislation aimed at implementing such Directive proposals nor would such Directive proposals be able to set aside tax treaties of the Member States due to the prohibition of reverse vertical direct effect. The consequence would then be that achievement of the result of Directives aimed at increasing the tax burden of taxpayers in a way that requires the setting aside of tax treaties, can only be achieved if Member States amend such tax treaties (or amend their superior status under the Member State perspective).

## CHAPTER 10
# Recommendations

It follows from Chapter 9 that there may be situations wherein a Directive cannot affect the application of a tax treaty in such a way that application of such a treaty allows for the result of such Directive to be achieved. With respect to Intra-EU Treaties, this would especially be the case if a Directive requires a result that requires an increase of the tax liability of a taxpayer whereas such an increase of tax liability would be incompatible with the obligations arising from an Intra-EU Treaty. In such a situation, the result of a Directive is not achieved as a result of the (continued) application of an Intra-EU Treaty under the rules of public international law and the laws of the EU. In section 10.1, recommendations are formulated with a view to ensuring that the application of an Intra-EU Treaty is affected in such a way that its application cannot conflict with, and as such jeopardise achieving the result of, a Directive.

With respect to Extra-EU Treaties, it follows from Chapter 9 that their application cannot be affected under the rules of public international law. Under the laws of the EU, the same applies with respect to (pre-accession) Extra-EU Treaties falling within the (temporal and substantive) scope of Article 351 TFEU. Pursuant to this provision of the TFEU, the rights of, and obligations towards, third states shall also not be affected by the Directives under the laws of the EU. As such, the effect of the Directives on the application of pre-accession Extra-EU Treaties, to the extent that it concerns the rights of, and obligations towards, third states, under the laws of the EU, i.e., none, is identical to the effect that such Directives would have under public international law, i.e., none. Whereas the effect of the Directives is identical with respect to (rights and obligations of) Extra-EU Treaties that fall within the scope of Article 351 TFEU, this is not, in principle, the case for those (rights and obligations of) Extra-EU Treaties falling outside the scope of Article 351 TFEU. Under the laws of the EU, the application of such latter treaties can be affected. This is due to such Extra-EU Treaties being subject to the primacy of conflict rule and, as such, having to be set aside by the laws of the EU, including the Directives, to the extent that their application would be incompatible with the result to be achieved under a directly effective provision of a Directive (provided such primacy does not result in the imposition of an obligation on the taxpayer). It thus follows that the scope of Article 351 TFEU, essentially, determines the extent to which the effect of the Directives on Extra-EU Treaties under the laws of the EU can exceed the effect of such Directives under public international law. With respect to such scope, it follows from Chapter 9 that an analogous application of Article 351 TFEU must be rejected. Taking into account, however, that the Commission has adopted the view that Directives should only affect post-Directive Extra-EU Treaties under Article 351 TFEU,[814] section 10.2 provides recommendations aimed at clarifying the extent to which a Directive would be intended to affect the application of Extra-EU Treaties in light of the rejection of an analogous application of Article 351 TFEU. This chapter ends with a comment on the combined effect of the recommendations set out in sections 10.1 and 10.2 (section 10.3).

## 10.1 RECOMMENDATIONS WITH RESPECT TO INTRA-EU TREATIES

Whereas the *lex posterior* and *lex specialis* conflict rules of public international law may be able to affect the application of Intra-EU Treaties in such a way that they are only applicable to the extent compatible with the Directives, such application is only considered 'arguable'. As such, it cannot be excluded such conflict rules of public international law would not be able to, at all times, ensure that Intra-EU Treaties are inapplicable to the extent required for achieving the result of a Directive. Hence, the rules of public international law may not be able to ensure that Intra-EU Treaties cannot jeopardise achievement of the result of a Directive. Taking into account that Intra-EU Treaties may thus (continue to) stand in the way of achieving the result of a Directive, the following two recommendations are made:

(a) The conclusion of a multilateral treaty between all Member States that provides that all, at that time concluded, Intra-EU Treaties shall apply in so far as compatible with the Directives (or EU law in general).
    A draft multilateral treaty to that effect, based on the multilateral treaty concerning the termination of bilateral investment treaties, has been included in Annex 4. The conclusion of such a multilateral treaty providing for the priority of the Directives over pre-existing Intra-EU Treaties would ensure that such Intra-EU Treaties are only applicable under public international law to the extent compatible with present and future Directives.
(b) The inclusion of a subordination clause in each future Intra-EU Treaty. Such a clause would then grant priority to Directives (or EU law in general) in the event that the provisions of the Intra-EU Treaty would be incompatible with the obligations arising from a Directive (or EU law in general). A draft subordination clause, based on the subordination clauses in Hungarian tax treaties, is provided below:

814. *See* Room Document # 1, Working Party on Tax Questions – Direct Taxation, Proposal for a CCCTB of 15 January 2013, p. 7.

*'The provisions of this treaty shall apply to the extent that they are compatible with any present or future obligation arising from membership of either Contracting State of the European Union.'*

The inclusion of such a subordination clause would ensure that each Intra-EU Treaty would not be applicable, under public international law, to the extent incompatible with earlier as well as later (obligations relating to the) Directives. As such, Member States would ensure that the obligations arising from Intra-EU Treaties under public international law would not be able to prevent them from complying with their obligations under EU law. The result would then be that the Directives - or EU law in general - would be de facto superior, under public international law, to Intra-EU Treaties containing such a subordination clause.[815]

These recommendations, if implemented together, would ensure that Intra-EU Treaties are only applicable to the extent compatible with the (result of the) Directives as a matter of public international law. As a consequence, there would be no need to rely on the 'arguable' analogous application of the *lex posterior* conflict rule of Article 30 VCLT 1969 or the 'arguable' application of the *lex specialis* conflict rule in order to ensure that, as a matter of public international law, Intra-EU Treaties are inapplicable to the extent required for the purposes of achieving the result of a Directive. Instead, the inapplicability of such treaties would be provided for by the provisions of the Intra-EU Treaties themselves (as affected by the multilateral treaty set out in Annex 4). As such, if both recommendations were implemented, it would be ensured that Intra-EU Treaties would not, or no longer, be able to jeopardise achievement of the result of the Directives.

815. It is acknowledged that subordination clauses may also be relevant for Extra-EU Treaties. The inclusion of a subordination clause in Extra-EU Treaties would, for example, ensure that - present or future - Extra-EU Treaties providing for an exemption with respect to income that must be taxed under a Directive would be inapplicable. As such, a subordination clause in an Extra-EU Treaty would also ensure that the application of such treaties is affected in such a way that the result of the Directives would be achieved at all times. Notwithstanding the relevance of subordination clauses with respect to Extra-EU Treaties, it should be acknowledged that the inclusion of such a clause would de facto allow for future EU law legislation to override pre-existing Extra-EU Treaties. From the perspective of third states, this outlook may not be very attractive, especially given the fact that their consent is not required for the adoption of such future EU law legislation. Hence, third states may not be willing to agree to a subordination clause. The situation of Member States with respect to a subordination clause in their Intra-EU Treaties is different. First, Member States must have expressed their consent to a Directive before it can be adopted. Hence, they can influence the extent to which a Directive would require the inapplicability of their Intra-EU Treaties. Second, contracting states to an Intra-EU Treaty are both required to achieve the result of a Directive. As such, both contracting states would have an interest in including a subordination clause. This is different or third states given that they are under no obligation to achieve the result of a Directive or to ensure that the Member State is able to achieve such result.

## 10.2 RECOMMENDATIONS WITH RESPECT TO EXTRA-EU TREATIES

With respect to the effect of the Directives on the application of Extra-EU Treaties, it has been concluded that only (rights of, and obligations towards, third states under) pre-accession Extra-EU Treaties shall not be affected by the (primacy of the) Directives. It follows, however, from room documents that the Commission Services – within the context of the CCCTB proposal (2011) – expressed the view that post-accession, pre-Directive Extra-EU Treaties would also not be affected by the CCCTB directive. It was explicitly noted in such documents that it 'has been accepted that the ambit of the rule [of Article 351 TFEU] extends to the entire body of EU law which exists at a certain point in time (i.e., acquis Communautaire). It follows that, to examine the status of a DTC between a Member State and a third country under the CCCTB, one shall first check whether the DTC pre-dates the adoption of the CCCTB Directive in Council'.[816] In light of the rejection of such an (analogous) application of Article 351 TFEU in this thesis, this author recommends that future Directive(s) (proposals) contain a clause explicitly addressing the extent to which a Directive is intended to affect treaties concluded with third states. For that purpose, it is recommended to include the following clause into Directives:

> **Article X.I.**
>
> **Relationship with tax treaties concluded with third states prior to the adoption of this Directive**
>
> This Directive does not apply to the extent that it would affect the rights of, and obligations towards, third states under international agreements concluded by the Member States before the date of adoption of this Directive.

Article X.I is based on the assumption that a Directive would be intended to affect the application of later Extra-EU Treaties. It is, however, conceivable that a Directive would also be intended to, ultimately, affect earlier Extra-EU Treaties. If that is the case, a Directive provision could be inserted that resembles the second paragraph of Article 351 TFEU. With respect to this second paragraph, it has been concluded that it does not contain a clear deadline for taking the appropriate steps. Such a deadline could therefore be inserted in a Directive. As such, a provision resembling the second paragraph of Article 351 TFEU could be added to Article X.I, which would then read as follows:

> **Article X.I**
>
> **Relationship with international agreements concluded with third states**
>
> 1. This Directive does not apply to the extent that it would affect the rights of, and obligations towards, third states under international agreements concluded by the Member States before the date of adoption of this Directive.

816. *See* Room Document # 1, Working Party on Tax Questions – Direct Taxation, Proposal for a CCCTB of 15 January 2013, p. 7.

2. Without prejudice to paragraph 1, the Member States shall take the appropriate steps, including denunciation of tax treaties with third states, to ensure that the Directive is effective in the relations with all third states before [date].

Whereas the previous recommendations were based on the assumption that a Directive should affect later Extra-EU Treaties, it is conceivable that no such intention exists. This has, for example, been the case with respect to the Significant Digital Presence Directive proposal. Article 2 of such Directive proposal provided that it would only apply to an Extra-EU Treaty if such a treaty 'includes provisions similar to Articles 4 and 5 of this Directive'. Moreover, a more specific intention to not affect earlier as well as later Extra-EU Treaties may be derived from Article 9(5) ATAD2. This provision stipulates that a Member State is not required to tax income attributable to a disregarded permanent establishment if 'the Member State is required to exempt the income under a double taxation treaty entered into by the Member State with a third country'. Article 9(5) ATAD2, similar to Article 2 of the Significant Digital Presence Directive proposal, refers to Extra-EU Treaties in general and, as such, does not draw a distinction between earlier and later Extra-EU Treaties. In the absence of such a distinction, a Directive (provision) seems to indicate that it is not intended to affect the rights of and obligations towards, third states under both existing and future Extra-EU Treaties. If it would indeed have been the intention of such Directive proposal or such Directive to not have an effect on both existing and future Extra-EU Treaties, it might have been more clear to confirm this intended effect in a more explicit way. The benefit of such an explicit confirmation would be that it indicates that Member States would be authorised to, for example, conclude Extra-EU Treaties providing for an exemption of profits attributable to a disregarded permanent establishment, which confirmation would now only seem implicit based on the wording of Article 9(5) ATAD2. If, however, a Directive would be intended to preclude the conclusion of such a treaty, it is recommended to include Article X.I because it follows explicitly from such provision that post-Directive Extra-EU Treaties should be affected by the Directive. Alternatively, if it is intended that a Directive should affect none of the Extra-EU Treaties, Article X.II below could be adopted. This provision would, effectively, provide for wider protection than Article 351 TFEU. Whereas Article 351 TFEU merely provides that the rights of, and obligations towards, third states under pre-accession Extra-EU Treaties shall not be affected by, in this case, a Directive, Article X.II essentially extends such protection to all, pre-accession and post-accession, as well as all pre-Directive and post-Directive, Extra-EU Treaties. As such, Article X.II would not preclude Member States from concluding Extra-EU Treaties that, for example, provide for an exemption of profits attributable to a disregarded permanent establishment.

**Article X.II**

**Relationship with international agreements concluded with third states**

This Directive does not apply to the extent that it would affect the rights of, and obligations towards, third states under international agreements concluded by the Member States before as well as after the adoption of this Directive.

The recommended Articles X.I and X.II would provide the Commission, as the organ having the (exclusive) right to put forward proposals for Directives,[817] with a toolbox that allows it to clarify the way in which a Directive is intended to affect Extra-EU Treaties. If it would make use of such toolbox, there would no longer be uncertainty as to the 'required' effect of a Directive on the application of Extra-EU Treaties. If it is intended that a Directive should not affect pre-Directive Extra-EU Treaties only, Article X.I could be included in a Directive proposal. If a Directive should, ultimately, also affect situations covered by pre-Directive Extra-EU Treaties, it could specifically provide for a deadline before which Member States must have amended (or terminated) such Extra-EU Treaties. Finally, if a Directive is not intended to affect the application of Extra-EU Treaties at all, Article X.II could be inserted.

## 10.3 REFLECTION ON THE EFFECT OF THE RECOMMENDATIONS

If the recommendations set out in sections 10.1 and 10.2 were adopted, the consequence would be that tax treaties concluded by the Member States would no longer be able to jeopardise achievement of the result of a Directive. This can be illustrated as follows.

If the recommendations of section 10.1 would be implemented, each conflict between obligations under an Intra-EU Treaty and a Directive would be resolved – under public international law – by granting priority to the Directive. As such, the application of each Intra-EU Treaty would be affected by the Directives – under public international law – to the extent that its application would be incompatible with the result to be achieved under such Directives. This, in turn, would seem to entail that the question of whether tax treaties are superior vis-à-vis national legislation aimed at implementing a Directive becomes irrelevant. This is due to such tax treaty being inapplicable to the extent required by the Directive that such national legislation seeks to implement. Hence, the recommendations of section 10.1 with respect to Intra-EU Treaties would ensure that all Member States would be able to achieve the result of the Directives, irrespective of the superiority of such treaties in their national legal orders. In other words, the recommendations of section 10.1 would ensure that Intra-EU Treaties can no longer jeopardise the achievement of the result of a Directive by the Member States.

If the recommendations of section 10.2 were implemented, to the extent that it concerns Article X.I, it would be ensured that Directives do not require Member States to violate the rights of or obligations towards, third states under pre-Directive Extra-EU Treaties.[818] This, in turn, entails that conflicts cannot arise between a pre-existing Extra-EU Treaty and a Directive (because the result to be achieved under such Directive does not apply to the extent that it would affect the rights of or obligations towards, third states under pe-existing Extra-EU Treaties). In the absence of such a conflict, Member States would be able to comply with both the Directives and the pre-Directive

817. *See*, to this effect, Article 289 TFEU in connection with Article 115 TFEU.
818. The same applies with respect to Article X.II. Such Article X.II would, however, also extend to post-Directive Extra-EU Treaties.

Extra-EU Treaty at the same time notwithstanding that a Directive would also be intended to relate to situations that may fall within the scope of Extra-EU Treaties in general.

Adopting Article X.I in Directives does not, however, prevent any conflicts from arising between Extra-EU Treaties and Directives. This is due to post-Directive Extra-EU Treaties falling outside its scope. The starting point, from the perspective of the laws of the EU, would, however, be that such conflicts should not arise because Member States are precluded from concluding Extra-EU Treaties that are incompatible with their obligations under the laws of the EU. Therefore, such conflicts should, in principle, not arise. If, however, conflicts would arise, the recommended Article X.I does not protect post-Directive Extra-EU Treaties. In light of the purpose of the Directive, as follows from Article X.I, being aimed at affecting such Extra-EU Treaties, this would not, however, seem to raise any issues from the perspective of the EU. By concluding an incompatible post-Directive Extra-EU Treaty, the Member State concerned would have violated its obligations under the laws of the EU. As such, Article X.I would not be able to prevent any international responsibility from arising under Extra-EU Treaties, but it would at the very least clarify with respect to which type of Extra-EU Treaties, i.e., post-Directive Extra-EU Treaties, such responsibility may arise. As such, the Directive would at least provide explicit evidence of its intended effect vis-à-vis Extra-EU Treaties as opposed to leaving such effect open.

In sum, the recommendations of section 10.1 are aimed at ensuring that the application of Intra-EU Treaties is affected by a Directive to the extent required for achievement of the result of such a Directive while the recommendations of section 10.2 are aimed at clarifying the extent to which the application of Extra-EU Treaties shall not be affected by the Directives. If both recommendations are implemented, the consequence would be that the application of Intra-EU Treaties would, at all times, be compatible with the result to be achieved under the Directives while it is also clear that, in principle, Extra-EU Treaties should not be affected by the Directives (either due to the Directive providing that such treaties shall not be affected or due to Member States being precluded from concluding such Extra-EU Treaties).

# Appendices

## Annex 1

# Overview of the EU Tax Treaty Network

## 1 INTRODUCTION

For the purposes of various sections of this thesis, the timing of the conclusion of a tax treaty as compared to accession to the EU or adoption of a Directive may be relevant (*see*, to that extent, sections 3.2.2.3 (Article 3(2) OECD Model), 3.4.2.2.2 (Article 31(3)(c) VCLT 1969), 6.4.2 (Article 30 VCLT 1969) and 7.2.2.1 (Article 351 TFEU)). Based on such relevance, and in the absence of a study – at least to the present author's knowledge – regarding the order of conclusion of a tax treaty, accession to the EU and adoption of a Directive, the present author has studied such order for the purposes of this thesis. The purpose of such study was to provide insight into the relative importance, reflected by the number of treaties that would be 'earlier' or 'later', of the 'timing' or 'sequence' questions with respect to the various rules discussed in this thesis. Annex 1 sets out the methodology used for such purpose (section 2), as well as the findings resulting from the application of such methodology (section 3).

## 2 METHODOLOGY

- The relevant tax treaties have been identified by means of the IBFD Tax Treaty Database (14 June 2022). In this database, the tax treaties concluded by the Member States have been identified by means of the following general filters: '*Treaty Subject: Income/Capital*', and '*Treaty status: In Force*'. With such filters, the filter '*Country/Jurisdiction*' has been used to only search for the tax treaties concluded by the Member States. Application of these filters has resulted in 1,849 tax treaties in force on 14 June 2022.[819]

819. *See* tab: 'Annex 1 | Directives', cell: 'C7' in the excel file that can be accessed via https://doi.org/10.17026/dans-zku-ckqy.

- In order to be able to determine the order of conclusion of the identified tax treaties, accession of the Member State(s) to the European Union, and adoption of the Directives (that are currently in force), the starting point has been the year in which a tax treaty (in force on 14 June 2022) or an accession treaty, including for these purposes the Treaty of Rome,[820] has been signed and the year of adoption of a Directive by the Council.[821] The reason for adhering to these dates, as opposed to, for example, the entry into force of the tax treaty, accession treaty, and the Directive, is that signing and adoption reflect the moment on which the intention to be bound by the relevant treaty, agreement, or Directive has been expressed.
- In determining whether a tax treaty is 'earlier' as compared to an accession treaty or a Directive, it has been assumed that this would be the case if the tax treaty has been concluded in any year prior to the year in which such agreement was signed or the Directive adopted. As such, if a tax treaty has been signed in the same year as an accession treaty would have been signed, or a Directive would have been adopted, it is regarded as 'later' as compared to such an agreement or Directive. The rationale for adopting this assumption is that negotiations regarding accession to the European Union or adoption of a Directive usually take quite some time, entailing that the (future) Member State(s) was (were) aware – at the time of conclusion of the tax treaty – of its future EU commitments.
- Amendments to the tax treaties in force on 14 June 2022 by means of protocols or other means, have not been considered for the purposes of determining the order of such treaties, accession to the European Union, and the adoption of Directives. This is due to such amendments generally not going as far as replacing substantial parts of the tax treaties. As such, it would seem safe to assume that the tax treaty as originally concluded remains unchanged for the most part.
- All items of information were manually coded in an excel database freely available online through DANS, the Netherlands Centre of Expertise and Repository for Research Data.[822]

820. The relevant years are thus: 1957 (Treaty of Rome concluded by Belgium, France, Germany, Italy, Luxembourg, and the Netherlands), 1972 (accession Denmark and Ireland), 1979 (accession Greece), 1985 (accession Spain and Portugal), 1994 (accession Austria, Finland and Sweden), 2003 (accession Czech Republic, Cyprus, Estonia, Latvia, Lithuania, Hungary, Malta, Poland, Slovenia, and Slovak Republic), 2005 (accession Bulgaria and Romania), and 2011 (accession Croatia).
821. The relevant years, for the Directives currently in force, are 2003 (Interest and Royalties Directive (2003/49/EC)), 2009 (Merger Directive (2009/133/EC)), 2011 (Mutual Assistance Directive (2011/16/EU) and Parent-Subsidiary Directive (2011/96/EU)), 2014 (amendment of Parent-Subsidiary Directive (2014/96/EC)), 2015 (amendment of Parent-Subsidiary Directive (2015/121 (EU)), 2016 (ATAD1 (EU) 2016/1164), and 2017 (ATAD2 (EU) 2017/952) and Arbitration Directive ((EU) 2017/1852).
822. DANS, The Effect of Directives in the Area of Direct Taxation on the Interpretation and Application of Tax Treaties, https://doi.org/10.17026/dans-zku-ckqy. As entries were manually coded, all errors in the database are the author's only.

# 3 RESULTS

## 3.1 Intra-EU Treaties and Extra-EU Treaties

| *Intra-EU Treaties and Extra-EU Treaties* | | |
|---|---|---|
| | *Number of Treaties* | *% of Total Treaties* |
| Intra-EU Treaties | 342 | 18.5 |
| Extra-EU Treaties | 1507 | 81.5 |
| | 1849 | 100.0 |

The first distinction that can be drawn is between those tax treaties concluded with other Member States (so-called Intra-EU Treaties) and third states (so-called Extra-EU Treaties). This distinction is especially helpful in demonstrating the relevance of, for example, the Directives when interpreting tax treaties as (i) context within the meaning of Article 3(2) OECD Model (section 3.2.3.1), (ii) context of Article 2(2) MLI (section 3.3), and as relevant rules of international law applicable in the relations between the parties (section 3.4.2.2.2), as well as for the relevance of such Directive within the context of its effect on the application of a tax treaty (*see* section 6.4).

## 3.2 Pre-accession and Post-accession Tax Treaties

| *Pre-accession and Post-accession Treaties* | | | | | |
|---|---|---|---|---|---|
| | *Number of Total Treaties* | *Pre-accession Treaties* | | *Post-accession Treaties* | |
| | | *Number of Treaties* | *% of Total Treaties* | *Number of Treaties* | *% of Total Treaties* |
| Intra-EU Treaties | 342 | 233 | 68.1 | 109 | 31.9 |
| Extra-EU Treaties | 1,507 | 413 | 27.4 | 1,094 | 72.6 |
| | 1,849 | 646 | 34.9 | 1,203 | 65.1 |

The second distinction that is drawn is that between tax treaties concluded before accession (so-called pre-accession treaties) and after accession of a state to the EU (so-called post-accession treaties). Based on such distinction, it can be established whether the duty of Union loyalty and the general obligation to achieve the results of directives (either under Article 189 Treaty of Rome or, after its replacement, (now) Article 288 TFEU) has arisen before or after the conclusion of a tax treaty. This is relevant for sections 3.2.2.3 (Article 3(2) OECD Model), 3.4.2.2.2 (Article 31 VCLT 1969), 6.4.2.2.1 (Article 30 VCLT 1969), and 7.3.3.2 (Article 351 TFEU).

### 3.3 Pre-Article 288 TFEU and Post-Article 288 TFEU Tax Treaties

Based on section 6.2.1.1.1, the relevant treaty for the purposes of determining whether the obligation to achieve the result of a Directive is 'successive' to a tax treaty is not necessarily the accession treaty. This is due to Article 189 Treaty of Rome having been replaced by (now) Article 288 TFEU in 1992 by means of the Treaty of Maastricht. Hence, a conflict between the obligations relating to the Directives and a tax treaty, is to be regarded as a conflict with the Treaty of Maastricht and not the Treaty of Rome. This entails that, for the purposes of Article 30 VCLT 1969, a distinction should be drawn between 'pre-Article 288 TFEU tax treaties' and 'post-Article 288 TFEU tax treaties'.

*Earlier and Later Treaties as Compared to Article 288 TFEU*

| | | *Pre-288 TFEU* | | *Post-288 TFEU* | |
|---|---|---|---|---|---|
| | *Number of Treaties* | *Number of Treaties* | *% of Total Treaties* | *Number of Treaties* | *% of Total Treaties* |
| Intra-EU Treaties | 342 | 251 | 73.4 | 91 | 26.6 |
| Extra-EU Treaties | 1,507 | 626 | 41.5 | 881 | 58.5 |
| | 1,849 | 877 | 47.4 | 972 | 52.6 |

### 3.4 Tax Treaties as 'Earlier' Vis-à-Vis the Directives

#### *3.4.1 Intra-EU Treaties as 'Earlier' Vis-à-Vis Accession or the Directives (Analogous Application of Article 30 VCLT 1969)*

In section 6.4.2.2.5, it is concluded that an analogous application of Article 30 VCLT 1969 is 'arguable' (or: 'conceivable'). In order to demonstrate the relevance of such conclusion versus a 'regular' application of Article 30 VCLT 1969, this section provides an overview of the number of Intra-EU Treaties that are 'earlier' as compared to a Directive (based on its date of adoption). The starting point in this respect is that an Intra-EU Treaty will, in any event, be 'earlier' if it concerns a pre-accession treaty. This is due to the circumstance that such treaties have been concluded by states that, at the time of such conclusion, were not yet Member States and, as such, not bound by the Directives. They only became bound by such Directives after the conclusion of an accession agreement. With respect to such pre-accession treaties, it thus follows that they are – irrespective of the date of adoption of a Directive – 'earlier' as compared to (becoming bound to) the Directives. With respect to the remaining post-accession Intra-EU Treaties, the table below sets out the number of additional post-accession Intra-EU Treaties that have been concluded before each relevant Directive ('# (additional) earlier treaties'), as well as the total number of Intra-EU Treaties concluded before each relevant Directive ('cumulative').

| *Number of Intra-EU Treaties 'Earlier' for Analogous Application of Article 30 VCLT 1969* | | | |
|---|---|---|---|
| | *(Additional) Earlier Treaties* | *Cumulative* | *% of Total Treaties* |
| Pre-accession Intra-EU Treaties | 233 | 233 | 68.1 |
| Interest and Royalties Directive (2003/49/EC) | 37 | 270 | 78.9 |
| Merger Directive (2009/133/EC) | 35 | 305 | 89.2 |
| Mutual Assistance Directive (2011/16/EU) and Parent-Subsidiary Directive (2011/96/EU) | 6 | 311 | 90.9 |
| Parent-Subsidiary Directive (2014/96/EU) | 16 | 327 | 95.6 |
| Parent-Subsidiary Directive (2015/121 (EU)) | 2 | 329 | 96.2 |
| ATAD1 ((EU) 2016/1164) | 4 | 333 | 97.4 |
| ATAD2 ((EU) 2017/952) and Arbitration Directive ((EU) 2017/1852) | 3 | 336 | 98.2 |

### *3.4.2 Intra-EU Treaties as 'Earlier' Vis-à-Vis Article 288 TFEU or the Directives (Analogous Application of Article 30 VCLT 1969)*

Whereas section 3.4.1 in Annex 1 focused on determining the number of Intra-EU Treaties concluded before accession of the Directives, this section aims to provide the same overview for the number of Intra-EU Treaties concluded before (now) Article 288 TFEU or the Directives (*see* section 3.3 of Annex 1).

| *Number of Intra-EU Treaties 'Earlier' for Analogous Application of Article 30 VCLT 1969* | | | |
|---|---|---|---|
| | *Number of (additional) Earlier Treaties* | *Cumulative* | *% of Total Treaties* |
| Pre-Article 288 TFEU Intra-EU Treaties | 251 | 251 | 73.4 |
| Interest and Royalties Directive (2003/49/EC) | 19 | 270 | 78.9 |
| Merger Directive (2009/133/EC) | 35 | 305 | 89.2 |
| Mutual Assistance Directive (2011/16/EU) and Parent-Subsidiary Directive (2011/96/EU) | 6 | 311 | 90.9 |

| Number of Intra-EU Treaties 'Earlier' for Analogous Application of Article 30 VCLT 1969 | | | |
|---|---|---|---|
| | *Number of (additional) Earlier Treaties* | *Cumulative* | *% of Total Treaties* |
| Parent-Subsidiary Directive (2014/96/EU) | 16 | 327 | 95.6 |
| Parent-Subsidiary Directive (2015/121 (EU)) | 2 | 329 | 96.2 |
| ATAD1 ((EU) 2016/1164) | 4 | 333 | 97.4 |
| ATAD2 ((EU) 2017/952) and Arbitration Directive ((EU) 2017/1852) | 3 | 336 | 98.2 |

### *3.4.3 Extra-EU Treaties as 'Earlier' Vis-à-vis the Directives (Analogous Application of Article 351 TFEU)*

In section 7.2.2.1.2, an analogous application of Article 351 TFEU has been discussed. The table below seeks to provide an understanding of the relevance of an analogous application of Article 351 TFEU in terms of treaties 'protected' from the primacy of each Directive.

The starting point in determining this number is the number of post-accession Extra-EU Treaties (*see* section 7.2.2.1). Under an analogous application of Article 351 TFEU, post-accession Extra-EU Treaties would also be 'protected' from the primacy of the Directives if they are concluded before the date of adoption of a Directive. The table below sets out the number of additional treaties that would be 'protected' by the rule of Article 351 TFEU in the event of an analogous application of this provision:

| Number of Extra-EU Treaties 'Earlier' for Analogous Application of Article 351 TFEU | | | |
|---|---|---|---|
| | *Number of (Additional) Earlier Treaties* | *Cumulative* | *% of Total Treaties* |
| Pre-accession Extra-EU Treaties | 441 | 441 | 27.4 |
| Interest and Royalties Directive (2003/49/EC) | 443 | 884 | 58.7 |
| Merger Directive (2009/133/EC) | 214 | 1,098 | 72.9 |
| Mutual Assistance Directive (2011/16/EU) and Parent-Subsidiary Directive (2011/96/EU) | 119 | 1,217 | 80.8 |
| Parent-Subsidiary Directive (2014/96/EU) | 48 | 1,265 | 83.9 |

| *Number of Extra-EU Treaties 'Earlier' for Analogous Application of Article 351 TFEU* | | | |
|---|---|---|---|
| | *Number of (Additional) Earlier Treaties* | *Cumulative* | *% of Total Treaties* |
| Parent-Subsidiary Directive (2015/121 (EU)) | 75 | 1,340 | 88.9 |
| ATAD1 ((EU) 2016/1164) | 29 | 1,369 | 90.8 |
| ATAD2 ((EU) 2017/952) and Arbitration Directive ((EU) 2017/1852) | 47 | 1,416 | 94.0 |

## ANNEX 2

# Overview of Amendments to Extra-EU Treaties

### 1 INTRODUCTION

The present thesis addresses the effect of the Directives on the interpretation and application of tax treaties. It follows from section 7.2.2.1.3 that it may be relevant in this respect whether a pre-accession Extra-EU Treaty has been amended after the accession of the relevant Member State to the EU. The present section seeks to provide an overview of the amendments to such Extra-EU Treaties, as in force on 14 June 2022, by means of (i) bilateral amendments (section 2) and (ii) amendments by means of the MLI (section 3).

### 2 METHODOLOGY

- The relevant tax treaties have been identified by means of the IBFD Tax Treaty Database (14 June 2022). In this database, the tax treaties concluded by the Member States have been identified by means of the following general filters: '*Treaty Subject: Income/Capital*', and '*Treaty Status: In Force*'. With such filters, the filter '*Country/Jurisdiction*' has been used to only search for the tax treaties concluded by the Member States. Application of these filters has resulted in 1,849 tax treaties in force on 14 June 2022.[823]
- From these 1,849 tax treaties, 1,507 have been concluded by a Member State and a third state (*see* Annex 1, section 3.1).
- From these 1,507 Extra-EU Treaties, 441 tax treaties have been concluded prior to the accession of the Member State (section 3.2).

823. *See* tab: 'Annex 1 | Directives', cell: 'C7' in the excel file that can be accessed via https://doi.org/10.17026/dans-zku-ckqy.

- With respect to each of these 441 pre-accession Extra-EU Treaties, it has been determined whether it has been amended. Bilateral amendments have been based on the IBFD Tax Treaty Database. The criterion for a bilateral amendment was whether such database provides the following with respect to a treaty: '(*as amended through [year]'*). For amendments by means of the MLI, the relevant criterion has been whether the IBFD Tax Treaty Database provided that the MLI was *'in effect'* on 14 June 2022.
- With respect to the 64 pre-accession Extra-EU Treaties that have been amended bilaterally, it has furthermore been assessed whether such amendment took place before or after accession of the relevant Member State to the EU. An amendment has been considered as having occurred before accession if the relevant protocol or other means of amendment has been signed before the year of accession. As such, any such amendment in the year of accession is considered as a post-accession amendment.
- All items of information were manually coded in an excel database freely available online through DANS, the Netherlands Centre of Expertise and Repository for Research Data.[824]

## 3 RESULTS

Based on the methodology adopted above, it follows that of the 66 pre-accession Extra-EU Treaties that have been amended, 55 have been signed after the accession of the relevant Member State to the EU. As such, it is with respect to such 55 pre-accession Extra-EU Treaties that the nature of the amendments, as well as the negotiations themselves, may be relevant in light of the *Open Skies* judgments as discussed in section 7.2.2.1.3. With respect to the 148 pre-accession Extra-EU Treaties that have been amended by the MLI, the same applies because the MLI was signed after the most recent accession treaty in 2011.

824. DANS, The Effect of Directives in the Area of Direct Taxation on the Interpretation and Application of Tax Treaties, https://doi.org/10.17026/dans-zku-ckqy. As entries were manually coded, all errors in the database are the author's only.

ANNEX 3

# Overview *Lex Posterior* and Sources of Public International Law

## 1 INTRODUCTION

In section 6.4.2.2.1, it is submitted that there is no case law of the ICJ, ECtHR and arbitral tribunals confirming an application of the *lex posterior* rule to conflicts between (earlier) treaties and (later) decisions of international organisations. This Annex 3 sets out the methodology adopted for the purposes of ascertaining whether the ICJ, ECtHR and arbitral tribunals applied the *lex posterior* rule to such conflicts (section 2), as well as the results of adopting such methodology (section 3).

## 2 METHODOLOGY

(i) For the purpose of identifying judgments of the ICJ, ECtHR or an arbitral tribunal wherein the *lex posterior* rule would have been applied to conflicts between a treaty and a decision of an international organisation, the assumption has been made that such courts or tribunals would have made reference to the term '*lex posterior*'.

(ii) The rationale for this assumption is that a conflict between a treaty and a decision of an international organisation falls outside the wording of Article 30 VCLT 1969 and that, for that reason, the ICJ, ECtHR or an arbitral tribunal would refer to the broader principle of '*lex posterior derogat legi priori*' or, at least, to the principle '*lex posterior*'.

(iii) Based on the assumption that the ICJ, ECtHR or an arbitral tribunal would have referred to the term '*lex posterior*', this term – between quotation marks – has been used as the relevant search term for the purposes of identifying judgments wherein the *lex posterior* rule would have been applied to conflicts between a treaty and a decision of an international organisation.

(iv) Having established the relevant search term, a search has been performed with this term in the following databases:
- for the ICJ: https://www.icj-cij.org/advanced-search;
- for the ECtHR: https://hudoc.echr.coe.int/eng#;
- for arbitral tribunals: https://www.italaw.com/search/site.[825]

(v) The search performed in the database of the ICJ for '*lex posterior*', under the '*exact word or phrase*', gave rise to 32 results (on 14 September 2022); the search performed in the database of the ECtHR for '*lex posterior*', under '*Text*', gave rise to 31 results (on 14 September 2022); the search performed in the database for arbitral tribunals for '*lex posterior*' gave rise to 71 results (on 14 September 2022).

(vi) With respect to each of these 134 results, the following results have been eliminated for the purposes of determining whether the ICJ, ECtHR or an arbitral tribunal would have used the term '*lex posterior*' within the context of a conflict between a treaty and a decision of an international organisation:
- the result was published in a language other than English (or Dutch);[826]
- the result did not concern a judgment or decision of the ICJ, ECtHR or arbitral tribunal but, for example, a report of a public hearing or documents submitted by (one of the) parties.[827]

(vii) After application of these filters, 7 judgments of the ICJ, 18 of the ECtHR and 46 judgments of arbitral tribunals remained. With respect to each of such judgments, it has then been determined within which context reference has been made to the term '*lex posterior*'. The outcome of such determination is set out in section 3.

## 3 RESULTS

### 3.1 ICJ

Based on analysis of the paragraphs of the seven judgments of the ICJ wherein reference is made to the term '*lex posterior*', the following picture emerges:

825. The reason for using https://www.italaw.com/search/site has been that this database allows for full text searches. The database of the ICSID (https://icsid.worldbank.org/cases/case-database) does not seem to allow for full text searches given that application of the search term '*lex posterior*' results in '*Case count: 0*'.
826. Application of this filter entailed that 7 ICJ results, 18 ECtHR, and 5 arbitral tribunal results had to be eliminated.
827. Application of this filter entailed that 19 additional ICJ results (12 results reflecting oral proceedings and 6 reflecting written proceedings), 0 ECtHR results, and 12 arbitral tribunal results (2 surrejoinders, 1 counter-memorial, 1 affirmation, 1 excerpts of award, 1 expert declaration, 1 expert opinion, 1 affidavit, 1 notice of petition to confirm, 1 respondent's reply, 1 statement of dissent) had to be eliminated.

| *Reference to* Lex Posterior *in the Context of:* | *Number of Judgments Wherein the Reference Is Made* | *Sources of (Public) International Law* |
|---|---|---|
| A treaty and (unilateral) declarations of states within the meaning of Article 36(2) ICJ Statute[828] | 4 | Treaty and (coincidental) unilateral declarations of state consent |
| A (system of a) treaty and (the system of) the UN Charter | 2 | Two (systems of) treaties |
| General remark that *lex specialis* and *lex posterior* are metanorms of conflict resolution | 1 | None |

The table illustrates that the ICJ has not referred to the term *lex posterior* in the context of treaties and decisions of international organisations. It does seem, however, that the ICJ has made such references in the context of different sources of public international law, i.e., in the context of a treaty and unilateral declarations under Article 36(2) ICJ Statute. With respect to the four results wherein references are made to the term *lex posterior* in such context, the following can be noted. First, in the judgment regarding *Maritime Delimitation in the Indian Ocean (Somalia v. Kenya)*, the reference to the term '*lex posterior*' relates to an argument made by Kenya in connection with a reservation made in respect of its declaration within the meaning of Article 36(2) ICJ Statute, made on 19 April 1965.[829] In such reservation, Kenya accepted the jurisdiction of the ICJ over all disputes arising after 12 December 1963 other than disputes in regard to which the parties to the dispute have agreed or shall agree to have recourse to some

828. The legal status of declarations within the meaning of Article 36(2) ICJ Statute seems to be not clear-cut. They have been described by the ICJ, 26 November 1984 (*Nicaragua v. United States of America*), Jurisdiction of the Court and Admissibility of the Application, p. 419, para. 59 as 'facultative, unilateral engagements that States are absolutely free to make or not to make'. This is also recognised by C. Tomuschat in: The Statute of the International Court of Justice: A Commentary (3rd Edition) (Zimmermann, Tams, Oellers-Frahm & Tomuschat eds), 2019, para. 73 who notes that declarations under Article 36(2) ICJ Statute 'are by essence unilateral acts, issued under the authority of State sovereignty'. Bearing this unilateral nature in mind, it can still be argued that 'to the extent that the declarations coincide, a consensual bond is formed between the States concerned which fulfils the general requirement for the exercise of jurisdiction by the [ICJ] …' (C. Tomuschat in: The Statute of the International Court of Justice: A Commentary (3rd Edition) (Zimmermann, Tams, Oellers-Frahm & Tomuschat eds), 2019, para. 73). The unilateral declarations within the meaning of Article 36(2) ICJ Statute do not, however, seem to necessarily qualify as 'treaties' or 'international agreements'. Tomuschat (para. 73) notes, for example, that they resemble 'to some extent a multilateral treaty', whereas R. Kolb, 2013, p. 456 considers such declarations as 'complex acts and not simple bilateral or multilateral agreements'.

829. *See* ICJ, 2 February 2017, Preliminary Objections (Maritime Delimitation in the Indian Ocean (*Somalia v. Kenya*), Judgment, p. 10, para. 1. For completeness' sake, Somalia made its declaration on 11 April 1963.

other method or methods of settlements.[830] According to Kenya, the conclusion of UNCLOS by, *inter alia*, Kenya and Somalia on 10 December 1982 constituted a later agreement between Kenya and Somalia to have recourse to some other method of settlement. In order to substantiate such argument, Kenya put forward the argument that the UNCLOS should take priority over the declarations within the meaning of Article 36(2) ICJ Statute because it is, *inter alia*, the *lex posterior* as compared to such declarations. The ICJ did not agree, however. It held that the wording of the reservation indicated that '*whether a particular agreement between the Parties falls within Kenya's reservation does not turn on the degree of specificity or the date of that agreement, but must be answered by examining the content of the particular agreement*'.[831] As such, the ICJ rejected the application of the *lex posterior* conflict rule to the situation of unilateral declarations within the meaning of Article 36(2) ICJ Statute and a later treaty in this case due to the wording of the relevant declaration. Given that such rejection was based on the wording of the reservation in the unilateral declaration of Kenya, it would seem that this judgment does not indicate a principal ruling on the question of whether a later treaty can, or cannot, take priority over earlier unilateral declarations within the meaning of Article 36(2) ICJ Statute under the *lex posterior* rule.

The second reference to *lex posterior* is found in a dissenting opinion of Judge Robinson in *Maritime Delimitation in the Indian Ocean (Somalia v. Kenya)*. In this opinion, Judge Robinson states that he agrees with '*the majority's rejection in paragraph 120 of Kenya's argument that its reservation "attaches special significance to an agreement to a method of dispute settlement that is lex specialis and lex posterior in relation to the Parties' optional clause declarations".*' The reference to *lex posterior* in this dissenting opinion thus occurs within the context of the judgment of the ICJ and, therefore, does not reflect a decision on the question of whether the *lex posterior* rule could have been applicable to the situation of a later treaty and unilateral declarations within the meaning of Article 36(2) ICJ Statute.

The third and fourth references to the term *lex posterior* by the ICJ appear in the judgment of the ICJ in *Territorial and Maritime Dispute (Nicaragua v. Colombia)* and the summary thereof. In this judgment, the term *lex posterior* is used within the context of the argument Colombia that the so-called Pact of Bogotá, the American Treaty on Pacific Settlement, should take precedence over declarations made by Nicaragua and Colombia within the meaning of Article 36(2) ICJ Statute and would, therefore, constitute the ICJ's title of jurisdiction.[832] In response to this argument, the ICJ ruled that the Pact of Bogotá, as well as on the basis of the declarations within the meaning of Article 36(2) ICJ Statute, '*represent two distinct bases of the Court's jurisdiction which are not mutually exclusive*'.[833] As such, the ICJ did not rule on the question of whether

830. Regarding such reservation, *see* ICJ, 2 February 2017, Preliminary Objections (Maritime Delimitation in the Indian Ocean (*Somalia v. Kenya*), Judgment, p. 17, para. 31.
831. *See* ICJ, 2 February 2017, Preliminary Objections (Maritime Delimitation in the Indian Ocean (*Somalia v. Kenya*), Judgment, p. 47, para. 120.
832. *See* ICJ, 13 December 2007 (Territorial and Maritime Dispute (*Nicaragua v. Colombia*)), Preliminary Objections, Judgment, p. 42, paras 125-126.
833. ICJ, 13 December 2007 (Territorial and Maritime Dispute (*Nicaragua v. Colombia*)), Preliminary Objections, Judgment, p. 45, para. 136.

the Pact of Bogotá took priority over the earlier declarations within the meaning of Article 36(2) ICJ Statute as *lex posterior*. Instead, it assessed whether it had jurisdiction under both the Pact of Bogotá as well as under such declarations. In that respect, the ICJ concluded that it had neither jurisdiction under the Pact of Bogotá or Article 36(2) ICJ Statute due to there being no legal dispute between the parties.[834]

Whereas it might have seemed, at first glance, that the ICJ has made reference to the term *lex posterior* in the context of different sources of public international law, i.e., in the context of a treaty and unilateral declarations under Article 36(2) ICJ Statute, the analysis above reveals that it has not applied the *lex posterior* rule to conflicts between such sources. As such, these cases do not provide support for concluding that the ICJ has applied the *lex posterior* conflict rule to conflicts between different sources of public international law.

## 3.2 ECtHR

Based on analysis of the paragraphs of the 18 judgments of the ECtHR wherein reference is made to the term '*lex posterior*', the following results can be presented regarding the context wherein reference is made to such term:

| *Reference to* Lex Posterior *in the Context Of:* | *Number of Judgments Wherein the Reference Is Made* | *Sources of (Public) International Law* |
|---|---|---|
| Provisions of national law | 13 | None |
| Provisions of national law and a treaty (under domestic law) | 5 | Treaty and no source of public international law |

It follows from this table that the ECtHR has not referred to the term *lex posterior* in the context of conflicts between two sources of public international law. As such, it has not referred to the term *lex posterior* in the context of a treaty and a decision of an international organisation.

## 3.3 Arbitral Tribunals

Based on an analysis of the paragraphs of the 46 judgments of arbitral tribunals wherein reference is made to the term '*lex posterior*', the following results emerge regarding the context wherein reference is made to such term:

834. ICJ, 13 December 2007 (Territorial and Maritime Dispute (*Nicaragua v. Colombia*)), Preliminary Objections, Judgment, p. 46, para. 138.

| *Reference to* Lex Posterior *in the Context Of:* | *Number of Judgments Wherein the Reference Is Made* | *Sources of (Public) International Law* |
|---|---|---|
| Energy Charter Treaty and (accession to) the EU Treaties | 25 | Two treaties |
| Bilateral Investment Treaty and (accession to) the EU Treaties | 16 | Two treaties |
| ICSID Convention and (accession to) the EU Treaties | 1 | Two treaties |
| Bilateral Investment Treaty and a contract by a company with a government | 4 | Treaty and no source of public international law |

It follows from this table that arbitral tribunals have not referred to the term *lex posterior* within the context of treaties and decisions of international organisations. Additionally, it also follows from this table that arbitral tribunals have not referred to the term *lex posterior* in the context of two different sources of public international law. It has either referred to such term with respect to two treaties or within the context of a treaty and a contract between a company and a government, which contract does not qualify as a source of public international law.

## 4 CONCLUSION

It follows from the preceding sections 3.1 through 3.3 that, based on the methodology set out in section 2, the ICJ, ECtHR and arbitral tribunals have not applied the *lex posterior* rule to conflicts between treaties and decisions of international organisations. They also indicate that the *lex posterior* rule has not been applied by such courts and tribunals to conflicts between different sources of public international law.

Annex 4

# Draft Agreement for the Amendment of Intra-EU Treaties

**AGREEMENT**

for the amendment of Bilateral Tax Treaties between the Member States of the European Union

THE CONTRACTING PARTIES,
THE KINGDOM OF BELGIUM,
THE REPUBLIC OF BULGARIA,
THE CZECH REPUBLIC,
THE KINGDOM OF DENMARK,
THE FEDERAL REPUBLIC OF GERMANY,
THE REPUBLIC OF ESTONIA,
THE HELLENIC REPUBLIC,
THE KINGDOM OF SPAIN,
THE FRENCH REPUBLIC,
THE REPUBLIC OF CROATIA,
THE ITALIAN REPUBLIC,
THE REPUBLIC OF CYPRUS,
THE REPUBLIC OF LATVIA,
THE REPUBLIC OF LITHUANIA,
THE GRAND DUCHY OF LUXEMBOURG,
HUNGARY,
THE REPUBLIC OF MALTA,
THE KINGDOM OF THE NETHERLANDS,
THE REPUBLIC OF POLAND,
THE PORTUGUESE REPUBLIC,
ROMANIA,
THE REPUBLIC OF SLOVENIA and

THE SLOVAK REPUBLIC

HAVING in mind the Treaty on European Union (TEU) and the Treaty on the Functioning of the European Union (TFEU) and general principles of Union law,

HAVING in mind the rules of customary international law as codified in the Vienna Convention on the Law of Treaties (VCLT),

RECALLING that the Court of Justice of the European Union (CJEU) held in Case C-478/07 Budějovický Budvar that provisions laid down in an international agreement concluded between two Member States cannot apply in the relations between those two States if they are found to be contrary to the EU Treaties,

RECOGNISING that provisions of bilateral tax treaties between the Member States of the European Union (intra-EU bilateral tax treaties) contain clauses that may be contrary to provisions of directives adopted in the field of direct taxation,

CONSIDERING that some of the directives in the field of taxation are aimed at limiting the benefits of intra-EU bilateral tax treaties for individuals,

RECALLING that the CJEU has also held in Joined Cases C-115/16, C-118/16, C-119/16 & C-299/16 N Luxembourg 1 that the principle of legal certainty precludes directives from being able by themselves to create obligations for individuals and therefore from being capable of being relied upon per se by the Member State as against individuals.

CONSIDERING that not applying an intra-EU bilateral tax treaty in the relations between two Member States on the basis of that it is contrary to a directive is precluded by the principle of legal certainty if the non-application of the intra-EU bilateral tax treaty is detrimental for an individual,

RECOGNISING that without amendments of intra-EU bilateral tax treaties, the achievement of the result of provisions of directives in the field of direct taxation is jeopardised,

SHARING the common intention to not apply intra-EU bilateral tax treaties to the extent such application would jeopardise the achievement of the result of directives in the field of direct taxation,

CONSIDERING that the references to the European Union in this Agreement are to be understood also as references to its predecessor, the European Economic Community and, subsequently, the European Community, until the latter was superseded by the European Union,

HAVE AGREED UPON THE FOLLOWING PROVISIONS

**Section 1**

**Definitions**

For the purposes of this Agreement, the following definitions shall apply:

a) 'Intra-EU Bilateral Tax Treaty' means any tax treaty listed in Annex A;
b) 'VCLT' means the Vienna Convention 1969, done in Vienna at 23 May 1969.

## Section 2

***Provisions regarding the amendment of intra-EU bilateral tax treaties***

*Article 2*

*Amendment of intra-EU bilateral tax treaties*

1. Intra-EU Bilateral Tax Treaties, as concluded before the date of this Agreement, shall apply only to the extent that their provisions are compatible with any obligation arising from membership of the European Union of the Contracting Parties.
2. It is understood that any obligation arising from membership of the European Union of the Contracting Parties includes any obligation arising from legal acts of the Union referred to in Article 288 of the TFEU.
3. This Agreement shall constitute, with respect to each individual intra-EU bilateral tax treaty, a successive treaty relating to the same subject matter within the meaning of Article 30 of the VCLT.

## Section 3

**Final provisions**

*Article 3*

*Depositary*

1. The Secretary-General of the Council of the European Union shall act as Depositary of this Agreement.
2. The Secretary-General of the Council of the European Union shall notify the Contracting Parties of:
   (a) any decision on provisional application in accordance with Article 9;
   (b) the deposit of any instrument of ratification, acceptance or approval in accordance with Article 7;
   (c) the date of entry into force of this Agreement in accordance with Article 8(1);
   (d) the date of entry into force of this Agreement for each Contracting Party in accordance with Article 8(2).
3. The Secretary General of the Council of the European Union shall publish the Agreement in the *Official Journal of the European Union.*

*Article 4*

*Annex*

The annex to this Agreement constitutes an integral part thereof.

*Article 5*

*Reservations*

No reservations shall be made to this Agreement.

*Article 6*

*Dispute settlement*

1. Disputes between the Contracting Parties concerning the interpretation or application of this Agreement shall, if possible, be settled amicably.
2. If a dispute between the Contracting Parties cannot be settled amicably within 90 days, the dispute shall, on the request of one of the Contracting Parties to the dispute, be submitted to the CJEU in accordance with Article 273 TFEU.
3. For greater certainty, this Article constitutes a special agreement between the Contracting Parties within the meaning of Article 273 TFEU.

*Article 7*

*Ratification, approval or acceptance*

This Agreement shall be subject to ratification, approval or acceptance.

The Contracting Parties shall deposit their instruments of ratification, approval or acceptance with the Depositary.

*Article 8*

*Entry into force*

1. This Agreement shall enter into force 30 calendar days after the date on which the Depositary receives the second instrument of ratification, approval or acceptance.
2. For each Contracting Party which ratifies, accepts or approves it after its entry into force in accordance with paragraph 1, this Agreement shall enter into force 30 calendar days after the date of deposit by such Contracting Party of its instrument of ratification, approval or acceptance.

*Article 9*

*Provisional application*

1. The Contracting Parties, in accordance with their own constitutional requirements, may decide to apply this Agreement provisionally. The Contracting Parties shall notify the Depositary of any such decision.
2. When both parties to an intra-EU bilateral tax Treaty have decided to apply this Agreement provisionally, the provisions of this Agreement shall apply in respect of that Treaty 30 calendar days from the date of the later decision on provisional application.

*Article 10*

*Authentic texts*

This Agreement, drawn up in a single original in the Bulgarian, Croatian, Czech, Danish, Dutch, English, Estonian, French, German, Greek, Hungarian, Italian, Latvian, Lithuanian, Maltese, Polish, Portuguese, Romanian, Slovak, Slovenian and Spanish languages, the text in each of these languages being equally authentic, shall be deposited in the archives of the Depositary.

# Bibliography

Adamczyk, Ł. & Majdanska, A., The Sources of EU Law Relevant for Direct Taxation in: Introduction to European Tax Law on Direct Taxation (Lang, M., Pistone, P., Schuch, J. & Staringer, C., eds), Wien: Linde Verlag 2014.

Alvarez, J.E., International Organizations as Law-Makers, Online: Oxford University Press 2005.

Ariginelli, P., Multilingual Tax Treaties: Interpretation, Semantic Analysis and Legal, Online: IBFD 2015.

Ariginelli, P., The ATAD and Third Countries in: The External Tax Strategy of the EU in a Post-BEPS Environment (Jiménez, A.M., ed.), Online: IBFD 2019.

Arnull, A., What Is a General Principle of EU Law? in: Prohibition of Abuse of Law: A New General Principle of EU Law? (De la Feria, R. & Vogenauer, S., eds), Oxford: Hart Publishing 2011.

Arnold, B.J., International Tax Primer, Alphen aan den Rijn: Kluwer Law International 2019.

van Asselt, H., 'Managing the Fragmentation of International Environmental Law: Forests at the Intersection of the Climate and Biodiversity Regimes', New York University Journal of International Law and Politics 2012/4.

Aust, A., Modern Treaty Law and Practice, Cambridge: Cambridge University Press 2013.

Avella, F., 'Using EU Law to Interpret Undefined Tax Treaty Terms: Article 31(3)(c) of the Vienna Convention on the Law of Treaties and Article 3(2) of the OECD Model Convention', World Tax Journal 2012/6.

Avery Jones, J.F., Berg, C.J., Depret, H., Ellis, M., Fontaneau, P., Lenz, R., Miyatake, T., Roberts, S.I., Sandels, C., & Strobl, J., 'The Interpretation of Tax Treaties with Particular Reference to Article 3(2) of the OECD Model – Pt I', British Tax Review 1984/1.

Avery Jones, J.F., Berg, C.J., Depret, H., Ellis, M., Fontaneau, P., Lenz, R., Miyatake, T., Roberts, S.I., Sandels, C., & Strobl, J., 'The Interpretation of Tax Treaties with Particular Reference to Article 3(2) of the OECD Model – Pt II', British Tax Review 1984/2.

Avery Jones, J.F., The Interaction Between Tax Treaty Provisions and Domestic Law in: Tax Treaties and Domestic Law (Maisto, G., ed.), Online: IBFD 2006.

Avery Jones, J.F., 'A Fresh Look at Article 3(2) of the OECD Model', Bulletin for International Taxation 2020/11.

Avery Jones, J.F., & Hattingh, J., Global Tax Treaty Commentaries: Treaty Interpretation, Online: IBFD 2021.

Baerentzen, S., Lejour, A. & Van 't Riet, M., 'Limitation of Holding Structures for Intra-EU Dividends: An End to Tax Avoidance?', World Tax Journal 2020/5.

Baker, P., Double Taxation Conventions, London: Sweet & Maxwell's Tax Library 1996.

Baker, P., 'Multilateral Tax Treaties', Bulletin for International Taxation 2021/11 & 12.

Bernhardt, R., 'Interpretation and Implied (Tacit) Modification of Treaties – Comments on Arts. 27, 28, 29 and 38 of the ILC's 1966 Draft Articles on the Law of Treaties', Zeitschrift für Ausländisches Öffentliches Recht und Völkerrecht 1967/27.

Bobek, M., The Effect of EU Law in the National Legal Systems in: European Union Law (Barnard, C. & Peers, S., eds), Oxford: Oxford University Press 2017.

Borgen, C.J., Treaty Conflicts and Normative Fragmentation in: The Oxford Guide to Treaties (Hollis, D.B., ed.), Oxford: Oxford University Press 2012.

Bosman, R.A., Other Income under Tax Treaties, Online: Kluwer Law International 2015.

Bosman, R.A., Formele aspecten van het multilaterale instrument, MBB 2017/4.

Bosman, R.A. & Pötgens, F.P.G., Belastingverdragen in: De toekomst van de vennootschapsbelasting (van de Streek, J., ed.), Online: Kluwer 2017.

Bossuyt, J., The Legal Status of Extrinsic Instruments for the Interpretation of Tax Treaties, Online: IBFD 2021.

Boulogne, G.F., Shortcomings in the Merger Directive, Alphen aan den Rijn: Kluwer Law International 2016.

Boynes, N.D., France in: IFA Cahiers 2020 – Volume 105A: Reconstructing the Treaty Network, Online: IFA 2020.

Bracco, P., Italy in: IFA Cahiers 2010 – Volume 95A: Tax Treaties and Tax Avoidance: Application of Anti-avoidance Provisions, Online: IFA 2010.

Brauner, Y. & Kofler, G., The Interaction of Tax Treaties with International Economic Laws in: Global Tax Treaty Commentaries, Online: IBFD 2022.

Brauner, Y., 'The True Nature of Tax Treaties', Tax Treaty Monitor 2020/1.

de Broe, L., Chapter 16: Should Courts in EU Member States Take Account of the ECJ's Judgment in the Danish Beneficial Ownership Cases When Interpreting the Beneficial Ownership Requirement in Tax Treaties? in: Current Tax Treaty Issues (Maisto, G., ed.), Online: IBFD 2019.

de Broe, L., Chapter 23: Resolving Conflicts between Secondary EU Law and Commitments of Member States under Tax Treaties in: Building Global International Tax Law: Essays in Honour of Guglielmo Maisto (Pistone, P., ed.), Online: IBFD 2022.

Broekhuijsen, D.M., 'A Modern Understanding of Article 31(3)(c) of the Vienna Convention (1969): A New Haunt for the Commentaries to the OECD Model', Bulletin for International Taxation 2013/9.

Broekhuijsen, D.M., A Multilateral Tax Treaty: Designing an Instrument to Modernise International Tax Law, Alphen aan den Rijn: Kluwer Law International 2018.

Brokelind, C., Coordination of Negotiation of Member States' Double Tax Treaties with Third States in: The External Tax Strategy of the EU in a Post-BEPS Environment (Jiménez, A.M., ed.), Online: IBFD 2019.

van den Bruggen, E., 'Good Faith in the Application and Interpretation of Double Taxation Conventions', Bulletin for International Taxation 2003/1.

van den Bruggen, E., 'Unless the Vienna Convention Otherwise Requires: Notes on the Relationship Between Article 3(2) of the OECD Model Tax Convention and Articles 31 and 32 of the Vienna Convention on the Law of Treaties', European Taxation 2003/5.

Capotorti, F., Legal Problems of Directives, Regulations and Their Implementation in: Making European Policies Work: The Implementation of Community Legislation in the Member States (Volume I) (Siedentopf, H. & Ziller, J., eds), London: SAGE Publications 1988.

Chand, V., 'Exit Charges for Migrating Individuals and Companies: Comparative and Tax Treaty Analysis', Bulletin for International Taxation 2013/4/5.

Chand, V., Turina, A. & Romanovska, K., 'Tax Treaty Obstacles in Implementing the Pillar Two Global Minimum Tax Rules and a Possible Solution for Eliminating the Various Challenges', World Tax Journal 2022/2.

Churchill, R.R. & Foster, N.G., 'European Community Law and Prior Treaty Obligations of Member States: The Spanish Fisherman's Cases', The International and Comparative Law Quarterly 1987/3.

Claes, M., The Primacy of EU Law in European and National Law in: The Oxford Handbook of European Union Law (Arnull, A. & Chalmers, D., eds), Oxford: Oxford University Press 2015.

Conway, G., EU Law, Abingdon: Routledge 2015.

Cordewener, A., The Interest and Royalty Directive in: European Tax Law (Wattel, P.J., Marres, O.C.R. & Vermeulen. H., eds), Alphen aan den Rijn: Kluwer Law International 2018.

Corredor Velásquez, D.O., 'Tax Treaty Interpretation: Interaction Between Article 3(2) Organisation for Economic Co-operation and Development Model Convention and Article 31 Vienna Convention', Intertax 2016/12.

Craig, P., 'The Legal Effect of Directives: Policy, Rules and Exceptions', European Law Review 2009/3.

Crawford, J., The Sources of International Law in: Brownlie's Principles of Public International Law (Crawford, J., ed.), Oxford: Oxford University Press 2019.

Dashwood, A., Dougan, M., Rodger, B., Spaventa. E. & Wyatt, D., Wyatt and Dashwood's European Union Law, Oxford: Hart Publishing 2011.

David, E., Treaties and Third States in: The Vienna Convention on the Law of Treaties (Corten, O. & Klein, P., eds), Oxford: Oxford University Press 2011.

Dimopoulos, A., 'The Validity and Applicability of International Investment Agreements Between EU Member States under EU and International Law', Common Market Law Review 2011/1.

Distaso, M. & Russo, R., 'The EC Interest and Royalties Directive – A Comment', European Taxation 2004/4.

Docclo, C., 'EU-richtlijnen inzake BEPS en belastingverdragen: een moeilijk huwelijk', Fiscoloog 2017/406.

Dörr, O. & Schmalenbach, K., Vienna Convention on the Law of Treaties: A Commentary, Berlin: Springer 2018.

Douglas-Scott, S., Constitutional Law of the European Union, London: Longman 2002.

Douma, S.C.W. & Engelen, F.A., Introduction in: The Legal Status of the OECD Commentaries (Douma, S.C.W. & Engelen, F.A., eds), Online: IBFD 2008.

Douma, S.C.W., 'Gevoegde zaken N Luxembourg 1 e.a., BNB 2020/9.

Dourado, A.P., Kofler, G., Reimer, E., Rust, A., Ismer, R. & Ruß, J., Article 3 in: Klaus Vogel on Double Taxation Conventions (Reimer, E. & Rust, A., eds), Alphen aan den Rijn: Wolters Kluwer Law & Business 2022.

Dubuisson, F., Art. 59 1969 Vienna Convention in: The Vienna Convention on the Law of Treaties (Corten, O. & Klein, P., eds), Oxford: Oxford University Press 2011.

Eckes, C., 'Case C-188/07, Commune de Mesquer v. Total France and Total International Ltd., Judgment of the Court (Grand Chamber) of 24 June 2008 [2008] ECR I-4501; Case C-301/08, Iréne Bogiatzi v. Deutscher Luftpool, Société Luxair, European Communities, Luxembourg, Foyer Assurances SA, Judgment of the Court (Fourth Chamber) of 22 October 2009', Common Market Law Review 2010/3.

Eckes, C., The Role of the European Court of Justice in: International Law as Law of the EU (Cannizzaro, E., Palchetti, P. & Wessel, R.A., eds), Leiden/Boston: Martinus Nijhoff Publishers 2011.

Eckes, C. & Wessel, R.A., An International Perspective in: Oxford Principles of European Union Law: The European Union Legal Order (Vol. I) (Schütze, R. & Tridimas, T., eds), Oxford: Oxford University Press 2018.

Eckes, C., 'The Autonomy of the EU Legal Order', Europe and the World: A Law Review 2020/1.

Edvinsson, D., Sweden in: IFA Cahiers 2020: Volume 105A – Reconstructing the Treaty Network, Online: IFA 2020.

Eeckhout, P., External Relations of the European Union, Oxford: Oxford University Press 2011.

Engelen, F.A., Interpretation of Tax Treaties under International Law, Online: IBFD 2004.

Engelen, F.A., Vleggeert, J. & Vergouwen, T.M., 'Belastingverdragen en voorrang van richtlijnen op het gebied van directe belastingen', WFR 2019/257.

Farmer, P., The Impact of EC Law on Groups of Companies in: International and EC Tax Aspects of Groups of Companies (Maisto, G., ed.), Online: IBFD 2008.

Fernandes, J.A. & De Sousa de Camara, F., Portugal in: IFA Cahiers 2010 – Volume 95A: Tax Treaties and Tax Avoidance: Application of Anti-avoidance Provisions, Online: IFA 2010.

Finke, J., Regime-Collissions: Tensions Between Treaties (and How to Solve Them) in: Research Handbook on the Law of Treaties (Tams, C.J., Tzanakopoulos, A. & Zimmermann, A., eds), Cheltenham: Edward Elgar Publishing 2014.

Franklin, C.N.K., 'Flexibility vs. Legal Certainty: Article 307 EC and Other Issues in the Aftermath of the Open Skies Cases', European Foreign Affairs Review 2005/10.

Gardiner, R.K., Treaty Interpretation in: The Oxford Guide to Treaties (Hollis, D.B., ed.), Oxford: Oxford University Press 2012.

Gardiner, R.K., Treaty Interpretation, Oxford: Oxford University Press 2015.

Gasbarri, L., 'Regime Interactions and the Dual Legality of EU Law: The Case of Slovak Republic v. Achmea', The Global 2018 (accessible via: https://theglobal.blog/2018/04/26/regime-interactions-and-the-dual-legality-of-eu-law-the-case-of-slovak-republic-v-achmea/).

Geiger, R., Article 351 [Former Agreements of Member States] in: European Union Treaties (Geiger, R., Khan, D.-E. & Kotzur, M., eds), Munich: C.H. Beck 2015.

Glinksi, C., 'Achmea and Its Implications for Investor Dispute Settlement', Legal Studies Research Paper Series, Paper No. 2019/70.

de Graaf, A.C.G.A.C., De invloed van het EG-recht op het internationaal belastingrecht: beleids- en marktintegratie, Deventer: Kluwer 2004.

de Groot, I.M., 'Aan doorstroomvennootschap betaald dividend; misbruik van recht', NLF 2019/0597.

de Groot, I.M., 'Implementation of the Controlled Foreign Company Rules in the Netherlands', Intertax 2019/8 & 9.

Gutmann, D., Chapter 18: Is the Methodology of Tax Law Interpretation Still Able to Preserve the European Union's Tax Identity? in: Building Global International Tax Law: Essays in Honour of Guglielmo Maisto (Pistone, P., ed.), Online: IBFD 2022.

Hage, J., 'The Logic of Analogy in the Law', Argumentation 2005/4.

Haket, S., 'Coherence in the Application of the Duty of Consistent Interpretation in EU Law', Review of European Administrative Law 2015/2.

Hartley, T.C., The Foundation of European Union Law, Oxford: Oxford University Press 2010.

Haslehner, W.C., 'A Multilateral Interpretation of the Multilateral Instrument (and Covered Tax Agreements)?', Bulletin for International Taxation 2020/4 & 5.

Haslehner, W.C., The General Scope of the ATAD and Its Position in the EU Legal Order in: A Guide to the Anti-Tax Avoidance Directive (Haslehner, W.C., Pantazatou, K., Kofler, G. & Rust, A., eds), Cheltenham: Edward Elgar Publishing Limited 2020.

Haslehner, W.C., Introduction in: Klaus Vogel on Double Taxation Conventions (Reimer, E. & Rust, A., eds), Alphen aan den Rijn: Kluwer Law International 2021.

Helminen, M., Chapter 17: The Principle of Elimination of Double Taxation under EU Law - Does It Exist? in: Principles of Law: Function, Status and Impact in EU Tax Law (Brokelind, C., ed.), Online: IBFD 2017.

Helminen, M., EU Tax Law - Direct Taxation, Online: IBFD 2021.

Herdegen, M., Interpretation in International Law in: Max Planck Encyclopedias of International Law (Wolfrum, R. ed.), 2013.

Hindelang, S., 'Conceptualisation and Application of the Principle of Autonomy of EU Law – the CJEU's Judgment in Achmea Put in Perspective', European Law Review 2019/3.

Hinnekens, L., 'Compatibility of Bilateral Tax Treaties with European Community Law: The Rules', EC Tax Review 1994/4.

Hinnekens, L., 'The Uneasy Case and Fate of Article 293 Second Indent EC', Intertax 2009/11.

Hohenwarter, D., Austria in: Tax Treaties and Domestic Law (Maisto, G., ed.), Online: IBFD 2006.

Hoor, O.R. & Medler, A., Luxembourg in: IFA Cahiers 2020: Volume 105A – Reconstructing the Treaty Network, Online: IFA 2020.

Huhn, W., 'The Stages of Legal Reasoning: Formalism, Analogy, and Realism', Villanova Law Review 2003/1.

van Hulten, L.C. & Korving, J.J.A.M., 'Svig og misbruk: de Deense antimisbruikzaken', WFR 2019/129.

Jennings, R. & Watts, A., Oppenheim's International Law (Vol. I), London: Longman 1992.

Jiménez, A.J.M., Beneficial Ownership – Global Tax Treaty Commentaries in: Global Tax Treaty Commentaries – Global Topics, Online: IBFD 2022.

Kellerbauer, M. & Klamert, M., Article 351 TFEU in: The EU Treaties and the Charter of Fundamental Rights: A Commentary (Kellerbauer, M., Klamert, M. & Tomkin, J., eds), Online: Oxford Scholarship 2021.

Kelsen, H., Principles of International Law, New York: Rinehart & Company Inc 1952.

Klabbers, J., Treaty Conflict and the European Union, Cambridge: Cambridge University Press 2008.

Klabbers, J., An Introduction to International Institutional Law, Cambridge: Cambridge University Press 2009.

Klabbers, J., Beyond the Vienna Convention in: The Law of Treaties Beyond the Vienna Convention (Cannizzaro, E., ed.), Oxford: Oxford University Press 2011.

Klabbers, J., 'Unity, Diversity, Accountability: The Ambivalent Concept of International Organisation', Melbourne Journal of International Law 2013/6.

Klabbers, J., Advanced Introduction to the Law of International Organizations, Online: Edward Elgar Publishing 2015.

Klabbers, J., Sui Generis? The European Union as an International Organization in: A Companion to European Union Law and International Law (Patterson, D. & Söderston, A.), Chichester: Wiley Blackwell 2016.

Klabbers, J., International Law, Cambridge: Cambridge University Press 2017.

Klamert, M., The Principle of Loyalty in EU Law, Oxford: Oxford University Press 2014.

Kofler, G.W., Direct Applicability and Direct Effect in: Principles of Law: Function, Status and Impact in EU Tax Law (Brokelind, C., ed.), Online: IBFD 2014.

Kolb, R., The International Court of Justice, Oxford: Hart Publishing 2013.

Kolb, R., The Law of Treaties: An Introduction, Cheltenham: Edward Elgar Publishing 2016.

Kolozs, B. & Koszegi, A., Hungary in: IFA Cahiers 2010 – Volume 95A: Tax Treaties and Tax Avoidance: Application of Anti-avoidance Provisions, Online: IFA 2010.

Kontou, N., The Termination and Revision of Treaties in the Light of New Customary International Law, Oxford: Clarendon Press 1994.

Koops, C.E., Contemplating Compliance: European Compliance Mechanisms in International Perspective, Amsterdam: University of Amsterdam 2014.

Koronczioví, A. & Kacaljak, M., 'GAAR as Tax Treaty Override: Slovak Perspective', Economics and Social Issues Review 2017/3.

Koszowski, M., Analogical Reasoning in Law, Newcastle-upon-Tyne: Cambridge Scholars Publisher 2019.

Koutrakos, P., EU International Relations Law, Oxford: Hart Publishing Ltd. 2006.

Krenzler, H.G. & Landwehr, O., 'A New Legal Order of International Law': On the Relationship Between Public International Law and European Union Law after Kadi in: From Bilateralism to Community Interest: Essays in Honour of Bruno Simma (Fastenrath, U., Geiger, R., Khan, D.-E., Paulus, A., von Schorlemer, S. & Vedder, C., eds), Oxford: Oxford University Press 2011.

ter Kuile, B.H., 'Juridische aspecten van de fiscale soevereiniteit in de interne markt' WFR, 1991/10.

Lang, M., Introduction to the Law of Double Taxation Conventions, Amsterdam: IBFD 2016.

Lang, M., 'Tax Treaty Interpretation – A Response to John F. Avery Jones', Bulletin for International Taxation 2020/11.

Lasinìski-Sulecki, K. & Morawski, W., Poland in: IFA Cahiers 2020 - Volume 105A: Reconstructing the Treaty Network, Online: IFA 2020.

Lavranos, N., 2022, Lex Superior: How EU Law Trumps Investment Law (28 June 2022), Thomson Reuters. Practical Law. Arbitration Blog.

Lenaerts, K. & Gutiérrez-Fons, J.A., 'The Constitutional Allocation of Powers and General Principles of EU Law', Common Market Law Review 2010/6.

Lenaerts, K. & van Nuffel, P., European Union Law, London: Sweet & Maxwell 2011.

Lenaerts, K. & Gutiérrez-Fons, J.A., 'To Say What the Law of the EU Is: Methods of Interpretation and the European Court of Justice', EUI Working Papers 2013/9.

Lenaerts, K. & van Nuffel, P., Europees Recht, Antwerpen - Cambridge: Intersentia 2017.

Lenaerts, K. 'The Autonomy of European Union Law', Post AISDUE 2019/I.

Linderfalk, U., 'Who Are "The Parties" Article 31, Paragraph 3(c) of the 1969 Vienna Convention and the "Principle of Systemic Integration" Revisited', Netherlands International Law Review 2008/3.

Linn, A., Germany in: IFA Cahiers 2010 - Volume 95A: Tax Treaties and Tax Avoidance: Application of Anti-avoidance Provisions, Online: IFA 2010.

Lindroos, A., 'Addressing Norm Conflicts in a Fragmented Legal System: The Doctrine of Lex Specialis', Nordic Journal of International Law 2005/1.

Lowe, V., International Law, Oxford: Oxford University Press 2007.

Maisto, G., Chapter 25: Counteracting Tax Treaty Abuses from a European Perspective: Frictions and Interactions Between the OECD PPT and the ATAD GAAR in: Thinker, Teacher, Traveler: Reimagining International Tax Essays in Honor of H. David Rosenbloom (Kofler, G., Mason, R. & Rust, A., eds), Online: IBFD 2021.

Manzini, P., 'The Priority of Pre-existing Treaties of EC Member States Within the Framework of International Law', European Journal of International Law 2001/4.
Marres, O.C.R., Chapter 16: CCCTB and Tax Treaties in: The KPMG Guide to the CCCTB, 2012 (accessible via: https://assets.kpmg.com/content/dam/kpmg/pdf/2012/10/ccctb-part3-v2.pdf).
Marres, O.C.R. & de Groot, I.M., 'Combatting Abuse by Conduit Companies. The Doctrine of Abuse under EU Law and Its Influence on Tax Treaties', European Taxation 2021/8.
Matz-Lück, N., Conflicts Between Treaties in: The Max Planck Encyclopedias of International Law (Wolfrum, R. ed.), Oxford: Oxford University Press 2010.
Mayer, F.C., Van Gend en Loos: The Foundation of a Community of Law in: The Past and Future of EU Law: The Classics of EU Law Revisited on the 50th Anniversary of the Rome Treaty (Maduro, M. & Azoulai, L., eds), Oxford: Hart Publishing 2010.
McLachlan, C., 'The Principle of Systemic Integration and Article 31(3)(c) of the Vienna Convention', International and Comparative Law Quarterly 2005/2.
McNair, P., The Law of Treaties, Oxford: Clarendon Press 1961.
Meessen, K.M., 'The Application of Rules of Public International Law Within Community Law', Common Market Law Review 1974/4.
de Melo, C.R. & Ramos, T.C., Portugal in: IFA Cahiers 2020 – Volume 105A: Reconstructing the Treaty Network, Online: IFA 2020.
Merkouris, P., Article 31(3)(c) of the VCLT and the Principle of Systemic Integration, London: Queen Mary University of London 2010.
Message, N., France in: Tax Treaties and Domestic Law (Maisto, G., ed.), Online: IBFD 2006.
Michaels, R. & J. Pauwelyn, J., 'Conflict of Norms of Conflict of Laws? Different Techniques in the Fragmentation of International Law' (accessible via: https://scholarship.law.duke.edu/cgi/viewcontent.cgi?referer=&httpsredir=1&article=2933&context=faculty_scholarship).
Mifsud, I., Constitutional Law in Malta, Alphen aan den Rijn: Kluwer Law International 2022.
Molnar, T., The Interplay Between the EU's Return Acquis and International Law, Northampton: Edward Elgar Publishing 2021.
Moser, K., 'Recent Developments and Challenges Regarding Exit Taxes in the Context of Tax Treaties: Article 13 of the OECD Model and Change of Residence', Bulletin for International Taxation 2019/10.
Müller, D., EU Law and Arbitration Under International Investment Instruments: The Surprising Award in Green Power v. Spain (28 June 2022), Jus Mundi 2022.
Mus, J.B., Conflicts Between Treaties in International Law, Netherlands International Law Review 1998/2.
Navez, E.-J., Belgium in: Taxation of Companies on Capital Gains on Shares under Domestic Law, EU Law and Tax Treaties (Maisto, G., ed.), Online: IBFD 2013.
Nevill, P., The European Union as a Source of Public International Law, Hungarian Yearbook of International Law and European Law 2013.

Niemelä, P., The Relationship of EU Law and Bilateral Investment Treaties of EU Member States: Treaty Conflict, Harmonious Coexistence and the Critique of Investment Arbitration, Helsinki: University of Helsinki 2017.

Noone, D. & Quinn, A., Ireland in: IFA Cahiers 2010 – Volume 95A: Tax Treaties and tax avoidance: application of anti-avoidance provisions, Online: IFA 2010.

Öberg, M-L., 'Autonomy of the EU Legal Order: A Concept in Need of Revision?', European Public Law 2020/3.

Odermatt, J., 'When a Fence Becomes a Cage: The Principle of Autonomy in EU Externa Relations Law', EUI Working Papers 2016/7.

Odermatt, J., 'Is EU Law International? Case C-741/19 Republic of Moldova v Komstroy LLC and the Autonomy of the EU Legal Order', European Papers 2021/3.

Oppenheim, L.F., International Law. A Treatise (Vol. I), London: Longmans, Green 2012.

Orakhelashvili, A., The Interpretation of Acts and Rules in Public International Law, Oxford: Oxford University Press 2008.

Orakhelashvili, A., Application and Interpretation of Treaties, s.2 Application of Treaties, Art. 30 1969 Vienna Convention in: The Vienna Conventions on the Law of Treaties (Corten, O. & Klein, P., eds), Oxford: Oxford University Press 2011.

Pancham, S., Permanent Establishment Mismatches under ATAD II in: The Implementation of Anti-BEPS Legislation in the European Union: A Comprehensive Study (Pistone, P. & Weber, D., eds), Online: IBFD 2018.

Pantaleo, L., 'Member States Prior Agreements and Newly EU Attributed Competence: What Lesson from Foreign Investment', European Foreign Affairs Review 2014/2.

Panzeri, I. 'Tax Treaties Versus EU Law: Which Should Prevail?', European Taxation 2021/4.

von Papp, K., 'Solving Conflicts with International Investment Treaty Law from an EU Law Perspective: Article 351 TFEU Revisited', Legal Issues of Economic Integration 2015/4.

Pauwelyn, J., Conflict of Norms in Public International Law: How WTO Law Relates to Other Rules of International Law, Cambridge: Cambridge University Press 2003.

Pellet, A. & Müller, D., Article 38 in: The Statute of the International Court of Justice: A Commentary (3rd Edition) (Zimmermann, A. Tams, C.J., Oellers-Frahm, K. & Tomuschat, C., eds), Online: Oxford University Press 2019.

Peters, F.G.F. & Roelofsen, A., Netherlands in: IFA Cahiers 2010 – Volume 95A: Tax Treaties and Tax Avoidance: Application of Anti-avoidance Provisions, Online: IFA 2010.

Pirlot, A., When EU Law and International Law Pursue Seemingly Contradictory Paths: A Mapping of Potential Conflicts in Tax Matters in: European Tax Integration: Law, Policy and Politics (Pistone, P., ed.), Online: IBFD 2018.

Pit, H.M., The EU Arbitration Convention, Groningen: Rijksuniversiteit Groningen 2017.

Pötgens, F.P.G. & Vergouwen, T.M., 'Supreme Court Issues Third Ruling on Fictitious Wage and Tax Treaties: Decision of the Netherlands Supreme Court of 18 November 2016, BNB 2017/34', European Taxation 2017/8.

Pötgens, F.P.G., Chapter 20: How the EU Tax Arbitration Directive Relates to Other International Dispute Resolution Mechanisms: A Dutch Perspective in: Building Global International Tax Law: Essays in Honour of Guglielmo Maisto (Pistone, P., ed.), Online: IBFD 2022.

Pötgens, F.P.G. & Vergouwen, T.M., De toenemende invloed van de EU-wetgever op belastingverdragen in: Jubileumbundel 150 jaar WFR (Jansen, J.J. & Stevens, L.G.M., eds), Deventer: Kluwer 2022.

Prechal, S., 'Joined Cases C-397/01 to C-403/01, Bernhard Pfeiffer et al', Common Market Law Review 2005/5.

Prechal, S., Directives in EC Law, Oxford: Oxford University Press 2009.

Prost, M., Sources and the Hierarchy of International Law: Source Preferences and Scales of Values in: The Oxford Handbook of the Sources of International Law (Besson, S. & d'Aspremont, J., eds), Online: Oxford University Press 2018.

Resch, X.R., Tax Treaty Interpretation: The Meaning and Application of Article 3(2), Leiden: Tredition Gmbh 2020.

Ribes, A.R., Spain in: IFA Cahiers 2020 - Volume 105A: Reconstructing the Treaty Network, Online: IFA 2020.

Rosas, A., 'The Status in EU Law of International Agreements Concluded by EU Member States', Fordham International Law Journal 2011/5.

Rosenne, S., Breach of Treaty, Cambridge: Cambridge University Press 1985.

Rust, A., Germany in: Tax Treaties and Domestic Law (Maisto, G. ed.), Online: IBFD 2006.

Rust, A., Controlled Foreign Company Rule (Articles 7 and 8 ATAD) in: A Guide to the Anti-Tax Avoidance Directive (Haslehner, W.C., Pantazatou, K., Kofler, G. & Rust, A., eds), Cheltenham: Edward Elgar Publishing Limited 2020.

Sadat-Akhavi, S.A., Methods of Resolving Conflicts Between Treaties, Leiden/Boston: Martinus Nijhoff Publishers 2003.

Salmon, J., Art. 26 1969 Vienna Convention in: The Vienna Conventions on the Law of Treaties (Vol. I) (Corten, O. & Klein, P., eds), Oxford: Oxford University Press 2011.

Samson, M., 'High Hopes, Scant Resources: A Word of Scepticism about the Anti-Fragmentation Function of Article 31(3)(c) of the Vienna Convention on the Law of Treaties', Leiden Journal of International Law 2011/3.

Sands, P., 'Treaty, Custom and the Cross-Fertilization of International Law', Yale Human Rights and Development Law Journal 1998/1.

Sawyer, K., 'The Principle of "Interprétation Conforme": How Far Can or Should National Courts Go when Interpreting National Legislation Consistently with European Community Law?', Statute Law Review 2007/3.

Schermers, H.G. & Blokker, N.M., International Institutional Law, Leiden/Boston: Martinus Nijhoff Publishers 2011.

Schmidt, P.K., Denmark in: IFA Cahiers 2020 - Volume 105A: Reconstructing the Treaty Network, Online: IFA 2020.

Schütze, R., 'On "Federal" Ground: The European Union as an (Inter)national Phenomenon', Common Market Law Review 2009/4.

Schütze, R., European Law and Member State Agreements in: Foreign Affairs and the EU Constitution: Selected Essays (Schütze, R., ed.), Cambridge: Cambridge University Press 2014.

Schütze, R., European Union Law, Online: Cambridge University Press 2021.

Schwarzenberger, G., 'Myths and Realities of Treaty Interpretation: Articles 27-29 of the Vienna Draft Convention on the Law of Treaties', Virginia Journal of International Law 1968/1.

Simma, B. & Pulkowski, D., 'Of Planets and the Universe: Self-Contained Regimes in International Law', European Journal of International Law 2006/3.

Simma, B. & Kill, T., Harmonizing Investment Protection and International Human Rights: First Steps Towards a Methodology in: International Investment Law for the 21st Century: Essays in Honour of Christoph Schreuer (Binder, C., Kriebaum, U., Reinisch A. & Wittich, S., eds), Oxford: Oxford University Press 2009.

Simma, B. & Tams, C.J., Termination and Suspension of the Operation of Treaties, Art. 60 1969 Vienna Convention in: The Vienna Convention on the Law of Treaties (Corten, O. & Klein, P., eds), Oxford: Oxford University Press 2011.

Sinclair, I., The Vienna Convention on the Law of Treaties, Manchester: Manchester University Press 1984.

Smit, D.S., The Anti-Tax-Avoidance Directive (ATAD) in: European Tax Law (Wattel, P.J, Marres, O.C.R. & Vermeulen, H., eds), Deventer: Kluwer 2018.

Sorel, J.-M. & Eveno, V.B., Application and Interpretation of Treaties in: The Vienna Convention on the Law of Treaties (Corten, O. & Klein, P., eds), Oxford: Oxford University Press 2011.

Sunstein, C.R., 'On Analogical Reasoning', Harvard Law Review 1993/3.

Switzer, S., European Law Essentials, Edinburgh: Edinburgh University Press 2009.

Szudoczky, R., The Sources of EU Law and Their Relationship: Lessons for the Field of Taxation, Online: IBFD 2014.

Szudoczky, R. & Blum, D., Unveiling the MLI: An Analysis of Its Nature, Relationship to Covered Tax Agreements and Interpretation in Light of the Obligations of Its Parties in: International and EU Tax Multilateralism: Challenges Raised by the MLI (Dourado, A.P., ed.), Online: IBFD 2020.

Szurek, S., Article 11 in: The Vienna Conventions on the Law of Treaties (Corten, O. & Klein, P., eds), Online: Oxford University Press 2011.

Tiesinga, D. & Nuku, E., Netherlands in: IFA Cahiers 2020 – Volume 105A: Reconstructing the Treaty Network, Online: IFA 2020.

Timmermans, C.W.A., 'Directives: Their Effect Within National Legal Systems', Common Market Law Review 1997/4.

Tomuschat, C., Article 36 in: The Statute of the International Court of Justice: A Commentary (3rd Edition) (Zimmermann, A., Tams, C.J., Oellers-Frahm, K. & Tomuschat, C., eds), Online: Oxford University Press 2019.

Trstenjak, V., 'National Sovereignty and the Principle of Primacy in EU Law and Their Importance for the Member States', Beijing Law Review 2013/2.

Vergouwen, T.M. & Broekhuijsen, D.M., 'De duur van onderhandelingen van belastingverdragen', NLF-W 2022/5.

Villiger, M.E., Commentary on the 1969 Vienna Convention on the Law of Treaties, Leiden/Boston: Martinus Nijhoff Publishers 2009.

Vita, V., 'The Romanian Constitutional Court and the Principle of Primacy: To Refer or Not to Refer?', Germany Law Journal 2015/6.

Vleggeert, J., Over onafhankelijkheid, de verschaling van het fiscale debat en wat we daaraan kunnen doen, Leiden: 2020.

Vleggeert, J., Een burgerperspectief op belangenverstrengeling, Leiden: 2022.

Vogel, K., 'Double Tax Treaties and Their Interpretation', Berkeley Journal of International Law 1986/1.

Vogel, K. & Prokisch, R.G., General Report in: Interpretation of Double Taxation Conventions, Online: IFA 1993.

Vöneky, S., Analogy in International Law in: Max Planck Encyclopedias of International Law, Online: Oxford Public International Law 2008.

de Vos, P. & Docclo, C., Belgium in: IFA Cahiers 2020 – Volume 105A: Reconstructing the Treaty Network, Online: IFA 2020.

Vranes, E., 'Lex Superior, Lex Specialis, Lex Posterior – Zur Rechtsnatur der 'Konfliktlösungsregeln', Zeitschrift für ausländisches öffentliches Recht und Völkerrecht 2005/2.

Vranes, E., 'The Definition of "Norm Conflict" in International Law and Legal Theory', European Journal of International Law 2006/2.

Vranken, J., 'Exciting Times for Legal Scholarship', Recht en Methode in onderzoek en onderwijs 2012/2.

Ward, D.A., Avery Jones, J.F., de Broe, L., Ellis, M.J., Goldberg, S.H., Killius, J., Gall, J.-P.L., Maisto, G., Miyatake, T., Torrione, H., van Raad, C. & Wiman, B., The Interpretation of Income Tax Treaties with Particular Reference to the Commentaries on the OECD Model, International Fiscal Association 2005.

Warner, J.P., 'The Relationship Between European Community Law and the National Laws of Member States', The Law Quarterly Review 1977/93.

Wessel, R.A., 'Studying International and European Law: Confronting Perspectives and Combining Interests', Grotius Centre Working Paper Series No. 2018 2018/071 PIL.

de Witte, B., Direct Effect, Primacy, and the Nature of the Legal Order in: The Evolution of EU Law (Craig, P. & De Búrca, G. eds), Oxford: Oxford University Press 2011.

de Witte, B., The European Union as an International Legal Experiment in: The Worlds of European Constitutionalism (De Búrca, G. & Weiler, J.H.H., eds), Cambridge: Cambridge University Press 2012.

de Witte, B., EU Law: Is It International Law? in: European Union Law (Barnard, C. & Peers, S., eds), Oxford: Oxford University Press 2017.

Wouters, J., Ryngaert, C., Ruys, T. & de Baere, G., International Law: A European Perspective, Oxford: Hart Publishing 2019.

Zaimaj, A., Italy in: IFA Cahiers 2020 – Volume 105A: Reconstructing the Treaty Network, Online: IFA 2020.

# Table of Cases

# Table of Legislation

## EU Legislation

**Other**

# Table of Treaties

# Documents Published by Governments or International Organisations

European Union, 2003, Voting Result, 3 June 2003, session 2513, regarding the Council Directive on a common system of taxation applicable to interest and royalty payments made between associated companies of different Member States, Document 5926/3/03, 146

European Union, 2005, EC Law and Tax Treaties - Annex A: The Articles of the OECD Model Convention. A Community Perspective (TAXUD E1/FR DOC (05) 2306/A), 4, 17

European Union, 2009, Report from the Commission to the Council in accordance with Article 8 of Council Directive 2003/49/EC on a common system of taxation applicable to interest and royalty payments made between associated companies of different Member States, 43

European Union, 2011, Proposal for a Council Directive on a Common Consolidated Corporate Tax Base (CCCTB) (COM(2011) 121), 81, 193

European Union, 2011, Voting Result, 17 February 2011, no. 6695/11, regarding Council Directive on administrative cooperation in the field of taxation and repealing Directive 77/799/EEC, 146

European Union, 2011, Voting result, 30 November 2011, no. 17931/11, Council Directive on the common system of taxation applicable in the case of parent companies and subsidiaries of different Member States (Recast), 146

European Union, 2013, Room Document # 1, Working Party on Tax Questions - Direct Taxation, Proposal for a CCCTB of 15 January 2013, 264, 266

European Union, 2014, Voting Result, 5 December 2014, no. 11621/1/14, regarding the Council Directive amending Directive 2011/96/EU on the common system of taxation applicable in the case of parent companies and subsidiaries of different Member States, 146

European Union, 2015, Voting result, 2 February 2015, no. 5636/15, regarding the Council Directive amending Directive 2011/96/EU on the common system of taxation applicable in the case of parent companies and subsidiaries of different Member States, 146

European Union, 2016, Voting Result, 13 July 2016, no. 11171/16, regarding Council Directive laying down rules against tax avoidance practices that directly affect the functioning of the internal market, 146

European Union, 2017, Voting Result, 29 May 2017, no. 9740/17, regarding Council Directive amending Directive (EU) 2016/1164 as regards hybrid mismatches with third countries, 146

European Union, 2017, Voting Result, 10 October 2017, no. 13104/17, regarding the Council Directive on Tax Dispute Resolution Mechanisms in the European Union, 146

European Union, 2018, Proposal for a Council Directive laying down rules relating to the corporate taxation of a significant digital presence (COM(2018) 147 final), 81

European Union, 2019, Commission Notice on the recovery of unlawful and incompatible State aid (2019/C 247/01), 29

European Union, 2021, Proposal for a Council Directive on ensuring a global minimum level of taxation for multinational groups in the Union, COM(2021) 823 final, 5, 221, 235

European Union, 2021, Proposal for a Council Directive laying down rules to prevent the misuse of shell entities for tax purposes and amending Directive 2011/16/EU, COM(2021) 565 final, 2021/0434 (CNS), 193

ILC, 1964, Summary record of the 772nd meeting (Extract from the Yearbook of the International Law Commission), 74

ILC, 1966, Yearbook of the International Law Commission, Volume II, 61, 69, 72–75, 77, 147

ILC, United Nations Conference on the Law of Treaties, First session, 26 March - 24 May 1968, A/CONF.39/C.1/SR.33, 33rd meeting of the Committee of the Whole75

United Nations Conference on the Law of Treaties, Second session, Vienna, 9 April-22 May 1969, Summary of the plenary meetings and of the meetings of the Committee of the Whole, 135

ILC, 1969, United Nations Conference on the Law of Treaties, 85th meeting of the Committee of the Whole, A/CONF.39/C1/SR.85, 132, 135

ILC, 2001, United Nations Conference on the Law of Treaties, 91st meeting of the Committee of the Whole, A/CONF.39/C.1/SR.91, 123, 126

ILC, 2001, Draft articles on Responsibility of States for Internationally Wrongful Acts with commentaries, 183, 197, 198

ILC, 2006, Report of the International Law Commission, Fifty-eight session, No. 10 (A/61/10), 70

ILC, 2006, Fragmentation of International Law: Difficulties arising from the diversification and expansion of international law, Report of the Study Group of the International Law Commission (Finalized by Martti Koskenniemi), A/CN.4/L.682, 61, 67, 83–85, 119–121, 126, 131–133, 136–138, 147, 179, 180, 182, 183, 185, 187, 196

OECD [illegible] on Tax Treaty [illegible] of the OECD Council [illegible] October 2014 [illegible]
OECD 2015, Developing a Multilateral [illegible] Effectual Tax Treaties, Action 15 2015 Final Report [illegible]
OECD 2017, 2017 Update to the OECD Model Tax Convention 21 November 2017 [illegible]
OECD 2021, [illegible] of the Contracting Parties of the Multilateral [illegible] Multilateral Convention to Implement Tax Treaty Related Measures to Prevent Base Erosion and Profit Shifting [illegible] and Implementation [illegible] Approved [illegible] the [illegible] 5 May 2021 [illegible]
[illegible]
[illegible]
[illegible]
[illegible]

## SERIES ON INTERNATIONAL TAXATION

1. Alberto Xavier, *The Taxation of Foreign Investment in Brazil,* 1980 (ISBN 90-200-0582-0).
2. Hugh J. Ault & Albert J. Rädler, *The German Corporation Tax Law with 1980 Amendments,* 1981 (ISBN 90-200-0642-8).
3. Paul R. McDaniel & Hugh J. Ault, *Introduction to United States International Taxation,* 1981 (ISBN 90-6544-004-6).
4. Albert J. Rädler, *German Transfer Pricing/Prix de Transfer en Allemagne,* 1984 (ISBN 90-6544-143-3).
5. Paul R. McDaniel & Stanley S. Surrey, *International Aspects of Tax Expenditures: A Comparative Study,* 1985 (ISBN 90-654-4163-8).
6. Kees van Raad, *Nondiscrimination in International Tax Law,* 1986 (ISBN 90-6544-266-9).
7. Sijbren Cnossen (ed.), *Tax Coordination in the European Community,* 1987 (ISBN 90-6544-272-3).
8. Ben Terra, *Sales Taxation. The Case of Value Added Tax in the European Community,* 1989 (ISBN 90-6544-381-9).
9. Rutsel S.J. Martha, *The Jurisdiction to Tax in International Law: Theory and Practice of Legislative Fiscal Jurisdiction,* 1989 (ISBN 90-654-4416-5).
10. Paul R. McDaniel & Hugh J. Ault, *Introduction to United States International Taxation* (3rd revised edition), 1989 (ISBN 90-6544-423-8).
11. Manuel Pires, *International Juridicial Double Taxation of Income,* 1989 (ISBN 90-6544-426-2).
12. A.H.M. Daniels, *Issues in International Partnership Taxation,* 1991 (ISBN 90-654-4577-3).
13. Arvid A. Skaar, *Permanent Establishment: Erosion of a Tax Treaty Principle,* 1992 (ISBN 90-6544-594-3).
14. Cyrille David & Geerten M.M. Michielse (eds), *Tax Treatment of Financial Instruments,* 1996 (ISBN 90-654-4666-4).
15. Herbert H. Alpert & Kees van Raad (eds), *Essays on International Taxation,* 1993 (ISBN 90-654-4781-4).
16. Wolfgang Gassner, Michael Lang & Eduard Lechner (eds), *Tax Treaties and EC Law,* 1997 (ISBN 90-411-0680-4).
17. Glória Teixeira, *Taxing Corporate Profits in the EU,* 1997 (ISBN 90-411-0703-7).
18. Michael Lang et al. (eds), *Multilateral Tax Treaties,* 1998 (ISBN 90-411-0704-5).
19. Stef van Weeghel, *The Improper Use of Tax Treaties,* 1998 (ISBN 90-411-0737-1).

20. Klaus Vogel (ed.), *Interpretation of Tax Law and Treaties and Transfer Pricing in Japan and Germany,* 1998 (ISBN 90-411-9655-2).
21. Bertil Wiman (ed.), *International Studies in Taxation: Law and Economics; Liber Amicorum Leif Mutén,* 1999 (ISBN 90-411-9692-7).
22. Alfonso J. Martín Jiménez, *Towards Corporate Tax Harmonization in the European Community,* 1999 (ISBN 90-411-9690-0).
23. Ramon J. Jeffery, *The Impact of State Sovereignty on Global Trade and International Taxation,* 1999 (ISBN 90-411-9703-6).
24. A.J. Easson, *Taxation of Foreign Direct Investment,* 1999 (ISBN 90-411-9741-9).
25. Marjaana Helminen, *The Dividend Concept in International Tax Law: Dividend Payments Between Corporate Entities,* 1999 (ISBN 90-411-9765-6).
26. Paul Kirchhof, Moris Lehner, Kees van Raad, Arndt Raupach & Michael-Rodi (eds), *International and Comparative Taxation: Essays in Honour of Klaus Vogel,* 2002 (ISBN 90-411-9841-5).
27. Krister Andersson, Peter Melz & Christer Silfverberg (eds), *Liber Amicorum Sven-Olof Lodin,* 2001 (ISBN 90-411-9850-4).
28. Juan Martín Jovanovich, *Customs Valuation and Transfer Pricing: Is It Possible to Harmonize Customs and Tax Rules?,* Second Edition, 2018 (ISBN 978-90-411-6134-5).
29. Stefano Simontacchi, *Taxation of Capital Gains under the OECD Model Convention: With Special Regard to Immovable Property,* 2007 (ISBN 978-90-411-2549-1).
30. Michael Lang, Josef Schuch, & Claus Staringer (eds), *Tax Treaty Law and EC Law,* 2007 (ISBN 978-90-411-2629-0).
31. Duncan Bentley, *Taxpayers' Rights: Theory Origin and Implementation,* 2007 (ISBN 978-90-411-2650-4).
32. Sergio André Rocha, *Interpretation of Double Taxation Conventions: General Theory and Brazilian Perspective,* 2008 (ISBN 978-90-411-2822-5).
33. Robert F. van Brederode, *Systems of General Sales Taxation: Theory, Policy and Practice,* 2009 (ISBN 978-90-411-2832-4).
34. John G. Head & Richard Krever (eds), *Tax Reform in the 21st Century: A Volume in Memory of Richard Musgrave,* 2009 (ISBN 978-90-411-2829-4).
35. Jens Wittendorff, *Transfer Pricing and the Arm's Length Principle in International Tax Law,* 2010 (ISBN 978-90-411-3270-3).
36. Marjaana Helminen, *The International Tax Law Concept of Dividend,* Second Edition, 2017 (ISBN 978-90-411-8394-1).
37. Robert F. van Brederode (ed.), *Immovable Property under VAT: A Comparative Global Analysis,* 2011 (ISBN 978-90-411-3126-3).
38. Dennis Weber & Stef van Weeghel, *The 2010 OECD Updates: Model Tax Convention & Transfer Pricing Guidelines - A Critical Review,* 2011 (ISBN 978-90-411-3812-5).
39. Yariv Brauner & Martin James McMahon, Jr. (eds), *The Proper Tax Base: Structural Fairness from an International and Comparative Perspective— Essays in Honour of Paul McDaniel,* 2012 (ISBN 978-90-411-3286-4).
40. Robert F. van Brederode (ed.), *Science, Technology and Taxation,* 2012 (ISBN 978-90-411-3125-6).

41. Oskar Henkow, *The VAT/GST Treatment of Public Bodies*, 2013 (ISBN 978-90-411-4663-2).
42. Jean Schaffner, *How Fixed Is a Permanent Establishment?*, 2013 (ISBN 978-90-411-4662-5).
43. Miguel Correia, *Taxation of Corporate Groups*, 2013 (ISBN 978-90-411-4841-4).
44. Veronika Daurer, *Tax Treaties and Developing Countries*, 2014 (ISBN 978-90-411-4982-4).
45. Claire Micheau, *State Aid, Subsidy and Tax Incentives under EU and WTO Law*, 2014 (ISBN 978-90-411-4555-0).
46. Robert F. van Brederode & Richard Krever (eds), *Legal Interpretation of Tax Law*, 2014 (ISBN 978-90-411-4945-9).
47. Radhakishan Rawal, *Taxation of Cross-border Services*, 2014 (ISBN 978-90-411-4947-3).
48. João Dácio Rolim, *Proportionality and Fair Taxation*, 2014 (ISBN 978-90-411-5838-3).
49. Paulo Rosenblatt, *General Anti-avoidance Rules for Major Developing Countries*, 2015 (ISBN 978-90-411-5839-0).
50. Gaspar Lopes Dias V.S., *Tax Arbitrage through Cross-Border Financial Engineering*, 2015 (ISBN 978-90-411-5875-8).
51. Geerten M.M. Michielse & Victor Thuronyi (eds), *Tax Design Issues Worldwide*, 2015 (ISBN 978-90-411-5610-5).
52. Oktavia Weidmann, *Taxation of Derivatives*, 2015 (ISBN 978-90-411-5977-9).
53. Chris Evans, Richard Krever & Peter Mellor (eds), *Tax Simplification*, 2015 (ISBN 978-90-411-5976-2).
54. Reuven Avi-Yonah & Joel Slemrod (eds), *Taxation and Migration*, 2015 (ISBN 978-90-411-6136-9).
55. Alexander Bosman, *Other Income under Tax Treaties: An Analysis of Article 21 of the OECD Model Convention*, 2015 (ISBN 978-90-411-6610-4).
56. John Abrahamson, *International Taxation of Manufacturing and Distribution*, 2016 (ISBN 978-90-411-6664-7).
57. Frederik Boulogne, *Shortcomings in the EU Merger Directive*, 2016 (ISBN 978-90-411-6713-2).
58. Angelika Meindl-Ringler, *Beneficial Ownership in International Tax Law*, 2016 (ISBN 978-90-411-6833-7).
59. Andreas Waltrich, *Cross-Border Taxation of Permanent Establishments: An International Comparison*, 2016 (ISBN 978-90-411-6832-0).
60. Sergio André Rocha & Allison Christians (eds), *Tax Sovereignty in the BEPS Era*, 2017 (ISBN 978-90-411-6707-1).
61. Peter Antony Wilson, *BRICS and International Tax Law*, 2018 (ISBN 978-90-411-9435-0).
62. Louise Otis, Brigitte Alepin & Blanca Moreno-Dodson (eds), *Winning the Tax Wars: Tax Competition and Cooperation*, 2018 (ISBN 978-90-411-9460-2).
63. Marta Castelon, *International Taxation of Income from Services under Double Taxation Conventions: Development, Practice and Policy*, 2018 (ISBN 978-90-411-9594-4).

64. D.M. Broekhuijsen, *A Multilateral Tax Treaty: Designing an Instrument to Modernise International Tax Law*, 2018 (ISBN 978-90-411-9872-3).
65. John Abrahamson, *International Taxation of Energy Production and Distribution*, 2018 (ISBN 978-90-411-9101-4).
66. Leopoldo Parada, *Double Non-taxation and the Use of Hybrid Entities: An Alternative Approach in the New Era of BEPS*, 2018 (ISBN 978-90-411-9991-1).
67. Richard Snoeij, *International Tax Aspects of Sovereign Wealth Investors: A Source State Perspective*, 2018 (ISBN 978-90-411-9431-2).
68. Aleksandra Bal, *Taxation, Virtual Currency and Blockchain*, 2019 (ISBN 978-94-035-0103-1).
69. Werner Haslehner, Georg Kofler, Katerina Pantazatou & Alexander Rust (eds), *Tax and the Digital Economy: Challenges and Proposals for Reform*, 2019 (ISBN 978-94-035-0361-5).
70. Eva Escribano, *Jurisdiction to Tax Corporate Income Pursuant to the Presumptive Benefit Principle: A Critical Analysis of Structural Paradigms Underlying Corporate Income Taxation and Proposals for Reform*, 2019 (ISBN 978-94-035-0640-1).
71. Jérôme Monsenego & Jan Bjuvberg (eds), *International Taxation in a Changing Landscape: Liber Amicorum in Honour of Bertil Wiman*, 2019 (ISBN 978-90-411-9234-9).
72. Kasper Dziurdź, *Non-discrimination in Tax Treaty Law and World Trade Law: The Impact of Formal, Substantive and Subjective Approaches*, 2019 (ISBN 978-94-035-0904-4).
73. Félix Daniel Martínez Laguna, *Hybrid Financial Instruments, Double Nontaxation and Linking Rules*, 2019 (ISBN 978-94-035-1074-3).
74. Jan Gooijer, *Tax Treaty Residence of Entities*, 2019 (ISBN 978-94-035-1301-0).
75. John Abrahamson, *International Taxation of Banking*, 2020 (ISBN 978-94-035-1094-1).
76. Richard Krever & François Vaillancourt (eds), *The Allocation of Multinational Business Income: Reassessing the Formulary Apportionment Option*, 2020 (ISBN 978-94-035-0614-2).
77. Ajit Kumar Singh, *Exploring the Nexus Doctrine in International Tax Law*, 2021 (ISBN 978-94-035-3363-6).
78. Galya Savir, *Regulation and Tax in Space*, 2021 (ISBN 978-94-035-3393-3).
79. Rita Julien, *Credit Method Compatibility and Constraints under EU Law: An Analysis of the Case Law of the CJEU*, 2022 (ISBN 978-94-035-2363-7).
80. Sergio André Rocha & Allison Christians (eds), *A Multilateral Convention for Tax: From Theory to Implementation*, 2022 (ISBN 978-90-411-9428-2).
81. Brigitte Alepin, Lyne Latulippe & Louise Otis (eds), *Coordination and Cooperation: Tax Policy in the 21st Century*, 2022 (ISBN 978-94-035-3740-5).
82. Chunyang Zhang, *The Role of Tax Law in Mergers and Acquisitions: A Chinese Perspective*, 2022 (ISBN 978-94-035-3741-2).
83. Florian Navisotschnigg, *Substance in International Tax Law: DEMPE Approach, Substantial Activity Requirement and Beneficial Ownership*, 2022 (ISBN 978-94-035-4895-1).

84. Mees Vergouwen, *The Effect of Directives Within the Area of Direct Taxation on the Interpretation and Application of Tax Treaties*, 2023 (ISBN 978-94-035-0907-5).